Oxford University Press

Oxford   New York
Athens   Auckland   Bangkok   Bogotá   Buenos Aires   Calcutta
Cape Town   Chennai   Dar es Salaam   Delhi   Florence   Hong Kong   Istanbul
Karachi   Kuala Lumpur   Madrid   Melbourne   Mexico City   Mumbai
Nairobi   Paris   São Paulo   Singapore   Taipei   Tokyo   Toronto   Warsaw

and associated companies in
Berlin   Ibadan

Copyright © 2000 by Mia Elisabeth Bay

Published by Oxford University Press, Inc.
198 Madison Avenue, New York, New York 10016

Oxford is a registered trademark of Oxford University Press.

Library of Congress Cataloging-in-Publication Data
Bay, Mia.
The white image in the black mind : African-American ideas about
white people, 1830–1925 / Mia Bay.
p.   cm.
Includes bibliographical references and index.
ISBN 0-19-510045-X; ISBN 0-19-513279-3 (pbk.)
1. United States—Race relations.   2. Afro-Americans—Attitudes—
History—19th century.   3. Afro-Americans—Attitudes—History
—20th century.   4. Afro-Americans—Intellectual life.   5. Race
awareness—United States—History—19th century.   6. Race
awareness—United States—History—20th century.   7. Whites—
United States.   8. Whites in literature.   I. Title.
E185.61.B29   1999
305.8'00973—dc21   98-48935

1 3 5 7 9 8 6 4 2
Printed in the United States of America
on acid-free paper

Acknowledgments

This book had been a long time coming and has incurred many debts along the way. Friends and colleagues whose ideas and support have nourished this project go all the way back to my undergraduate days at University of Toronto, where Michael Wayne and John Ingham introduced me the study of African-American history, and Barrie Hayne supervised me in a senior essay that explored some of the themes covered in this book.

At Yale University, where this project began to take its final shape, I had the good fortune to be advised by David Brion Davis, whose support and encouragement helped me complete both my dissertation and its reincarnation as this book. Other Yale friends whose discussions and critical readings shaped this work include Jean Christophe Agnew, Jonathan Cedarbaum, Debbie Elkin, Jonathan Holloway, David Goldshalk, Stephanie Smallwood, Carol Sherriff, Ann Standley, Beth Wenger, and above all, Barbara Savage—a tremendously willing and generous reader from graduate school to the present day.

Since graduate school, more people than I could name here have aided me in thinking through the ideas explored here. Most notable have been my friends and colleagues at Rutgers, whose confidence in my work has often exceeded my own. In particular, I want to thank Bonnie Smith and the other members of the fabulous gender group for their comments on several chapters; Tom Slaughter, Paul Clemens, David Levering Lewis, and Rudy Bell for careful readings of the entire manuscript; Jennie Brier, Justin Hart, and Amina Pilgrim for superb research assistance; and Matt Matsuda, Carmen Whalen and Carolyn Brown for always cheering me on. In addition, I have to give special thanks to Beryl Satter. My best editor and a rock-steady friend, Beryl helped me survive this book. Likewise, Deborah Gray White has been a crucial friend, reader, and mentor throughout this project. In addition to lots of help and advice, Deborah, along with her daughters Asha and Maya, provided me with a warm and welcoming New Jersey home away from home during some of the late night hysteria that went into this book.

New colleagues, but old friends, Jennifer Morgan and Herman Bennett have been equally important to this work. In matters both intellectual and day-to-day, they supported me through every step of the book writing process while also hooking me up with other wonderful supportive friends, most especially Ms. Lisa Waller.

This book has also benefited from the generosity of a wide variety of scholars and institutions elsewhere. Many thanks to David Roediger, who has been instructive both in his own work and in his generous comments on mine. I am grateful to George Fredrickson not only for his reading of my manuscript but for tolerating my transposition of the title of his classic book, *The Black Image in the White Mind: The Debate on Afro-American Character and Destiny, 1817–1914*. My work owes an obvious debt to his. Other critics and readers of my work include Suzanne Lebsock, Thomas Trautman, Walter Johnson, Kathy Tanner, Martin Summers, and the fellows at Harvard University's Charles Warren Center, where I held a postdoctoral fellow in 1994–1995. Particularly helpful there were Laura Kalman, Steve Nissenbaum, Steve Biel, and the center's wonderful administrator Susan Hunt.

In addition to the Warren Center fellowship, this work has also been facilitated by a grant from the Provost's Office at Rutgers University and a J. Franklin Jameson Fellowship from the American Historical Association and the Library of Congress.

The research that went into this book could not have been completed without the aid from a large number of librarians and archivists. I am particularly indebted to the staffs of the manuscripts division of the Library of Congress and Boston Public Library's Rare Book Room, as well as the research librarians at Yale University's Sterling Memorial Library, the Harvard University Libraries, Howard University's Moorland-Springarn Research Center, and New York Public Library's Schomburg Center. Many thanks to Pamela Grieff of the Boston Atheneuem for her efficiency in helping me acquire a number of the pictures included in this book.

Friends and relatives have sustained and encouraged this project throughout. Among them are Laura Fuerstein, Kathryn O'Hara, Rose Stewart, Bill Moses, Elisabeth Abrams, Laura Saltz, Jude Lovrin, the late, much-loved John D'Amico, and my cousin Dauna Williams. Finally, let me thank my family, especially my parents. My father, Christian Bay, did not live to see this project completed. But his advice, encouragement, and love still sustained me throughout. And my mother, Juanita Bay, remains a constant source of support and inspiration.

New York, New York   M. B.
July 1999

Contents

THE WHITE IMAGE IN THE BLACK MIND

Introduction

Desegregating American Racial Thought

When Olaudah Equiano, an African who was captured and shipped to the New World in 1756, first saw the slave ship and its white crew, he fainted in fright. He was convinced that he and the other blacks he saw chained aboard the vessel would be eaten "by these white men with horrible looks, red faces, and long hair." No assurances from African slave merchants assisting with the loading of the slaver could convince Equiano or the rest of the ship's human cargo that they would not ultimately be consumed by "these ugly men."[1] Equiano's fear that his white captors were cannibals was a misapprehension widely shared among his countrymen from the interior of Africa, who were unfamiliar with whites. Many such captives, as historian Philip Curtin notes, "believed, on being shipped in slave vessels, that the white men were cannibals who had almost eaten up their countrymen and now came back to fetch black men to gratify their taste for human flesh."[2]

The unfavorable first impressions that Europeans made on many eighteenth- and nineteenth-century Africans, like the very different, but often equally unfavorable, first impressions Africans made on Europeans during the same era, were determined by the specific historical context that shaped the initial encounters between the two groups. Displaying a xenophobia perhaps natural to human beings everywhere, both groups found each other's looks distasteful, customs peculiar, and religious beliefs impious. But the specific suspicions they developed about each other were shaped by historical circumstances rather than psychic responses alone.

Europeans encountering Africans within the context of the international slave trade saw black people as brutish and bestial. As historian Winthrop Jordan observes, the parallels Europeans drew between Africans and apes may have received their initial impulse from the coincidence that some Europeans first encountered both black people and some of the most human-looking animals of the simian species at the same time and in the same part of the world.[3] But Europeans had no real difficulty distinguishing Africans from apes—indeed, the

3

growing value the former held as a commodity was no doubt the main reason that Europeans continued to see blacks as brute creatures.

Similarly, African fears about white cannibalism were rooted in a very specific historical context. As William Piersen points out, these fears had "antecedents in traditional African tribal animosities that placed the imputation of cannibalism on distrusted foreign peoples."[4] Moreover, African fears about cannibalism also arose from the circumstance that Africans taken by the Europeans were usually never seen again. One captured African reported that his people, the Foleys of West Africa, had a great horror "for the state of slavery amongst the English; for they generally imagined, that all who were sold for slaves, were generally eaten or murdered, since none had ever returned."[5]

Unlike the white suspicions about the place of black people in the human family—which would flourish in the slave societies that developed in the Americas—African misapprehensions about white cannibalism gave way in the New World. Encountering the grim realities of forced labor, enslaved Africans eventually realized that being eaten by white people was the least of their worries. Yet the character of white people would remain a concern for both these unwilling black immigrants and their American-born offspring, particularly in the United States, where African-Americans would live as a racial minority set apart by law, class, and condition from a highly color-conscious white majority. What new ideas about white people did these Africans and their descendants develop once in America? At present, this question meets a profound historical silence.[6] While there is a vast scholarly literature on American conceptions about race, most of this literature focuses on white American ideas about black people.[7]

This book aims to recapture the biracial history of American ideas about race by exploring how black Americans have perceived white Americans. More specifically, *The White Image in the Black Mind* is a study of oral and written commentary on white people in African-American culture between 1830 and 1930. The study picks up more than a half century after the experience that Equiano records for the simple reason that firsthand testimony of black life from the early years of American settlement is extremely scarce. Much as we might like to chart exactly how Africans' perceptions of white people changed as they became African-Americans, most of what we know about black life and thought during the seventeenth and eighteenth centuries comes through the eyes of white observers. Accordingly, the book begins its story in the nineteenth century, when black sources of African-American thought and folk belief are far more abundant.

The rich nineteenth- and early twentieth-century sources this study draws upon include the writings of black thinkers and novelists and narratives composed by ex-slaves. It also employs extensive oral testimony on the black experience available in sources ranging from court records to the accounts of black life and culture recorded by folklorists, amateur historians, and federal Works Project Administration interviewers in the late nineteenth and early twentieth centuries. In recent decades, historians have used these resources to uncover more about slave life and culture, and about the black experience in emancipation and Reconstruction, than earlier generations of historians, who eschewed such eyewitness testimony, ever seemed to envision possible.

Even with this documentary record, however, this study faced formidable difficulties when it came to evidence. "What a record could the victims of this terrible hatred present against the dominant race," the black abolitionist Sarah Parker Remond mourned in 1866. "It will never be written. It can never be written."[8] Remond's lament expressed her frustration with the antiblack politics of presidential Reconstruction and questioned whether language could even capture white injustice. At the same time, she also voiced a simple truth. Throughout much of this country's history, the vast majority of black Americans have been neither literate nor in any position to be at all candid in expressing their views of white character.

Consequently, the African-American discussion of white people *as a race* has never been anywhere near as vocal, voluminous, or well-publicized as has been white American thinking on black racial traits. Discussions of the Negro were ubiquitous among nineteenth-century whites who studied, reviewed, condemned, and sometimes even celebrated the black body and the black mind in a wide variety of contexts. Over the course of the century, the character and capacities of black people were assessed and evaluated by Southern slaveholders, defended by white abolitionists, examined and measured by white scientists, and debated and decried in American politics. At the same time, African-Americans captured the imagination of white Americans. Black people are ubiquitous in white American art and letters, where the African-American presence, as Toni Morrison points out, provides "a fabricated brew of darkness, otherness, alarm and desire that is uniquely American."[9]

African-Americans, by contrast, had far less to say about white Americans. Too powerless to lash out at white people freely, and forever required to defend themselves against racism's charges, African-Americans never inscribed white images across their culture and imaginative life. On the contrary, explicit commentary on white people is scant and often veiled in black thought. African-Americans had a number of obvious reasons to be reticent on the subject of white people. For one thing, when they recorded their thoughts—on paper or otherwise—nineteenth-century African-Americans often addressed an audience that included whites as well as blacks. As slaves, and later as sharecroppers, most blacks of the era had little title to privacy. Their songs, sayings, and spirituals were rarely sealed off from white listeners, and it was white listeners who collected most of our con-

temporary record of slave music and testimony. Likewise, even articulate blacks of the nineteenth century frequently directed their arguments toward a white audience. Much of their literature consists of
petitions, protests, and artistic productions designed to draw white attention to racial injustice.[10]

So this book must acknowledge from the outset that the historical
evidence on its subject is fragmented and incomplete. In particular,
much of antiwhite sentiment contained in nineteenth-century black
popular culture may be forever obscured by the constraints of expe-
diency and audience that shape our record on nineteenth- and early
twentieth-century black racial thought. Also rare is any commentary
on whites from middle-class black women, whose ability to speak
freely about white people was hindered by nineteenth-century gender
etiquette, as well as the dictates of prudence. Bent on honoring the
domestic ideals of true womanhood, nineteenth-century black women
often avoided public discussion of the subject of race. Black women
had yet to define themselves in the public sphere; as Anna Julie Cooper
complained in 1892, they were "mute and voiceless."[11]

Despite such lacunae, neither antiwhite sentiment nor African-
American women's perspectives on whites are totally obscured from
our record of nineteenth-century African-American life and thought.
Black hostility toward whites is freely expressed in a number of
sources, ranging from the testimony of slave rebels to black abolitionist David Walker's fiery abolitionist manifesto, *Appeal to the Colored Citizens of the World*. And along with earlier black women writers such as
Maria Stewart, Anna Julia Cooper sought to document the "exact
Voice of the Black Woman" on "our Nation's problem."[12] Moreover, as
we shall see, race, rage, and the concerns of black men and women
alike manifest themselves in disguised and indirect ways in what political theorist James C. Scott would call the "hidden transcript" of
African-American history—in the dissident political culture, to which
African-Americans, like other oppressed peoples, gave covert expression in their folklore, jokes, songs, and religious beliefs.[13]

If nothing else, African-Americans who grew up under slavery and
segregation could not defend themselves against racist doctrine without discussing the character of white people. In their attempts to
rebut and refute white claims against their race, black Americans were
inexorably drawn into a debate over the character of the races, which
led them to make revisionist assessments of both races. Writing in
1829, David Walker wondered whether white people were "*as good by
nature* as we are or not*" in thundering reply to Thomas Jefferson,
whose *Notes on Virginia* suggested that the black race was inferior to all
other races. Meanwhile, enslaved African-Americans asked the same
question more covertly. Meditating on the slaveholders' version of
Christianity, they sang: "Jordan's stream is wide and deep, / Jesus
stand on t'oder side. . . . I wonder if my maussa deh."[14] Speaking in

1850, ex-slave James W. C. Pennington elegantly summarized the intellectual contest that lay at the heart of black America's struggle against racial domination. When the "proud and selfish Anglo-Saxon seized upon the Negro to be used merely as a beast," the self-educated fugitive told an audience abroad, "he was soon alarmed to find that he must undertake the difficult task of forging chains for a mind like his own. That Herculean work was undertaken and from that moment to the present slavery has literally been A WAR OF MINDS."[15] The war over the capacities of black people that Pennington describes has raged on both during slavery and long after. It is of central concern here, for more than anywhere else, this battleground is where the African-American discussion of white people emerges.

Overview

> By means of what the white man imagines the black man to be the black man is enabled to know who the white man is.
>
> James Baldwin, *Notes of a Native Son*[16] (1955)

African-American discussions of whiteness are embedded within a larger story about black resistance to racism. Nothing about white people—their looks, their skin color, their customs—struck African-Americans as forcibly as the implacable hostility whites directed against them. It carried an oppressive force that was not just political but challenged the very humanity of African-Americans and left them struggling to redefine both themselves and the dominant race as kith and kin in the same human family. " 'He has no rights, &c.'—'He is inferior order of being'—'No ancestral line, worthy of consideration, &c. &c.' " was how Robert Purvis, a wealthy black Philadelphian, summarized the "falsities and blasphemies" in which "the enslavers & haters of the black man seek their apologies and defense" in 1860.[17] Less privileged blacks heard still worse; the slaves were often told that blacks were not even human. "Dey jus like animals, not like other folks," ex-slave Fannie Moore was told by her master's mother, who believed that "niggers didn't need nothin' to eat."[18]

In face of such absurdities, African-Americans never even had the option of remaining silent on the subject of white people or their racist views. Free, literate blacks contested the racial ideology of white scientists, politicians, and proslavery polemicists, producing a black literature on ethnology—the nineteenth-century "science of the races." Meanwhile, unlettered African-Americans, who formed the majority of nineteenth-century America's black population, were largely unfamiliar with both the rhetoric of black intellectuals and the white racial theories they debated. But they, too, were acutely aware that white people held their race in low esteem. In addition to complaining that white people did not see blacks as human beings, they speculated on the mysteries of white power and authority, taking comfort in their belief that whites and blacks alike would ultimately answer to the same God. Black ideas about white people are inextricably entwined in this history of African-American intellectual resistance to racism. Organized in three thematic and loosely chronological parts, this book chronicles that history and the black commentary on white people inscribed therein.

The book opens by considering ideas about race and white people among nineteenth-century black intellectuals. Drawing on the writings and speeches of the many African-American thinkers who critiqued white racist doctrine, Part I examines the image of white people in African-American ethnology. A rearguard defense of black humanity, African-American ethnology was devoted primarily to defending the place of black people in the human family. Written almost exclusively by black men, it sought to uphold the status of black men among "the races of men." A challenge to white supremacy's gendered hierarchies of racial difference, black ethnology was also a rich site for black assessments of white people. As they defended their own history, origins, and racial character, black thinkers produced revisionist assessments of both races. Challenging the racial ideologies of their day, they argued that the character of the Anglo-Saxon race compared unfavorably with the better nature of their own race.

In Part II the book maps the place of race among the unlettered slaves and freedpeople who formed the vast majority of nineteenth-century America's black population. Whereas educated blacks read and debated racist doctrine, slaves and ex-slaves drew their information about race from different sources. Reading racism from the comments and actions of whites around them, rather than from anything written, they observed that white people treated black people more like farm animals than human beings. They did not question the humanity of white people themselves but instead emphasized their own. Whites, these African-Americans sometimes observed, were distinguished from black people mainly by power and privilege—which they often abused. Drawing on the authority of a religious tradition that taught them "we are the people of God," they questioned the morality of white injustice, predicting a divine punishment that would leave few whites unscathed.

Part III, the book's final section, provides a brief overview of the changing images of whites in early twentieth-century black thought. Between 1900 and 1925, both black and white ideas about race began to be reshaped by new scientific ideas, as well as demographic and social changes that reconfigured American race relations. Starting at the turn of the century, the racial determinism of the nineteenth century entered a slow decline as social scientists began to equate race with culture rather than with biology. Meanwhile, the actual relationship between the races was transformed by the massive migration of Southern blacks to the cities of the North that began during World War I. Not surprisingly, these changes in American racial thought and race relations were felt most acutely in the black community. Although glad to see racial determinism go, black intellectuals had to rethink their own ideas before they could see culture, rather than race, as the major arbiter of human differences. By contrast, other sectors of the black community went the opposite direction. The 1920s saw the rise of a variety of new black separatist movements in the urban North. Followers of movements such as Marcus Garvey's Universal Negro Improvement Association and Moorish Science Temple embraced race as an organic and divinely ordained distinction between human beings and denounced the historical and religious character of white people.

The story that this book ultimately tells is more difficult to summarize than its chapters. Shrewd, desperate, and determined critics of racist ideology, the African-Americans who grew up under slavery and segregation challenged the meaning of race itself when they contested white supremacy. Stripping white theories of black inferiority down to the self-interested and dehumanizing stories that gave them life, they suggested that white Americans deemed blacks a lesser species only to rationalize their own exploitation and abuse of people of color. "Of one blood God hath created all nations to dwell on the face of the earth," countless black thinkers proclaimed, citing the wisdom of Acts 17:29 to counter white claims that the African race was inferior to and distinct from their own.

Yet even as they emphasized the shared blood and lineage of blacks and whites, African-Americans often questioned the innate moral character of the white race. If whites were not better than blacks, they ended up suggesting, they might be worse. Such judgments reflected not only the many injustices that African-Americans suffered in the hands of the white race but also the fragile and elusive character of the racial equality to which African-Americans have always aspired. For as American educator Jacques Barzun wrote many years ago in his classic book on race:

> Equality is neither provable nor disprovable. This is so for groups and individuals alike. Equality is not a scientific but a political idea, and it is valid only when one assumes it, as in the Declaration of Independence and the French Declaration of the Rights of Man.[19]

Such assumptions of equality were rare in nineteenth-century America, and they remain so today. In their place, we have racial ideologies, not all of which have been fully mapped. The white image in the black mind is one of them.

I

WHITE PEOPLE IN
BLACK ETHNOLOGY

The catastrophe of American slavery . . . must be understood as a bloody history of atrocity, of stripping a people of cultural identity, then grotesquely caricaturing them in the national (white) imagination. The burden on the free, literate black population was staggering—to lead the antislavery effort, counteract the ideology of racism, and prove themselves worthy of equality.

Charles Johnson, Being and Race (1988)

ONE

✽

"Of One Blood God Created All the Nations of Men"

*African-Americans Respond to the Rise
of Ideological Racism, 1789–1830*

In 1779 a group of Connecticut slaves petitioned their state's general assembly with the protest "that we are the Creatures of that God who made of one Blood, and Kindred all the Nations of the Earth; we perceive by our own Reflection that we are endowed with the same Faculties as our masters, and there is nothing that leads us to a Belief, or Suspicion, that we are any more obliged to serve them, than they us."[1] In protesting that they were no different than their white masters, these African-American slaves spoke to the heart of the issue that would frame American debates over the status of black people in the nation's life and politics through the slavery era and long after. Were the races the same? Or were black people natural underlings whose inferior capacities doomed them to forever serve the white race?

It is difficult to say just when these debates over the differences between the races began. Clearly, slavery pitted blacks and whites against each other from its inception. But the question of when the distinctions of nationality, religion, and condition of servitude that separated the first generation of Euro-American colonists from their black bondspeople were superseded by distinctions understood as "racial differences" defies any easy answer. Historians have long been unable to agree whether America's African and African-American population came to be seen as different and inferior as a result of the emergence of chattel slavery in the American colonies, or whether the development of racial slavery was fueled by such prejudices. One general point of consensus does emerge within this "chicken-and-egg" controversy, however.[2] Whatever racism's origin, a rationalized ideology of black inferiority did not develop until the early nineteenth century.

Certainly, as the Connecticut slaves were all too aware, a "societal racism—the treatment of blacks as if they were inferior for reasons of race"—existed in America long before then.[3] However, published arguments identifying black men and women as an inherently inferior order of people whose natural incapacities justified their enslavement were rare before the 1820s. "Articulate whites" of the earlier period, historian George Fredrickson explains, "were characteristically unable, and perhaps even unwilling, to defend their anti-Negro predispositions by presenting anything that resembled a 'scientific' or philosophical case for the innate moral and intellectual inferiority of the Negro race."[4]

As the nineteenth century progressed, this reticence gave way dramatically. Before the century was even half over, a constellation of religious, historical, and biological theories positing the natural inferiority of persons of African descent would come to be embraced as time-honored truths by white Americans. In the first half of the century, racist ideology provided a rationalization for the enslavement of African-Americans in the South and for the marginal position accorded to free blacks in the North. After the Civil War, this ideology reached new heights in a society where racial proscription continued to govern the social and economic relations between white and black people.

No Americans followed the rise of this ideological racism more closely than black Americans, whose affront at their white contemporaries' attacks on the status of black people in the human family is resoundingly expressed in their oratory and protest thought. From the outset, they opposed the "destructiveness, and bitter malignity of prejudice," contesting racist ideology as it developed and mourning the ready acceptance it found among their white countrymen.[5] In particular, educated blacks were both well versed in, and preoccupied with, white racist doctrine. Their engagement with the subject was as unavoidable as it was unwelcome. Over the course of the nineteenth century, according to Alexander Saxton, "racism became part of that massive synthesis of physical, biological and historical explanation that nineteenth-century science bequeathed to humanity. It then confronted every informed person, white or non-white, in the dual guise of existing social reality and established scientific knowledge."[6]

For all its power, however, racism did not confront the white and the nonwhite in the same way. In an era when even white "friends of the Negro" would slowly come to accept the prevailing social and scientific arguments for black inferiority, African-Americans challenged white racial ideology from its eighteenth-century origins onward. Even before published arguments for black inferiority began to appear, both free blacks and slaves were all too aware of white prejudices against them, and they spoke out in self-defense. With the rise of ethnology, the now discredited "science of the human races," in the early nineteenth century, they went on the offensive, attacking the writings of white scientists and proslavery polemicists. Black writers opposed this new scientific racism by crafting their own version of ethnology, which defended the origins, ancestry, and human capacities of the black race. Their arguments were drawn from scriptural history and the scientific writings of eighteenth-century European and American naturalists, who took a far more egalitarian view of the human family than their successors would. Steeped in tradition, these black ethnological arguments emerged early in the nineteenth century and changed little thereafter. In place by 1830, the arguments that African-American intellectuals made against black inferiority upheld eighteenth-century wisdom about the unity of the human family and the equality of all men under God. Cobbled together out of old ideas, these arguments nonetheless came to sound increasingly original as the white society began to subscribe to a new and more racially divided view of human origins and relations.

Black racial thought has been neglected in both the study of American racial thought and the study of African-American intellectual history. Yet it is crucial here, for the responses of African-Americans to the rise of ideological racism created the forum for public discussions of white people as a race among black Americans. In speaking out to oppose white allegations of black inferiority, African-Americans of all classes were drawn into a discussion of the character of the races and of the differences that might divide them. Much of what they said about white people cannot be understood without reference to this larger discussion, the genesis of which this book will begin by tracing. In particular, the earliest African-American responses to the rising chorus of white American arguments for the innate and irradicable inferiority of the black race merit close attention here. Forged between 1789 and 1830, these responses introduce many of the arguments and issues that framed nineteenth-century black racial thought.

"In What Single Circumstance Are We Different from Mankind?": Black Americans Confront the Ethnological Case against the Negro

One of Thomas Jefferson's less-celebrated distinctions is a pioneering contribution to American racial thought. In his *Notes on Virginia*, the father of American democracy made one of the earliest American arguments for black inferiority. Written in the 1780s, Jefferson's widely read book was not a proslavery document. Jefferson disliked slavery himself and did not think men could be rightfully enslaved whatever their natural capacities, but he had little admiration for black people. In *Notes on Virginia* he advanced, "as a suspicion only, that the blacks, whether originally a distinct race, or made distinct by time and circumstances, are inferior to the whites in the endowments both of body and mind." He prefaced this speculation with an additional qualification:

> The opinion that they are inferior in the faculties of reason and imagination, must be hazarded with great diffidence. To justify a general con-

clusion, requires many observations, even where the subject may be submitted to the anatomical knife, to optical glasses, to analysis by fire or by solvents. How much more then where it is a faculty, not a substance, we are examining; where it eludes the research of all the senses, where conditions of its existence are various and variously combined; where the effects of those which are present or absent bid defiance to calculation.[7]

In Winthrop Jordan's assessment, "Until well into the nineteenth century, Jefferson's judgment on that matter, with all its confused tentativeness, stood as the strongest suggestion of inferiority expressed by any native American."[8]

Nonetheless, early black writing and oratory reveal that eighteenth-century African-Americans were troubled by a growing awareness that their inherent human capacities were being called into question. In a 1779 petition to the New Hampshire legislature, nineteen slaves from New Hampshire wanted to know "from what authority" their owners assumed "power to dispose of our lives freedom and property." Did it come from Christianity or law, they wondered, quickly rejecting these ideas in turn. Did it come from "the volumes of nature," they then asked. Their answer reflected their consciousness that their humanity was under attack: "No, here, we can read with others, of this knowledge; slavery cannot wholly deprive us; here we know that we ought to be free agents, here we feel the dignity of human nature; here we feel the passions and desires of men, though checked by the rod of slavery; here we feel a just equality; here we know that the God of Nature made us free."[9]

Former slaves Absalom Jones and Richard Allen challenged racist assessments of black capacities still more directly in an essay published in the back of their *Narrative of the Proceedings of the Black People, During the Late Awful Calamity in Philadelphia*. After recording the good works performed by black Philadelphians during the yellow fever epidemic that swept the city in 1793, these two leaders of Philadelphia's Free African Society challenged "those who stigmatize us as men, whose baseness is incurable [to] try the experiment of taking a few black children, and cultivate their minds with the same care, and let them have the same prospect in view, as you would wish for your own children, you would find upon the trial, they were not inferior in mental endowments."[10] Moreover, even in this early period, a number of black writers clearly felt the need not only to defend their race's innate abilities but also to affirm the Negro's place in the human family. In 1789 one ex-slave complained:

Can it be contended, that a difference of colour alone can constitute a difference in species?—if not, in what single circumstance are we different from mankind? what variety is there in our organization? what inferiority of art in the fashioning of our bodies? what imperfection in the faculties of our minds?—Has not a negro eyes? has not a negro hands, organs, dimensions, senses, affections, passions?[11]

The experience of slavery no doubt fueled such questions. But even blacks who lived outside of bondage seemed fully aware that an ideology of black inferiority was being forged around them. Benjamin Banneker, who lived between 1731 and 1807, was a free black who achieved considerable renown as a mathematician, astronomer, and inventor. Despite his own success, Banneker clearly feared that Jefferson's doubts about the intellectual capacities of the black race were widely shared. Hoping to change Jefferson's mind, Banneker sent him a copy of his own soon-to-be-published *Almanac*, along with a letter that gently rebuked Jefferson for underestimating black intelligence. In the letter Banneker lamented "that we are a race of beings, who have . . . long been considered rather as brutish than human, and scarcely capable of mental endowments." He hoped that Jefferson would

embrace every opportunity, to eradicate that train of absurd and false ideas and opinions, which so generally prevails with respect to us; and that your sentiments are concurrent with mine, which are that one uniform father hath given being to us all; and that he hath not only made us all of one flesh, but that he hath also, without partiality, afforded us all the same sensations and endowed us all with the same faculties; and that however variable we may be in society or religion, however diversified in situation or color, we are all in the same human family.[12]

Jefferson's response to Banneker, in turn, illustrated how difficult it would be for African-Americans to prove their equality to unsympathetic whites. Jefferson's reply was cordial. He wrote Banneker, "Nobody wishes more than I do to see proofs as you exhibit, that nature has given to our black brethren, talents equal to those of other colors of men, and that the appearance of a want of them is owing merely to the degraded condition of their existence." He also allowed his reply to be published in a pamphlet, alongside Banneker's letter, and even commended the self-taught scientist's mathematical skills to the Marquis de Condorcet, one of Jefferson's French correspondents. A more private letter, however, written over a decade later, calls the sincerity of Jefferson's enthusiasm into question. Railing against a defense of the intellectual capacities of black people written by the French revolutionary Abbé Henri Grégoire, Jefferson told his friend Joel Barlow that Banneker's *Almanac* proved nothing.[13] "We know he had spherical trigonometry enough to make almanacs, but not without the suspicion of aid from Ellicot who was his friend and neighbor, and never missed an opportunity of puffing him." Still more dismissively, he added, "I have had a long letter from Banneker, which shows him to have a mind of a very common stature indeed."[14]

Unshakable doubts about black capacities such as Jefferson's were so prevalent in the eighteenth century that even some white Americans found it necessary to defend the African race's innate capacities. As the century progressed, for example, white proponents of slave conversion became increasingly likely to stress that black ignorance arose "not from Want of Capacity, but from Want of Instruction."[15] Meanwhile, less sympathetic whites had increasingly far-reaching doubts about whether blacks could ever be equal to whites. Although the scriptural account of human origins still prevailed, biblical wisdom about the unity of humankind was under attack in some quarters even at this early date—as can be seen in Samuel Stanhope Smith's references to theories that held the races to be descended from separate creations in his 1787 *An Essay on the Causes of Variety of the Complexion and Figure in the Human Species*.[16]

These black and white defenses of black humanity and capacity for improvement reveal that even though a scientific case for Negro inferiority had yet to be developed, and a proslavery ideology based on racial difference was still confined to the inchoate realm of Southern practice and tradition, new questions were being asked about the place of black people in human society. Moreover, they show how the racial turn the slavery issue took during the Revolutionary era carried both blacks and whites with it. African-Americans did not invent racist ideology. Yet, in their bitter opposition to slavery and racism, articulate blacks of this era were drawn into a debate over black racial capacities from which they would not soon escape.

Part of the problem was that racism and antiracism grew up together. Both racist ideology and the countervailing arguments for a human equality transcending color and condition made by African-Americans and their white allies came out of the same Revolutionary era intellectual ferment. Moreover, these opposing arguments were shaped in similar ways by the enormous impact that the European Enlightenment had on thinkers on both sides of the Atlantic. A rethinking of the relationship between God, nature, reason, and man, the Enlightenment led Euro-American thinkers to replace theological interpretations of human life with scientific ones. As the natural laws of physiology replaced the hand of Providence in post-Enlightenment discussions of human history, race acquired a whole new meaning that would be exploited by both friends and foes of black equality.

On the one hand, the European breakthroughs in biological science that followed the Enlightenment ultimately paved the way for scientific racism. On the other, the new interest in man as a physical being ushered in by this rational, secular age did not dictate the hierarchical distinctions between men of different colors that would later prevail. The interest that Enlightenment era thinkers took in the physical side of human nature and in man's place in the natural world led them to devise systems of classification for people parallel to those they developed to study the animal kingdom. Yet "classification of mankind by color and physical type . . . did not necessarily imply a ranking within the species by relative superiority."[17] And although many of the eighteenth-century classifiers held the physical and mental characteristics of non-European peoples in low esteem, few believed that these racial characteristics heralded innate and immutable distinctions between the races. According to Fredrickson, "The dominant eighteenth-century view was that racial characteristics were not innate but rather the result of environmental factors, such as climate and social habits."[18]

This environmentalist theory of human differences was the first truly racial conception of mankind insofar as it set out to explain race as a fundamental and important distinction between human beings. It developed on the heels of the "gradual decomposition of religious beliefs" in the West, beliefs that held variety in the human species to be an inexplicable manifestation of the Creator's mysterious will.[19] Environmentalist thinkers argued that the influence of environment on people evolved into "biological types peculiar to their own geographical areas and that each exhibited a peculiar culture."[20] While this new biological conception of man, with its emphasis on physical characteristics, could and would be used to support the idea that blacks were inferior, it also gave ready support to those who would argue that all people were the same under the skin.

Indeed, in the eighteenth century, environmentalist ideas provided ammunition for intellectual assaults on slavery articulated by both blacks and whites. The men and women in the antislavery movement reaffirmed the traditional scriptural conception of all people as children of God. And they posed environmental explanations of the Negro's color and physiognomy to those who sought to argue that Africans were both so degraded and so different from Europeans that they should be seen as a lower species of people, suited only for perpetual slavery. In combination with natural-rights philosophy, environmentalist ideas formed the basis for ideological opposition to slavery in Revolutionary era America.

Thus, the post-Enlightenment shift from theological to biological thinking was initially employed in arguments for the equality of the races. As Winthrop Jordan has pointed out, however, environmentalist defenses of the unity of mankind would ultimately be transformed by the addition of biology. The writings of Princeton College philosopher and theologian Samuel Stanhope Smith are a case in point. Smith's major work on environmentalism was his *Essay on the Causes of the Variety of Complexion and Figure in the Human Species* (1787), a scriptural defense of unity of the human family. By 1810, Smith evidently felt that this work required additional proof and republished his *Essay* in a greatly expanded form. Twice as long as the original, his second edition "unwittingly demonstrated that the question of human equality had moved to new ground." Writing in reference Smith's second edition, Jordan explains:

From the facts of natural history Smith spoke for an equality among men which derived from their corporeal sameness. Rather than equal before God, men were equal before their environment. The *fact* that all men became darkened by exposure to the sun was of a significantly different order than the *fact* that all men came to face the justice of God — except of course, that both facts entailed a universally shared experience. Men had been created equal by the Creator, yes, but the evidence for this creation now lay in man's physical being.[21]

This shift in the intellectual terrain on the subject of equality is faithfully reflected in early writing by African-Americans. From the late eighteenth century onward, blacks protesting slavery and racial discrimination pointedly reaffirmed the legitimate place of their race in the human species and cited the physical and mental characteristics shared by both races as evidence. "Has the GOD who made the white man and the black, left any record declaring us a different species?" asked black Philadelphian James Forten in 1813. "Are we not sustained by the same power, supported by the same food, hurt by the same wounds, wounded by the same wrongs, pleased by the same delights, and propagated by the same means?"[22] In 1813 George Lawrence declared that the "most prominent arguments" for black inferiority "are lighter than vanity for vacuous must the reasons of that man have been . . . who dared assert that genius is confined to complexion or that nature knows difference in the immortal soul of man. No! the noble mind of Newton could find room, and to spare within the tenement of many an injured African."[23]

Arguments in defense of black equality that rested solely on the overarching spiritual equality of all men would become increasingly rare as the century progressed. From 1787 onward, following the publication of Jefferson's *Notes on Virginia* and Smith's *Essay*, the natural capacities of black people were debated in American magazines and newspapers. At issue was not just the status of the Negro in American scholarly discourse. Slavery and the slave traffic were contentious issues in the nation's polity in the debates over the Constitution, as well as in later ones over the abolition of the slave trade.

Public debate over the question of whether blacks were the equal of whites reflected political concerns in the new republic as well as the new biological cast understandings of human nature were beginning to acquire. The debate also signaled that the Negro's capacity was becoming the central issue for spokesmen on both sides of the slavery debate. David Brion Davis explains:

> The strategy of Revolutionary debate left little ground for an abstract or generalized discussion of slavery. Given the widespread enthusiasm for liberty and equal rights, it was difficult for an apologist to show that the freedom of some Americans depended on the exploitation of others. . . . The abolitionists, by resting their case on the highest moral principles, helped to isolate the Negro's supposed incapacity for freedom —

whether inherent or the result of long oppression—as the only obstacle to emancipation. . . . Both parties in the Revolutionary debate helped make race the central excuse for slavery.[24]

The racial terms of the debate, as unfavorable as they were to black people, were something that nineteenth-century African-Americans could not escape. Well aware of the circularity of the racist argument against abolition, early black spokesmen were frustrated by the absurdity of the case they had to confront. "Will you," complained Richard Allen, the senior bishop of Philadelphia's African Methodist Church, "because you have reduced us to the unhappy condition our color is in, plead our incapacity for freedom . . . as a sufficient cause for keeping us under the grievous yoke?"[25] At the same time, however, African-Americans also felt compelled to provide evidence to disprove the mounting belief in black inferiority among white Americans.

Racist questions about black capacities were so pervasive by the early decades of the nineteenth century that they dogged Northern free blacks even as they celebrated emancipation holidays commemorating the end of the slave trade and abolition in their states. In memorializing these occasions, speakers such as Adam Carman, who in 1811 commemorated the fourth anniversary of the abolition of the slave trade in New York, found it necessary to address the "reproach" that branded blacks "an inferior species of human beings." "All such censures as we have long labored under," Carman scoffed, "are the firstborn of absurdities; for our mental faculties are as capacitious, and just as open to impression from precept and example as any nation that ever breathed the vital air."[26] Turn-of-the-century emancipation day orators also "proclaimed the glories of ancient Egyptian and Ethiopian civilizations." Such claims likewise aimed to counter white racism, while simultaneously reflecting the importance that Africa held in the collective identity of urban free blacks. Emancipation day orators celebrated their race's African past to disprove the charge, as William Hamilton put it in 1809, "that we have not produced any poets, mathematicians, or any to excel in any science whatever."[27]

Black secular organizations, such as mutual aid societies, also felt this need to answer white questions about black capacities. These organizations characteristically had poignant goals beyond the usual programs for community welfare of similar organizations in the white community. According to Benjamin Quarles, organizations such as the African societies of Providence and Boston and the Brown Fellowship Society of Charleston "were bent on demonstrating that blacks as a class were, if given the opportunity, prepared to assume the full responsibilities of freedom and citizenship, thus disputing the argument that blacks would never amount to anything."[28] Organized by women as well as men, these voluntary associations also included black literary groups and moral reform societies. Whatever their cause or constituency, all shared a commitment to a philosophy of racial uplift.[29] The educational and civic objectives they pursued were designed to ensure that the education and deportment of black people would counter all white suspicions against them. For example, the founders of the Female Literary Association of Philadelphia, one of the earliest black educational societies for women, considered it their "duty . . . as daughters of a depised race, to use our utmost endeavors to enlighten the understanding, to cultivate the talents entrusted to our keeping, that by so doing, we may in a great measure, break down the strong barrier of prejudice, and raise ourselves to an equality with those of our fellow beings, who differ from us in complexion."[30]

"A Clap of Thunder":
Free Black Opposition to Colonization

In addition to attempting to break down white prejudices through self-improvement and self-cultivation, free blacks also attacked such prejudices directly. As early as the 1820s, African-Americans began to craft sustained arguments contesting the ethnological case against the Negro then emerging in white America. The most immediate impetus for this development was a renewed discussion among both blacks and whites on the nature of racial differences that arose in response to the activities of the American Colonization Society (ACS). Founded in 1816, the ACS was a simultaneously visionary and conservative benevolent movement bent on ridding America of both slaves and slavery by sending all American blacks back to their "homeland." Removed to Africa, advocates of colonization argued, Christianized American blacks would contribute to the conversion and redemption of Africa. The long-range goal held by the Protestant clergy who made up the organization's leadership was to lead American slaveholders into the gradual and voluntary emancipation of all American slaves. What made the ACS's plans so utterly objectionable to free blacks was not so much this improbable vision as the organization's short-term goal. It planned to begin this reverse diaspora by transporting the country's free blacks to Africa.

Ironically, the colonization movement met intense opposition from both proslavery spokesmen and free blacks. Many proslavery apologists could not countenance the abolition of slavery, however gradual or voluntary. Meanwhile, free black opposition to colonization first mobilized in Philadelphia, where black residents held four mass meetings between 1817 and 1819 to condemn colonization. "The plan of colonizing," they objected in one of these protests, "was not asked for by us; nor will it be required, in our present or future condition, as long as we shall be permitted to share the protection of the excellent laws and just government which we now enjoy."[31] The sentiment expressed in Philadelphia was soon echoed in other black communities from Baltimore to

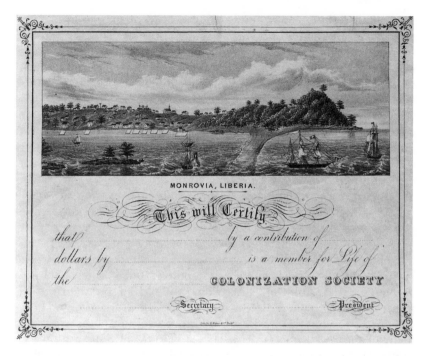

MONROVIA, LIBERIA.

Receipt form for donations to the Colonization Society. The illustration presents an idyllic view of Monrovia, Liberia (Boston Athenæum).

Boston. From the beginning, free blacks feared that they might be compelled to emigrate—a fear that was only strengthened when they watched the federal government forcibly remove the last of the South's Indian inhabitants to new lands in the West in the 1830s.

Although free blacks were never threatened with removal by force, their alarm over colonization made them acutely aware of just how tenuous was their place in American society. The ACS, they realized, did not consider them Americans. As they affirmed their identity as Americans, and their right to a future on the American continent, the free blacks of antebellum America were drawn into a debate with white Americans about race and identity, and the place of black people in American society, which ultimately led them to lay out their thoughts on these subjects at length in ethnological literature and other writings. According to Leonard Sweet, opposition to the "meaning, methods, and motives of the American Colonization Society did more to generate black solidarity and engender a sense of identity among the black community than any other single issue in the first half of the nineteenth century."[32]

The ACS's activities spurred black Americans to develop specific and detailed arguments for their own equality because both the rhetoric and the goals of the organization were shaped by deeply racist ideas and assumptions. The removal of free blacks would accomplish nothing toward the colonizationists' antislavery goals, but it would rid the nation of a "degraded" people seen to represent a threat to the social order. Like other white Americans, the ACS's members believed that the very existence of free blacks challenged the stability of American society, especially in the South, where they were widely suspected of encouraging slave insurrections. The ACS's most fundamental objection to free blacks, however, was quite simply their race. The colonizationists assumed that black people could never be incorporated into American society. Although few of the early colonizationists argued that blacks were innately inferior to whites, they believed that blacks would never thrive in America because white prejudices against them could never be eradicated.

George Fredrickson writes that, "insofar as colonizationists affirmed or implied that there was an inevitable and legitimate white prejudice against black skin, they succumbed . . . to a protoracist form of biological determinism."[33] According to Fredrickson, their racism stopped short of biological determinism because they attributed both the low condition of American blacks and white prejudices against them to the social effects of slavery. Advocates of colonization expressed great admiration for the "African genius" and argued that once in the hospitable environment of their "native" land black Americans "would soon rise rapidly in the scale of existence, and soon become equal to the people of European origin, so long their masters and oppressors."[34]

The colonizationist panegyrics to a proud black past in Africa would be cited in defense of the Negro race by egalitarian-minded whites and blacks for many years to come—often without attribution or acknowledgment of their source. Despite its complimentary language, however, early colonizationist propaganda was never taken seriously by free blacks. Indeed, from the outset the free black community perceived the colonization movement as an attack on the character of their race. From their first mass meeting onward, free black opponents of the ACS denounced colonization as an "unmerited stigma attempted to be cast upon the reputation of the free people of color."[35] Further evidence that they understood the ACS's program as a racial slight can be seen in the fact that not all of the ACS's black foes objected to emigration per se. Some of black Philadelphia's most vociferous anti-colonizationists, for example, had endorsed an earlier emigration promoted by black ship captain and businessman Paul Cuffe.[36]

Widespread opposition to colonization gave impetus to the development and articulation of black racial thought. The racial ideas and assumptions that lay behind the white colonizationists' complimentary language and antislavery sentiment made the ACS all the more dangerous: it could not be ignored. "We call upon the learned author of the 'address' for the indication of the distinction between us and other men," Samuel Ennels and Philip Bell wrote in answer to an 1831 publication produced by the New York Colonization Society. "There are different colors among all species of animated creation. A difference in color is not a difference of species. Our structure and organization are the same, and not distinct from other men; in what respects are we inferior?"[37] Black critics also challenged the inconsistency of the colonizationists' racist logic. Speaking before a national free black convention in 1834, William Hamilton charged that the colonization movement was "one thing in the south and another in the north." He complained that

> it sometimes represents us as the most corrupt, vicious, and abandoned class of men in the community. Then again we are kind, meek, and gentle. Here we are ignorant, idle, a nuisance, and a drawback on the resources of the community. But as abandoned as we are, in Africa we shall civilize and Christianize all that heathen country.[38]

Free black resistance to colonization also inspired far more extended critiques of white racist ideology, beginning with the publication of *Freedom's Journal*, the nation's first black newspaper. Founded in 1827 by Samuel Cornish, who resigned his pastorate at New York's First Colored Presbyterian Church to work full-time editing his new publication, *Freedom's Journal* was launched with the support of other leading black New Yorkers. The paper aimed to speak for the whole free black community. "We wish to plead our own cause," began the first page of the first issue. "Too long others have spoken for us. Too long has the publick been deceived by misrepresentations." Above all, the misrepresentations that Cornish and his backers sought to address centered around race and colonization. Cornish's friend and successor at the First Colored Presbyterian, Theodore Wright, later recalled that *Freedom's Journal* "came like a clap of thunder" at a time when free black opponents to colonization despaired of ever making themselves heard. Fearing coercive measures, they "used to meet together and talk and weep and . . . knew not what to do."

> They could not gain access to the public mind: for the press would not communicate the facts of the case—it was silent. In the city of New York, after a large meeting, where protests were drawn up against colonization, there was not a single public journal in the city, secular or religious, which would publish the views of the people of color on the subject.[39]

When *Freedom's Journal* "announced the facts for the case, our entire opposition," it became a forum for free black racial thought as well as African-American opposition to colonization. For Cornish's editorial policy reflected his utter rejection of the colonizationists' conviction that African-Americans could never win the respect of their white countrymen. "*To concede so much to prejudice is to deify it*," he maintained. Accordingly, he supported his paper's anticolonization message with discussions of African-Americans' origins and capabilities designed to illustrate their legitimate place in American society. "We have ever held that all men are equal by nature," he editorialized, emphasizing that the historical achievements of the black race compared favorably with those of other races. In ancient times "our now despised race were the inventors of different arts and sciences, while the rest of the now civilized world were sunk in darkness and ignorance." Colonizationists and other proponents of African-American inferiority, Cornish argued, always looked only to the ignorant and degraded condition of the American slave for evidence of black capacity. They omitted "through ignorance or illiberality what ancient sages have written . . . concerning this very 'wooly haired thick lipped, flat nosed, coal black race.' "[40] Intent on setting the facts straight, and rehabilitating the black race in the eyes of the world, *Freedom's Journal* presented arguments on the color of mankind at Creation, the genealogical descent of black people in the Bible, the ethnological status of the Egyptians, and the influence of environment on human variation. The discussions of racial subjects in *Freedom's Journal* set the broad outlines for African-American discourse on these subjects for many years to come.

"The Mutability of Human Affairs": Early Black Ethnology

Like the more racist ethnology that prevailed in the white community, black ideas about the origin and character of the races blended scientific explanation, history, and scriptural doctrine. One of the earliest examples of black ethnology is a long essay entitled "The Mutability of Human Affairs," which was published serially in *Freedom's Journal* during 1827. Written by John Russwurm, a West Indian–born graduate of Bowdoin College who was the junior editor of *Freedom's Journal*, this essay covered themes that would recur through black ethnological literature for the rest of the century.

Among the first African-Americans to receive a bachelor's degree from an American college, the well-educated young Russwurm was not as firmly set against colonization as Cornish and most other black leaders. Indeed, he would ultimately outrage his contemporaries by embracing colonizationism and departing for Africa. But so long as he wrote for *Freedom's Journal*, Russwurm remained in the anticolonization camp. Prior to his defection, his opposition to colonization was ingenious. His articles converted the colonizationist paeans to the glories of the Africa into arguments for black equality.

Russwurm modeled "The Mutability of Human Affairs" after Constantin-François Volney's *Ruins*, a 1791 meditation on the rise and fall of empires. Like the French philosopher, Russwurm began by mourning the fall of empires past, although his reverie focused pri-

Drawing of John Russwurm (courtesy of Widener
Library, Harvard University).

marily on the decline of Egypt. Upon a recent viewing of an Egyptian
mummy, he wrote, his "thoughts were insensibly carried back to former times when Egypt was in her splendor."[41] Russwurm's opening
set the stage for his argument that the ancient Egyptians were black
and closely related as a people to the ancient Ethiopians—whose very
name meant black. Thus claiming Egyptian heritage for himself and
all of Africa's children, he mourned "her present day degradation,
while reflecting on the mutability of human affairs, and upon the present condition of a people, who, for more than one thousand years,
were the most civilized and enlightened." By viewing the accomplishments of the races through the lens of time, Russwurm sought to
prove that the African race was not inferior. Africa's peoples had been
brought low by the same "mutability" that attended not only "the fortunes of their descendants, but [of] other nations also."

The Egyptians, Ethiopians, and their black African descendants,
Russwurm emphasized, were descendants of Ham by way of his son
Cush, whose progeny left a more illustrious record in biblical history
than the white branch of the human family—that is, the descendants
of Japhet. Moving from these historical and scriptural arguments for
black equality, Russwurm finished with a scientific argument. He
asserted that mankind was originally neither black nor white but

copper-colored, and that the physical differences between the races were caused by the environment. The ancient Egyptians became black in Africa as a result of the effects of that continent's hot climate on bile. Likewise, Europeans could permanently darken with prolonged exposure to the equatorial sun.[42]

Russwurm's arguments were not new. His scientific theory was, as Jane H. Pease and William H. Pease point out, "in harmony with theories well known to Americans at the period"—in particular, the climatist environmentalism of Samuel Stanhope Smith. Likewise, the historical and scriptural case he made for a glorious black past drew on ideas that had been around for quite some time. As Russwurm noted with reference to Herodotus, classical authors often referred to the Egyptians as a people of color and admired the achievements of both the Egyptians and the Ethiopians. On the basis of such evidence, eighteenth-century authors such as Volney viewed both peoples as black. Indeed, in reflecting on the fall of various empires, the French philosopher marveled that in "that narrow valley, watered by the Nile, . . . a people, now forgotten, discovered, while others were still barbarians, the elements of arts and sciences; a race of men now rejected from society for their *sable skin and frizzled hair,* founded the study of the laws of nature and those civil and religious systems which still govern the universe."[43] Similarly, Russwurm's contention that black Africans were descended from Noah's son Ham, whose progeny's achievements were recorded in the Scriptures, also drew on traditional wisdom. Starting in the fifteenth century, Europeans had identified the Hamites as a Negro people, although they had little to say about the achievements of the Hamites and viewed their color as a curse.[44]

Russwurm's early articulation of what would become the basic tenets of black ethnological self-defense illustrates how African-Americans built their case for equality of the races on eighteenth-century ideas. In the 1820s these ideas were still influential among whites as well and were most notably presented to further the colonizationist's arguments against the growing body of proslavery ideology that presented the Negro as inferior by nature and, therefore, a natural slave.[45] However, some of these ideas were already losing authority in white America. George Fredrickson writes, "Environmentalist philosophy was beginning to erode by 1810; by then, increasing doubts were being expressed about the naive eighteenth-century theory that differences in pigmentation were a comparatively short-range result of climate and other environmental factors."[46] Likewise, the eighteenth-century scriptural and historical arguments that Russwurm made on behalf of his race were becoming increasingly outmoded.

Indeed, Russwurm's mournful reflections on the mutability of human affairs were cleverly designed to challenge a complex constellation of unfavorable new ideas about the history and origins of the black race that was emerging in white America as he wrote his articles.

As can be seen in Russwurm's commentary, by the 1820s the rather positive eighteenth-century assessment of the ancient past of the black race, seen in European authors such as Volney, had few adherents in America. "Mankind," Russwurm complained, "generally allows that all nations are indebted to the Egyptians for the introduction of the arts and sciences; but they are not willing to acknowledge that the Egyptians bore any resemblance to the present race of Africans: though Herodotus, 'the father of history,' expressly declared that the Egyptians had black skins and frizzled hair."[47]

At stake in Russwurm's complaint was far more than ancient history. As he meant to show by emphasizing the mutability of human affairs, the fact that Egypt—the world's earliest civilization—developed in Africa confounded white American claims for the permanent and irradicable inferiority of the black race. If the Egyptians were even remotely related to African-Americans, proslavery apologists could not claim that the black race had always been ignorant and servile. Russwurm's point was a concern among white Americans as well, as is evident in his claim that they refused to acknowledge the color of the Egyptians.

In claiming Cush and Mizraim as the original ancestors of the black race, Russwurm may also have been addressing other questions about the biblical descent of the African race. Right through the nineteenth century, white Southerners often spoke of African-Americans as the children of Ham, who was father to Cush and Mizraim. This identification ran counter to any claims for a white Egypt, since, as Russwurm noted, biblical evidence suggests that these two sons of Ham founded Egypt and Ethiopia. Unlike Russwurm, however, white Southerners did not invoke this genealogy to tie the black race to Egypt. Leaving this connection aside, they stressed the Hamitic origins of the black race because they believed that black people were heir to an ancient and tragic legacy: namely, the "curse of Ham."[48] This article of faith was derived from a strange and confusing Old Testament story in which Noah cursed his son Ham after Ham was so immodest as to look upon his father's naked body when Noah was drunk and lay uncovered in his tent. The venerable old patriarch laid his punishment not on Ham directly but on Ham's son Canaan, decreeing that Canaan be "the slave of slaves."

Once seen by Europeans as a curse on the Slavs from the Black Sea region, who were widely enslaved in the late Middle Ages, the European myths about the curse of Ham were transferred to the African race with the rise of racial slavery. Not surprisingly, the African version of the story proved particularly popular in the United States, where the story of Ham's curse served as a convenient rationalization for the low status of black people in American society. In "The Mutability of Human Affairs," Russwurm did not address the question of whether the curse of Ham applied to black people directly, as many later black authors would do. But in addition to emphasizing that Africa rose and fell like other empires, he was careful to point out that the black race descended from Cush and Mizraim—both sons of Ham, but not the one named in Noah's curse.[49]

The questions about the origins and ancestry of the black race that Russwurm addressed in his series were soon to be neatly resolved in the minds of proslavery apologists such as Josiah Nott and George Gliddon by the theory of polygenesis, the doctrine of separate creations. According to this theory, black people were created separately from white people. Not even the descendants of Adam and Eve, blacks had no place in the Bible, and they appeared in Egypt only as the servants of a fair-skinned ruling race. Polygenesis would not receive its full scientific articulation until the 1840s and 1850s, when Nott, Gliddon, and Samuel Morton—the pioneers of what came to be known as the American school of ethnology—published a series of works arguing for the separate origins of the races.[50] But white Americans had evidently begun to entertain Thomas Jefferson's speculation that blacks might be "originally a distinct race" well before then. Already in 1827, Russwurm was concerned about such speculations. "The people of color are ignorant and degraded," he wrote, rehearsing white racist doctrine

> nothing can ever be made of them—God formed them to serve their fairer brethren—endowed them with faculties little superior to the tribe of Ourang Outangs. They want all the inner feelings of men—are an insensible and ungrateful race—and to render these prejudices still stronger, the craniologist exclaims, their retreating foreheads evidently denote them another race, something between man and brute creation![51]

Freedom's Journal folded just two years after it began and was succeeded only briefly by *The Rights of All,* another Cornish-led paper. Meanwhile, just as *Freedom's Journal* was folding, John Russwurm stunned the New York free black community, and hastened the paper's demise, by converting to colonizationism in 1829 and leaving for Liberia shortly thereafter.[52] But the black dialogue on ethnology that Russwurm had contributed to in *Freedom's Journal* would continue, rehearsing scriptural, historical, and environmental arguments for black equality that were increasingly at variance with white American racial thought. Indeed, arguments such as Russwurm's would seem increasingly crucial to the free black struggle for equality, since, even as they held fast to their old arguments for racial equality, black observers could not fail to notice the ominous developments in white racial thought.

Starting in the 1830s, the growth of an immediatist abolition movement among Northern whites inspired increasingly heated debates over slavery and black capacities. Led by William Lloyd Garrison, a New England journlist and evangelical reformer, a small group of white Northerners began to see the gradual emancipation plans favored by colonizationists as an immoral response to the sin of slavery. Denouncing gradual emancipation as an expedient, rather than a righteous means of eradicating bondage, these white reformers joined free blacks in calling for an immediate end to slavery. Never numerous, white abolitionists had an impact that belied their numbers. In 1831 Garrison founded the first white abolitionist newspaper, the *Liberator*, which would provide a forum for the opinions of black as well as white abolitionists right through to the passage of the Thirteenth Amendment in 1865. Along with other white abolitionists, Garrison also formed a new organization called the American Antislavery Society (AAS) in 1833. The AAS promoted and publicized the abolition of slavery with innovative techniques drawn from British reformers' successful campaign to abolish slavery in the West Indies.[53] Members of the AAS canvassed the North, distributing antislavery literature, organizing affiliates, and circulating antislavery petitions. This energetic white support was more than welcome among Northern free blacks, who were among Garrison's most devoted supporters. However, white abolitionism brought new enemies as well as new allies into the black struggle for freedom. Alarmed by the increasingly radical tone of Northern antislavery sentiment, white Southerners and their supporters began to come up with increasingly elaborate and racist justifications for slavery.

In the face of militant white opposition to slavery, supporters of the institution felt compelled to provide racial rationalizations for the enslavement of black people. Whereas Thomas Jefferson had lamented both black deficiencies and slavery, Southern intellectuals of the 1830s increasingly presented black deficiencies as a justification for slavery, arguing that black people were unfit for freedom. These Southern apologists were not the only proponents of racist dogma. Antiblack sentiment was rising in the North as well, where the abolitionist movement was unpopular enough to inspire mob violence against white and black abolitionists alike.

The wave of Revolutionary era egalitarianism that had led the Northern states to abolish slavery at home was all but gone by the 1830s. In the wake of emancipation, Northern blacks found persecution and exclusion. Disenfranchised in all but a few Northern states, they could not bear arms in the state militias, nor testify against whites in court. Generally unwelcome in white society, blacks could not count on being able to use public services—including schools—which were frequently segregated or set aside for whites. A myriad of local ordinances, varying from place to place, restricted where blacks could live, work, travel, and even gather in public. Outside abolitionist circles, white Northerners shared their Southern counterparts' conviction that blacks were a grossly inferior race that could never hope to interact with white people on equal terms.[54]

Proslavery and antiblack arguments for African-American inferiority were, of course, rejected by white abolitionists, but the attitudes and actions of individual whites in the abolitionist movement often failed to live up to the movement's egalitarian ideology. While staunchly antislavery, white abolitionists were less reliable as allies against racism. Indeed, blacks sometimes found themselves unwelcome in the new white abolition societies that began to proliferate after 1830. Established in 1835, the Ladies' New York Antislavery Society was one such organization. Led by white middle-class evangelicals, the society opposed the "social mixing" of the races and effectively excluded black members.[55] At the same time, even integrated abolitionist organizations did not always admit African-Americans on equal terms. African-Americans were allowed only a limited role in the decisions made by many abolitionist organizations and rarely held positions of authority within them.[56] Moreover, as the abolitionist movement grew, it attracted white supporters whose antislavery politics did not always entail a strong commitment to black equality. "Three years ago, when a man professed to be an Abolitionist we all knew where he was. He was an individual who recognized the identity of the human family," Theodore S. Wright commented in 1837, lamenting the changing composition of the abolitionist movement. "Now a man calls himself an abolitionist and we know not where to find him." Wright linked this change to the increasing popularity of the movement, noting: "A rush is made into the abolition ranks. Free discussion, Anti-Texas, and political favor converts are multiplying." He went on to recommend that "every man who comes into this society ought to be catechized. It should be ascertained whether he looks upon man as man, all of one blood and one family."[57] The same year Samuel Cornish expressed similar concerns with reference to the benevolent whites in the American Union for the Improvement of People of Color. Cornish thought the members of this organization had no hope of being serviceable "until they have buried their prejudice of heart, and learned to view [blacks], as brethren of the same family and the same blood, with themselves."[58]

In the face of a colorphobia so ubiquitous that it even compromised their white allies in the antislavery movement, black thinkers became ever more determined to uphold traditional wisdom about the unity of the races. The subject was too important to be left in the hands of unreliable white allies. As the 1830s began, this point was emphasized by a remarkable black Bostonian named David Walker. Between September 1829 and the beginning of 1830, Walker published and amended three editions of a fiery manifesto entitled *Appeal to the Colored Citizens of the World*. His *Appeal* denounced slavery, colonization, and racial discrimination, calling for increased black opposition to all three. The most vehement abolitionist tract of its day, Walker's *Appeal* was banned in the South because it called for violent

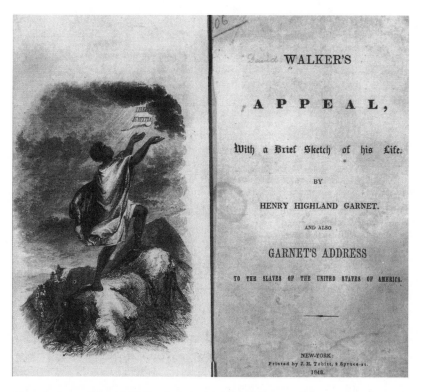

Frontispiece of David Walker's *Appeal* (1829) (Library of Congress).

resistance to slavery. A champion of intellectual as well as physical resistance to white oppression, Walker also encouraged black contributions on the subject of ethnology. "We and the world," Walker wrote in his *Appeal*," wish to see the charges of Mr. Jefferson refuted by the blacks *themselves*, according to their chance; for we must remember that what whites have written respecting this subject, is other men's labours and did not emanate from blacks."[59] Laying the groundwork for such contributions himself, Walker reviewed the history of the races in his *Appeal*, defending the black race with some of the same arguments used by Russwurm, while raising some new questions about the character of the white race.

"Whether They Are as *Good* as Ourselves": David Walker's *Appeal*

Born in Wilmington, North Carolina, in 1785, David Walker was the son of free black mother and a slave father. Little is known about his early life, but by the late 1820s Walker had settled in Boston, where he made his living as the proprietor of what was known as a "slop shop"—a used-clothing store that specialized in outfitting sailors.[60] Also a prominent antislavery activist, Walker was the Boston agent for *Freedom's Journal*, which he sold out of his Brattle Street store. Hence, it is not surprising to find him rehearsing some of the same ethnological arguments for black equality advocated in *Freedom's Journal*.

Like John Russwurm, Walker assumed that the African race descended from Ham and that all the races were of one blood. Debunking another racist canard, he also noted that blacks were not "the seed of Cain," stained dark so they might be known as slaves, as "ignorant and avaricious" whites sometimes claimed. "Man, in all ages and all nations of the earth, is the same," Walker declared, outraged that anyone could think otherwise. "See the inconsistency of the assertions of those wretches," he wrote of white Americans. "They beat us inhumanely, sometimes almost to death, for attempting to inform ourselves, by reading the *Word* of our Maker, and at the same time tell us that we are beings *void of intellect*!!!"[61]

To the contrary, wrote Walker, the black race had once led the world in learning and civilization. As Russwurm had done, he traced the history of the African race back to the mighty civilizations of ancient Egypt, noting that it had once ridden high, only to be plunged into an "almost impenetrable abyss" by the "wheel of events." Depressingly ignorant and degraded in the present day, African-Americans were further tormented by being told that "they are an *inferior* and *distinct race* of beings," a lie that Walker feared blacks would "swallow by and by." Nothing could be further from the truth. "When we take the retrospective view of the arts and sciences—the wise legislators —the Pyramids, and other magnificent buildings—the turning of the channel of the river Nile, by the sons of Africa or of Ham, among whom learning was originated, and carried thence into Greece, where it was improved upon and refined," Walker argued, blacks had no cause to be ashamed of their heritage. History testified to "the renown of that once mighty people."[62]

Interestingly, as he proclaimed his people's Egyptian heritage, Walker also revealed how new this understanding of black history was among the African-Americans of his era. Widely popularized by Afrocentric thinkers today, the idea that the black race had ancestral ties with Egypt was not a traditional theme in African-American culture when Russwurm and Walker wrote. As they converted to Christianity in the eighteenth century, enslaved African-Americans had made the story of the Exodus their own. But far from tracing their ancestry to Egypt, black Americans identified with the Hebrews, whose escape from slavery they hoped to emulate. As an early champion of his people's ancient heritage in Egypt, therefore, Walker first had to explain the connection between the two peoples:

> Some of my brethren do not know who Pharoah and the Egyptians were—I know it to be a fact, that some of them take the Egyptians to have been a gang of *devils*, not knowing any better, and that they (Egyptians) having got possession of the Lord's people, treated them *nearly* as cruel as *Christian Americans* do us, at the present day. For the information of such, I would only mention that the Egyptians, were Africans or coloured people, such as we are.[63]

New in the 1830s, the idea that Egyptians were black would become a commonplace among educated African-Americans as the nineteenth century progressed. Following Walker and Russwurm's lead, many generations of subsequent black thinkers would invoke the accomplishments of a black Egypt to counter charges that their race had always been a servile one.

In addition to endorsing the Egyptian ancestry and Hamitic descent of the black race, Walker raised another subject that would loom large in nineteenth-century black ethnology, namely, the racial character of white people. Going one step further than Russwurm, who defended the African race without casting aspersions on the character of the white race, Walker countered white assertions of black inferiority with questions about white racial capacities. Disdainful of white pretensions of superiority, most especially "Mr. Jefferson's remarks respecting us," Walker wondered whether whites might be the inferior race.[64] "The whites have always been an unjust, unmerciful, avaricious and bloodthirsty set of beings, always seeking after power and authority," he argued in his *Appeal*.

> We view them all over the confederacy of Greece, where they were first known to be any thing, (in consequence of education) we see them there, cutting each other's throats—trying to subject each other to wretchedness and misery—to effect which, they used all kinds of deceitful, unfair, and unmerciful means. We view them next in Rome, where the spirit of tyranny and deceit raged still higher.—In fine we view them in Europe, together with what were scattered about in Asia and Africa, as heathens, and we see them acting more like devils than accountable men. But some may ask, did not the blacks of Africa and the mulattoes of Asia, go on in the same way as whites did of Europe[?] I answer, no—they were never half so avaricious, deceitful and unmerciful as whites, according to their knowledge.[65]

On the basis of his review of white history in Europe and America, Walker turned Jefferson's suspicions of black inferiority around, solemnly concluding, "I therefore, in the name and fear of the Lord God of Heaven and of earth, divested of prejudice either on the side of my colour or that of the whites, advance my suspicion of them, whether they are as *good by nature* as we are or not."[66]

David Walker died shortly after his *Appeal* was published, succumbing swiftly and unexpectedly to a stomach ailment toward the end of June 1830. Many Boston blacks attributed his death to poison, believing him murdered by one of his many proslavery enemies. Despite his tragic and mysterious death, the issues Walker raised in his *Appeal* lived on. Answering Walker's call for black contributions on ethnology, black leaders and thinkers wrote extensively on the origins and character of the races throughout the antebellum period and beyond. In doing so, they would build on the scriptural and environmental arguments for black equality first set in place during early nineteenth-century black struggles against slavery, discrimination, and colonization.

Also set in place early on were some of the ironies and contradictions that would bedevil black ethnologists as they expanded upon themes first laid out in Walker's *Appeal* and Russwurm's articles. As Walker's manifesto reveals, one of the overwhelming ironies in black ethnology was that African-Americans fought white allegations of black inferiority with arguments that were not always traditional to African-American culture, nor even wholly their own. The eighteenth-century environmentalism black intellectuals invoked against accusations that black people were an inferior order of beings was lifted from the ideas of eighteenth-century naturalists. And African-American claims to Egyptian ancestry were inspired by white attacks on the historical achievements of the African race, rather than any oral tradition among African-Americans.

Moreover, Walker's *Appeal* also shows that African-Americans bent on proving black equality would not necessarily escape the concept of race altogether. As will be apparent in upcoming chapters, the African-Americans who wrote on ethnology were, to some degree, ensnared by the idea of race even as they sought to refute racism's insult to their humanity. For the historical and environmentalist defenses of black humanity in black ethnology stressed the equal excellence of the races, while not necessarily affirming the actual identity of black and white men and women. White and black people were the products of different histories and different environments, many nineteenth-century African-American writers emphasized in defense of their race's color and condition: they were different but equal. Yet these black-authored arguments for difference and equality were beset by some of the same difficulties contained in the late nineteenth-century white segregationist doctrine of "separate but equal." Equality does not easily coexist with difference or separation.

The contradictions between difference and equality are easily seen in Walker's *Appeal*, for he argued that the races were equal while also suggesting that blacks were better than whites. He asked, "How can the preachers and people believe the Bible? Does it teach them any distinction on account of man's colour?" His answer was a resounding no. Yet, as we have seen, when he reflected on the history of the white race and the current injustices practiced by his white fellow Americans, he was less than egalitarian himself: he repeatedly questioned "whether they are as good as ourselves."[67]

"Facts as Clear as Daylight": Racial Difference in Black Ethnology

"Posterity will find it difficult to believe," wrote the Haitian ex-slave Pompée-Valentin Vastey in 1817,

> that in an age like ours, there are men, who call themselves philosophers, willing to reduce human beings to an equality with brutes, merely for the sake of sanctioning the abominable privilege of oppressing a large portion of mankind. While I am writing I can scarcely refrain from laughter, at the absurdities which have been published on this subject. Learned authors and skillful anatomists, have passed their lives discussing facts as clear as daylight, and in dissecting the bodies of men and animals in order to prove that I, who am now writing, belong to the race of Ourang-Outangs.[68]

Vastey's outrage was echoed throughout the nineteenth century by American blacks who, above all else, spoke out on the subject of race to resist the terrible insult thrown up against them by those who sought to cast their race as a lesser species. "None but APES will doubt for but a moment but what man is man everywhere," wrote antislavery lecturer David Ruggles in 1834, mocking the slur cast on his race by those who questioned the status of black people in the human family.[69]

Mockery and scorn, however, were small weapons to carry into battle against the growing authority of racist ideology in nineteenth-century America. As we have seen, black Americans felt compelled to disprove, rather than dismiss, even the earliest, tentative arguments for black inferiority made by white Americans such as Thomas Jefferson. And they would continue to feel compelled to address white racist doctrine throughout the nineteenth century. Building on the scriptural and environmental defenses of black equality first seen in *Freedom's Journal*, black thinkers developed a distinctive black ethnology that provides rich evidence about black ideas about race in general, and white people in particular.

Like David Walker, later black thinkers would also wonder whether whites might be the truly inferior race. Yet they would also voice the most ringing denunciations of race as fallacy heard in nineteenth-century America. Within this profoundly ambivalent racial discourse, black ideas about white people took shape. In refuting and rebuting antiblack doctrine, African-American intellectuals questioned the whole idea of race. Yet their challenges to white racist doctrine sometimes reified the concept of race. Rather than abandoning racial distinctions, black thinkers revised them, presenting the black race as a more-than-equal, redeemer race. Whites, they often suggested, were overly aggressive and lacking in moral virtues that were natural to black people—"Angry Saxons," as a twentieth-century heir to this tradition quipped.[70] The next chapter will trace the emergence of the redeemer race and those Angry Saxons.

TWO

𝒮ℓ

The Redeemer Race and
the Angry Saxon

*Race, Gender, and White People
in Antebellum Black Ethnology*

Government requires make believe. Make believe that the King is
divine, make believe that he can do no wrong or make believe that the
voice of the people is the voice of God. Make believe that the people
have a voice or make believe that the representatives of the people are
the people. . . . Make believe that all men are equal or make believe that
they are not.

Edmund Morgan, *Inventing the People:
The Rise of Popular Sovereignty in England and America*[1]

By the 1830s, Jefferson's tentative suspicion that black people might
be inferior to white people was emerging as one of America's governing fictions—one of the "make believes" of government that Edmund
Morgan talks about. Ironically, the fiction at the heart of the caste system that emerged in this new nation's industrializing democracy was
nothing modern but an old "Phoenician thing," described in Plato's
Republic more than two thousand years earlier. In a dialogue with his
disciple Glaucon on how to create a great republic, the great philosopher Socrates argues that the creation of an ideal society might require an "audacious fiction." A stable and orderly society, the philosopher maintains, must rest on class divisions. So the citizens in the ideal
republic will be divided by education and merit into three ranks:
rulers, auxiliaries, and craftsmen. But the republic will prosper only if
its citizens accept their ranks. Unable to devise any logical reason for
citizens to acquiesce to the three unequal ranks, Socrates proposes a
"noble lie":

> They [the citizens] are to be told that their youth was a dream, and their
> education and training which they received from us, an appearance
> only; in reality during all that time they were being formed and fed in
> the womb of the earth. . . . Citizens, we shall say to them in our tale, you
> are brothers, yet God has framed you differently. Some of you have the

power of command, and in composition of these he has mingled gold, wherefore also they have the greatest honor; others he has made of silver, to be auxiliaries; others again who are to be husbandmen and craftsmen he has composed of brass and iron; and the species will generally be preserved in the children. . . . An oracle says that when a man of brass or iron guards the State, it will be destroyed.

Socrates then asks Glaucon, "Is there any possibility of making our citizens believe it?" "Not in the present generation," Glaucon replies. "There is no way of accomplishing this; but their sons may be made to believe in the tale, and their son's sons, and posterity after that."[2]

Substitute "genes for metal," as Stephen Jay Gould has pointed out, and Socrates' tale might well apply to nineteenth-century America. But did Glaucon's prediction come true? Perhaps it did for white Americans, whose whiteness was indeed precious currency. But black people—the closest American equivalents to Socrates' men of brass and iron—had little incentive to buy the story. Not even secure within the lowly ranks assigned to Socrates' iron and brass husbandmen and guardsmen, they confronted a far more insidious fiction than the story the Greek philosopher told—a fiction that put them entirely outside the polity in many ways. In the antebellum era, even free black people were not considered American citizens, according to Supreme Court Justice Taney's infamous 1957 *Dred Scott* ruling, which declared that African-Americans as a group "had no rights which the white man was bound to respect."[3] Moreover, throughout the century all African-Americans, enslaved or otherwise, were subject to a variety of legal, political, and civil restrictions. Worst of all, perhaps, was that the American version of the lie put them not only outside the polity but also outside of the human community. "Have they not, after having reduced us to the deplorable condition of slaves under their feet, held us up as originally descending from the tribes of *Monkeys* or *Orang-Outangs*?" David Walker asked.[4]

"Us is human flesh," the slaves claimed, and likewise free and educated African-Americans spoke out all through the nineteenth century to repudiate white attempts to place the black race outside of the human family.[5] But, as a survey of antebellum black writing on ethnology and race can show, race's "audacious fiction" held some ideas that educated blacks found difficult to altogether escape. Written by black leaders and thinkers who were all too well versed in the specific scientific and scriptural arguments made by white racists, black ethnology sought to answer racism's charges directly. Rejecting the values assigned to the races in white racial thought, the African-Americans who wrote ethnology refused to be placed at the bottom of a hierarchy of the races. Yet they did not always rule out the possibility of racial differences—the citizens composed of brass and iron might still be distinguished from the classes made of silver and gold, provided all the metals were precious.

In attempting to revise the values that white Americans assigned to the races, black intellectuals struggled with multiple meanings that race held in American culture—meanings that further complicated and obfuscated the racial fiction that they faced. In particular, these critics of racism had to face the fact that what was at stake in the American debates over who qualified for citizenship was not just color or even race. Also at issue in these debates was manhood—a prerequisite for citizenship rights in nineteenth-century American political culture. Defined by race as well as gender, "manhood rights" traditionally "inhered to white males, only." As Gail Bederman points out:

> Framers of the state constitutions in sixteen northern and western states explicitly placed African-American men in the same category as women, as "dependents." Negro males, whether free or slave, were forbidden to exercise manhood rights—to vote, hold electoral office, serve on juries, or join the military. Similarly, white working men insisted that, as men, they had claim to manly independence that women and Negro men lacked. The conclusion was implicit but widely understood: Negro males, unlike white males, were less than men.[6]

Implicit in law, this conclusion was explicit in much of white racial thought. Written almost exclusively by white men, the white supremacist literature of the nineteenth century asserted that blacks were inferior to whites in much the same way that women were inferior to men—less intelligent and rational, more childlike and emotional.

Meanwhile, African-Americans were well aware that white attempts to place black people outside the polity rested, above all, on a denial that black males possessed all the qualities of men. To be sure, black women were sorely oppressed as well. Enslaved in the South and impoverished in the North, most African-American women were utterly excluded from the ideals white Americans invoked to define womanhood. They might be wives and mothers, as their society dictated that women should be, but the arduous work that most black women performed, combined with the low status of their race, exempted black women from fulfilling the nineteenth-century ideal of true womanhood. Whatever their feminine qualities, complained black Bostonian Maria Stewart in 1832, black women could never be ladies. "Let our girls possess whatever amiable qualities of soul they may; let their characters be as fair and spotless as innocence itself; let their natural taste and ingenuity be what it may; it is impossible for scarce an individual among them to rise above the condition of servants."[7] Yet Stewart and other nineteenth-century black activists ultimately saw the disabilities suffered by black women as arising from the degradation of black men.

"Have the sons of Africa no souls? Feel they no ambitious desires? Shall the chains of ignorance forever confine them?" asked Maria Stewart, who lambasted black men for not doing more to vindicate their race and elevate their women and children. Women could only do so much, Stewart argued, embracing the domestic ideals of true womanhood. Black women could "strive to excel in good housewifery, knowing that prudence and economy are the road to wealth," she suggested. They could raise funds for colored schools. But ultimately the larger task of raising "your sons and daughters from the horrible state of servitude and degradation in which they are placed" lay with black men. "It is upon you that woman depends; she can do little besides using her influence."[8]

Black men clearly accepted this judgment. Indeed, they often questioned their own manhood when they reflected on the low status of African-Americans in American society. "Are we MEN!!—I ask you, O my Brethren! are we MEN?" was the question David Walker put to the "men of color" he addressed in his *Appeal*. "How can we be so *submissive* to a gang of men, whom we cannot tell whether they are *as good* as ourselves or not, I never could conceive."[9] Like his suspicions about whether whites were "*as good* as ourselves," Walker's question "Are we MEN?" would resonate throughout nineteenth-century black writing on race—long outlasting Walker himself. During this era, African-American literature on ethnology and race, like its white counterpart, was written almost exclusively by men and aimed to find a place for black men among the "races of men."

Forced to defend their claims to manhood, as well as their place in the human family, the black men who wrote ethnology became enmeshed in a complex discourse about race, gender, and difference that frequently led them to racial fictions of their own. Some of these men struggled to debunk race as a concept, but they all stopped short of rejecting the notion of racial differences altogether. Moreover, although they were highly aware of the ideological interests that white comparisons between the races served, African-American leaders and thinkers were ultimately unable to eschew such comparisons themselves.

As a result, their arguments for racial equality were always ambivalent and self-contradictory. Some conceded that in their present low estate, African-Americans were only potentially equal to white people; others shared Walker's suspicion that black people might be better than white people. Long-suffering and virtuous, the latter thinkers argued, blacks constituted a "redeemer race": a people who had once led the world and were destined to lead it again. Replete with gentle virtues lacking in the Anglo-Saxon race, the moral and pious "redeemer race" was celebrated by black authors as an alternative to both white supremacy and the masculine values associated with the white race.

A revision of the American racial hierarchy, as well as a critique of the brutal behavior of white Americans toward African-Americans, the racial self-image that emerged in black ethnology reveals limits that circumscribed African-American challenges to racism's audacious fiction. Crafted to counter white assertions that black people might have been "originally . . . distinct"—as Jefferson put it—black ethnology emphasized the original unity of the human family without claiming that the races were identical.[10] As African-American authors juggled equality and difference, black ethnology became a rich site for racial imagery and discourse, on which African-American ideas about white and black people were mapped in counterpoint.

Abolitionism, Proslavery Science, and the Rise of Black Ethnology

Black efforts at racial self-vindication were needed more urgently than ever in the years that followed David Walker's death in 1830. As white Americans continued to debate the morality of slavery and the nature of black capacities, American science began to lend increasing support to racist ideas. By the 1840s, scientific claims for black inferiority had become commonplace. In pioneering new studies of anatomy, craniology, and human development, American scientists compared the races and invariably found that the Negro came up short. So short, in fact, that some scientists questioned whether blacks and whites were even remotely related.

The most influential of these scientists was Dr. Samuel Morton of Philadelphia, one of the founders of the American school of ethnology. A man of Quaker upbringing with no evident personal interest in slavery, Morton was a craniologist who collected and studied human skulls for insights into ethnology. Morton took the cranium to be an accurate measure of human moral and mental capacities and further hypothesized that the races varied significantly by skull size. Published in an 1839 volume entitled *Crania Americana*, his collection of skull measurements dovetailed nicely with popular prejudices: Caucasians had the largest skulls, blacks the smallest, and Indians were in between.

In addition to providing what was hailed as definitive scientific evidence of black inferiority, Morton's research fueled white doubts about the place of blacks in the human family.[11] Decades earlier Jefferson had speculated that blacks might be originally distinct from whites. Now Morton, whose work with ancient and modern skulls led him to believe that different races had not changed much over time, began to share the founding father's suspicions. Collaborating with George Gliddon, an Egyptologist who provided him with mummy skulls and other archaeological evidence, he set out to assess the antiquity of the races. In his second book, *Crania Aegyptiaca* (1844), Morton concluded that racial distinctions were indeed ancient and enduring.[12] The Egyptians were not black, he argued, and the black people who lived in Egypt had occupied servile positions, much like their American counterparts.[13] From there it was but a short step for

Morton and other members of the American school to conclude that blacks were the product of a separate creation—too different and distinct from whites to share the same ancestry.

Enthusiastically promoted by proslavery advocates such as Dr. Josiah Nott, who was a leading exponent of the new ethnology, the theory of polygenesis struck other Americans as rank heresy. The Bible recorded only one Creation; there could be no more. Even the perennially proslavery George Fitzhugh was slow to embrace this pluralist theory of human origins on the grounds that it was "at war with scripture, which teaches us that the whole human race descended from a common parentage," although he eventually did so.[14] Controversial even among slavery's supporters, polygenesis never displaced the traditionally accepted account of human origins—monogenesis. Nor did it displace other more traditional explanations of Negro inferiority, such as the story of the curse of Ham, which remained popular in the South.

But the American school of ethnology's findings proved influential all the same. Proslavery and antiblack thinkers did not have to embrace the theory of polygenesis to make use of ethnological evidence for black inferiority. Monogenist Southerners incorporated the new ethnology into the story of Ham, rendering blacks servile by both biology and divine decree.[15] And white Americans in general were open to the scientific proof of black inferiority that Morton offered in *Crania Americana* and *Crania Aegyptiaca*. The statistical charts that these books contained, which ranked the races by skull size, were widely respected and reproduced. Indeed, according to biologist Stephen Jay Gould, Morton's charts "outlived the theory of separate creations, and were reprinted repeatedly during the nineteenth century as irrefutable 'hard' data on the mental worth of the races."[16]

Now thoroughly discredited, the data collected by Morton and other nineteenth-century scientists no longer testify to anything but how powerfully science can be shaped by preconceived ideas. Gould, who has revisited Morton's data, describes his results as "a patchwork of fudging and finagling in the clear interest of controlling *a priori* convictions."[17] But in the antebellum period, what we now call scientific racism was the *science* of its day. The polygenesis-monogenesis controversy aside, data for black inferiority went largely unchallenged, except among free blacks who observed the increasing racial bias in American science with alarm and disappointment.

"We had hoped for much from science," mourned a writer in *Colored American* in 1839, reviewing a physician's report on the New York Colored Orphan's Asylum that attributed high mortality rates among the orphans to peculiarities in the constitution their race. "We had fondly dreamed that she would ever rear her head far above the buzz of popular applause, or the conflicting opinion of the moral world; it is therefore almost with the anguish that springs from a blasted hope that we view this first, however flimsy, attempt to demean her to the contemptible office of pandering to public prejudices."[18] Other blacks could hardly contain their contempt for the new ethnology, or the causes it was being used to support. "Ninety-nine out of every hundred of the advocates of a diverse origin of the human family, are among those who hold it the privilege of the *Anglo-Saxon* to enslave and oppress the African" was Frederick's Douglass's cynical assessment of white ethnology.[19]

Bitterly aware that they were under attack from all corners, African-American leaders and thinkers did more than just complain. They expanded on their own discourse on ethnology, presenting ever more detailed rebuttals to racist theories such as polygenesis. Like white ethnology, black ethnology blended science and Scripture, but black and white practitioners told very different stories about the history and capacities of the races. White scientists took the inferiority of the African race as a given, sometimes even presenting the inferiority of black people as evidence showing that blacks were the product of a separate creation. By contrast, African-American ethnologists denied such charges and defended the place of black people in the human family. Expanding on the defense of eighteenth-century environmentalism laid out by John Russwurm, black thinkers presented their own accounts of the history and origins of races. Their revisionist accounts of human ethnology challenged both white science and white supremacy, sometimes even predicting "the destined superiority of the Negro race."

Unembarrassing the Origins of the Colored People: Black Ethnology in the 1830s and 1840s

One of the earliest black ethnologists was Robert Benjamin Lewis, a Maine resident of mixed African and Indian descent. A jack-of-all-trades, Lewis made his living painting, papering, and whitewashing houses, cleaning carpets, crafting baskets, caning chairs, and fixing parasols and umbrellas. In 1836 he added a new trade to his repertoire when he became an author and traveled through New England on annual tours, selling a book he had written.[20] Entitled *Light and Truth: Collected from the Bible and Ancient and Modern History, Containing the Universal History of the Colored and the Indian Race, from the Creation of the World to the Present Time*, Lewis's four-hundred-page volume was the first book-length work in black history and ethnology.

Echoing John Russwurm and other black writers who had covered these subjects in *Freedom's Journal* a decade earlier, Lewis emphasized the past achievements and illustrious ancestry of the colored race. Like them, he argued that the Egyptians had descended from the Ethiopians, and that the Ethiopians were the children of Ham. However, Lewis went one step further than the earlier writers in his discussion of the origins of the races. He maintained that the Garden of Eden was in Ethiopia and that God had created Adam from "the rich and *black* soil" of the land.[21] Although *Light and Truth* contains no mention of polygenesis, Lewis's account of human origins virtually turned the doctrine of separate creations on its head. Blacks became the first family, and Lewis further insisted that all the early nations were colored: "Greece, Europe, and NORTH AND SOUTH AMERICA WERE SETTLED BY DESCENDANTS OF EGYPT," he proclaimed.[22]

Light and Truth did not complete its reversal of white racial theory by suggesting that whites were the product of a separate creation. Rather, Lewis's account of human history says nothing about how or when the white race originated. Over all, except for a brief reference to Greek "aborigines," whom he described in graphically unflattering terms, Lewis simply left out white history—much as white writers did the African and African-American past. "Extremely barbarous," the early Greeks "wandered in the woods, without law or government, having little intercourse with each other. They clothed themselves with the skin of beasts; retreated for shelter to rocks and caverns; and lived on acorns, wild fruits, raw flesh and even devoured the enemies they slew in battle."[23] By contrast, Lewis's account of the ancient history of the colored race was expansive and glorious. Recoloring the heroes of the Bible and the ancient world, Lewis maintained that Plato and Julius Ceasar were Ethiopians, and that Moses, Solomon, and many other luminaries were men of color. Moreover, in a section entitled "The Hair on Men's Heads," he went further still, arguing that biblical descriptions of the hair of both Christ and God himself showed that the Almighty and his Son were colored also.[24]

Light and Truth provides an early example of how easily African-American efforts to rebut white racial doctrine could shade into a black chauvinism that mirrored the very racist logic it opposed. Racism could be reversed more readily than it could be controverted. The disconcerting parallels between Lewis's extravagant claims for the colored races and the historical claims made by white writers did not go unnoticed. No stranger himself to claims for black superiority, Martin Delany lambasted Lewis for mirroring the errors of prominent American Egyptologist George Gliddon, who "makes all ancient black men *white*." "So this colored man makes all the ancient great white men *black*," Delany noted in 1852. "Gliddon's idle nonsense had found a capital match in the production of Mr. Lewis' 'Light and Truth' and both should be sold together."[25]

Light and Truth met a better reception elsewhere. The book went through at least three editions. Initially published in four installments by Lewis himself, it was republished in a one-volume edition in 1844 by a "Committee of Colored Men"; the committee also issued a second edition. Endorsing Lewis's pantheon of colored heroes, these publishers explained that they offered the book in order that "a correct knowledge of colored and Indian people ancient and modern, may be extended freely, unbiassed [*sic*] by any prejudicial effects from descent or station." Indeed, thanks to Lewis's annual book tours, *Light and Truth* may well have been the most widely circulated of the nineteenth-century black publications on ethnology.

Other early works of black ethnology both recognized the existence of the white race and offered more measured assessments of the relationship between the races. Even as they insisted that all the races were of one blood, however, African-American writers were often far from sure that the races were identical. Published in 1837, Hosea Easton's *Treatise on the Intellectual Character, and Civil and Political Condition of the Colored People of the United States* offers a case in point. Easton, who led an African Methodist Episcopal Zion Church in Hartford, Connecticut, did not make all black men white. Indeed, Easton, who came from a Boston family with a history of "aggressive protest against white racism," attacked the very idea of race distinctions.[26] Citing the authority of the Scriptures—as did all the participants in the nineteenth-century debates over ethnology—Easton insisted that since God had made all men of one blood there could be no innate differences among the races. Human complexions varied, as did the texture of human hair, but such distinctions were "casual or incidental," and of no more consequence than the color variations seen in some species of flowers. "Were I to be asked why my hair is curled," said Easton "my answer would be because God gave nature the gift of producing variety."[27]

Easton further argued that white theories about the racial peculiarities of black people were "the production of modern philosophy, bearing date with European slavery." The widespread conviction that blacks endured heat better than whites, he noted by way of example, was but one of the confabulations that arose with the slave trade. It gave the slave traders "a plea of justification" for carrying Africans across the sea to work the temperate plantations of the New World, and it proved equally useful to the American planters who grew rich off the profits of slave-grown cotton, rice, indigo, tobacco, and sugar. "It must be that God had made [Africans] on purpose for that," wrote Easton, parroting the smug logic of proslavery apologists; "hence, it is no harm for us to act in accordance with the purpose of God." Likewise, the ubiquitous white complaint that blacks were lazy invariably sustained rationalizations for forced labor: "If they are not made to work for us, they will not work at all, and &c." White theories about the origins of the races were equally self-serving, argued Easton, presenting American ethnology as his example:

> There could be nothing more natural, than for a slaveholding nation to indulge in a train of thoughts and conclusions that favored their idol, slavery. It becomes the interest of all parties, not excepting the clergy, to

sanction the premises, and draw the conclusions, and hence teach a rising generation. What could better accord with the objects of this nation
with reference to blacks, than to teach their little ones that the negro is
part monkey?[28]

Easton's incisive analysis of the functions of prejudice appears to
challenge the existence of racial differences—to expose race as a social construction as modern scholars have done. But elsewhere in his
Treatise, Easton reenvisions racial differences rather than repudiating
them. Weaving the traditional components of the African-American
ethnological defense into a dizzyingly complex theory of racial development, Easton presents blacks and whites as having different tem-
peraments as well as a different past, present, and future.

All the nations were of one blood, argued Easton, but the races that
had descended from the sons of Noah had charted different paths.
The descendants of Ham, who founded Africa, had a far more illustrious history than the children of Japhet's son Javan, who was the
father of the Greeks. Africans had dominated the ancient world,
building a mighty empire in Egypt and "carrying the blessings of civilization to Greece." But then this cultivated and "unwarlike people"
had been overtaken by the Europeans, whose "innate thirst for blood
and plunder" drove them to roam the earth in search of conquests
and colonies. The fortunes of the races seesawed. Africa was "robbed
of her riches and honors, and sons and daughters, to glut the rapacity of European bigots."[29]

The Africans lost their kingdoms, their history, and even their
racial integrity to the European advance, wrote Easton, who believed
American slaves were physically and intellectually inferior to both whites
and blacks who had never been enslaved. The African-American
slave population was indeed degraded, the freeborn Easton conceded, sounding for all the world like a white racist when he listed
the "lineal effects" of slavery. "Contracted and sloping foreheads"
were among the characteristics that slavery imposed on African-
Americans, along with "prominent eyeballs; projecting under-jaw;
certain distended muscles about the mouth, or lower parts of the
face; thick lips and flat nose[s]; hips and rump projecting; crooked
shins; flat feet, with large projecting heels [and] half destroyed, dis-
cordant minds." But these characteristics did not stem from any
"original hereditary cause." They were the product of slavery, which
caused suffering so acute it maimed the unborn. Exposed to the elements, frightened, brutalized, and overworked, slave mothers did
not give birth to normal children—"Unnatural causes produce unnatural effects." Fortunately, these effects could be reversed. A thoroughgoing environmentalist, Easton believed that the ill effects of the
slave environment would disappear once that environment disap-
peared, providing white Americans were willing to stimulate the "genius" of the race.[30]

"Nothing but liberal, generous principles, can call the energies of an African mind into action," wrote Easton, sketching a vision of a black people as a gentle race whose redemption would mark the beginning of a millennial era. Casting black people as the barometer of human goodness, he maintained that Africa would not rise until "other nations have learned to deal justly with her from principle. . . . When that time shall arrive, a lapse of but a few generations will show the world that her sons will again take the lead in the field of virtuous enterprise, filling the front ranks of the church, when she marches into the millennium."[31]

In Easton's teleology of race development, African-Americans were likewise the measure of American justice and would not achieve their full potential until slavery and color prejudice were eradicated in both the North and the South. "Merely to cease beating the colored people and leave them in their gore, and call it emancipation is nonsense," said Easton, who clearly thought that the Northern states had not done enough for their ex-slave population. African-Americans would not be redeemed until "all that slavery had taken away from them" had been restored. Whites would have to "act the part of the good Samaritan" and provide remedies for the degradation they had imposed on all African-Americans. Easton did not state exactly what these remedies would be, but he insisted that if whites would but "do unto others as they would that others should do unto them," they would see a wondrous transformation in America's black population. Not only would the "innate principles of moral, civil and social manhood" be kindled anew among black Americans; their very physiognomies would change. Freed from the scourges of slavery and color prejudice, African-American countenances would "brighten with joy," "narrow foreheads, which have hitherto been contracted for want of mental exercise, would begin to broaden," and eyeballs once "strained to prominence by a frenzy excited by the flourish of the whip" would recede."[32]

In part, Easton's premillenarian message was no doubt designed to foster hope among African-Americans and inspire antislavery whites to redouble their efforts. His argument that the eradication of slavery and race prejudice would purge the nation of its sins was in keeping with the spirit of religious reformism that swept the Northeast on the heels of the Second Great Awakening. It was an age of messianism, millenarianism, and apocalyptic visions, when the reborn sought to prepare for and speed the Lord's return by improving themselves and others.

More than a by-product of this religious moment, however, Easton's work provides an early articulation of what was to become one of the central themes in nineteenth-century black racial thought. Merging revisionist ethnology with messianic themes of social liberation and racial redemption that already had deep roots in black culture,

Easton portrayed his people as a redeemer race. Peaceful and long-suffering, he suggested, people of African descent had unique characteristics that would put them at the forefront of the human race come Judgment Day. Easton's promise of a black redemption echoed the hopes of African-American slaves who had long embraced the book of Exodus as a parable for their own destiny. It likewise echoed one of the other canonical texts in nineteenth-century black religion: the obscure prophecy of Psalm 68:31, which reads, "Princes shall come out of Egypt and Ethiopia shall soon stretch her hands out to God."[33] Fueled by such traditions, messianic ethnology would become a dominant theme in black thought over the course of the nineteenth century, flourishing particularly among postbellum black nationalists such as Alexander Crummell and James T. Holly, who believed that African-Americans were destined to create a great Christian empire in Africa.[34]

In addition to this millenarian vision, messianic ethnology also carried a message about the character of white people that would become increasingly specific over time. If blacks were a gentle, spiritual, almost feminine, redeemer race, whites might well be their irredeemable opposite. Easton certainly appeared to think so at times. Besides blaming Africa's decline on the rapaciousness of Europe, he painted a grim portrait of the past and present character of the white race. Destabilizing the dominant culture's ideas about gender as well as race, Easton presented the male qualities that so many white thinkers celebrated as evidence of the superiority of their race in the worst possible light. Echoing Lewis's description of the aboriginal Greeks, Easton claimed that whites were descended "from a savage race of men" who made their living "traversing the woods and wilds, inhabiting rocks and caverns, a wretched prey to wild beasts and to one another." European civilization had improved briefly during the glory days of Greece and Rome, but whites soon reverted to their old ways. By the Middle Ages, "all Europe exhibited a most melancholy picture of Gothic barbarity," wrote Easton. "Drawn from their homes by a thirst for blood and plunder," the Goths, Vandals, Saxons, and "other fierce tribes" roamed the European continent, reducing great numbers of their people to servitude.[35]

All in all, Easton described the European ancestors of white Americans as an unrelentingly destructive race, which put conquest and acquisition above all ends. He further suggested that white Americans were little different than their savage forebears. "It is not a little remarkable" observed Easton,

> that in the nineteenth century a remnant of this same barbarous people should boast of their national superiority of intellect, and of wisdom and religion; who, in the seventeenth century, crossed the Atlantic and practiced the same crime their barbarous ancestry had done in the fourth, fifth, and sixth centuries; bringing with them the same boasted

spirit of enterprise; and not unlike their fathers, staining their route with blood, as they have rolled along, as a cloud of locusts, towards the West.[36]

Easton's appraisal of the white race as an overly aggressive group of marauders echoed David Walker's judgment that whites were always more brutal and avaricious than blacks. In Easton's account of human history, as well as those of many black authors who wrote after him, the gentle virtues of black people stood in marked contrast to the aggressive and domineering spirit of the white race.

Shot through with contradictions, Easton's contrast between the womanly values he ascribed to black people and the domineering savagery he condemned in the white race was no brief for a reassessment of the genders. Rather, he called for revision of the gender hierarchies underlying racist ideology. At the same time, however, Easton's celebration of the feminine virtues of the redeemer race ran contrary to the antiracist arguments that he and most other black abolitionists favored. If the races were the same but for "incidental" variations in skin color and hair texture, as Easton himself argued, how could blacks possess a special temperament and destiny that distinguished them through all human history?

The contradictions between equality and difference remained unreconciled in Easton's account of human ethnology, much as they had in Walker's *Appeal*. Difficult to reconcile, equality and racial difference would clash again and again in nineteenth-century black ethnology, with the latter often being defined by contrasting sets of gendered racial characteristics. These clashes between racial difference and equality are not surprising, since the African-Americans who wrote ethnology invariably felt compelled both to explain why black people were different and to prove that they were equal. Little wonder that African-American attempts to vindicate the race were often replete with arguments for the moral supremacy of black people. Laying claim to the virtues of the weak (women) and the power of the righteous, Easton and other black evangelicals revised the racial hierarchy to favor their long-suffering race over its white oppressors. This strategy held a certain appeal even among thinkers who were not convinced that the black race had special gifts, as can be seen in the work of James W. C. Pennington.

Pennington, who published his *Text Book of the History of the Colored Race* in 1841, was also a minister in Hartford, where he presided over a Congregationalist church.[37] Probably acquainted with Easton, Pennington was almost certainly familiar with his work, since the publication of Easton's *Treatise* "was a landmark event for the Hartford black community."[38] Despite the men's common profession and milieu, Pennington's *Text Book* did not endorse his colleague's vision of African-Americans as a downtrodden redeemer race. A fugitive slave from Maryland who served as a blacksmith prior to his escape, Pennington shared neither Easton's conviction that the present-day victims of slavery were degraded nor his belief that the black race had special redemptive characteristics. Grounded in the here and now, the main aim of Pennington's *Text Book* was to refute white arguments for black inferiority.

His book illuminates the central role that history held in racist doctrine, for Pennington could not vindicate his race without delving into the past. In order to make a case for racial equality, he had to confront an assortment of arguments slighting the history and ancestry of the black race—to "unembarrass the origin . . . of the colored people." "We are not the seed of Cain as the stupid say," he noted tartly, working his way through a dismally demeaning roster of theories about black people; Cain's offspring perished in the deluge. Nor were black people doomed to servility by an ancient curse, he argued, pointing out that proslavery interpretations of the curse of Ham did not mesh with the story itself. Noah's curse was on Ham's son Canaan, not his brother Cush, who settled Ethiopia. Those who believed in the curse were at the very least "mistaken in their game" and must "discharge the Africans . . . and go and get the Canaanites." Moreover, as a justification for slavery the whole story was absurd. In the Bible, Noah's curse fell on Canaan alone, not on his descendants, and may not even have been carried out. Would God empower the curses of a drunken patriarch? "Is the spirit of wine the spirit of God?" Moving onto secular history, Pennington concluded his rebuttal by dismissing claims that racial slavery developed because Africans were suited to slavery. "Slavery had its origin on this continent," he countered, "not with Africans for slaves, but with the aborigines!"[39]

In discussing the history of the colored race, Pennington, like the black authors who preceded him, claimed Egyptian ancestry for his race. Citing the authority of Herodotus, he argued that Egypt was a mixed-race society where Ethiopians and Egyptians—both descendants of Cush—intermingled. "The arts and sciences had origins with our ancestors," he proclaimed, lauding the accomplishments of these civilizations, "and from them have flown forth to the world."[40] Pennington drew no conclusions about the comparative merits of the races from this history, however. Unlike Easton, who insisted that "the Egyptians alone have done more to cultivate such improvements as comports to the happiness of mankind, than all the descendants of Japhet put together," Pennington remained steadfastly egalitarian. To him, the accomplishments of the Egyptians proved only *"that intellect is identical in all human beings, and the contrary opinion is an absurdity."*[41]

Intent on minimizing racial distinctions, Pennington also felt compelled to explain the causes of color. Defending eighteenth-century environmentalism, Pennington ridiculed the white scientists of the nineteenth century who sought other explanations for the color of the African race. "The subject has first been mystified and then declared difficult," he wrote, insisting that the correlations between climate and color were obvious. Were not Africans from the torrid regions of West Africa blacker than those who hailed from the more temperate zones on the eastern coast of the continent? "I would far sooner be a black man with common sense than a white man with a head full of non-sense," Pennington concluded.[42]

"NO MAN IS ANYTHING MORE THAN A MAN, NO MAN IS LESS THAN A MAN" was the simple, but embattled, proposition espoused by Pennington's *Text Book*.[43] Yet by the late 1840s, after years of battling white clergy who refused to categorically disavow slavery, and wondering whether slavery would ever end, Pennington began to sound less certain that the races were identical. Following in Easton's footsteps, Pennington began to embrace the idea that the black race had unique and redemptive characteristics. Most of all, Pennington was impressed by his own race's ability to endure adversity and suffering. In 1848 he told a white missionary who had claimed that the "weaker races" were dying out that the African race would never expire. To the contrary, wrote Pennington:

> I am quite thankful that God had endowed the race of Ham with a constitution so remarkable for endurance; a constitution which not only fits him to be the Anglo-Saxon of the tropical region, but which also enabled him for centuries to give, in this and in other parts of the world where the odds of climate and relative position are against him, incontestable proof of the possession of an undying manhood, by surviving the successive shocks of Anglo-Saxon wrath and oppression.[44]

By 1850 Pennington was convinced that the heroic endurance and resistance displayed by enslaved African-Americans was evidence of the greatness of their race. A wanted man himself, Pennington aided dozens of other black fugitives, and he was convinced that the courage and ingenuity displayed by these men and woman was testimony to the intelligence and righteousness of the race. Blacks would prevail in America, he told an antislavery audience, because they had a special appreciation for "the true Christian law of *moral power*, . . . the law of *forgiveness* and endurance of wrong."[45] Above all, Pennington's optimism about his race's future was grounded in his faith in divine justice. He was confident that a just God would never permit white American oppressors to destroy the colored race. But he took additional comfort in the virtue of his people, sharing in Easton's vision of a black millennium.

Pennington's and Easton's hopes for the redeemer race, along with their ambivalence about race distinctions, were echoed by Henry Highland Garnet. A contemporary of Pennington's, Garnet was a prominent minister and abolitionist. An educated and scholarly New Yorker by the time he entered his twenties, Garnet had arrived in that city at the age of nine when his entire family escaped from their owner's plantation in Maryland. Ordained as a Presbyterian minister after graduating from the Oneida Institute in upstate New York, Garnet retained bitter memories of slavery. In 1843 the crusading minister scandalized white and black reformers alike by inciting the slaves to revolt and kill their masters.[46] Garnet's discussion of ethnology, delivered at a meeting of the Female Benevolent Society in Troy, New York, five years later, was less incendiary, but it presented a very conflicted account of the unity of the races.

Garnet began his speech by attempting to dispense with racial distinctions altogether. He apologized for using the word *races*, which he described as "one of the improper terms of our times." "There was but one race, as there was but one Adam," Garnet proclaimed. "Children of one father," all human beings originally shared the same reddish complexion. The color differences that had developed since then were but an unaccountable and unimportant manifestation of the Lord's will. Moreover, white and colored races were hardly separate anyway, said Garnet, surveying the American scene. Race mixture was rampant, and it was not always possible to "draw the line between the Negro and the Anglo-Saxon"—"*The Western World is destined to be filled with a mixed race.*"[47]

Yet Garnet went on to undercut his own argument by defending some of the more essentialist tenets of black ethnology. Despite his insistence that race was an inconsequential and highly mutable category, he presented the black race as an eternally distinct people whose unbroken lineage began with Adam and would carry through to Judgment Day. The African race descended from Ham, whose progeny founded both Egypt and Ethiopia, said Garnet, outlining what had become the standard account of black history in African-American ethnology. A once mighty people, blacks had not been despised in the ancient world. Solomon's favorite wife was black, as was the wife of Moses; the Egyptian queen Cleopatra was also black, as was the great conqueror Hannibal. Echoing Easton's hopes, Garnet predicted that the black race would rise again. White Americans would suffer for their sins come Judgment Day, he intimated, whereas African-Americans could look forward to redemption. "There are blessings yet in store for our patient race," Garnet intoned. Just as the sky turns clear after a thunderstorm, "so shall this race come forward to reoccupy their station of renown."[48]

By contrast, the racial merits of whites and Indians did not assure them any similar future, claimed Garnet, seemingly contradicting his earlier predictions of a polyglot, raceless world. "The Red Men of North America," wrote Garnet, echoing a common white view of the Indians as a vanishing race," are retreating from the approach of the white man. They have fallen like Aztecs on the ground on which they first took root, and on the soil on which their foliage shaded." The Indians of the United States would disappear from their native land as had their Latin American counterparts, mowed down by white settlement. They would be survived by the more hardy colored race, a people who flourished despite being "transplanted in a foreign land," clinging and growing with the "oppressor as wild ivy entwines around the trees in the forest."[49]

Meanwhile, however closely entwined, blacks and whites were also different. "The besetting sins of the Anglo-Saxon race are, the love of gain and the love of power," Garnet claimed, further refining his distinction between the races. Likewise, his dismal account of white history strengthened his contrast between the patient and moral colored race and its white brethren. "When the representatives of our race were filling the world with amazement," he said, referring back to the days of Hannibal, "the ancestors of the now proud and boasting Anglo-Saxons were among the most degraded of the human family. They abode in caves underground, either naked or covered in the skins of wild beasts. Night was made hideous by their wild shouts, and the day darkened by the smoke which arose from the bloody altars on which they offered human sacrifice."[50]

Despite their insistence that the races were the same, black ministers such as Garnet, Pennington, and Easton often ended up suggesting that blacks and whites had distinct qualities that had divided them in the past and would continue to do so in the future. Patient, long-suffering, and good, black people were a special redeemer race; whereas white people—or white men in particular, since the warring Europeans described in black ethnology always appear to be male—were brutal, domineering, and virtually irredeemable. In drawing this contrast, and in identifying blacks as a chosen people who held a special place in God's favor, these black ministers may appear to be making religious arguments rather than racial ones. Such a distinction would have been meaningless in their day, however, for these men wrote well before contemporary distinctions between science and religion took shape. Even polygenesis, a theory that many antebellum-era Americans considered heretical because it contradicted the Scriptures' account of human genesis, was predicated on the assumption that white people descended from Adam and Eve. Moreover, well into the nineteenth century American thinkers—both black and white—would continue to blend science with the Scriptures.

What was distinctive about black ethnology, then, was not its mixture of scientific and religious ideas but its emphasis on two not always compatible themes: human sameness and racial distinctions. Whether they celebrated their race's redemptive qualities, bemoaned the present-day condition of African-Americans, or attacked the character of the white race, black thinkers invariably conceded that blacks and whites were not quite the same, while simultaneously insisting that they were equal. These competing claims to equality and difference run through virtually all nineteenth-century black racial thought, including the more secular accounts of racial development offered by a variety of African-American laymen.

Black Ethnology and the Sectional Crisis: The 1850s

More focused on the worldly status of their race than on any sort of racial redemption, increasing numbers of nonclerical blacks addressed ethnological issues as the nineteenth century progressed. From the mid-1840s until the Civil War, black interest in ethnology was renewed time and again by the continuing political crises over slavery—crises that provoked ever more rancorous debate over the relative merits of the races. These years marked the high tide of proslavery thought as well as black ethnology. Under siege by abolitionists, the peculiar institution had begun to require energetic defense. No longer opposed by white radicals alone, slavery was increasingly unpopular among ordinary Northerners, who distrusted the growing political power and expansionist spirit of the slave South.

Confronted by broad-based opposition for the first time, the South rallied around slavery as never before. Distinguished Southern intellectuals touted the scriptural, economic, and moral virtues of slavery, taking on its defense as a "sacred vocation."[51] Slavery was "an institution of divine origin," these thinkers proclaimed, "manifestly designed and used by an all-good creator to forward his beneficent purposes."[52] Proslavery thinkers insisted that slavery was an ideal institution that served the interests of both the masters and the slaves. In return for their labor, slaves were guaranteed food, clothing, and shelter under the stewardship of a benevolent master. Unlike the white workers of the North, the slaves were not exploited by a master class with no direct interest in the health and survival of their workforce. Slavery created a *"community* of interests" between the masters and the slaves, relegating each group to its proper place in a harmonious and well-ordered society.[53] At the heart of the proslavery argument was a sometimes implicit, and often explicit, assumption of black racial inferiority. Both the place of slaves in Southern society and their acceptance of it were predicated on the black race being a dependent and inferior people, who would benefit from the stewardship of the white race.

Consequently, Southern thinkers looked to ethnology for scientific proof of slavery's divine sanction. If science could confirm the hierarchy of the races, who could say American slavery was anything but a righteous institution that organized the races according to their natural gifts? Inequality, science would show, was part of God's plan. Slavery was sanctioned by both science and the Scriptures, Southern apologists insisted, using ethnology to unite religion and science in defense of the peculiar institution. Ethnological discussions of black inferiority appeared regularly in leading Southern journals such as *De Bow's Review* and were also reprinted in proslavery collections.[54] A number of slavery's most energetic defenders, including Josiah Nott, Samuel Cartwright, and, by the 1860s, George Fitzhugh, embraced polygenesis wholeheartedly, arguing that blacks were a distinct and degraded species; others dodged the origins controversy but made strong arguments for black inferiority all the same. "The African, if not a distinct, is an inferior, race," ill suited to "any other condition but slavery," wrote South Carolina politician and planter James Henry Hammond in 1845, fudging the origins issue much as Jefferson had done half a century earlier.[55]

Little wonder, then, that black thinkers such as Pennington insisted that a correct knowledge of ethnology and black history was "vital to the right state of mind on the total subject of human rights." The "Fugitive Blacksmith" also hoped to see these issues fully explored by "someone more competent" than himself, and as the antebellum period progressed his hopes were met.[56] Endlessly discussed by proslavery thinkers and abolitionists, ethnology and the history of the races became popular lecture subjects throughout the Northern states— among both blacks and whites. The African-Americans who addressed these subjects included some of the earliest black men of science, such as John Rock and James McCune Smith, who both held medical degrees; Martin Delany, who attended Harvard Medical School briefly before being forced out on account of his race; as well as the untrained but brilliant ex-slave Frederick Douglass. Other now-obscure black men spoke on ethnology as well, but not all black discourse on this subject has survived. Recording a vanishing tradition in 1901, black librarian Daniel Murray, who was born in the 1850s, noted that during the antebellum era a number of African-American lecturers were "famous" for their mastery of ethnology, but "the high cost of printing [restricted] their reputation to the oral tradition."[57]

One carrier of this lost tradition was Dr. John Rock himself, whose numerous speeches on ethnology have not survived. A freeborn black who grew up in Salem, Rock was well known in his day. A prominent abolitionist, he had training in dentistry and received a medical degree from the American Medical College in Philadelphia in 1852. In 1861 he conquered yet another field, becoming the first African-American to be admitted to the Massachusetts bar. During the 1850s, Rock, whose multifaceted professional work was hindered by ill health and racial discrimination, began to devote his considerable talents and scientific expertise to lecturing on ethnology. His most popular speeches covered themes that had become traditional in black ethnology. Speaking before audiences throughout New England and in several of the western states, Rock's topics included "The Unity of the Races," "The Light and Shade of the African Character," "Races

Portrait of John Rock (Boston Athenæum).

and Slavery," and "The Varieties in the Human Family."[58] Well received, Rock's speeches were lauded in the Massachusetts press for their "superior scholarship and careful research."[59] Indeed, his lecture "The Unity of the Human Races" was so widely acclaimed "that he was invited to deliver it before the Massachusetts legislature, which he did to a crowded audience in the Lower Chamber of the State Capitol, April 24, 1856."[60]

Despite their renown, Rock's lectures have left hardly a trace. Only the titles of his speeches, not their content, were recorded in the nineteenth-century newspapers that announced his lectures and praised his oratorical skills. The one place we get some inkling of the character of his ideas is a fleeting citation in the *Liberator*. In 1858 Garrison's paper published a transcript of Rock's remarks before an abolitionist meeting commemorating the eighty-eighth anniversary of the Boston Massacre. There Rock, who spoke briefly due to poor health, gave voice to a sardonic black chauvinism that skewered white supremacy by reversing it. "If old Mother Nature had held on as well as she commenced," he told an audience that included the leading white abolitionists of the day, "we should have few varieties of races."

> When I contrast the fine tough muscular system, the beautiful rich color, the full broad features, and the gracefully frizzled hair of the Negro, with the delicate physical organization, wan color, sharp features and lank hair of the Caucasian, I am inclined to believe that when the white man was created, nature was pretty well exhausted—but determined to keep up appearances, she pinched up his features and did the best she could under the circumstances.[61]

Hardly a serious statement of his views on ethnology—although it did address the much discussed question of which race came first—Rock's comment drew laughter from his mixed audience. He then went on to disavow that color distinctions held any real meaning. Condition rather than color was what determined the status of American men. "In this country where money is the great sympathetic nerve which ramifies society, and has a ganglia in every man's pocket, a man is respected in proportion to his success in business," Rock remarked. "When the avenues of wealth are opened to us, we will then become educated and wealthy, and then the roughest looking colored man you ever saw, or ever will see, will be pleasanter than the harmonies of Orpheus, and black will be a very pretty color."[62]

Little more can be said about Rock's views on ethnology or the oral tradition that produced his lectures, since the other black luminaries alluded to by the librarian Daniel Murray have vanished in obscurity. But contemporaries such as James McCune Smith and Frederick Douglass left more ample records of their views on ethnology. As these African-American thinkers grappled with this subject during the tense years leading up to the Civil War, like their predecessors they continued to juggle the competing claims of equality and difference, counterbalancing assertions that the races were identical with claims that their own race had unique gifts.

By far the most prolific black student of ethnology in the antebellum era was James McCune Smith, a New York physician, reformer, editor, and essayist who was the first black American to earn a medical degree.[63] Smith, who received his degree in Glasgow in 1837, after being rejected by medical schools in the United States on account of his race, devoted his scientific career to disproving some of white ethnology's more outrageous claims. He may have found this mission frustrating, since he had a keen appreciation for the absurdity of his era's racial science and at times seemed tempted to dismiss it altogether. Early in his career, he seemed to do just that. Speaking in upstate New York at the Phylomathean Society and Hamilton Lyceum in 1841, he skewered the whole concept of race with one incisive observation. "Learned men," he told his audience,

Dr. James McCune Smith (courtesy of Widener Library, Harvard University).

in their rage for classification, and from a reprehensible spirit to bend science to pamper popular prejudices, have brought the human species under the yoke of classification, and having shown to their own satisfaction a diversity in the races, have placed us in the very lowest rank. Now if this were true, and we were in reality such inferior beings, we would of necessity fall into this low rank in the social scale without the aid of laws. There is no law in these states to prevent dogs & monkeys from voting at the polls.[64]

As his career progressed, however, Smith was not content to simply make light of the racial thought of his day. The African-American of his generation most well qualified to challenge white ethnology's arguments for the biological inferiority of black people, he attempted to take on mainstream science on its own terms, with interesting results. Over the course of his career, Smith developed an elaborate theory of the relationship between race and climate, which in some sense sought to replace the prevailing "yoke" of racial classification with a more fluid classification scheme of his own.

In a series of articles and scientific studies published during the 1840s and 1850s, Smith discussed racial distinctions as a physician, eschewing the historical and scriptural questions so common to nineteenth-century ethnology. He used his knowledge of anatomy to critique the work of contemporary ethnologists such as John Augustine Smith. Like many white scientists of his day, the latter maintained that there were significant physical differences between white and black people, and that the skull of the Negro more closely resembled that of an ape than that of any member of the Caucasian race. Mc-Cune Smith challenged the purely conjectural science behind such claims, arguing that competent research could prove no osteological differences between the races, especially with regard to the size and shape of their crania. He further argued that even if it could be proved that black people had different facial angles than whites, such differences could not be assumed to show anything about black intellectual abilities, since there was no proof that facial angle was an indication of intelligence or brain capacity.[65]

James McCune Smith also devoted considerable energy to the study of climate and longevity—subjects that on first glance might seem to have little to do with racial differences. But in the racially charged atmosphere of the 1840s, when it was widely alleged that black people were naturally suited to the temperate climate of the slave South and ill suited to both Northern climates and Northern freedoms, the relationship between climate and longevity was a race question. Smith set to solve it by using population statistics from the 1830 census to calculate the average life spans of people living in the Northern and Southern United States and in the nations of Europe. He concluded that climate was indeed a key determinant of longevity. In particular, he found that cold climates "unquestionably diminish the longevity of mankind." But he discovered no evidence that blacks were especially susceptible to the rigors of a cold climate. On the contrary, he found that whereas the Indo-European races lived longest in cool climates, flourishing in regions where the average annual temperatures ranged between forty-five and fifty degrees Fahrenheiht, black people prospered in almost any climate. They outlived Southern whites, despite the latter's "more favorable circumstances," and held their own elsewhere.[66]

Smith's conclusions on climate and longevity contained an implicit argument for the superiority of African-Americans over white Americans—at least with regard to life span. Smith did not dwell on this point, however, unlike his colleague Martin Delany, who gleefully maintained, with reference to his people's ability to survive in cold weather as well as in the tropical climates thought to be deadly to white people, "We are a *superior race*, being endowed with properties fitting us for *all parts* of the earth, while they are only adapted to *certain* parts."[67] Instead, toward the end of the 1850s, Smith reworked his researches on climate into a theory of climate and civilization. His theory sought an answer to the perennial question of nineteenth-century ethnology: the question, as Smith put it, of "whether human advancement be the result of the innate superiority of any portion of the human race, or whether it results from adventitious phenomena."[68]

Not surprisingly, Smith embraced the latter proposition. In an article entitled "Civilization: Its Dependence on Physical Circumstances," published in the *Anglo-African Magazine*, he argued that the effects of climate and environment were what distinguished peoples from each other. A thoroughgoing environmentalist, like most nineteenth-century African-Americans who wrote on ethnology, Smith was convinced that climate governed both human physical and intellectual development, consequently dictating the character of human civilizations from place to place. In human beings as an aggregate, "physical vigor in mankind" went hand in hand with intellectual vitality.[69]

Smith went on to explain how climate created the distinctive racial characteristics and civilizations among the peoples of the various temperature zones. He held that very cold climates demanded rapid combustion in the human respiratory system to maintain body temperature. Much nourishment was needed to support such combustion, and even with sufficient nourishment, "so much of the blood is consumed in respiration, that too little is left for the full development of the human frame: hence the large appetites and small stature of the hyperborean races." Worse still, cold hampered the strength and intellectual powers of these races as well, said Smith, who cited the research of the French astronomer and statistician Quételet to demonstrate the formidable barriers to civilization facing the inhabitants of northern regions. Quételet, he explained, had demonstrated that while men peaked in physical strength at age twenty-five, and in intellectual power between thirty and thirty-five, they reached their peak in their ability to endure cold at age seventeen and were never so resistant thereafter. Accordingly, in "extremely cold climates, the mass of the population are cut off before reaching twenty-five years of age—and hence do not reach the maximum of physical or intellectual power."[70]

Very hot climates, while not as lethal, were also debilitating. The air in the tropics "contains more vapor of water and consequently less oxygen, than the air of temperate regions." This deficiency, Smith believed, caused slow combustion of the lungs, and hence "a smaller development of physical strength," in the inhabitants of tropical regions. Even black people, whose dark skin contained "an elaborate refrigerator" consisting of non-heat-conducting carbon or charcoal directly under its surface, suffered ill effects in hot climates. The "dark races in hot climates have flattened chests, from the relatively less exercise or expansion of their lungs in breathing."[71] Fortunately, the ill effects of a tropical climate were easily reversed by relocating, as could be seen by the example of blacks in the United States. "The colored population," wrote Smith, enslaved and free, of Maryland and Virginia, are descendants of those who, from 50 to 200 years ago, were removed from the African coast. This Afric-American race, are not only far superior, in physical symmetry and development to the pure African now found on the coast, but actually equal in these respects the white race of Old Dominion, who have never lived in any but a temperate clime.[72]

For Smith, environmentalism was not only a theory of human development; it also held the long-term solution to America's race problem. What diverse environments had made different, a common environment would make the same. Thomas Jefferson had been wrong to predict that black and white Americans would never be able to co-exist, Smith wrote in a stinging critique of the "Fourteenth Query" in Jefferson's *Notes on Virginia*. In his now-infamous discussion of American race relations, Jefferson maintained that the "deep-rooted prejudices entertained by whites," coupled with the "ten thousand recollections, by the blacks, of the injuries they have sustained; new provocations; the real distinctions which nature has made; and many other circumstances, will divide us into parties, and produce convulsions, which will probably never end but in the extermination of the one or the other race." With this grim future in mind, Jefferson looked upon blacks as unassimilable people and asked, "What further is to be done with them?"[73]

Smith replied that Jefferson need not ask, "How shall we get rid of them?" since there was "nothing in the races themselves" that prohibited their dwelling in harmony. Any muscular or osteological peculiarities that might be noticed among some blacks were caused by malnutrition. Moreover, the dark skin that distinguished African-Americans from their white countrymen was already giving way in North America's temperate environment. "The Ethiopian can change his skin," asserted Smith.[74] Even the Negro's woolly hair would soon straighten itself out under the salubrious influence of America's climate and culture, and Smith thought that "[t]his must be consolatory to those who have gazed upon this, to them, insurmountable difficulty in the way of incorporating blacks in to the state." Moreover, he maintained that these changes were already under way: "Anyone whose observation extends twenty years back, must observe that the hair of the colored population of the United States is growing more and more straight. This is partly the result of extreme culture on their part, and partly the result of the climatic or geological influences under which they live."[75]

Smith rejected the notion of the innate superiority of any race and predicted a raceless future, in which Americans would become one people under the beneficent influence of the American climate and culture. In doing so, he clearly addressed the scientifically literate men of his day. The premises behind his theories about climate were widely accepted. The idea that blacks were better able to withstand warm weather than whites but worse off in the cold was a common-place in antebellum medicine.[76] Moreover, white thinkers, such as J. Hector St. John de Crèvecoeur had previously hailed the emergence of robust and distinctive new American people on the North American continent.[77] Smith merely took such environmentalist ideas to their logical extreme, claiming—as had the white eighteenth-century environmentalist Samuel Stanhope Smith—that blacks would also be transformed by the beneficent influence of their New World environment.

In doing so, McCune Smith revealed the limitations inherent to any environmentalist defense of human equality. Environmentalist theories of human difference did not rule out the possibility of significant distinctions between the races—indeed, environmental determinism was usually invoked to explain these differences. Nor did environmentalism preclude the notion of superior and inferior races, providing such distinctions were not asserted to be permanent. Indeed, all these caveats were evident in Smith's own theories. His understanding of the effects of climate allowed for substantial, albeit impermanent, racial differences in physical strength and intellectual vigor between blacks and whites. Moreover, his theories left open the possibility that a substantial portion of the world's black population was distinctly inferior. He avoided any concession of inferiority or difference in American blacks by emphasizing the wondrous improvement seen in the "Afric-American race" as a result of the civilizing influence of climate.[78] But blacks in Africa were apparently doomed to savagery so long as they remained in the tropical climate of their native land.

These weaknesses in the environmentalist argument for human equality would become especially noticeable in late nineteenth-century black writing on racial issues. At that time black thinkers such as George Washington Williams and Alexander Crummell would simultaneously defend the innate equality of their race, embrace the contemporary social Darwinist understanding of black people as a backward race, and predict "the destined superiority of the Negro."[79] But even in the antebellum era, environmentalism's weaknesses as a defense of human equality confused and complicated black ethnology's definition of racial equality, as can be seen in the ethnological writings of Frederick Douglass and Martin Delany.

These two prominent black leaders expressed very different views on race and ethnology. Contrasting characters, these two men clashed on many subjects during their long public careers. A fugitive slave of mixed parentage, Douglass expressed little attraction toward the mystical and racialistic side of black uplift. He denounced racial pride as "ridiculous," failed to identify with Africans, and dismissed the whole issue of racial differences succinctly. "Wherein does the white man differ from the black?" he asked. "Why one is white and the other black.

Martin Delaney (courtesy of the Photographs and Prints Division, Schomburg Center for Research in Black Culture, The New York Public Library, Astor, Lenox, and Tilden Foundations).

Well what of that? Does the sun shine more brightly on one than it does on the other?"[80] By contrast, the freeborn Delany, who laid proud claim to unalloyed African ancestry, was practically a black supremacist. In 1865 he declared with swaggering pride in the *Liberator*, "We barely acknowledge the whites as equals—perhaps not in every respect."[81] Their politics were equally distinct. Sometimes known as the "father of black nationalism," Delany was an enthusiastic advocate of black separatism and emigration for most of his life, whereas Douglass was a vociferous opponent of both.[82] For all their differences, however, both men took an active interest in ethnology, which they employed to very different ends. In doing so, they revealed the indeterminate character of African-American ethnology: the environmentalist arguments that antebellum black authors used to defend the unity of the races were flexible enough to support both Delany's black chauvinist, separatist agenda and Douglass's far less racialist arguments for black integration.

Born in what is now West Virginia, and raised in Pennsylvania, Delany came to ethnology with some scientific training. As a young man, he apprenticed as a doctor in Pittsburgh and then enrolled in Harvard Medical School. His medical career ended abruptly after one semester, when he was forced out of Harvard by angry white students bent on preserving the school's color barrier. Thereafter, he devoted himself to a career of writing, editing, and political activism.[83] He served as a major in the Union Army during the Civil War and went on to hold several political appointments, including the position of minister and general consul to Haiti in 1891. Long after his medical career ended, Delany retained his interest in science and would publish a lengthy treatise on racial differences entitled *Principia of Ethnology* in 1879.

Well before then, however, Delany was interested in racial differences and convinced that black and white people were quite distinct. He never questioned the central tenet of nineteenth-century black ethnology—that "God has made of one blood all the nations that dwell on the face of the earth." Nor did he challenge the environmentalist orthodoxy in black thought: his *Principia* held that the different races were created by the effects of climate and intermixture. Despite his rejection of pluralism, however, Delany was convinced that the races had become physically and mentally different.

In an 1852 pamphlet entitled *The Condition, Elevation, Emigration, and Destiny of the Colored People of the United States*, Delany insisted that blacks were "physically superior to either the European or American [Indian] races—in fact physically superior to any living race of men." Along with changes in climate, blacks could endure changes in "habits, manners and customs, with infinitely less injury to their physical systems than any other people of God's earth." He also believed the colored races were "especially susceptible to religion."[84] Delany argued that blacks should accept their differences, cultivate their talents, "and develop them in their purity." "In truth," he declared in 1852, "we are not identical with the Anglo-Saxon, or any race of the Caucasian or pure white type in the human family, and the sooner we know and acknowledge this truth the better for ourselves and prosperity."[85]

Whites and blacks were not just different but wholly incompatible, Delany further argued in an essay written two years later. In "The Political Destiny of the Colored Race on the American Continent," he presented a sweeping indictment of the history of the white race:

> We regret the necessity of stating the fact that for more than two thousands years, the determined aim of the whites has been to crush the colored races wherever found. With a determined will they have sought and pursued them in every quarter of the globe. The Anglo-Saxon has taken the lead in this work of universal subjugation. But the Anglo-American stands preëminent for deeds of injustice and acts of oppression, unparalleled, perhaps, in annals of modern history.[86]

Some of the special qualities that Delany identified in black people were closely tied to the political future he envisioned for his race. His 1852 argument that blacks were superior to whites when it came to tolerating a variety of climates supported his emigrationist aspirations. Once a supporter of African emigration, by the 1850s Delany had become suspicious of the American Colonization Society's attempts to get free blacks to resettle in Liberia. Accordingly, his claims about climate were linked to an alternative emigration proposal. He suggested that African-Americans leave the United States, but not the New World. In particular, he called for emigration to countries in a number of temperature zones, including Canada, the West Indies, and Central and South America. Blacks were a hardy, robust people who could flourish outside Africa, said Delany, countering white colonizationists' claims that blacks were ill suited to live anywhere else. They no more needed to return to their original homelands to prosper than did the Europeans.

Although they furthered his emigration schemes, Delany's racial theories cannot be seen as purely expedient. Whereas the father of black nationalism's separatism waxed and waned throughout his long career as a political activist, his race pride did not. A man who could trace his ancestry back to Gullah chieftains and African princes, Delany took tremendous pride in both his personal heritage and that of his race. An admiring 1868 biography by Frances Rollin refers to Delany's "pride of race, which even distinguishes him from the noted colored men of his time." And Frederick Douglass commented less reverentially, "I thank God for making me a man simply; but Delany always thanks him for making him a *black man*."[87]

Consistently critical of Delany's black chauvinism, Douglass accused Delany of going "about the same length in favor of blacks, as the whites have in favor of the doctrine of white superiority. He stands up so straight that he leans back a little."[88] Although "he understood his people's need for dignity and self-respect," Douglass was always suspicious of race pride—whether it be white or black.[89] Late in his life, especially during the virulently racist post-Reconstruction era, Douglass repeatedly warned black Americans against excessive self-celebration. "Do we not know that every argument we make, and every pretension we set up in favor of race pride is giving the enemy a stick to break our own heads?" he queried in 1889.[90] But, as his strictures against Delany show, his distaste for black chauvinism dated back far earlier.

In part, Douglass's antipathy toward race pride was very likely a product of his own complicated sense of racial identity. For Douglass, a mulatto who thought he might be the son of his white owner, identification with the black race was never unconflicted. Moreover, it evolved and changed throughout his long life, further complicating his sentiments on race pride. Less changeable was his commitment to a black American nationality, which gave him further cause to oppose Delany's black chauvinism as well as his separatist philosophy and emigration schemes. Throughout his career, Douglass counseled African-Americans to remain in the United States and to avoid forming separate social and political organizations. "Our Union is our weakness," was how he summed up his integrationist philosophy in 1889. "A nation within a nation is an anomaly. There can be but one American nation . . . and we are Americans."[91]

Not surprisingly, Douglass was even more impatient with advocates of white superiority than he was with black chauvinists. Dismissing the American school of ethnology as "Southern pretenders to science," he wrote:

> If the origins and motives of most works opposing the unity of the human race could be ascertained, it may be doubted whether one such work could boast an *honest* parentage. Pride and selfishness, combined with mental power, never want for theory to justify them—and when men oppress their fellow men, the oppressor ever finds, in the character of the oppressed, a full justification.

A trenchant critic of both white superiority and the whole idea of race, Douglass went so far as to suggest that no one could speak objectively on the subject of ethnology. Even his own views on the unity of the human family, he modestly conceded, were open to "the suspicion that *'the wish is the father of the thought.'*" Meanwhile, racism made white scientific theories wholly unreliable. "It is the province of prejudice to blind; and the scientific writers not less than others, write to please as well as to instruct, and even unconsciously to themselves, (sometimes), sacrifice what is true to what is popular."[92]

Given Douglass's disdain for race pride and his disavowal of racial differences, along with his doubts that anyone could make objective pronouncements about race, one might expect him to shun the subject of ethnology altogether. But he did not. All too aware that few Americans shared his belief that racial distinctions were absurd—including his black abolitionist colleague Martin Delany—Douglass also knew that arguments for black racial inferiority were used to justify slavery and discrimination. Scholarship on racial difference was important, he acknowledged in 1854: "The relation subsisting between white and black people of this country is the vital question of the age. In the solution of this question, the scholars of America will have to take a vital and controlling part. This is the moral battle field to which their country and their God now call them. In the eye[s] of both the neutral scholar is an ignoble man."[93]

Accordingly, Douglass spoke out regularly on ethnology, and admitted to a lifelong interest in the subject.[94] "The Races of Man" was one of his few prepared speeches that he gave repeatedly at public engagements. And when he was invited to give the commencement ad-

Frederick Douglass. Engraving by J. C. Buttre in *Autographs for Freedom* (1854) (Boston Athenæum).

dress at Western Reserve College in 1854, he refined this old standby for an academic audience. No scientist, Douglass prepared a more scholarly version of his speech by studying the works of prominent white ethnologists such as Samuel Morton, whom he criticized, as well as by consulting with Dr. M. B. Anderson, a white ethnologist who helped him select his reading list.[95] In all likelihood, he also consulted his old friend James McCune Smith, whose work he cites.[96]

Entitled "The Claims of the Negro Ethnologically Considered," Douglass's carefully prepared address consisted of a series of arguments quite standard to the ethnological defense of the black race by the 1850s. He affirmed the "oneness of the human family," denouncing the "Notts, Gliddens, Agassiz, and the Mortons" and their "profound discoveries in ethnological science." Different climates and environments, not different origins, explained the physical distinctions between the races, wrote Douglass, echoing the environmentalist ethnology of James McCune Smith. Moreover, polygenesis was not only wrong but also heretical, he noted, declaring that "the credit of the Bible is at stake" in the controversy over the origins of the different races. In addition to invoking environmentalist and religious defenses of human unity traditional to nineteenth-century black ethnology by midcentury, Douglass echoed earlier black thinkers by insisting that ancient Egyptian civilization came out of Africa. "Egypt is in Africa," he observed sarcastically. "Pity that it had not been in Europe or Asia, or better still, America!" The Egyptians were not white, and none of Morton's and Gliddon's elaborate arguments about the ethnicity of the Egyptians could get around the fact that ancient Egyptians would be seen as Negroes in modern America.[97]

Douglass was probably the shrewdest contemporary critic of his era's science of the races-black or white. Yet neither his low opinion of ethnology as a science nor his concern about whether anyone could practice it objectively prevented him from offering his own scientific conjectures about racial traits and inheritance. For instance, he asserted that "intellect is uniformly derived from the maternal side" and, therefore, that the tendency of white Americans to ignore the Negro blood in intelligent persons of mixed heritage was contradicted by the fact that "mulattos, in this country, may almost wholly boast Anglo-Saxon male ancestry."[98] Moreover, Douglass's suspicion that race distinctions were primarily dictated by ideological interests did not prevent him from making his own invidious distinctions between the races.

Leaning in the opposite direction from Martin Delany, Douglass ultimately presented the black race as only potentially equal to more advantaged white Europeans and Americans. Emphasizing that ill treatment, as well as poor climate, could compromise the physical and intellectual character of a people, Douglass painted a dismal picture of black Americans. "The form of the Negro," he told his audience at Western Reserve College,

> has often been the subject of remark. His flat feet, long arms, high cheek bones, and retreating forehead, are especially dwelt upon, to his disparagement. . . . I think it will ever be found that the well or ill condition of any part of mankind, will leave its mark on the physical as well as on the intellectual part of man. A hundred instances might be cited of whole families who have degenerated, and other[s] who have improved in personal appearance, by a change of circumstances.

Douglass qualified this comment with the parenthetical affirmation that he believed the black race would "one day be as illustrious" as the white.[99] But his acceptance of racist assessments of black physiognomy is still striking, especially given that he argued in the same lecture that the American school of ethnology's use of comparative anthropometric measurements between blacks and whites to demonstrate the superiority of whites was methodologically unsound.

Moreover, Douglass was not sure African-American physical deficiencies were attributable solely to slavery. Like James McCune Smith, Douglass believed that the races were shaped by their physical circumstances. He was also convinced that the African continent had provided a most unfortunate environment for the development of the black race. "Need we go behind the vicissitudes of Barbarism for an explanation of the gaunt, wiry appearance of some genuine Negroes?" he asked. "Need we look higher than the vertical sun, or lower than the damp, black soil of the Niger, the Gambia, the Senegal, with their heavy and enervating miasma, rising ever from the rank growing and decaying vegetation, for an explanation of the Negro's color?"[100] Douglass's low opinion of contemporary Africans was further revealed when, in entertaining a worst-possible-case scenario at the end of his lecture, he asked:

> What if the Negro may not be able to prove his relationship to Nubians, Abyssinians and Egyptians? What if ingenious men are able to find plausible objections to all arguments maintaining the oneness of the human race? What, after all, if they are able to show very good reasons for believing the Negro to have been created precisely as we find him on the Gold Coast—along the Senegal and the Niger—I say, what of all this?

Thus, while Douglass accused whites of looking for justifications for oppression "in the character of the oppressed," he did not take this insight to its logical conclusion when it came to assessing ethnology's case against the Negro. Indeed, by the end of his lecture, his argument for human unity had retreated to the low ground that blacks need not be either equal to whites or identical in their origins, to deserve just treatment: "A diverse origin does not disprove a common nature, nor does it disprove a united destiny."[101]

Despite his brilliant assessment of the fictions and contradictions of white racial theory, Douglass was not immune to the racial fallacies of his day. In "The Claims of the Negro Ethnologically Considered," he failed to challenge some of his white contemporaries' negative stereotypes about black people, especially about Africans. Moreover, for all his suspicions about the accuracy and objectivity of white assessments of blacks, he frequently displayed an unquestioning acceptance of the dominant culture's description of other ethnic and racial groups. Both in his lecture on ethnology and elsewhere, Douglass employed a panoply of racial and ethnic stereotypes when discussing other peoples of color. At Western Reserve University, he lauded his own race's powers of endurance and adaptation over those of "his tawny brother the Indian" who "dies under the flashing glance of the Anglo-Saxon."[102] Elsewhere, he described Chinese immigrants as "gentle and inoffensive," as well as "dexterous of hand, patient of toil, marvelously gifted in the power of imitation, and have but few wants." And, in an 1871 editorial on Mexico, entitled "Our Southern Sister

Republic," he suggested that Mexicans' slow progress toward democracy was due to "their comparatively low state of civilization, the demoralizing influence of long continued Spanish tyranny, and perhaps a deficiency inherent to the Latin races."[103]

Douglass's dispassionate and rather harsh assessment of his own race in "The Claims of the Negro Ethnologically Considered" may have been partly dictated by his white audience, before whom he clearly wished to sound as objective and impartial as possible. Recapitulating the lecture before a black audience in 1865, he would sound more enthusiastic about the achievements of "our race."[104] However, Douglass was not just playing to his audience. His assessments of Africans and African-Americans in the lecture reflected his own cultural biases in favor of Euro-American culture, which he, like many black Americans of his day, saw as the pinnacle of civilization. The fact that he could work such biases into an attack on white ethnology reveals the weaknesses of the environmentalist defense of human equality that Douglass and so many other black thinkers invoked. Environmentalism, as Douglass scholar Waldo Martin notes, allowed Douglass to believe in both "racial equality and cultural hierarchy. Although he agreed that each race had its special gifts, he believed human mental and moral endowments to be a function of environment and, consequently, alterable."[105]

Race, War, and Manhood: Black Racial Thought during the Civil War Era

By the end of the 1850s, a distinct set of black and white racial stereotypes had emerged in black ethnology. Although they questioned the whole concept of racial differences, African-American thinkers tended to present the races in counterpoint. Doubters such as Douglass aside, most black thinkers identified unique characteristics in each race, rather than insisting that the races were identical—which even Douglass did not do. Black people had certain natural gifts that the white race failed to appreciate, thinkers from Hosea Easton to Martin Delany proclaimed. Moral, pious, and benevolent, black people were less aggressive than Anglo-Saxons. A redeemer race, people of African descent were destined by both Providence and their own God-given gifts to endure and survive slavery and oppression, and to lead mankind toward the millennium. By contrast, whites were all but irredeemable. Greedy and warlike, whites had been savages in Europe, and they still terrorized blacks and other people of color.

At its most chauvinistic, antebellum black ethnology revalued the hierarchy of the races, presenting black people as different and better than white people. Revising, rather than rejecting, the dominant society's racial rankings, African-American thinkers insisted that men made of brass and iron might be better than men made of gold. In doing so, however, these thinkers laid claim to a racial superiority riddled with contradictions. Their characterizations of the white race as amoral, aggressive, acquisitive, and proud usually coexisted uneasily with arguments for racial equality and human sameness. By assigning transhistorical characteristics to the races, African-American thinkers seemingly undercut their own environmentalist explanations of human differences. If the influence of diverse climates and environments was the sole cause of racial differences, why were the characters of the races eternally distinct?

Moreover, the contradictions between equality and difference were not the only contradictions in black racial thought. The contrast that black thinkers made between the feminine black race and the masculine white race presented its own problems as well—especially appearing, as it did, amid an almost exclusively male-authored debate with white men over what kind of racial manhood American citizens should display. Antebellum African-Americans' claims to being a morally superior redeemer race sometimes came dangerously close to some less flattering white racial stereotypes about the Negro.

After all, nineteenth-century African-American thinkers were hardly alone in characterizing their own race as the more feminine of the races. Indeed, blacks' worst detractors often excoriated them for being cowardly, weak, overly emotional, and unintelligent—qualities also associated with women. Meanwhile, more sympathetic whites, such as the abolitionists, came up with more positive assessments of the Negro race. But even the white abolitionists who championed the black race often discounted black manhood when celebrating the gentle virtues of the Negro. As George Fredrickson has shown, from the 1840s onward many Northern abolitionists adopted a doctrine of "romantic racialism," which "acknowledged permanent racial differences but rejected the notion of a clearly defined racial hierarchy." Adherents of this doctrine characterized the black race as naturally gentle, submissive, affectionate, and religious. Although the characteristics that romantic racialists celebrated in blacks were in many respects strikingly similar to the virtues black thinkers claimed on behalf of their race, white thinkers tended to stress the womanly characteristics of the Negro far more emphatically than any of their black counterparts. "The negro is superior to the white man—equal to the white woman," proclaimed Theodore Tilton, editor of the *New York Independent*, in a speech entitled "The Negro," delivered in 1863. "It is sometimes said . . . that the negro is the feminine race of the world. This is not only because of his social and affectionate nature, but because he possesses that strange moral instinctive, insight that belongs more to women than to men."[106]

Especially during the Civil War years, such compliments must have seemed backhanded at best.[107] Indeed, it was during these years that the pitfalls inherent to claiming a gentler black masculinity became acutely evident to African-Americans. As the conflict loomed, aggression and masculinity were at a premium in American society.[108] With the North and the South meeting on the battlefield rather than in the court of public opinion, a reputation for gentle virtues did not stand the Negroes in good stead. Indeed, African-Americans were initially judged insufficiently manly to serve in the Union Army. Northern policy makers' resistance to black recruits had other sources, the most important being fears that enlisting black men "would suggest a measure of [racial] equality most Northern whites refused to concede."[109] Another major obstacle to black enlistment, however, was that many Northern whites suspected that blacks were too cowardly and servile to make good soldiers.

Although black soldiers had fought in both the Revolutionary War and the War of 1812, questions about the race's courage in combat were commonplace among white Americans. Well before the Civil War, even devout white abolitionists such as Theodore Parker were prone to suggesting that blacks remained in bondage at least partly on account of their meek and mild temperament. While he professed great admiration for the black race's *"superior[ity] in sentiment and affection,"* Parker was convinced that "'the stroke of the ax would have settled the [slavery] question long ago, but the black man would not strike.'" Similarly, Thomas Higginson, a fiery white abolitionist who in 1862 would lead the first black regiment of Southern recruits (the First South Carolina Volunteers), initially had his doubts about black soldiers. Unlike Parker, Higginson freely admitted that black docility, if it existed, was nothing to be admired. "If the truth were told," he wrote in an article published a year before he took command, "it would be that the Anglo-Saxon despises the Negro because he is *not* an insurgent, for the Anglo-Saxon would certainly be one in his place."[110]

Higginson would ultimately change his mind about the character of black men. By the war's end, battlefield experience with the South Carolina Volunteers had convinced him that blacks were neither "more nor less courageous than whites."[111] Moreover, once permitted to do so, approximately 180,000 free blacks and slave fugitives served in the Union Army. Despite "unequal pay, severely limited opportunities for advancement, inadequate equipment, and inferior medical care," these black soldiers fought bravely. By the end of the war, even Northern whites admitted "the use of black soldiers to be a resounding success."[112]

Not surprisingly, the wartime controversies over African-American enlistment, and the war itself, completely displaced ethnological concerns among black intellectuals. During the war, African-American leaders and thinkers abandoned scholarship and contrasts between the races in favor of encouraging and defending black enlistment in the Union Army. Rallying around the Union cause, they emphasized that black men were no different than any other men. "Why does the government turn down the Negro?" asked Frederick Douglass in 1861. "Is he not a man? Can he not wield a sword, fire a gun, march and countermarch, and obey orders like any other?"[113]

The gentle redeemer race, however, and its corollary, the Angry Saxon, would resurface in black thought soon after the enlistment controversy was settled. Such images, along with African-American interest in ethnology, rebounded as the war began to free the slaves. Emancipation brought no end to racism: political and scientific attacks on the Negro reached a new zenith in the second half of the nineteenth century. As white racist doctrine was repeatedly reshaped by the differing ideological currents of emancipation, Reconstruction, and redemption, African-American thinkers continued to elaborate on the defenses of their race first set in place during the turn-of-the-century struggles against colonization. Still wrestling with questions of equality and difference, they also resurrected the antebellum era comparisons between the redeemer race and the aggressive Anglo-Saxon just discussed here. Indeed, with the failure of Reconstruction and the rise of unparalleled white racist violence thereafter, postbellum black Americans had ever more reason to wonder whether whites were somehow aggressive and immoral by nature. In so doing, late nineteenth-century black thinkers would build on antebellum images to paint an ever more unflattering portrait of white people.

THREE

*

"What Shall We Do with
the White People?"

*Whites in Postbellum
Black Thought*

In the winter of 1860, just as the debate over the place of black people in American society was reaching new heights among a divided
white electorate, a black correspondent for the *Anglo-African Magazine*
considered the question from the other side: "What shall we do with
the white people?" asked William J. Wilson, a Brooklyn schoolteacher
and civic leader who wrote under the pseudonym "Ethiop." This
"grave question" required consideration, Ethiop maintained, for white
people in America were a "failure" of grand proportions. "Discontent
and disaffection have marked [their] every footstep," and not even
their possession of almost the entire North American continent could
bring them peace. Was there any hope for this unruly race? "For
many centuries now have they been on this continent; and for many
years have they had entire rule and sway; yet they are to-day no
nearer the solution of the problem, *'are they fit for self-government'*—
than they were at the commencement of their career."[1]

Ethiop had no satisfactory answers to his own question. The colonization of the white race was out of the question. "Plans for the removal of these white people," he noted with wry reference to the activities of the American Colonization Society, "as all such schemes
are—such for example as these people have themselves laid for the
removal of others in their midst—would be wrong in conception, and
prove abortive in attempt." Yet he could not reconcile the right of
white people to remain in America with their tendencies toward "the
exhibition of prejudices, bitter hates, fierce strifes, dissensions, op-
pressions, [and] frauds." He closed by exhorting his readers to grapple with this dilemma: "Let our constant thought be, *what for the best
good of all should we do with White people?*"[2]

Clearly, much of Ethiop's essay is tongue-in-cheek. His central
question of "what to do with the white people," as well as his prediction that, left to their own devices, whites would soon arrive at "sure

and certain barbarism," satirically reversed contemporary pronouncements made about the Negro by whites. Nonetheless, Ethiop's question was at least half serious. His discussion of the evils of white people is quite sober, and his essay does not simply reverse the racial hierarchy of the day. Unlike white critics of black people, Ethiop cast no slur on the intellectual faculties or physical appearance of the white race. Indeed, he referred to white Americans as a people gifted by "manifold blessings, physical and intellectual," a gift for material progress, as well as great energy and force of character. Yet, for him, these virtues in white people were entirely overshadowed by their group's fractious and unpleasant disposition. "Restless, grasping, unsatiated, they are ever on the look out for not what is, or ought to be theirs, but for what they can get."[3] American white people were "in inclination if not habit, marauders," and their path on "the direct road to barbarism" seemed unstoppable. At best Ethiop speculated in closing, one could hope: "Who knows but that some day, when, after they shall have fulfilled their mission, carried arts and sciences to their highest point, they will make way for a milder and more genial race, or become so blended with it, as to lose their own peculiar and objectionable characteristics."[4]

Ethiop was by no means the first nineteenth-century black commentator to identify peculiar and objectionable racial characteristics in white people. As we have seen, the era's black writing on race includes a discussion of the racial characteristics of white people that can be traced back at least as far as David Walker's 1829 *Appeal to the Colored Citizens of the World*. There, Walker expressed his doubts about whether whites were "*as good by nature* as we are," and in doing so opened up a question that would reverberate through nineteenth-century black writing on race.[5] Such questions about the character of the white race defied an easy answer, particularly because most black authors were committed to defending the unity of the races and consequently sought to minimize rather than maximize racial distinctions. While always resistant to the unflattering notion of a separate creation, these educated African-Americans did not rule out the possibility of racial differences entirely. Framing their discussions within an environmentalist understanding of human development that did not preclude the possibility that descendants of the same ancestors might become different over time, black thinkers frequently assumed that the black and white races had developed their own distinctive characteristics. Indeed, as the century progressed, black thinkers became increasingly likely to forge racial explanations for the oppressive behavior of whites. In doing so, they created a discussion of whiteness that exhibited a number of forms: ranging from direct attacks on the characteristics of white people, such as the one voiced by Ethiop, to evaluations of the white race that emerge only between the lines of black authors' representations of their own people.

Parody, sarcasm, and anger abound in this black commentary on the dominant race. In discussing white people, nineteenth-century African-Americans often met the insults of white racism with insults of their own. However, the ideas that black thinkers employed in these mudslinging contests bear examination. Like Ethiop, most African-American thinkers did not simply reverse the contemporary racial hierarchy when they presented critical perspectives on white people. Although black critics might well have found cause to question the human nature or divine origins of their white oppressors, they did not try to turn the tables by suggesting that white people were of a lower or different species. Instead, they forged a critique of the white race designed to fit within the confines of their monogenist and environmentalist understanding of human ethnology. Shaped by different lineages, histories, and environments, the children of Ham and Japhet were equally human but not the same.

Assertions that the races differed were commonplace in black ethnology by the 1850s, as were unfavorable contrasts between the aggressive, domineering white race and Ham's gentle descendants. White people were a hyperaggressive, acquisitive, and domineering race, antebellum era authors such as Hosea Easton suggested, too close to the barbarity of their Anglo-Saxon ancestors to achieve any true civilization. In the postbellum era such suggestions proliferated in black thought, creating a distinctive critique of the Anglo-Saxon race. Part social commentary, part racial ideology, this critique condemned the aggressiveness and brutality of the white race during a period in which white violence against blacks and other people of color was endemic. At the same time, black thinkers' assessments of the white race also gave voice to the gender anxieties of black men who sought to assert their own manhood in a nation where white men laid exclusive claim to both civilization and manliness. In challenging the Anglo-Saxon ideal, African-American thinkers sought to create a place for black men among "the races of men." An exploration of their commentary on whiteness provides a chronicle of their efforts.

"Is There Anything So Peculiarly Blessed in Color?" Black Views on White Skin

What, if anything, was the significance of the white race's color for black Americans? As the celebrated phenomenon of light-skinned blacks "passing" in the white population demonstrates, racial differences in skin color were essential to maintaining the legal, social, and civil divisions that white Americans used to separate the two races during slavery and segregation. Skin color was, in fact, the only distinction between races that white Americans could rely on to distinguish blacks from whites, despite the efforts of white ethnologists to identify a range of racial traits peculiar to black people. This badge of inferiority, the color of the Negro, was also something that white Americans emphasized as one of the black race's great deficits.

Antislavery pioneer Benjamin Rush, who clearly shared his friend Thomas Jefferson's distaste for "that immovable veil of black which covers all the emotions of the other race," even went so far as to ask, "Is the color of the Negroes a disease?"[6] Like Jefferson, Rush assumed that the color of black people was so unappealing that even African-Americans disliked it. Accordingly, in a letter sent to Jefferson in 1797, the humanitarian Rush encouraged "attempts to cure this disease of the skin in negroes," the success of which would not only aid the cause of antislavery but also "add greatly to their [black people's] happiness, for however well they appear to be satisfied with their color, there are many proofs of their preferring that of the white people."[7]

Nobody took up Rush's call to cure the disease of the black race's color, but all evidence suggests that white Americans continued to find the complexion of the Negro unlovely well into the nineteenth century and beyond. For instance, Congressman Frank Clark of Florida told the House of Representatives in 1908 that black inferiority could be seen in the color and physical features of the black race, as well as in the race's lesser intelligence. "If God had intended these two races to be equal," declared Clark, "He would have so created them." Instead, God gave "the Caucasian a handsome figure, straight hair, regular features, high brow and superior intellect," while the Negro received "a black skin, kinky hair, thick lips, flat nose, low brow, low order of intelligence, and repulsive features."[8] Color was never the only failing of the colored races, whether black or red, but it was a failing accorded considerable importance in white American racial thought. Commenting on this phenomenon in his historical study of scientific racism, *The Mismeasure of Man* (1981), Stephen Jay Gould recounts that in his research for this work

> I have been much struck by the frequency of such aesthetic claims as a basis of racial preference. . . . many astute intellectuals never doubted the equation of whiteness with perfection. Franklin at least had the decency to include the original inhabitants in his future America; but, a century later, Oliver Wendell Holmes rejoiced in the elimination of the Indians on aesthetic grounds: ". . . and so the red-crayon sketch is rubbed out, and the canvas is ready for a picture of manhood a little more like God's own image."[9]

By contrast, the physical difference of color between the races, which struck so many white commentators so forcibly, never became a central subject in black discussions of racial difference. What Winthrop Jordan has called "the primacy of color in the white man's mind, the long-standing feeling that the most Negro thing about the Negro was his blackness," is not echoed in black thought about white people.[10] Nineteenth-century black intellectuals frequently questioned white people's innate morality and humane sensibility, but they rarely derided white people on account of their complexion. Indeed, they had little to say about the color of the white race.

In tracing the descent of their own race, as we have seen, black writers during the antebellum era frequently maintained that Adam was a man of color. Anxious to counter persistent claims that black people did not descend from humanity's first family, black authors would continue to present theories on the coloring of Adam and his family throughout the nineteenth century—the most elaborate being J. F. Dyson's *A New and Simple Explanation of the Unity of the Human Race and the Origin of Color* (1886). Contrary to Euro-American traditions which held that white was the natural color of man, and that all variations were, as one eighteenth-century thinker put it, "actual marks of degeneracy in the human form," black thinkers invariably insisted that at least one member of the original pair must have been a person of color.[11] Dyson, for instance, thought that Adam was red, on etymological grounds—the name means red in Hebrew—and Eve was white, and that their offspring were a variety of colors, a combination that over time gave rise to white, yellow, red, brown, and black races. But arguments such as Dyson's made no claims to the primacy of blackness, or even to the superiority of colored skin. Indeed, Dyson suggested Eve was endowed with fair skin to make her attractive to Adam: "What color is more attractive than white?" he asked.[12]

More reluctant than Dyson to concede that whiteness held any special attractions, most African-American intellectuals discussed the subject of the color differences between the races only when they felt compelled to note that there was nothing wrong with their own color. For instance, Benjamin Banneker began his 1792 letter to Thomas Jefferson, who had recorded his lack of enthusiasm for the black complexion in *Notes on Virginia*, "Sir, I freely and cheerfully acknowledge that I am of the African race, and in the color that is natural to them the deepest dye."[13]

In defending their own color, black authors emphasized mainly that they were pleased by their own complexions. At an 1858 abolitionist meeting commemorating the Boston Massacre, John Rock declared he was not troubled if some white people did not appreciate his own dark complexion, for such individuals lacked "good taste." As we have seen, Rock then went on to tell his largely white audience that he was not "particularly pleased" with the "wan color" and general appearance of white people, presenting a humorous summary of white deficiencies that drew laughter from his audience.[14] But even humorously negative comments on the color of whites are rare in nineteenth-century African-American discourse on race. Expressing a more typical view on color differences, a correspondent to the *Colored American* who wrote under the name "Sidney" observed only that most blacks were free of the colorphobia against dark skin so common in white

America: "The color God had given us, we are satisfied with; and it is a matter of little moment to us, who may be displeased with it."[15] Likewise, David Walker bristled at Jefferson's suggestion that "it is unfortunate for us that our Creator has been pleased to make us *black*." Unfortunate for whom? asked Walker. "We wish to be just as it pleased our Creator to have made us."[16]

At least one white racial theorist recognized that differently complected peoples of the world generally esteemed their own complexions over the coloring of any other group. J. F. Blumenbach, the founder of anthropology, observed "that toads must view other toads as paragons of beauty."[17] And nineteenth-century white friends of the Negro occasionally advanced arguments for aesthetic relativism—with more enthusiasm than Blumenbach's—in the black race's defense. For instance, Harvey Newcombe, a minister who published an anonymous tract protesting color discrimination in America's churches, argued that "ideas of beauty are capricious; being affected by prevailing tastes and prejudice."[18] Newcombe went on to cite evidence from Equiano's narrative and the writings of the French naturalist Abbé Grégoire to show that white people presented a shocking appearance to eighteenth-century Africans encountering Europeans for the first time. These arguments for aesthetic relativism, however, were rarely picked up by American blacks.[19]

Evidence that literate blacks were familiar with such arguments can be seen in the early black newspaper *Freedom's Journal*, which printed comments by white travelers who remarked on the universal preference that peoples across the world displayed for human coloring in their own likeness.[20] But the only reflection on this subject by a black author in the *Journal* was a sardonic comment from Haitian author Pompée-Valentin Vastey. "The ex-colonists say we are inferior to the White," wrote Vastey,

> because we have, according to them, features less agreeable, a black skin and curly hair. I will observe in answer that the same prejudice with respect to whites prevails among blacks, who think of themselves as infinitely handsomer, and far more favoured by nature; a prejudice which is strengthened by the frequent instances in which they fall under their own observation.

Vastey went on to testify that a distaste for white skin was common in Haiti, where black skin was considered far more beautiful, and that "our Haitian painters depict the Deity and Angels black while they represent the Devils white."[21]

If similar prejudices against white skin existed among American blacks, they were not recorded by African-American intellectuals, who actively disavowed color prejudice of all kinds.[22] As a result, throughout the nineteenth century black thinkers had very little to say, good or bad, about the complexion of white people. This omission might be attributed to discretion—black thinkers no doubt felt compelled to exercise some restraint in criticizing the racial characteristics of the dominant group. But any hesitancy African-Americans might have felt about criticizing white people cannot account for their near-total silence on the subject of color. Black authors from David Walker to Harvey Johnson condemned white people for a variety of racial characteristics other than color throughout the nineteenth century.

The absence of black commentary on the color of white people poses a challenge to scholars who would maintain that color differences have a transhistorical psychological resonance, and that groups react badly to people who differ greatly from themselves in somatic norms.[23] Clearly, the psychological ramifications of color differences look very different from the black side. Whatever white color meant to nineteenth-century black people, black thinkers did not record the kind of deeply emotional responses to the phenomenon of color difference that were recorded by white American intellectuals such as Jefferson.

The "primacy of color in the white man's mind" may require more explanation than any absence of evidence for a similar preoccupation in the minds of African-Americans. However, it is worth noting that the catholic attitudes of nineteenth-century African-Americans on the subject of color differences were entirely in accord with the environmentalist explanation of human differences, which the vast majority of them endorsed. According to environmentalism, skin color was caused by climate, and neither the color of black people nor the color of white people was of any great consequence. "Now it takes all sort of people to make a world," declared a colored subscriber who wrote under the name "Euthymus" in the *Liberator* in 1831. Given that "the diversification of color in the human species" was very probably the result of "climate and the mode of life," Euthymus stated, "I would gladly learn in the book of God or nature, that color is the standard of relative rank in the scale of humanity, and how this scale is graduated. . . . Why is color in one a mark of superiority, and in another an indenture of servitude?"[24] Similarly, a commentator writing in the *Anglo-African Magazine* in 1859 under the initials "S.S.N." argued that white and black Americans alike ought to drop hyphenated designations such as Anglo-Saxon and Anglo-African, which did not accurately describe the descent of these mingled peoples. "Is there anything so peculiarly blessed about color," asked this writer, "that we must never clothe ourselves with our proper citizenship . . . ?"[25] Throughout the nineteenth century, black commentators continued to disavow that variations in skin color held any significance. Even Henry MacNeal Turner, the Pan-Africanist bishop of the A.M.E. Church who used to tell his congregation that "God is Negro," made no case for the superiority of black skin over white. In an 1873 lecture on ethnology entitled *The Negro in All Ages*, Turner expressed doubts about whether either black or white was the original and natural color of the human species. "Indeed they are not colors," he noted, "they are both extremes of colors. And if it is a matter of astonishment why a man should be black, it is equally wonderful, why a man should be white. . . . But if there is any natural color, I believe the Indian or Japanese have it; and not the black or the white man."[26]

This lack of interest in the color of the white race was also in accord with the conviction often voiced by black spokesmen of the period, that condition rather than color was the source of their race's debasement. The elusive John Rock was not alone in thinking, "When the avenues of wealth are open to us, . . . black will be a very pretty color."[27] Frederick Douglass expressed the same sentiment—stating, "with a hundred thousand dollars . . . I could make a black man very white"—as did a host of other antebellum African-Americans.[28] Such sentiments served as an incentive for black economic self-improvement throughout this period and beyond.[29] When men such as Rock and Douglass argued that prejudice and colorphobia were not natural, but arose out of the low circumstances in which American whites saw people of color, they held out the hope that if black Americans could just improve their condition, white society would no longer hold their color against them.

This hope continued to be expressed in black self-improvement doctrines voiced by race leaders throughout the nineteenth century. In the postbellum era such hopes appeared increasingly unfounded as black people continued to be the subject of intense color prejudice despite the emergence of a class of propertied blacks. As George Levesque points out in his discussion of antebellum black ideology, even before the disappointments of the post-Reconstruction era, black aspirations to transcend color prejudice through economic and educational self-improvement appear quixotic in hindsight. For all their refinements, none of the very accomplished black reformers of the era, such as Frederick Douglass and John Rock, escaped racial discrimination in their personal lives. Moreover, discrimination effectively prevented many blacks from bettering their circumstances. Color prejudice and condition could form a vicious circle, as Douglass himself pointed out, complaining of the white race in 1841: "You degrade us, and then ask us why we are degraded—you shut our mouths, and then ask us why we don't speak—you close your colleges and seminaries against us, and then ask us why we don't know more."[30] Levesque suggests that Douglass and other blacks clung to "the self-improvement formula" despite its obvious flaws because they realized "if the color argument were conceded, then blacks had (for obvious reasons) lost all control over their eventual assimilation into the society of their birth."[31]

Black and White Bodies

Color was only one of a number of physical differences thought to be associated with race in nineteenth-century America. Indeed, for many white Americans, color and low intelligence were only the beginning of the Negro's deficiencies. Historian I. A. Newby points out that, beyond color, the "whole gamut" of the Negro's "physical features, from the top of his frizzled head to the bottom of his prehensile big toe, likewise attested to his inferiority."[32] Scientific arguments of this character were first articulated in America by Dr. John Augustine Smith, who, Winthrop Jordan explains, aimed to prove that the "anatomical structure" of the "European" was "superior" to that of the Asiatic, Indian, and Negro, "or, at least, that it is further removed from the brute creation."[33] Among other things, Smith argued that black inferiority was manifest in various distinctive characteristics of the race's physical structure such as longer arms, differently shaped legs, and low facial angles. Discussion of, and research on, the Negro's many presumed physical deficiencies continued throughout the nineteenth century and reached its peak in turn-of-the-century white racial thought when scientific authors such as Frederick Hoffman and Robert Bennett Bean offered up everything from the size and shape of black people's skulls to "the broad grin characteristic of the Black Race" as evidence of black inferiority.[34]

By contrast, African-Americans who wrote and spoke about racial differences had only a little more to say about physical differences in feature and frame than they did about the pale complexions of white people. They addressed these perceived differences (many of which have been proved to be mythological) for much the same reason as they addressed color differences. Their discussions of the anatomy and physiognomy of races primarily served to defend the equal merits of their own racial characteristics. As we have seen earlier, in the antebellum era James McCune Smith and Martin Delany pointed to the physical strength of members of the Northern black community as evidence against white predictions that the black race could survive neither freedom nor the colder climate north of the Mason-Dixon line. Ever enthusiastic about his race, Delany went so far as to claim that its ability to withstand both cold and hot climates showed that "we are a *superior race*."[35] Smith, however, made no such claims. And the white race's supposed inability to tolerate heat—a physical difference between the races widely assumed as fact by commentators of both races— was not celebrated as evidence of white inferiority by any nineteenth-century African-American intellectuals other than Delany.[36]

At the same 1858 meeting where he disparaged the white race's "wan complexion," Rock also said he thought the black race was better favored by nature than the white race, whose physical organization he described as "delicate" and marred by lank hair and "sharp," "pinched up" features.[37] But Rock's negative opinion of the appearance of his white countrymen's hair and facial features, like his criticism of their complexions and Delany's claim for the physical superiority of his race, was a perspective rarely aired in nineteenth-century black racial thought. Far from identifying any physical peculiarities in white people, most black thinkers, bent on proving the unity of the human family, argued that black and white people were utterly identical under the skin. "Analyze a black man, or anatomize him, and the result of the research is the same as analyzing or anatomizing a white man," wrote Hosea Easton in 1837.[38] Easton's assertion of the identity of the races under the skin was repeated over and over again in black ethnology during the next century or so, sometimes in amazing detail. For example, a 1905 work by black churchman and academic Joseph Hayne included a chapter entitled "The Black Man's Heart and Stomach, the Same as Those of White Men."[39]

The demands of the environmentalist argument for human unity may have required nineteenth-century African-American thinkers to stifle any ethnocentric disparagement of the physical appearance of the Caucasian race. After all, so many of the physical characteristics that whites cited as evidence of black inferiority, such as complexion, hair texture, and facial features, provided evidence of difference only, and could just as easily have been incorporated into arguments for white physical inferiority—had black thinkers chosen to make such arguments. One can even get some sense of how such an argument might read in an unusual fantasy piece written by "Ethiop," which appeared in the *Anglo-African*. In this story, entitled "Year 4,000: The Amecan's, or the Milk White Race," African-Americans who have outlasted white people by virtue of their superior physical and mental qualities look back on their white oppressors of olden days, who are recalled to be "terrible to look upon, yea even fearful."

> They had *milk white skins*, and their faces were like the chalk of foreign hills, yea like unto an evil spirit; their hair was long and strait and uncomely; and in hue as the yellow or red clay of our fields. . . . And their faces were long and narrow, and their noses sharp and angular, and their nostrils thin; so also were the lips of their sunken mouths. . . . They had sharp white teeth, like unto the teeth of the shark; and their eyes were as blue as the cloudless sky, and sometimes as leaden as when it was overcast; and their brows were large even unto hiding their eyes.[40]

However, this passage is quite singular. Even in nineteenth-century African-American fiction, white characters are often frightening in behavior, but rarely so in visage. As we have seen, in black ethnology any criticism of the physical traits of whites is even more rare.

Indeed, while maintaining that all races shared common origins and had the same measure of human potential, some black thinkers seemed less than confident that the black physiognomy was the equal of the white in the here and now. In his book on the "antecedents and achievements of the colored race," entitled *The Rising Son* (1876), William Wells Brown wrote that African-Americans carried not only the "indelible mark of barbarism left upon the features of the Africans" but also the "indelible imprint of the task master." He contrasted their appearance with that of the "Anglo-Saxon [who], by his rise on the scale of humanity, has improved his features, enlarged his brain, and brightened his intellect."[41]

Although rarely focused on the physical characteristics of white people, the arguments that Brown and a number of other black ethnologists made for the unity of the human family at times appear to concede the white assumptions that "the white man's characteristics, as the racists described them, were the standard of excellence" for all mankind.[42] As noted in chapter 2, black thinkers such as Hosea Easton and Frederick Douglass accepted many aspects of white ethnology's catalog of black physical deficiencies. Indeed, these men, and other African-American writers as well, proffered explanations of racial difference designed to explain how blacks had degenerated from a norm that was, by implication, white. For example, in the chapter "The Causes of Differences in Human Features," William Wells Brown provided an explanation of the characteristic facial features of African-Americans. In considering the black countenance, Brown explains, one must take into account the ill effects of slavery. Moreover,

> It must also be remembered that in Africa, the people, whether living in houses or in the open air, are oppressed with a hot climate, which causes them to sleep, more or less, with their mouths open. This fact alone is enough to account for the large wide mouth and flat nose; common sense teaching us that with the open mouth, the features must fall.[43]

Likewise, the Reverend J. F. Dyson considered the issue of black facial features and declared without much equivocation or explanation: "I am of the opinion that thin lips and sharp noses are the normal characteristics of the human family." Dyson went on to provide a number of explanations for the abnormal features seen in men and women of African descent, including an explanation of the African mouth even more Lamarckian than Brown's, although different in its particulars:

> The thickness of the African's lips resulted, no doubt, from their practice of sucking saps and wines from palms and various other trees, which is a common practice among them. If any one doubts whether this will produce thick lips then let him suck his own lips or press them hard with his palm while reading this, and he will discover when he ceases that they are swollen.[44]

The fact remains, however, that if some nineteenth-century African-American thinkers preferred the physical features of the white race, they did not express their admiration at length. The primary issue in black discussions of the physical differences between the races, just as in white discussions of these differences, was the appearance and physiognomy of black people. White racial theorists from John Augustine Smith, at the beginning of the nineteenth century, to a host of turn-of-the-century social scientists such as Robert Bennett Bean identified physical differences between the races primarily to prove that black people were a step closer to animals than were white people. The time-honored Euro-American suspicion that black people were close kin to the simian species received strong reinforcement from late nineteenth- and early twentieth-century understandings of evolution.

African-Americans abhorred and protested white racial theorists' insults to their humanity. Paradoxically, however, when they assumed that white physical features were the normal human features from which black people had degenerated, Dyson and a number of his black colleagues seem to distance their people from the imputation of anthropoid characteristics through a disturbingly self-abnegating argument. Black people's membership in the human species was above question, they appeared to be saying, because they used to look more like white people.

The implicit admission of the possibility of white physical superiority inherent in such arguments suggests that blacks were not immune to the overwhelming preference for the form and features of the white race emanating from the dominant culture. Certainly, some nineteenth-century African-Americans feared that black people had adopted the white race as their physical ideal. "The white man's idea of beauty," wrote black churchman and academic Joseph Hayne in 1887,

> his estimate of standards of excellence are assuredly that of the Negro as it is his own. All pictures of great men who have ever lived; all pictures in geographies are white. Hannibal of Carthage, the Egyptians, the conceivers and dispensers of civilization, the Sphinx at Memphis, are all painted white. So even our own children are thus educated to despise themselves because black is made to represent evil, and respect white because all accomplishments of man are represented to be the results of that race born white.[45]

Hayne, who wrote at least four works recording the honorable lineage and ancient accomplishments of his race, evidently doubted whether the revisionist ethnology and historiography he and other nineteenth-century black authors produced had much impact.[46]

The influence of Hayne and others is difficult to assess. More to the point, one must keep in mind that when it came to revisionist scientific arguments documenting the physiological equality of black people, the race got only modest support from even these stalwart defenders. Nineteenth-century African-Americans brought limited resources into their confrontation with arguments for white physical superiority made by scientific racists of the day. They questioned both the logic and the data used by these scientists but generally lacked the scientific credentials to produce countervailing evidence of their own.[47] It is therefore surely no coincidence that during the years in which white scientists busied themselves measuring the black body and weighing the black brain, the racial characteristics African-American thinkers most often scrutinized in white people were not corporal characteristics that could be measured and weighed.

"From Whence Sprang the Anglo Saxon Race?": Whites in Post-Emancipation Black Ethnology

From the early nineteenth century onward, then, most American thinkers believed racial differences amounted to more than variations in color and physiogomy. Black and white commentators alike asserted that races were divided by differences in character, temperament, "genius," and a host of other traits invisible to both the eye and the scalpel. By the end of the century, I. A. Newby suggests, many white thinkers found such intangible traits "more fundamental than the dissimilarity of curly blond hair and kinky black wool."[48] Meanwhile, the intangibles of racial difference were still more important in African-American racial thought. To black thinkers, most of whom insisted that the physical dissimilarities between the races were of no great consequence, distinctions in matters such as character and temperament were the only admissible fundamental racial differences.

Accordingly, when antebellum era African-American intellectuals turned their attention to the white race, they did not dwell on color or physique. As we have seen, their discussions of white people focused on the history, character, and temperament of the white race. As might be expected, they frequently found that the character and temperament of the dominant group left much to be desired. Ethiop's 1860 characterization of his troublesome white countrymen as murderously aggressive and acquisitive marauders drew on images of white people already well established in African-American writing on race. Black thinkers would continue to emphasize the masculine traits of aggression and acquisitiveness as the racial traits most characteristic of white people throughout the second half of the century as well.

These continuities in nineteenth-century black racial thought are not surprising, for although the Civil War wrought momentous changes among African-Americans, it did not end white assaults on

African-American humanity and manhood. During the war, black thinkers had predicted that black participation in the Union Army would vindicate the race. "Go quickly to fill up the first colored regiment from the North," Frederick Douglass urged after the Union Army finally began to recruit black men in 1862. "The chance is now given to you to end your degradation, and to rise in one bound from social degradation to the plane of equality with all other varieties of men."[49] Such predictions, however, never came true. As historian David R. Roediger suggests, "the fact of emancipation" may well have "called into question the tendency to equate blackness and servility" by teaching Northern whites that blacks were anxious to free themselves. Yet blacks who freed themselves were not always given credit for their own agency. Roediger writes, "Even the heroic actions of slaves fleeing from bondage were often cast as cowardly, confused, or lazy."[50] Likewise, the military exploits of black soldiers were sometimes transmuted into evidence of their racial deficiencies. "Blacks make excellent troops when well officered and disciplined," wrote one Union general; "*they are most easily ruled.*"[51]

In the long run, white Americans did not see the military contributions of black soldiers as proof of black manhood. Indeed, the contributions black soldiers made to the war were soon discounted and obscured by Northern and Southern whites anxious to reinstate the racial status quo. Bent on recovering their former superiority, Southern whites terrorized former soldiers and claimed that blacks had "fought no battles; or if engaged at all in such, they were trifling affairs."[52] Worse, the defeated South waged a systematic battle to resubjugate their recently freed slaves that ended with the defeat of Reconstruction and the rise of Jim Crow segregation. At the same time, the contributions of black soldiers were soon forgotten by Northern whites preoccupied by political struggles over the South's Reconstruction—struggles that ultimately exhausted their very limited enthusiasm for black civil rights.

Moreover, the Civil War and its aftermath ended up feeding the ever-increasing racism in American scientific thought. The Union Army advanced the cause of scientific racism by collecting anthropometric evidence believed to confirm the inferiority of black people. The United States Sanitary Commission, a semiofficial organization created to study the physical and moral condition of American soldiers, measured the troops from head to toe, generating the largest collection of anthropometric statistics ever assembled.[53] The most notable physical differences among whites, Indians, blacks, and mulattoes were variations in physical build, particularly through the arms and torso. Black soldiers, for example, were found to have longer arms and shorter bodies, on average, than their white counterparts. Where they found distinctions between the races, the white scientists who analyzed these data saw evidence of black inferiority, concluding the greater arm length of blacks marked their race as more anthropoid in development than the shorter-limbed white race. Likewise, the Provost Marshall-General's Bureau, another information-collecting branch of the Union Army, documented the inferiority of blacks and other people of color. The Union doctors surveyed by the bureau were convinced that the Negro could never hope to be the equal of the white man, and that mulattoes were physically and mentally inferior to both races. Published in the late 1860s, these army findings only added more weight to new and renewed questions about the character and capacities of blacks that surfaced during Reconstruction. Along with other scientific racist findings of the postbellum era, they reassured white Americans in both the North and the South that the millions of African-Americans emancipated during the war and its aftermath would be free but not equal.

Black emancipation posed more immediate questions than the long-term status of the races, however—questions that also evoked ethnological answers. Central among these was "Will the Negro work," a burning question among whites, who frequently had specific black labor arrangements in mind. In the North, this question reflected white anxieties that the freed people would migrate north, leaving the Southern cotton plantations untended and New England's cotton mills without raw materials; in the South, the issue was whether the freedpeople could be forced to work for what little white Southerners were willing to pay them. To their credit, Republican radicals opposed the draconian "Black Codes" enacted by the Southern states soon after the war, which used vagrancy and enticement laws to tie the freedpeople to their old plantations. In a series of acts passed between 1866 and 1870, the Republicans invalidated the Black Codes; passed the Fourteenth and Fifteenth Amendments, which extended citizenship and suffrage to black men; and imposed military rule through most of the South. Bent on forcing the South to accept black suffrage and Republican rule, the Republicans also set new rules for the readmission of the rebellious states into the Union. To rejoin the United States, the former Confederate states had to ratify the new amendments and renounce the leadership of former Confederates. The coalition of radical and moderate Republicans who imposed congressional Reconstruction on the unrepentant white South did so despite their own doubts about whether blacks were ready to assume the rights and obligations of citizenship. Anxious to restore order in the South, without letting the Confederacy reassemble itself, many Republicans saw black suffrage as a necessary evil. Only by extending the franchise to black men could the party restructure the Union under Northern hegemony.

Not surprisingly, Democrats and Southerners disagreed, blatantly appealing to the racial prejudices of whites in both sections as they voiced their objections. Denigrating the Negro's ethnological status anew, proslavery thinkers retailored their arguments for the post-emancipation era, while Northern democrats railed against the dangers of race mixture. Cherishing slavery as a lost ideal, white Southerners drew on the ethnological findings of physicians and other men of science to conclude that without the slaveowner to guide and protect them, the freedpeople would not survive. Russ James, a writer for *Scott's Monthly Magazine*, was convinced American blacks were on the road to extinction less than half a decade after the war. As a slave, he noted in 1868, the Negro had "obtained the knowledge of the true God; was affectionate to his family, and was immeasurably in advance of his ancestors, intellectually and morally." But freedom put an end to the race's improvement. Now, according to James,

> In many parts of the South, they are sinking into the most degrading and revolting superstition. . . . They have become insubordinate and habitual violators of law and order. Our prisons are swarming with them, while many have expiated a short, though bloody, career of crime upon the scaffold. As a race they are passing away rapidly, nearly one million having perished in the short space of three years.[54]

Less sentimental about slavery than their Southern counterparts, Northern Democrats also had ethnological objections to the elevation of the Negro. In particular, they warned that racial equality would lead to race mixture with a "semi-barbarous race of blacks who are worshippers of fetishes and polygamists." Black men would like nothing more than to "subject white women to their unbridled lust," according to Francis P. Blair, Democratic candidate for vice president in 1866. Opposing the Republican Reconstruction policies in the South, Blair warned that giving black men political rights would reverse the course of evolution. An early convert to Darwinism—on this subject at any rate—Blair prophesied that the amalgamation of the races would destroy the white race, eroding "the accumulated improvements of the centuries."[55]

In the face of ever changing and ever more scientifically authoritative claims against their manhood and their race, black intellectuals could only continue their long tradition of rebuttal and protest. Clinging to their conviction that "the efforts made by oppressed nations or communities to throw off their chains, entitles them to and gains them the respect of mankind," African-Americans commemorated the exploits of colored soldiers as evidence of the manliness of their race. Black authors such as William Wells Brown, Peter Clark, Edward Johnson, Joseph T. Wilson, and George Washington Williams wrote detailed accounts of the military achievements of the Negro in the Revolution, the War of 1812, and the Civil War.[56] Yet even as they created a genre chronicling the race's manly courage, some of these same authors presented white men as more manly still, reviving complaints about the white race seen in the antebellum era. Turning once again

William Wells Brown as he appears in his *Narrative of William Wells Brown, a Fugitive Slave* (1847) (Boston Athenæum).

to ethnology to answer the charges against their race, postbellum black writers continued to contrast the Negro's gentle virtues with the Anglo-Saxon's more aggressive temperament.

Such efforts began before the war had even ended and redoubled during Reconstruction, when struggles over black citizenship and political participation gave new life to old questions about the character and capacities of the black race. Speaking on behalf of a newly emancipated people, black leaders combed history and ethnology for evidence that a freedpeople could rise, while also reiterating time-honored arguments for the unity of the human family. Freedom brought new themes to black ethnology as well as reinvigorating old ones. In the face of prophecies that African-Americans would never be capable of rising to meet the demands of citizenship, African-Americans reminded whites that the Anglo-Saxon race had once been enslaved. As they described the white race's lowly past, they emphasized that early whites had been brutal and barbarous.

"From whence sprang the Anglo-Saxon?" asked ex-slave William Wells Brown in a book entitled *The Black Man: His Antecedents, His Genius, and His Achievements* (1863). Writing as the slave system was beginning to crumble, this abolitionist and antislavery lecturer, who also published one of the earliest African-American novels, sought to break the equation between race and slavery so entrenched in the minds of both black and white Americans. Reviewing the history of the Anglo-Saxon race, Brown drew on English and Roman historians for evidence of the Saxons' once lowly status. "'When Britons first became known to the Tyrian mariners,'" Brown said, quoting Mac-Cauley, "'they were little superior to the Sandwich Islanders.'" Citing the additional authority of Hume, he went on to describe the ancient Britons as a barbarous people who worshiped the Druids, wore the skin of wild beasts, and succumbed easily to the domination of first the Romans, then the Saxons. The Britons did not much impress their Roman conquerors, Brown reported with relish: the conquered islanders who were sent on to Roman slave markets were sold "very cheap on account of their inability to learn."

> Caesar, in writing home, said of the Britons, "They are the most ignorant people I have ever conquered. They cannot be taught music." Cicero, in writing to his friend Atticus, advised him not to buy slaves in England, "because," said he, "they cannot be taught to read, and are the ugliest and most stupid race I ever saw."[57]

Likewise, the eloquent A.M.E. minister Bishop Henry MacNeal Turner invoked similar images in 1868 when he defended the eligibility of black representatives for their seats in Georgia's reconstructed legislature. "Why did your forefathers come to this country?" Turner asked the all-white legislature:

> Did they not flee from oppression? They came to free themselves from the chains of tyranny, and to escape from the heel of the Autocrat. Why, sir, in England, for centuries together, men—and *white* men at that—wore metal collars around their necks, bearing, in graven characters, the names by which they were known. Your great and noble race were sold in the slave marts of Rome. . . . I say to you, white men, that the great deliverance of the recent past is not altogether dissimilar to the great deliverance of ancient times.[58]

Turner and the other black representative were seated in March 1869, after Congress intervened on their behalf. But their victory was short lived. They were ousted again in 1870, when the Democrats regained control of Georgia.

As Reconstruction collapsed around them, black thinkers continued to challenge white supremacy by emphasizing the base origins of the Anglo-Saxon race. In an 1873 work on ethnology composed in the wake of his unsuccessful career in politics, Turner compared the history of the races, concluding that "the Goths or Vandals of Europe, from whom our white friends are descended, are no more to be compared [with the ancient Africans], than I am to be compared with Isaac Newton."[59] His sentiments were echoed by the nationally circulated black Baptist newspaper *New National Era*, which denigrated white history in a series of articles entitled "The Descendants of Ham the Superior Race." "Ham and his descendants have been not the inferior, but the superior and the predominant race in all that part of the world's history where the family can be traced," wrote journalist J. W. Beckwith, who argued that the descendants of Japhet made a poor showing in the Bible and derived most of their civilization from earlier Hamitic civilizations.[60] Similarly, in a second work on ethnology, published in 1876, William Wells Brown again waxed eloquent on the inglorious history of the Anglo-Saxon race:

> Go back a few centuries, and we find their ancestors described in the graphic touches of Caesar and Tacitus. See them in the gloomy forests of Germany, sacrificing their grim and gory idols; drinking the warm blood of their prisoners, quaffing libations from human skulls; infesting the shores of the Baltic for plunder and robbery; bringing home the reeking scalps of enemies as an offering to their king.[61]

In addition to challenging white pretensions to innate superiority, Brown and other black writers discussed white history in order to show that any race could rise to power regardless of its origins. Brown urged his fellow African-Americans to study the rise of the Anglo-Saxon to a "refined, proud, haughty, and intellectual race." "As one man learns from another," he counseled, "nation learns from nation":

> There is nothing in race or blood, in the color of our features that imparts susceptibility of improvement to one race over another. The mind left to itself from infancy, without culture, remains blank. Knowledge is not innate. Development makes the man. As the Greeks, and Romans, and Jews drew knowledge from the Egyptians three thousand years ago, and the Europeans received it from the Romans, so must the blacks of the land rise the same way.[62]

Two decades later, black educator John Stephens Durham offered similar advice in *To Teach the Negro History* (1897). A prominent lawyer and diplomat as well as a teacher, Durham believed the education of the Negro should begin with a survey of European history. "To follow the European races through barbarism and slavery to the tribal and family state, to see how comparatively recently their social life was marked by fetish, polytheism, human sacrifices, perhaps, and certainly by family trees without clearly defined paternal roots," he suggested, "prepares one to overcome the soul-stifling influences of our daily experiences."[63]

Not all postbellum black thinkers found the history of the white race inspiring, however. Although the emancipation tempered his emigrationist zeal for a time, Martin Delany remained convinced whites had risen only at the expense of the African race. Appointed the first black major at the close of the Civil War, during Reconstruction Delany turned his attention to improving the condition of blacks in America, rather than encouraging them to leave. He worked for the Freedman's Bureau in South Carolina, "where he emerged as one of the most zealous African-American proponents of Reconstruction."[64] Yet even during the first few years after emancipation, when he was as optimistic as he would ever be about the future of blacks in American society, Delany remained pessimistic about white people. Described by one white officer as "a thorough hater of the white race," Delany lives up to that description in an essay he published in Frances Rollin's *Life of Major Delany* (1868).[65]

In "The International Policy of the World Toward Africa," Delany charged that racial slavery was created by the white nations of Spain, England, France, and Portugal with the express purpose of subjugating the African race. Throughout Europe, whites had once been enslaved, he explained, and white slaves were once deemed inferior beings in much the same way people of African descent were now thought of as a lesser race. British aristocrats used to claim that English peasants were "incapable of elevation [and] recorded and passed enactments against the Scotch and the Irish that they were innately inferior, totally insusceptible of instruction and civilization, calling them 'heathen dogs, fit for only slaves of the lowest order.'" In the long run, however, the European ruling classes had found it difficult to oppress their own people. The common people demanded their liberty, and "the elevated wealthy nobles could no longer bear to see the ignorant poor of his kinsmen degraded," wrote Delany, giving white Europeans credit for remarkable cross-class loyalties. "To longer deny them elevation was to disparage the genius and degrade the whole Caucasian race." Faced with this problem, France, England, Spain, and Portugal devised an ingenious solution. Selecting the African as "the victim of an international conspiracy," they replaced their white slaves with black ones, destroying Africa and degrading the African.[66]

The white rise to power was driven by "avarice and love of lucre" and was nothing to be emulated, in Delany's view. Whites could never be truly civilized, and their achievements would never equal those of the ancient Africans because they lacked essential virtues. "A people or race possessing in a high degree the great principles of pure ethics and true religion, a just conception of God, necessarily inherit the essential principles of the highest civilization," wrote Delany. "And is it not a known and conceded fact by all who are conversant with the African race, that he excels all other races in religious sentiments . . . ?"[67]

The image of whites in black ethnology did not improve after the defeat of Reconstruction. As Southern whites regained political power during last quarter of the nineteenth century, racist invective casting American black people as a bestial lower race reached new heights in American letters. Disenfranchised, segregated, and terrorized during the reascendance of home rule and white supremacy in the post-

Reconstruction South, blacks were also demonized in the press. Black males, in particular, were routinely depicted as sexual predators whose lust for white women both necessitated and justified a variety of repressive measures against them—up to and including lynching.[68]

By the late nineteenth century, blacks faced new scientific and religious assaults on their humanity as well. Probably the most egregiously racist production of the era was Charles Caroll's *The Negro Is a Beast*.[69] An old-fashioned polygenist, Carroll sought to reconcile his conviction that the races did not originate from the same ancestors with the biblical account of Creation through the simple expedient of classifying the Negro as an ape. Other white commentators allowed that blacks were human beings, but of a very primitive sort. Except among diehards like Carroll, pluralist theories gave way in the late nineteenth century, only to be replaced by Darwinian understandings of human development little more flattering to the black race. Broadly understood, Darwin's theory of evolution held that all human beings were related to animals, but late nineteenth-century white interpreters almost invariably assumed the "primitive races" were closer kin to the animal kingdom than to civilized people such as themselves. Indeed, to black thinkers, Darwinism as discussed by nineteenth-century whites held much the same import as polygenesis. "Look at the unreasonable and abominable distortion of truth that so many of our brothers in white resort to in order to prove the inferiority of the descendants of Ham," wrote black minister and theologian Joseph Hayne in an 1887 attack on the Darwinian understandings of Creation and human origins. "Have they not declared them a race that springs from baboons and apes, and can never be the equals of the white race?"[70]

Sounding the same alarm as so many earlier black thinkers, Hayne declared that the "much agitated question" of the Negro's origins "has become the first of all questions on the calendar now. . . . every thinker in the race is expected to take his place in the struggle to establish on the firm basis of historic facts the true status of Ham and his immediate descendants."[71] A prolific author, Hayne did his part, as did other blacks who wrote on black history and ethnology in the late nineteenth century.

"Modern Barbarians": Whites in Late Nineteenth-Century Black Thought

Indeed, black publications on the question of racial origins may well have reached their height during the post-Reconstruction era, when African-Americans felt compelled to defend themselves from both unflattering interpretations of Darwin and the "orgy of extreme racism" that accompanied the rise of the New South. Often written as a direct rebuttal to white supremacist charges against the race, black ethnology of the postwar era presented the races in counterpoint.[72] As always, post-Reconstruction black ethnology was dedicated to the defense of the Negro. But the African-Americans who wrote this literature invariably commented on the history, character, and temperament of white as well as black people. In doing so, they continued to weave a revisionist image of the white race in the name of black self-vindication.

Martin Delany further refined his case against the white race in the 1870s, when he retired from public life and wrote a detailed ethnological monograph explaining the differences between the races. Published in 1879, his *Principia of Ethnology: The Origin of the Races and Color with an Archaeological Compendium of Ethiopian and Egyptian Civilization from Years of Careful Examination and Enquiry* addressed all the usual concerns of black ethnology, while making what may well be the most unambiguous argument for the existence of permanent distinctions between the races by any nineteenth-century African-African. In this book Delany drew on his early medical training to present a scientific account of the history of the races. In keeping with the black ethnological tradition, Delany's *Principia* rejected pluralism, "making no apology for the liberal use of Creation as learned from the Bible." In all other respects, however, Delany found the races to be divided and distinct. Common origins did not make things the same, he suggested, expressing an almost Darwinian view of biological development. "Is it reasonable to suppose that there were necessarily original parents for all varieties in species of animals and vegetables?" he asked.[73]

Although Delany insisted that the divisions between the races were once permeable, he was equally convinced that the races of the present day would forever remain distinct and indestructible. The human family had divided into three "pure" or "sterling" races after the deluge, he explained, with the black, yellow, and white races descending from Ham, Shem, and Japhet, respectively. Once created, these divisions were irreversible: no amount of racial mixture could create a new race. "A general intermarriage of any two distinct races," Delany explained, "would inevitably result in the destruction, the extinction of the less numerous of the two; that race which preponderates entirely absorbing the other."[74]

In addition to being pure and distinct, Delany maintained, the three races were distinguished by their own "peculiar characteristics." In Delany's scheme the Creator's design was tidy. The "ardor and temperament of the races" was reflected in their coloring, which could be conveniently classified as "*positive, medium* and *negative*." These designations were determined by the amount of concentrated rouge, or "pigmentum nigrum," present in each race's skin, but they also reflected "the progress of the civilization propagated and carried forward" by each race. Color was character, and the future was clear: Ham's dark children were destined to redeem the world.[75]

Neither wholly coherent nor persuasive, Delany's account of the character of the races in *Principia* put a scientific gloss on the long-standing distinctions that he and other black writers often made between the redeemer race and the *"negative"* Anglo-Saxon. Delany never explained exactly why whites were negative—or, for that matter, what aspect of the yellow races, other than their color, made them *"medium."* But a familiar critique of the irredeemable Saxon was implicit throughout his description of the redeemer race. Africans were the most religious race; other races, most notably the oppressive white race, were less religious. The African race was endowed with "inherent faculties, designed by the Creator as essential to the divine plan for civilization"; the white race obviously failed to appreciate these inherent faculties.[76] Blacks who were the least contaminated by interaction and intermixture with whites, such as the Yorubas of West Africa, represented the best the race had to offer; the white race was a bad influence, both biologically and culturally.

Even during the difficult days that followed Reconstruction, few black thinkers were willing to make as much of racial distinctions as did Martin Delany, and fewer still shared his admiration of the African—"untrammeled in his native purity."[77] Nonetheless, even black authors who were not bent on exposing the deficiencies of white people or celebrating the purity of native Africans often presented historical descriptions of the white race that had much in common with Delany's depiction of whites as marauding predators. For instance, when William Wells Brown counseled African-Americans to follow the rise of Anglo-Saxons who used to drink from human skulls, he reinforced black ethnology's stock image of the white race as aggressive, bloodthirsty, and male. Similarly, other black admirers of the white race, such as Alexander Crummell, often reinforced rather than repudiated the image of the overly aggressive white race when they celebrated the primitive virtues of the Germanic tribes.

One of most distinguished black intellectuals of his day, by 1877 Alexander Crummell had combined his veneration for European culture and civilization with an unswerving conviction in the "destined superiority of the Negro."[78] Born in 1819 to free African parents, Crummell attended New York's African Free School along with Henry Highland Garnet, James McCune Smith, and Samuel Ringgold Ward. He went on to study at the Oneida Institute in upstate New York and then sought to complete his education at the (Episcopal) General Theological Seminary in New York. Refused admission there because of his race, Crummell trained on his own and was ordained by a sympathetic bishop. After completing his education at Cambridge University, Crummell went on to serve as a missionary in Liberia for sixteen years, returning to the United States in 1872. Subsequently, he founded St. Luke's Episcopal Church in Washington, D.C., where he served as pastor until shortly before his death in 1898. Throughout his long life, Crummell was active as a scholar and a lecturer, publishing many books and orations on Africa, race relations, and ethnology.[79]

Both an Anglophile and a race man, Crummell reconciled his belief in the destined superiority of the Negro race with his belief in the present-day superiority of the Anglo-Saxon race by adopting a cyclical theory of history. Like the great British statesman Benjamin Disraeli, whom he quotes on this point, Crummell was convinced that race was "the key to history."[80] Civilizations, or races—two terms that Crummell used interchangeably—rose and fell according to "God's disciplinary and retributive economy of races and nations." Thus, the ancient Egyptians, Abyssinians, and Babylonians had declined as a result of religious error, and the vast unconverted population of Africa languished in darkness, ruled by Moloch. By contrast, the European races had reaped the rewards of righteousness by embracing the "true and pure idea that God is a spirit."[81]

But Europeans had not always been so enlightened. "Their ancestors were barbarians," Crummell emphasized in 1854, sketching a familiar portrait of the white race's past "without commerce or enlightenment," who "worshipped dumb idols and bowed down in fear and awe to graven images." Only with the advent of Christianity did Europeans rise to "their present power and influence. . . . *as* Pagans they could never have *originated* nor retained commerce and civilization."[82] Although Crummell venerated the Protestant nations of Europe for creating the highest and most godly civilization yet achieved, his economy of "races and nations" was not simply an argument for the superiority of Protestant Christianity. Rather, Crummell was convinced that the destiny of any given race was determined by a seamless combination of religious and racial attributes. Europe rose on the strength of the "great sterling virtues" of its peoples, as well as their religious enlightenment. "The masterful nations," wrote Crummell, who argued that the African race was one of them, "are all more or less distinguished for vitality, plasticity, receptivity, imitation, family feeling, veracity and sentiment of devotion."[83]

Crummell explained that just as the racial gifts of Europeans flowered under Christianity, so too would those of the Negro. Like the Europeans, Africans possessed "conditions of character and of society, to which the divine purposes of grace and civilization are . . . especially fitted." Black people would not perish like the American Indians and other "weaker races," whose depravity prepared them for destruction. To the contrary, "the peculiar vitality" of the African race had enabled black people to survive "wave after wave of a destructive tempest." Adaptable, imitative, and naturally religious, black people had survived the rigors of the slave trade and European domination in Africa

Alexander Crummell (Moorland-Springarn Research Center, Howard University Archives).

and the Americas, as well their own "ancestral heathenism," without declining as a race. "Disciplinary and preparative," rather than punitive, "their history forecasted the greatness of the race."[84]

Crummell's theory of race neither necessitated nor implied any denigration of the white race. Indeed, he consistently presented the European civilization as a racial ideal. Nonetheless, his admiration for the white race did not prevent him from portraying white people as marauding conquerors. Throughout his career he consistently described the history of the white race in the same grim terms used by far more critical black commentators. Writing on Liberia in the 1860s, for example, Crummell presented a not entirely flattering homage to the virtues of the Anglo-Saxon race as embodied in the English language. While arguing that the English language was the language of freedom, wisdom, and true religion, and should be used in Liberia instead of the African languages native to the region, Crummell made the Anglo-Saxons themselves sound quite unpleasant. "Of all the races of men," he wrote, "none, I ween, are so domineering, none have a stronger and more exclusive sense of caste; none have a more contemptuous dislike of inferiority." He then went on to say that this robust race could "conquer" even their own fierce temperament when "chastened and subdued by Christianity." But elsewhere in his writings Crummell did not sound at all certain that they had ever managed to do so. In another essay written shortly afterward, Crummell argued that black Americans must lead the regeneration of Africa, since Europe's three-hundred-year history there was "a history of rapine and murder, and widespread devastation of families and the homes of simple and rude inhabitants. The whole coast, sir, had been ravaged wherever his [the European's] footsteps have fallen; and he had left little behind him but an exaggerated barbarism and an even deeper depth of ruin."[85]

Crummell would make similar comments about the domineering spirit and fierce disposition of the European races after he returned to the United States in the 1870s, creating an implicit contrast between the gentle character he ascribed to his own race and the aggressiveness of whites. At first glance his references to the fierceness of white people may seem difficult to reconcile with his veneration of Anglo-European civilization in America and abroad. Yet the contradictions entailed in lauding the white civilization while at the same time portraying white people as excessively aggressive may well have appealed to Crummell. They allowed him to believe that, with civilization, blacks could surpass the white race, leavening the Western tradition with gentle virtues lacking in the white European races. Crummell seems to suggest as much in his essay "The Destined Superiority of the Negro" (1877), in which he supports his central argument with a quote from a white British thinker. He cites a Dr. Raleigh, heard "at a recent meeting in London," who gushes: "Greece gave us beauty; Rome gave us power; the Anglo-Saxon race mingles and unites these; but in the African people there is a great gushing wealth of love which will develop wonders for the world."[86]

For most black thinkers, however, the aggressive Anglo-Saxon was rarely just a complement to the black race's better nature. One doubts whether even racial conservatives such as Crummell invoked the image of the aggressive Anglo-Saxon without making at least implicit reference to the long history of white violence against African-Americans and other people of color. Meanwhile, other black critics of the white race were quite explicit. For example, in 1879 the school paper of the Hampton Institute, the *Southern Workman*, ran an article on historic evils of the Anglo-Saxon race under the matter-of-fact title "Anglo-Saxon Brutality." The author of the article, who wrote under the initials "W.N.A.," argued that the Anglo-Saxon was, "of all the races, the most tender-hearted, humane, and sympathetic, so long as its own interests are not touched." However, "This race, in pursuit of its own advantages, or when it deems itself injured or insulted, is as brutal, obstinate, unjust, warlike and inhuman as any of the savage race of the world."

In W.N.A.'s account, the Anglo-Saxon race rarely manifested any of its good qualities. Presenting a review of Anglo-Saxon history already familiar in black writing on race, this author argued that the origins of the Anglo-Saxon people accounted for the race's perennially bad character: "It has been said, 'no wonder the Anglo-Saxons are brutes. They are the issue of Scandinavian pirates, Norman adventurers, and rough savages of Briton.'" W.N.A. further claimed this mixture created a "blood and iron" nature in the Anglo-Saxon. The "ferocious traits" of this nature could be seen in American Anglo-Saxon behavior toward blacks and Native Americans and in British Anglo-Saxon domination of India, exploitation of the Chinese, and mistreatment of the Maori people in New Zealand. W.N.A. held out the hope that these traits of the Anglo-Saxon civilization might be modified in the future:

> In founding nations, in building cities, in recovering the wilderness, in grappling with obstacles, in consolidating institutions, the aggressive traits of this race have been of great and splendid use. Now that it has settled itself, marking off its geographical claims, done its rough work, made itself supreme, and perhaps spent its brutality, there are indications of a rapid development in the qualities of generosity and humanity.[87]

Writing half a decade later, the Pan-Africanist J. T. Holly was equally critical of the white race's historical record and less hopeful about its future prospects. An advocate of Haitian emigration in the 1850s, Holly was looking toward less worldly solutions to racial injustice by the 1880s. In particular, he was confident that "the warlike Japhetic nations shall be overthrown at the battle of Armageddon" in a final reckoning that would be "carried on with a certain reference in the instruments employed to the tribal division in the humans race." Unveiling his "Divine Plan of Human Redemption in its Ethnological Development" in the *A.M.E. Church Review*, Holly prophesied that the "elect descendants of Ham" would lead the millennium, while unredeemably aggressive Japhetic nations would not even prosper from their own "evangelical zeal." Whites might have religion, but they lacked goodness:

> After nearly nineteen centuries of Gospel effort the Japhetic nations have not yet been able to realize among their most enlightened Christian nations, the second clause of the Angels' song sung at the birth of Christ, viz: "Peace on earth, good will towards men." On the contrary, the most warlike and predatory nations of this nineteenth century of

the grace of Jesus Christ are precisely the most enlightened Christian nations.

"All they that take by the sword shall perish by the sword," was Holly's gloomy prophecy for the white race.[88]

Holly's dire warning aside, attacks on the history, character, and temperament of the white race never became the main theme in nineteenth-century African-American racial thought: through the late nineteenth century, as earlier, black thinkers remained preoccupied with the ethnological defense of the Negro. Still, by the 1890s, discussions of whites as brutal and aggressive Anglo-Saxons were commonplace in black thought, appearing in a wide variety of contexts. One rather unlikely example is *A Voice from the South* (1892), a collection of essays written by African-American educator and activist Anna Julia Cooper. One of black feminism's foremothers, Cooper emphasized the unique concerns and educational needs of women throughout her essays and her career, arguing with reference to black women that they must be allowed to speak for themselves, since no one else could "fully and adequately reproduce the Voice of the Black Woman." Yet Cooper was capable of eliding race and gender herself when it came to comparing the races. For example, in her essay "Has America a Race Problem?" she describes the races in gendered racial stereotypes not unlike those used by male writers of both races. The white race's European ancestors have "huge white bodies, cool-blooded, with fierce blue eyes, reddish flaxen hair, ravenous stomachs, filled with meat and cheese, heated by strong drinks," Cooper writes, quoting a European authority. Masculine by lineage as well as by temperament, white people were the descendants of "brutal drunken pirates and robbers." By contrast, the black race possesses distinctly feminine-sounding virtues that, in a country where the races live side by side, can be hoped to mitigate the worst characteristics of the white race. "America needs the Negro for ballast if nothing else," Cooper concludes, envisioning a union between the two. "His tropical warmth and spontaneous emotionalism may form no unseemly counterpart to the cold and calculating Anglo Saxon."[89]

Ironically enough, this racial reconciliation was a marriage between men. Despite her calls for the recognition of African-American women in discussions of their race, Cooper herself found it difficult to carve out a place for women in the gendered racial stereotypes used by so many nineteenth-century black thinkers to represent the races. With reference to white people, however, this omission may not have troubled Cooper and her black contemporaries. The image of the Anglo-Saxon as a fierce barbarian no doubt seemed particularly appropriate in the 1890s—a decade when lynchings were occurring with unprecedented frequency, and racial violence against black people was endemic. As Gail Bederman has shown, during these years black journalist and activist Ida B. Wells employed similar metaphors in her brilliant campaign against lynching. Manipulating "dominant-middle class ideas about race, manhood, and civilization," Wells challenged the civility of the white Southern men who presented lynching as a manly and honorable response to black barbarism.[90] Lynching was not a civilized response to even the heinous crime of rape, Wells told audiences in England and the Northern states. Moreover, she pointed out, many lynching victims were not even accused of rape. Turning the Southern justification for lynching on its head, Wells defined lynching and the white Americans who tolerated it as barbaric. "Make your laws as terrible as you like against that class of crime [rape]," she wrote in 1894. "Devise whatever tortures you choose; go back to the most barbarian methods of the most barbarous ages; and then my case is just as strong. Prove your man guilty, first; hang him, shoot him, pour coal oil over him and roast him, if you have concluded that civilization demands this; but be sure the man has committed the crime first."[91]

Wells's black male contemporaries also described white violence in racial terms, holding up both lynching and American imperialism as evidence of Anglo-Saxon barbarism. In doing so, they perpetuated and strengthened a racial stereotype of white people that had become a well-established tradition in black thought over the course of the nineteenth century. To crusading black journalist John Edward Bruce the Euro-American was a "modern barbarian, who is dignified by the title of White citizen." Invoking white barbarism past and present in an 1890 speech before the Afro-American League, Bruce reflected:

> They now roast objectionable Negroes alive in certain portions of our God (?) blessed country. I have read of deeds of cruelty committed by one religious faction against another, of how thirty thousand were burned at the stake in one day. How men, women, and children were thrown from high eminencies upon wagons filled with sharp pointed spikes which lacerated their bodies and destroyed their lives; how men were hung with their heads downward until life was extinct; of Nero the tyrant and bigot who fiddled while the seven hilled city burned. But this modern Barbarism practiced on the Negro in Christian America by white men who boast of high civilization makes me "tremble for this country when I remember that God is just."

Echoing earlier black writers, Bruce insisted that white Americans were a distinctively vicious race, citing the nation's history as evidence. Both African-Americans and Native Americans, he maintained, had been victims of the white race's "rapacity and greed from the foundation of this Government to the present."[92]

In a slightly more roundabout way, an impertinent young man named William Edward Burghardt DuBois offered a similar criticism of the white race's temperament at his Harvard graduation in 1890. Honored by being among those graduates selected to give a brief oration at the commencement ceremony, DuBois boldly chose to address his elite white audience on the subject of Jefferson Davis. In a carefully worded speech DuBois described Davis as the "typical Teutonic hero," adding the sweeping caveat that "judged by the whole standard of Teutonic civilization, there is something noble about Jefferson Davis; and judged by every canon of human justice, there is something fundamentally incomplete about that standard." Advancing the critique of the historic behavior of the Anglo-Saxon race so often seen in nineteenth-century black thought, DuBois argued that the history of the race testified to the overly individualistic and aggressive character of Teutonic or Anglo-Saxon civilization. Somewhat obscurely, he recollected Europe's rise to power: "That brutality buried aught else beside Rome when it descended golden haired and drunk from the blue north has scarcely entered human imagination." And he bemoaned the negative influence of the Anglo-Saxon character on events in nineteenth-century America. "Individualism coupled with the rule of might," chided DuBois,

> it is this idea that has made the logic of even modern history, the cool logic of the Club. It made a naturally brave and generous man, Jefferson Davis—now advancing civilization by murdering Indians, now a hero of a national disgrace called by courtesy, the Mexican War, and finally, as the crowing absurdity, the peculiar champion of a people fighting to be free in order that another people not be free.[93]

Prominently featured in late nineteenth-century African-American protest thought, critiques of the brutal and aggressive Saxon remained a staple in late nineteenth-century black ethnology as well. Educator, editor, Baptist minister, and former slave Rufus Perry wove this theme into his 1893 tract entitled *The Cushite: or The Descendants of Ham as Found in the Sacred Scriptures and in the Writings of Ancient Historians*. A defense of the biblical account of the origins of the races, *The Cushite* was written by a "black men for black men" and aimed "to give them their proper or merited rank among the historical peoples of the earth." Like earlier black ethnologists, Perry never quite managed to reconcile equality and difference: he attacked the whole idea of racial difference, but he also drew racial distinctions of his own. Critiquing the concept of race in his first chapter, Perry drew attention to the inconsistencies in nineteenth-century racial thought. How many races were there? White authorities could not agree. "Naturalists and ethnographers have divided men into certain classes improperly called 'races.' 'Cuvier,' says Webster, gives 'three races; Pritchard, seven; Agassiz, eight; Pickering, eleven; and Blumenbach, five,' as given in our own school books." Despite his questions about the racial categories created by white scientists, Perry was by no means willing to abandon racial differences altogether. Instead, he clung to the scriptural version of race that nineteenth-century black thinkers had pieced together from the Bible—which he saw to be a transhistorical reality unconnected with racist ideology. "The primary divisions of men made by nature's color line are three," Perry insisted, because Noah had only three sons. The "covetuous Shem," the "predatory Japhet," and Ham, whose son Cush fathered the black race. Distinguished by great abilities and "a keen sense of right," the Cushites had "led the van for sixteen centuries." They created magnificent civilizations in Ethiopia and Egypt—a nation whose history whites now sought to claim as their own—only to be crushed in recent centuries by "the wide awake progeny of Japhet" who "set about to rob the Cushite of his liberty, and rob him of his name and fame."[94]

Perry cited an 1868 essay by Martin Delany to support a distinctively African-American account of the history of the races that had gained strength over time. Originating in the antebellum era as a Scripture-based rebuttal to the doctrine of polygenesis, black ethnology's account of history as a contest between the gentle and moral descendants of Ham and the predatory sons of Japhet lived on among educated blacks long after pluralism's scientific heyday. Moreover, it also came to shape the way educated African-Americans spoke about white people. Nourished by repetition, the hardening of America's color line after emancipation, and racial violence of the Jim Crow era, the image of the brutal and aggressive Anglo-Saxon ultimately became the dominant image of white people in nineteenth-century black discourse. "Take the white man in any stage of the world in which he has acted a part and he will show up as a law-breaker and a disturber of the general peace," was how Baltimore minister and civic leader Harvey Johnson summed up the black case against the white race in 1900. "He is not disposed to be at peace. He is never content or satisfied. He is everywhere in history creating a confusion[,] a turmoil, a rebellion. He is against law and order. He is as a race, cruel, heartless and bloodthirsty. With him it is rule or ruin."[95]

Although little known today, Johnson was well situated to sum up a century of black thought on whites. An influential Baptist leader and thinker whose connections extended far beyond Baltimore, Johnson participated in the turn-of-the-century meetings among black leaders at Niagara Falls that led to the formation of the National Association for the Advancement of Colored People (NAACP), and energetically opposed Jim Crow. Also a prolific writer, he published a number of works on ethnology and race relations, including several books and pamphlets devoted largely to the failings of white people. In works such as *The White Man's Failure in Government* and *Race Prejudice and Pride: On What are They Based? What Has the White man Ever done to*

Equal the Tremendous Achievements of the Sons of Ham? Johnson presented a detailed critique of whites. Bringing together nearly a century's worth of African-American ethnological and social commentary, Johnson questioned the origins, history, actions, and racial character of white people.[96]

Were white people even a race, he asked? Or had Japhet's white descendants adopted "the mysterious and fictive cognates" Aryan, Anglo-Saxon, and Caucasian because they had no history to boast of, only a barbaric record of slavery and brutality that could never rival the achievements of the sons of Ham?[97] And what were races, anyway? "If all nations of men are made up of one blood," as the Scriptures said, "then all nations are as one man."[98] Founded on "conjecture and supposition" rather than biblical authority, ethnology and anthropology were new sciences easily tailored to the "views, tastes, and opinions of the persons using them."[99] Taken together, Johnson's writings present a sophisticated critique of the white American racial thought of his day.

Like earlier black thinkers, however, Johnson deconstructed the concept of race only to rebuild it anew. Racial differences were not a matter of blood, bones, or color, Johnson argued, mocking white ethnologists for making distinctions between people that would sound ridiculous applied to any other species—who would ever believe a "negro horse" inferior to a horse of any other color? Divinely ordained, the distinctions within the human family were to be found in "the Bible narrative of the divisions of races." Noah's three sons, Shem, Japhet, and Ham, had fathered "historical races," which were different without necessarily being superior or inferior to each other. Johnson's assessment of the white race, however, suggested that he believed the races were far from equal.[100]

Just as Ethiop had done forty years earlier, Johnson argued that white people were a failure as a race and doubted whether they would ever be fit for self-government. Sounding familiar themes in the now time-honored black attack on the history, character, and temperament of the white race, Johnson wrote that the white man's history

> shows that his whole life or existence has been an irascible, competitive one; not evil in its early stages, but barbarous and degraded; and from that up through several intermediate steps to a hyper-semi-civilization which in turn is nothing more than refined barbarism; the principle with him is not cooperative and associate, but to compete on the principles of the "survival of the fittest," regardless of what becomes of his fellow and brother.[101]

Such sentiments would live on long after Johnson's era, particularly within a variety of twentieth-century black nationalist movements, to be discussed at greater length in the last section of this book. In the 1920s, Jamaican-born black nationalist Marcus Garvey set similar antiwhite imagery to poetry, writing:

Out of cold old Europe these white men came,
From caves, dens and holes, without any fame,
Eating their dead's flesh and sucking their blood,
Relics of the Mediterranean flood. . . .

They have stolen, murdered, on their way here,
Leaving desolation and waste everywhere;
Now boastingly telling what they have done,
Seeing not the bloody crown they have won.[102]

Such images also flourish to this day in the writings of Afrocentric thinkers who characterize the white race as the cold and brutal descendants of northern barbarians—"ice people." Both Garvey and contemporary Afrocentrists build on a nineteenth-century discourse about whites, which set these stereotypes in place. However enduring the nature of this black critique of the brutal Angry Saxon, it cannot be fully understood outside the historically specific circumstances in which it emerged. More grounded in ethnology, history, and religion than in Pan-Africanist politics, or any consistent adherence to black nationalism, nineteenth-century black thinkers' assessments of whites came out of their long and tenacious struggles to redefine both the meaning of race and the racial hierarchies of their day.

Anglo-Saxonism in Black and White

"What shall we do with the white people?" Ethiop asked in 1860, satirizing the debates among his white contemporaries over what to do with the Negro. However comic the question, it had no easy answer. Unlike the white thinkers, politicians, and voters who debated the future of the Negro, African-American intellectuals spoke to a constituency that lacked the political, economic, and social power to adjudicate, or sometimes even influence, the behavior of the dominant race. Instead, they could only wage desperate struggles against the strictures the white world imposed on their own people. Chief among these strictures was a racist ideology so pervasive that it challenged the very humanity of African-Americans, in word and deed. Buffeted by claims that their race was, as Frederick Douglass put it, "extreme brother to the ou-rang-ou-tang," African-Americans had to redefine both themselves and the Anglo-Saxon race before they could lay claim to the rights of citizenship. Resisting degrading definitions of their own race, as well as an Anglo-Saxon ideal that defined whites as "the extreme brother . . . to angels," the educated black leaders and thinkers considered in this chapter forged a distinctive racial ideology of their own.[103] Central to their revision of the racial hierarchies of their day was a challenge to the racial virtues of the Anglo-Saxon.

A distorted version of the manly figure celebrated by the dominant culture, the black version of the Anglo-Saxon was readily recognizable to whites and could be used as a vehicle for social criticism addressed to the majority group. Both Ida B. Wells's antilynching campaign and DuBois's graduation-day speech challenged the nationalist chauvinism of American whites, suggesting that Anglo-Saxon injustices toward the "weaker races" undermined white American claims for their superiority as a race and a nation. Of course, some white commentators believed that Anglo-Saxon might was what made the white American supreme. In particular, midcentury historians such as William Prescott, Francis Parkman, and John Lothrop Motely celebrated the triumph of the Anglo-Saxon or Germanic race, over both indigenous peoples and European competitors on the North American continent. Their romantic histories helped white America define itself by making "America's virtues racial rather than historical or environmental in origin."[104] But other whites occasionally conceded that the Anglo-Saxon race had its deficiencies, a concession black thinkers sought to enlarge upon.

Disturbed by slavery, expansionism, and the unfettered materialism of their age, white abolitionists such as Theodore Parker critiqued the white American "ethnological self-image." As we have seen, these antebellum era romantic racialists bemoaned the aggressive spirit of their own race, while praising the religious and affectionate temperament of the Negro. Sounding very much like one of his race's African-American critics when he spoke out against the expansion of slavery into the territories in 1854, Parker decried the Anglo-Saxon's "restless disposition to invade and conquer other lands; his haughty contempt of humbler tribes which leads him to subvert, enslave, kill, and exterminate; his fondness of material things, preferring those to beauty." Despite such recriminations, however, Parker and other romantic racists reconciled themselves to the deficiencies they identified in their own race with remarkable ease. To Parker the Anglo-Saxon, however violent, was also unique for "his love of personal liberty, yet coupled with most profound respect for peaceful and established law; his inborn skill to organize things to a mill, men to a company, a community, tribes to a federated state; and his slow, solemn, inflexible, industrious, and unconquerable will."[105] "I look with great pride on this Anglo-Saxon people," Parker wrote in a letter to an English friend in 1857. "It has many faults, but I think it is the best specimen of mankind which has ever attained great power in the world."[106] Confident in the overall superiority of their own race, Parker and other white social critics were never all that anxious to lay claim to the gentler virtues they admitted that Anglo-Saxons lacked. As George Fredrickson notes, "Meekness might be a virtue, but was it in fact the only virtue or even a cardinal one for those who celebrated its presence in the Negro?"[107]

By contrast, black thinkers were far more sincere and far-reaching in their critiques of the Anglo-Saxon race. Wholly suspicious of many of the Anglo-Saxon's self-proclaimed virtues, they balked at the notion that a commitment to civil liberty and representative government was an inbred trait of the Anglo-Saxon character. Black commentator Thomas Greathead Harper conceded that the Anglo-Saxons might venerate such ideals, but he questioned whether they ever achieved them. Whites ought to spend less time proclaiming their superiority over other races and more time on self-scrutiny, he suggested. The Anglo-Saxon

> does not see, or at any rate he appears not to see, that the comparison should be made, not between *his* conduct and the conduct of *other* races, but between the *Saxon's* ideals and the *Saxon's* conduct—between what the Saxon *professes to be* and what the Saxon *actually* is—between what the Saxon's systems of organization *ought to be* and what the exigencies of his *own* position compel the Saxon to make *his* institution *become*.[108]

Other African-Americans were still more cynical about the Anglo-Saxon good qualities. A.M.E. pastor Theopolis Gould Steward believed that many of the Anglo-Saxon virtues celebrated by white Americans existed nowhere "but in the dreams and fancies of self-applauding men." The Anglo-Saxons' civil liberties were always for themselves, accompanied by "subjugation, slavery, and death . . . for the rest of mankind," wrote Steward, who feared that advocates of Anglo-Saxon Christianity would not be satisfied until the "condemned, despised, hated, darker races will have been civilized off the face of the earth, and the whole world will be white."[109]

Brutal, arrogant, and selfish, the Anglo-Saxon described by black authors differed radically from the white ideal. Where the Anglo-Saxon was forceful, commanding, and resourceful, the "Angry Saxon" was violent, domineering, and overly materialistic. Embellishing such judgments with graphically unflattering descriptions of the white race's European antecedents, the black men who wrote about race and ethnology chipped away at white America's vaunted Anglo-Saxon ideal. At a time when white thinkers held up the ethnographic image of the Anglo-Saxon as a human ideal that no member of any other race could even hope to realize, African-American writers invoked a history of white savagery in the Middle Ages to recast the Anglo-Saxon ideal as a hyperaggressive, hypermasculine being who took his celebrated virtues of courage and manliness too far. I describe the Anglo-Saxon ideal in masculine terms quite deliberately here because, significant exceptions such as Anna Julia Cooper aside, in the almost exclusively male nineteenth-century discourse on race, African-American and white authors alike described their racial ideals as masculine. In this gendered discourse, the character of African-American men both as blacks and as males was at issue.

In calling into question the Anglo-Saxon as the manly ideal, the black men who wrote ethnology sought to create an alternative racial hierarchy. White men did not define the true racial ideal, they argued, for the brutal white race lacked important moral and spiritual qualities—qualities traditionally associated with the Negro. White and black women alike, by virtue of their female natures, might have been said to have some claim to these qualities, but the racial character of women was not a major subject of discussion in much of this masculine discourse on race. At issue was the meaning of manhood, and, more specifically, who should have access to all its privileges. The Anglo-Saxon virtues that whites celebrated as the pretext for their racial supremacy were male characteristics such as courage, manliness, intellect, and independence; likewise, the gentler ideals that male black writers argued should temper Anglo-Saxon manliness were also presented as masculine. As John Edward Bruce explained it, the problem with white men was that they did not follow the wisdom of the Nazarene: "As ye would that men should do unto you do ye even so unto them." Revealing a vision of the masculine ideal in which racial superiority and manliness were one and the same, Bruce predicted:

> If the American white man has the courage and the manliness to live up to this rule of conduct and right-living, he will have made good his boast of being the "superior race," and we shall hear less of lynching, and all the other iniquities which disgrace his civilization and belittle his manhood and humanity.[110]

White men, of course, never met Bruce's challenge. But by defining white men as hypermasculine, Bruce and other African-American intellectuals created an alternative understanding of race in which the masculinity and humanity of African-American men could be recognized.

Just how satisfying this endeavor was is difficult to assess. As Toni Morrison points out in a recent work of literary criticism, *Playing in the Dark: Whiteness and the Literary Imagination*, African-Americans have a different relationship to their culture's constructs of blackness and whiteness than do other Americans. For Morrison and, one could safely add, other black Americans throughout this country's history, the "vulnerability would lie in romanticizing blackness rather than demonizing it; vilifying whiteness rather than demonizing it."[111] This consideration of nineteenth-century black ideas about white people has revealed that during that era black intellectuals often succumbed to this vulnerability, and that they found some satisfaction in doing so. The particular form this vilification took, an attempt to identify white men as the real brutes in the hierarchy of color and gender at the heart of American racial ideology, rarely challenged the false assumptions about either race or gender at the core of this ideology. But, as Nancy Leys Stepan and Sander L. Gilman point out, the challenges mounted by blacks and other minorities to racist ideology "created modes of representation and knowledge essential to the stereotyped themselves."[112] By vilifying whiteness, black male writers sought to reclaim their own status as men in the face of their society's concerted effort to deny them legal, political, or social access to that rank.

II

**THE RACIAL THOUGHT OF
THE SLAVES**

A nigger may be humble and refuse to talk outside his race—
because he's afraid to, but you can't fool him about the white
man. And you couldn't fool him when he was a slave. He knows
the white man for what he is, and he knew him the same way
when he was a slave.

W. B. Allen, in *The American Slave*, v. 12.

From the early nineteenth century onward, the concept of race was
increasingly understood as a scientific phenonomen by educated
Americans on both sides of the color line—however differently they
may have interpreted it. Black and white thinkers alike discussed race
with reference to ethnological questions about the origins and history
of the races, identifying racial differences as part of the story of
human development. In doing so, they told a variety of competing
stories that all addressed the same basic issues: the extent and importance of racial differences, and the processes by which the races had
become different. But what of the slaves? Prior to the Civil War, the
vast majority of African-Americans were slaves. Approximately 4 million of the roughly 4.5 million African-Americans alive in 1860 were
born and raised in the slave South. Products of plantation society in
which most blacks were slaves, and all slaves were black, surely these
African-Americans, like their free Northern kin, pondered the character and cause of the physical and cultural differences their society
reified as race. How did they distinguish themselves from the white
Southerners who surrounded them? Did they see themselves as a
race? How did they explain racial distinctions?

These questions are crucial as we turn from the racial thought of
nineteenth-century black intellectuals to look at racial consciousness
in the larger black population. Unlike the small group of relatively
cosmopolitan and largely Northern black leaders and thinkers discussed thus far, the vast majority of African-Americans who lived between 1830 and 1925 never left the South. Most came into the world

enslaved, if they were born before the Civil War, and achieved free-dom only after emancipation, if they lived to see it. Both before and after slavery, nineteenth-century African-Americans lived unglam-orous lives dominated by unremitting toil. As slaves, and later as sharecroppers, most of them worked the land, planting and sowing the South's backbreaking cash crops—cotton, rice, and tobacco. Yet their life experiences embraced far more than the unbroken seasonal cycle of planting and harvesting traditional to agricultural labor. Black Americans whose lives spanned the midcentury were both wit-nesses and players in a series of dramas that transformed their region and their nation: the Civil War, emancipation, Reconstruction, and re-demption. It is against this momentous backdrop of change and up-heaval that we must investigate the racial thought of these Americans.

This is a daunting task, for in contrast to the black leaders and thinkers considered in previous chapters, who wrote extensively on race and on the character of white people, ordinary nineteenth-century African-Americans left a scarce and scattered record of their thoughts on race. Few could read and write, and even fewer commit-ted any of their thoughts to paper. Consequently, much of what we know about these men and women comes through a variety of indi-rect sources that offer only limited insight into what slaves thought about anything.

Take, for example, the plantation records that social historians have used to reconstruct day-to-day African-American life under slavery. Usually a compilation of the inventories, correspondence, daybooks, financial papers, and legal documents pertaining to a particular plan-tation's business, these records typically contain accounts of slave sales and purchases, births and deaths, infractions and punishments, as well as notes on the crops slaves produced and the supplies they con-sumed. Accordingly, they are rich sources of information on matters such as the work life of African-Americans under slavery, the condi-tions under which they lived and labored, and the patterns of sale, purchase, ownership, and reproduction that shaped the slave family.[1] Such records, however, are virtually devoid of direct evidence from the slaves themselves.

Such information can be found only in firsthand sources on slavery. Fortunately, such evidence exists in the form of fugitive slave narra-tives and autobiographies composed by former slaves, as well as a wide variety of oral testimony, including court testimony, folklore, slave songs, and interviews. Particularly rich oral testimony can be found in the federal Works Progress Administration's (WPA) Slave Narratives, a massive collection of interviews with ex-slaves conducted between 1935 and 1939.[2] Commissioned by the WPA's Federal Writ-ers' Project, a New Deal initiative designed to provide employment for Depression era writers, the Slave Narrative Project recorded the remembrances of the last surviving generation of ex-slaves in seven-

teen Southern and border states. All told, the writers and fieldwork-
ers who participated in the project turned in well over two thousand
interviews, creating the largest single body of evidence on American
slaves. These interviews provide rich evidence on how thousands of
ordinary African-African men and women understood their life experiences. In addition to autobiographical testimony by ex-slaves, the
materials collected by the WPA include slave tales, slave songs, and
black folklore.[3]

Both the oral testimony contained in the WPA collection and many
of the autobiographies written by ex-slaves were, of course, subject to
revision by white editors, be they the white interviewers who recorded
and transcribed most of the interviews or the abolitionist editors who
published the life histories of fugitive slaves. Moreover, the oral testimony collected by the WPA is further compromised by the influence
of what one scholar calls the "caste etiquette" of 1930s.[4] Conducted
during the golden age of Southern segregation, these interviews
brought the mostly white writers employed by the WPA into the
homes of elderly black men and women at a time when both law and
social custom limited contact between the races.

Especially in the Deep South, the freedpeople were often alarmed
by white visitors who arrived at their houses unexpectedly, asking
them questions about their lives. Some believed that, as government
employees, the WPA workers controlled welfare benefits, pensions,
and other government services. Consequently, respondents sometimes worried that what they said in their interviews might have far-
reaching repercussions—one woman was convinced that her household's electricity would be cut off as a result of her husband's testimony.[5]
The respondents' unease was often compounded by the behavior of
the interviewers. Hired at the state level, the interviewers varied from
state to state, but many had more training in the racial attitudes of
their day than in the collection of oral history. Most were native to
their regions, which meant that some were direct descendants of
slaveholders. Worse, some were convinced that they already knew all
about slavery, and therefore posed heavy-handed questions designed
to elicit specific answers. " 'Didn't you have a better time [during slav-
ery] than you do now, wasn't it an easier living?' " a white interviewer
asked Mississippi freedwoman Melissa Munson.[6] Others approached
the freedpeople with distaste." Adam Singleton is so black he shines;
all his teeth are gone," noted Mrs. William F. Holmes of Mississippi,
describing one of her interviewees. "He looks more like an ape than
any darky I've visited yet."[7]

The racism and condescension that emanated from some of the interviewers did not escape the ex-slaves, who often sound "polite,
guarded, and evasive" in the WPA transcripts.[8] But interviewer bias
complicates rather than invalidates the vast collection of evidence assembled by the WPA. For one thing, not all the interviewers were

white. The WPA collection contains a significant number of rich recollections recorded by African-American interviewers, including two
full volumes conducted by black researchers from Fisk University.[9]
Moreover, the testimony collected by the WPA is remarkably vast and
varied. Rosy accounts of slavery appear alongside reports of beatings,
torture, and sexual abuse—sometimes in the same interview. Respondents who sung the praises of their own masters often told blood-
curdling stories about what happened on neighboring plantations.
Some white interviewers were better than others, and the worst of
them elicited a variety of responses from the slave respondents. Ex-
slaves were not always willing to play along with their interviewers'
prejudices and preconceptions, as Miriam Logan of Ohio found out
when she interviewed two ex-slaves named Celia Henderson and
Samuel Sutter. "Neither [Celia] or Samuel had the kind of a story to
tell that I was expecting to hear from what little I know about colored
people," reported Logan. "I may have tried to get them on the songs
and amusements of their youth too often, but it seems that most that
they knew was work; did not sing or have a very good time."[10]

Despite their various shortcomings, the interviews conducted by
the WPA are especially useful to my exploration of the white image in
the black mind because they record the testimony of a whole generation of African-Americans who lived within the period covered by this
study. These men and women provide evidence on black folk thought
about race that cannot be obtained from the more educated and cosmopolitan authors of the slave narratives, whose pronouncements on
race and slavery were frequently shaped by high-minded white abolitionist editors and the genre conventions of the slave narrative
form.[11] The following chapters will therefore rely primarily but not
exclusively on the evidence in the WPA narratives to explore the place
of race in African-American folk thought.

FOUR

✍

"Us Is Human Flesh"

Race and Humanity in Black
Folk Thought

"Heap people says negro ent got no brains. . . . I suppose this is because they ent never carried out no Bizziness. Some negro don't know what it take to carry out bizziness. Mighty few knows the Lord Prayers. Thay go to bed like a hog & get up like a Dog," wrote ex-slave Charles Williams in his autobiography "I'se Much a Man."[1] In this strangely written and even more strangely spelled autobiography, the Mississippi-born Williams sought to show that he had "allers been quite in difference from the Most of Negro." Williams, who summarized the varied employments he pursued in the course of his life with the statement "I konker everything I lays my mits upon and all Kind of Job," received his early education from his slave mother and continued his education as a free man in his twenties when his mother drove him to school with a cowhide whip.[2] A man who took great pride his learning and abilities, Williams proclaimed, "Gentlemen, it ent the culard what make a man, it the callification [qualification]. . . . My Mind is what you may call Broad. It take to ecomardate my intelleck. You aurt to know that when a Negro boy remember every act he done sience he 5 year old till of 80, he is a man among men." Although he sought to set himself apart from "most Negroes," the concern Williams expressed by defining himself as a thinking human being, rather than an animal, was shared by countless black Americans of his generation. During the nineteenth century and beyond, a defense of black humanity reverberates throughout African-American culture, crossing class and regional lines and shaping the racial thought of the educated, the ignorant, and the in-between—such as Charles Williams.

Among black intellectuals, this defense of black humanity often took an ethnological form. In particular, black thinkers challenged the theory of polygenesis, which they understood as an allegation that black people were more closely related to the simian species than to the family of man. Outraged at this insupportable insult, nineteenth-century African-American writers turned to ethnology to define and defend the black race's place in the human family. In doing so, they redefined the place of the white race as well, creating a revisionist ideology that challenged white America's Anglo-Saxon ideal. Written by men, and for men, this black ethnological literature sought to create an alternative racial ideology in which the masculinity and humanity of black men could be recognized.

Charles Williams and other less educated and less ethnologically minded black men no doubt strove for such recognition as well. "When God pick up hand full dust & perform a Man, He did not perform only one & let it go at that," Williams emphasized in his autobiography. "He perform a worl full of mans."[3] But masculinity was not the central issue for Williams, who credited his strict mother with making "a man of me." As he explained it, she did so by teaching him a lesson that had nothing to do with gender. Affirming black humanity rather than black manhood, she instructed him: "If you is black as ace spade [ace of spades], yet you cin be relible and have some good morale & Pricciples and treat all boddies right." Williams's mother's lesson was one he ultimately endorsed, despite his attempts to distance himself from other blacks. In his reading of the Scriptures, Williams, like so many ex-slaves of his generation, upheld the God-given humanity of all black men and women. "So, sinner man," he wrote,

> God pick up handful of dust and perform you like a Man. You ourt to know that Christ didn make you to jest lay down like a hog or a Dog and be no more to you. It is a grand mistake on you side. Jest Keep the gate to you Mind open & see more better into the future. You ourt to know that God didn intend for His Son to go through all what he did without the Good Spirit come to visit every man & Woman.[4]

Like black intellectuals, Williams and other freedpeople sought to define themselves against the pervasive racist ideology that emanated from the white world around them. But the issues they faced were different from those tackled by black intellectuals who read and rebutted white ethnology and other racist doctrine. Indeed, the evidence in slave sources suggests that the slaves' conception of race lay outside the realm of the racial thought of the educated—be they black or white. As a largely unlettered people, for the most part these nineteenth-century African-Americans were unfamiliar with both the concept of ethnology and many of the specific theories invoked by the intellectuals of their day to explain the origins and character of the races. Not surprisingly, these black men and women did not need to hear about racist theories such as polygenesis, or read the writings of educated blacks who debated such theories, to know that white people held the character of their race in low esteem. But the fact that they rarely encountered such discourses meant that enslaved African-Americans developed their own understandings of racist doctrine and white superiority.

The black experience under slavery, one ex-slave warned his interviewer, could be told only by "somebody who wore the shoe."[5] His words are especially pertinent here, for racist ideology came across differently in subtle but important ways to those who had experienced slavery. The slaves' awareness of white racism required no knowledge of the pseudoscientific myths that white Americans employed to rationalize slavery and racial subordination. African-Americans who "wore the shoe" learned all they needed to know about race and racism from their condition of enslavement and their everyday interactions with whites and white society. Moreover, the lessons they learned gave them still more cause to defend the humanity of black people than reading racist doctrine did their educated and free brethren in the North. Both during slavery and long after, Southern race relations brought African-Americans and whites together on such radically unequal terms that black Southerners frequently had cause to wonder whether white people recognized black people as fellow members of the human species.

When they did so, they confronted race and racism in different ways than the educated blacks who read and rebutted racist doctrine. Steeped in a universalist understanding of Christianity and wholly unaware of scientific questions about the origins of the races, ex-slaves did not worry about tracing the biblical descent of their own race. Nor did they share the black intellectuals' anxieties about being mistaken for monkeys or apes—species largely unfamiliar to uneducated black Southerners. Instead, these African-Americans worried about being taken for animals of a different kind, complaining that whites made little distinction between black people and domestic animals. Throughout their oral testimony and their written accounts of bondage as well, former slaves compared the status of slaves to the condition of domestic animals. Rejecting the planter class's ideology of paternalism, which designated slaves the dependent children of their benevolent masters, ex-slaves found their analogy for the slave-master relationship entirely outside the familial realm. Identifying not with their masters' dependent children but with their masters' four-legged chattel, ex-slaves remembered being fed like pigs, bred like hogs, sold like horses, driven like cattle, worked like dogs, and beaten like mules.

The parallels that ex-slaves drew between their status as slaves and the subordination of domestic animals suggest that enslaved African-Americans confronted racial slavery as an institution that blurred the line between man and beast, while confusing other categories as well. Servitude, subjugation, and color, likewise, became overlapping categories in a society where all slaves were black, and most blacks were slaves. Amid this confusion of categories, the slaves highlighted one central fact: chattel slavery gave white people license to treat black people like beasts. The institution itself drew a line between the races that seemed to allow for the humanity of only one race. Hence, slave racial thought began with an assertion of sameness that embraced both blacks and whites. "Us ain't hogs or horses," argued the slaves. "Us is human flesh."[6]

Racial Myths in Slave Culture

Although they displayed little familiarity with the story of polygenesis, African-American slaves knew other racial myths. Like all peoples, they told tales that described the creation of the world and the origins of human beings. Not surprisingly, many of their stories addressed the issue of racial difference, providing a wide variety of explanations for the causes of color and other racial characteristics. Some of these black folktales echoed white racial myths, portraying blacks as an inferior or cursed population, while others took for granted that humanity began with the creation of the black race—only the characteristics of other races required explanation.

One reason that black folklore's explanations of racial distinctions are numerous is that they served a variety of functions in slave culture, some of which had only a tangential relationship to the explanation of racial difference. For example, slave children were sometimes told by blacks and whites alike that white babies were delivered by the stork but black infants came out of buzzards' eggs. "A snow white stork flew down from the sky. . . . To take a baby gal so fair, / To young missus, waitin there," recited Katie Sutton, remembering a song her mother had sung to her as a child. Entitled "A Slave Mammy's Lullaby," the song went on to tell the slave infant, "You was hatched from a buzzard's egg / My little colored chile." The refrain assured, "But you are jes as sweet to me / My little colored chile." Among other things, the story encapsulated in this song served to obscure issues of paternity and maternity in a community in which children could not always expect to be taken care of by their real parents. Katie Sutton learned the song from a mother she rarely saw because "she had to spend so much of her time at humoring the white babies and taking care of them." When her master and mistress told her and the other slave children that they were hatched by the buzzard and the white children were brought by the stork, Sutton reports, "We believed it." Likewise, the story could also be used to cloud the identity of fathers who could not be identified because they were white. On being introduced to her white father as a child, ex-slave Patience M. Avery told him, "I ain' got no father; I ain' got no father. No, I ain' got no father 'cause my mother told me dat de buzzards laid me an' de sun hatch me; an' she came 'long an' pick me up."[7]

Other slave tales dealt more directly with origins of the races. Like black intellectuals, enslaved African-Americans were familiar with

Anglo-American myths about Noah's curse on Canaan, the son of Ham. Indeed, some ex-slaves even accepted the story of Noah's curse on Ham as an explanation for the color and condition of their race. When asked by an interviewer from the WPA if she was taught to read in her slave days, Virginia-born Lizzie Grant replied:

> They [the white people] did not care if we could read or not, of course you know son we have been servants to the rest of the world ever since old Noah's son laughed at his father's nakedness and God turned his flesh black and told him for that act his sex would always carry a curse, and that they would be servants of the people as long as this old world in its present form remained.[8]

Alabama freedman Gus Rogers told the same story in more detail:

> God gave [religion] to Adam and took it away from Adam and gave it to Noah, and you know, Miss, Noah had three sons, and when Noah got drunk on wine, one of his sons laughed at him, and the other two took a sheet and walked backwards and threw it over Noah. Noah told the one who laughed, "Your children will be hewers of wood and drawers of water for the other two children, and they will be known by their hair and their skin being dark." So, Miss, there we are, and that is the way God meant us to be. We have always had to follow the white folks and do what we saw them do, and that's all there is to it. You just can't get away from what the Lord said.[9]

However, the Hamitic explanation for the origins and status of the races was by no means as ubiquitous in slave culture as it was in white Southern culture or among black intellectuals. The story of Noah's curse on Ham appears only a handful of times in the WPA testimony, and its tellers sometimes repeat directly from a white source—possibly to win the approval of a white interviewer. For instance, Alice Cole tells the tale ruefully after expressing her opinion that blacks ought to be allowed to vote. African-Americans ought to have rights in America like "every other color or race of people," the elderly freedwoman contended, especially since they were "captured and brought here in this country against their will." "But," Cole went on, in an abrupt return to racial deference, "is no use this old negro talking that way cause I'se had white men to tell me that we had a curse sent on us one time when Noah's son laughed at his father cause he was drunk and naked, all his children from that day on would be black and be servant of servants to the white man."[10] Moreover, despite their familiarity with the story of the curse of Ham, uneducated black Americans rarely identified themselves as his descendants.

In this respect they were unlike both the Southern whites who saw their black bondsmen as Ham's cursed children and the nineteenth-century black intellectuals who rejected the story of Noah's curse but embraced Ham as the father of Africa and Egypt. In contrast to the latter, who typically claimed Hamitic descent and celebrated the history of the Hamitic peoples, ex-slaves almost never referred to themselves as descendants of Ham. One South Carolina ex-slave asked her WPA interviewer which race the East Indians were descended from: "Ham, Seth, Japheth or what."[11] But I have been unable to find any other reference in slave sources to the three racial families so often discussed by black intellectuals.[12] Similarly, the slaves claimed no kinship with the Egyptians, the Hamitic ancestors whose achievements black intellectuals celebrated so proudly. To the contrary, African-American slaves identified with the ancient Israelites rather than the Egyptians. Appropriating the story of the Exodus as the expression of their own hopes for freedom and deliverance, the slaves celebrated Moses as "their ideal of all that is high, and noble and perfect in man" and abhorred his Egyptian oppressors.[13]

Derived largely from Southern whites, the story of Noah's curse on Ham was only one of the many explanations of racial differences discussed among the slaves. Others included self-denigrating tales such as the slave story reported in a South Carolina newspaper in 1828, which explained that black people were created by the devil in an attempt to imitate God's creation of Adam. But the devil did not have clay, so he used mud instead and substituted moss for hair. Not pleased by the figure he had created, "he kicked it in the shins and struck it on the nose, thus establishing the physical attributes of the black race." Historian Lawrence Levine notes of this tale and others like it:

> The importance of such patently white-influenced stories is obvious, but it would be a mistake to assume that the slaves invariably took them literally. There are indications that the blacks telling them frequently were aware of their original source. "En dat's how de w'ite man dun count fo' de nigger bein' on 'Arth," one black storyteller concluded such a story.[14]

Levine's suggestion that the slaves knew both black and white Creation stories is supported by the testimony of Charity More, a South Carolina freedwoman who reported that her father "had Bible tales he never told de white chillun," which included a story about how Adam was originally black and Eve ginger-colored, but after the original sin Adam was scared white.[15]

Such stories, Levine suggests, in which God began his Creation with the black race, are "perhaps more typical" of black culture than the white-influenced tales, and were certainly more original to it. One of the more widely told tales of this type was a story that began "once upon a time," when "ev'y person on God's green earth was black." These original black people lost their uniform hue when they came across a pond of water where you could wash yourself white. Wanting to "change deyselves den like dey always has," they flocked to the pond, which gradually ran out of water, leaving some yellow mulattoes and those who came last still black, except on the bottom of their hands and feet, where they walked "tryin' to git white."[16] In another enduring Creation legend, white people came about as a result of Cain's fratricide, which made him pale with horror and fear.[17]

Although their Creation stories varied, nineteenth-century black intellectuals and slaves alike often maintained that mankind descended from people of color. As we have seen, this belief was one of the arguments black thinkers marshaled against polygenesis, but its prevalence in black culture suggests it may have originated quite outside the confines of their debate with white ethnology. The idea of a black Creation appears to have been shared by a wide variety of people of African descent in the nineteenth century. During this period black Creation legends were also common in Africa, where white racial myths about the curse on Ham were also known, but the story about how Cain turned white after he murdered Abel was a more popular explanation for the origins of the color divisions in the human family. Levine comments, "Africans, both those who were forcibly taken from their homeland and those who remained to live in a colonized state, were the recipients of many of the same European racial myths and, it would appear, erected many of the same defenses against them."[18]

African-American folk culture's central defense against white racial myths, however, does not appear to have been any specific account of the origins or lineage of the races—a subject on which African-American storytellers appear to have neither sought nor reached consensus. Instead, African-American folk culture's central message about the relationship of the races was a simple affirmation of the God-given humanity of black people. In their religious worship, one freedwoman recalled, the slaves would invariably "sing an' shout. . . . dey would sing songs 'bout bein' God's children." Her recollection is confirmed by historians of slave religion, including Levine, who observes:

> The most persistent single image the slave songs contain is that of a chosen people. The vast majority of the spirituals identify the singers as "de people dat is born of God," "We are the people of God," "we are de people of de Lord," "I really do believe I'm a child of God," "I'm a child of God, wid my soul sot free," "I'm born of God, I know I am."

In designating themselves God's people, nineteenth African-Americans were by no means unique; many white Americans of this era expressed similar sentiments about themselves. But, as Levine also notes, this theme held special meaning in slave culture because it was expressed by a group of people "who were told endlessly that they were members of the lowliest of races." Among other things, the slaves' stress on the God-given humanity of African-American people suggests that although the slaves were not familiar with the notion of polygenesis, or the specific ideas coming out of the white science of ethnology, they were fully aware that white people questioned the status of black people in the human family. Surely it is no coincidence that African-Americans sang songs emphasizing that they were people, and born of God, at a time when white people speculated that the black race might have originated from a separate and lesser creation.[19]

The racist dogma the slaves heard and sought to combat appears to have been less specific than polygenesis but equally dehumanizing. Enslaved African-Americans complained over and over again in their written and oral testimony that white people did not see blacks as human beings, with human natures and souls. Ubiquitious in slave testimony, such complaints evolved out of the experience of racial slavery—of being enslaved as a people—and were voiced by even the most unacculturated American slaves.

For instance, once landed in the United States, the slave rebels who took over the slave ship *Amistad* in 1839 quickly began to wonder what kind of creatures white Americans took them for. Mendi-speaking natives of Sierre Leone, these kidnapped Africans had had few experiences with whites prior to their capture and detainment in New Haven. But as soon as they had acquired enough English to express themselves, they asked whether white Americans understood that the Mendi were people too. "Some people say Mendi people no got souls," KA-LE, one of the rebels, wrote to abolitionist sympathizer John Quincy Adams. "Why we feel bad we no got souls? We want to be free very much." Struggling with the new language, KA-LE went on to affirm again and again that his people were sentient and soulful human beings. Mendi people, he explained, *"think, think, think. . . .* Mendi have got souls. We think we know God punish us if we tell lie. We never tell lie we speak the truth. What for Mendi people afraid? Because they got souls."[20]

The perception formed so readily by the Mendi rebels of the *Amistad* that American white people did not understand that African people had souls was widely expressed among nineteenth-century African-Americans. Some ex-slaves derived this conviction directly from the religious teachings they heard from whites during their slave days. "In slavery they used to teach the Negro that they had no soul," recalled one ex-slave. "They said all they needed to do was to obey their mistress."[21] Oklahoma freedman Robert Burns and his fellow slaves heard similar doctrine from a white preacher, who informed them, "Only white people had souls and went to heaven. He told dem dat niggers had no more soul than dogs, and dey couldn't go to heaven any more than could a dog."[22] Such theology discouraged "Uncle Berry" Smith from going to church. He recalled of his plantation days, "De white preacher used to preach to de niggers sometimes in de white folks church, but I didn't go much. Dey tol' us we didn't have no souls den."[23]

Sermons informing the slaves that they had no souls would be dispiriting doctrine indeed, and it is clear that this theme was never meant to be a mainstay of the slaves' religious instruction. To the contrary, the Southern planters who offered spiritual instruction to their bondsmen and bondswomen hoped to make them better and more contented servants. After resisting slave conversion altogether during the colonial period for fear that it might jeopardize slavery, American masters embraced slave religion only after Southern clergy assured them that the religious instruction of Negroes was compatible with slavery, and would actually strengthen the institution. To prosper in the South, the various Protestant denominations that established themselves there had to convince slaveowners that Christianity could provide a useful means of controlling the slaves. By the nineteenth century, clerical advocates of slave religion had persuaded many masters that Christian teachings would lead the slaves to obey their owners "out of a sense of moral duty rather than fear."[24] Accordingly, the religious instruction of Negroes in the slave South centered around themes far more well-suited to the slaveowners' need for a well-behaved labor force than to any assertion that slaves had no souls would have been.

These themes included obedience, morality, humility, and the promise of a heavenly reward. As Blake Touchstone points out:

> The common denominator of the various white-sponsored religious activities for the slaves was the message: God wants you to be good, humble servants, patiently bearing your burdens on earth until your reward comes in the hereafter. Ministers and masters often chose biblical texts that directly supported this maxim, the master's view of slavery. Favorites were "Servants be obedient to their masters"; "Let as many servants as are under the yoke count their own masters worthy of all honor"; "In the sweat of thy face shalt thou eat bread, till thou return unto the ground"; "Render unto Caesar, the things which are Caesar's"; and "Well done, thou good and faithful servant."[25]

Such texts were prominently featured in slave catechisms such as that of Presbyterian minister Charles Colcock Jones. Published in 1834, Jones's *A Catechism for Colored Persons* provided slaveowners with a set of oral instructions designed to impart Christianity to the slaves.[26] Altering the Bible to suit the slaveholders' interests, one especially obliging Methodist minister devised this unorthodox catechism: "What did God make you for?" was one of his questions for the slaves, to which they were to answer: "To make a crop." To the question "What is the meaning of 'Thou shalt not commit adultery?'" they were supposed to reply: "To serve our heavenly Father, and our earthly master, obey our overseer, and not steal anything."[27]

What the slaves heard is another question, however. Slave religion emerged out of a symbiosis of white religious teaching, black interpretations of Christianity, and the African religious traditions the slaves brought from their homeland.[28] In addition, African-American bondspeople reinterpreted white Christianity in light of their experience with whites. Accordingly, slaves often heard messages that their owners did not intend them to hear in the carefully chosen texts of obedience and submission Southern whites selected for their indoctrination. Although religious, Georgia-born ex-slave John White refused his preacher's exhortations to "join up with the Lord" because he found the cleric's theology wholly unconvincing. "I never join because he don't talk about the Lord. Just about the Master and Mistress. How the slaves must obey around the plantation—how the white folks know what is good for the slaves. Nothing about obeying the Lord and working for him. I reckon the old preacher was worrying more about the bull whip than he was the Bible, else he say something about the Lord."[29]

As White's comments illustrate, slaves often understood and resented the political import of these white sermons. Moreover, some of them further understood the simplistic religious education they received in white churches as clear evidence that the white preachers did not recognize them as souls. "We went to a church there on the place," Wes Brady recalled. "You ought to have heard that 'Hellish' preaching. . . . 'Obey your Master and Mistress, don't steal chickens, don't steal eggs and meat,' and nary word 'bout having a soul to save."[30] Likewise, Margaret Nickerson of Florida recollected that when she "had church wid de white preachers," they preached obedience only and "never tole us nothin' 'bout Jesus."[31]

Moreover, since slaves who participated in white religious services usually did so on distinctly unequal terms, sitting apart from whites, or sometimes even listening to the sermon outdoors, some slaves took the message that whites did not recognize black slaves as human beings from their church experience itself. In the "white folks' church," South Carolina freedwoman Anna Morgan complained, the slaves "couldn't do nuthin'—jes sit dere. Dey could sing, an' take de sacrement; but didn't have no voice—jes like animals!"[32] Likewise, ex-slave Catherine Slim testified that, although she attended church with her masters, the religious teachings there did not seem to be directed at her. "Dey took me to church wid dem and dey put me behind de door," she recalled. "Dey tole me to set der till dey cum out. And when I see dem cumin' out to follow behind and get into de carrage. I dursent say nothin'. I wuz like a petty dog."[33]

The white church was only one of the many arenas in which nineteenth-century African-Americans found themselves treated as less than human. Indeed, the images that Catherine Slim and Anna Morgan invoke of black people being treated like animals were widely used by ex-slaves to describe their experiences with whites both during slavery and after. Comparisons between the treatment of blacks and the treatment of animals were employed by the ex-slaves to describe almost every African-American experience with white people; taken together, they shed light on how this group understood white racial ideology.

"The Same as Stock:" Animal Metaphors for Racial Subordination in Black Folk Thought

In describing childhood under slavery, Baily Cunningham recalled that both male and female slaves wore shirttails until they were twenty, and that he himself wore shoes for the first time only after he reached that age. "All under twenty," he explained, "were treated the same as the stock on the plantation."[34] Other ex-slaves detailed almost every aspect of slave childhood in similar terms. Slave children "slept on the floor like hogs. Girls and boys slept together."[35] Many freedpeople mentioned that as children they were provided with neither utensils nor dishes and instead ate out of troughs, "jest like de pigs."[36] On the plantation where Lizzie Williams grew up, slave children not only ate like animals but also ate with them. "Dey was a trough out in de yard," Williams remembered, where "dey poured de mush an milk in an us chillun an de dogs would all crowd 'round it an eat together. . . . we sho' had to be in a hurry 'bout it cause de dogs would get it all if we didn't."[37]

Freedpeople also compared their treatment to that of animals in describing specific incidents from their childhood years. Recalling lonely times as a little girl, one freedwoman explained, "When my white folks went on summer vacations—they was rich and traveled a great deal—mama always went along and she just left us children on the plantation just like a cow would leave a calf. She'd hate to do it though."[38] Similarly, a Fisk informant employed a whole menagerie of animal imagery to describe his difficult boyhood experience under slavery. "Them times peoples children was lousy as a pet pig," he said. "I worked at herding of the cows. Every morning I would go into the woods and drive them up. I was bare-footed as a duck. Sometimes I would drive the hogs out of their warm place to warm my feet."[39]

The parallels that ex-slaves drew between the treatment they received as children and the treatment of animals continued in their descriptions of adult slave life. The most famous American ex-slave, Frederick Douglass, began his classic autobiography by reporting that he had no accurate knowledge of his age and went on to explain, "By far the larger part of the slaves know as little of their ages as horses know of theirs."[40] Douglass introduces this metaphor early on to establish what will be one of the central themes in his elegantly written autobiography: the dehumanizing effects of slavery. But uneducated freedpeople invoked the same metaphor when they described their experience of slave life. Like Douglass, Lucie Ann Warfield did not know how old she was. She knew she was born in "Jass'min" County, Kentucky, but she could not "say what year, kaze white folks diden keep no 'count of dey slaves ages. Dey wuz jes' like chickens—like so many chickens."[41] "The masters kept records of ages of those born in their care," Arkansas ex-slave H. B. Holloway likewise explained to an interviewer. "Some of them did. Some of them didn't keep nothin'. Jus' like people nowadays Raised them like pigs and hogs."[42]

Ex-slaves employed similar animal imagery to describe many other aspects of their adult lives in bondage. Remembering simple things, such as what they ate and how they lived, time and again African-Americans described the slave experience with reference to the care and feeding of domestic animals. In some cases, freedmen and freed-women could not avoid these metaphors simply because their owners did in fact feed and house the slaves in much the same manner as their livestock. Arkansas freedwoman Mary Estes Peters, for example, ate out of a trough even as an adult, an experience she recalled with some bitterness. "They wouldn't let the slaves eat out of the things they ate out of," Peters commented. "Fed them just like they would hogs."[43] Other ex-slaves remembered eating the same food as the do-mestic animals on the plantation—animal-food, as opposed to the people-food that whites reserved for themselves. "The white folks et the white flour and the niggers et the shorts," reported one woman, adding, "The hogs was also fed the shorts."[44] Hal Hutson testified that he and his family of fifteen both ate and slept "like hogs" in their one-room cabin on a Texas plantation. All fifteen slept on the floor, crowded together like hogs in a pen, and received the same provi-sions as did their owner's hogs. "We never knew what biscuits were! We ate 'seconds and shorts' (wheat ground once) for bread."[45]

Moreover, even slaves who did not claim to have been treated like their owners' animals often compared their condition under slavery to the condition of domestic animals. Richard Toler noted that al-though black people never had "good times" before the Civil War, white slaveowners valued the slaves enough to keep them healthy. "They took care of us, though. As pa'taculah with slaves as with the stock—that was their money, you know."[46] Likewise, ex-slaves who had happy memories of eating well during their enslavement often emphasized that prosperous slaveowners kept their slaves and live-stock well fed and well tended. "Marster Levi kept his niggers fat, just like he keep his hogs and hosses fat, he did," one South Carolina freedman testified.[47] Such comparisons could, of course, go the other way: some former bondspeople wished they had fared as well as their masters' animals. Texas freedman Thomas Cole observed as much when he reported that adult slaves were treated much like mules except the "mules was fed good and slaves was sometimes half starved."[48]

Among other things, the prevalence and variety of references to domestic animals in slave testimony suggests that ex-slaves found animal husbandry to be the single most useful metaphor for understanding the intricacies of the slave-master relationship. An unsentimental assessment, this metaphor could capture the variety of experiences African-Americans had during slavery, as can be seen in the testimony of Foster Weathersby. A Mississippian, this freedman emphasized that the slave experience varied from plantation to plantation, largely because the slaveowners were not all the same. Using the analogy of animal husbandry, he explained: "Some Masters was kind to deir slaves and some was cruel, jes' lak some folks treat deir horses and mules—some like 'em and is good to 'em and some ain't."[49] Such comparisons, as Weathersby may have recognized, gained all the more power precisely because the slaves were not animals.

Nowhere, perhaps, did the slaves see themselves more closely akin to domestic animals than in the world of work. The vast majority of slaves were field workers who frequently labored right alongside the mules and horses to which they so often compared themselves. Like these work animals, black bondspeople performed labor for their white owners in return for care and feeding. But these similarities were not what inspired former bondspeople to say that they had been treated like animals during slavery. When the ex-slaves likened themselves to horses and mules, it was not to complain about performing unremunerated labor alongside these beasts of the field. Rather, what the slaves resented most were slaveowners who treated them like animals rather than workers. "Lord have mercy," Josephine Howard remembered of her slave days, "it sure was awful de way black folks was done. Dey wasn't nothin' de whites don't do to 'em—work em like dey was mules an' treat 'em jes' like dey don't have no feelin'."[50] Likewise, Ben Lawson recalled that, as a slave, "I was treated most harshly 'mongst a group of just white people . . . who seemed to think me de old work ox for all de hardest work."[51] Another ex-slave noted that although the slaveowners treated the slaves as well as they treated their stock, "the dog was supe'ior to us; they would take him in the house."[52]

Beyond work, the experience of bondage also suggested a world of other dehumanizing parallels between slaves and animals. The patrollers who enforced plantation discipline went around the country "just like dogs hunting rabbits."[53] Whites even referred to slaves as animals, according to one ex-slave, who complained that under slavery "we hardly knowed our names. We was cussed for so many bitches and sons of bitches and bloody bitches, and blood of bitches."[54] And some slaves remembered the white-officiated plantation marriages as illegitimate unions more suited to beasts than humans. "De white folks jes made niggers carry on like brutes," recalled Annie Boyd.

"One white man uster say ter nuther white man, 'My nigger man Sam wanter to marry yer nigger gal Lucy what does yer say' en if he said hit war all right why dat couple war supposed to be married."[55]

Above all else, however, African-Americans found themselves more akin to stock than to people during their days in the antebellum South because, unlike other Americans during that time, they could be bred, whipped, or sold. African-Americans who grew up under slavery remembered the indignity and anguish of these three experiences as treatment that made them feel they were regarded as no better than beasts.

Although the deliberate breeding of slaves was not a common practice in the antebellum South, some masters did bring male and female slaves together for the purposes of reproduction.[56] On the Texas plantation where Eliza Elsey was born, "Old Master Tom Smith" used to "take the strongest men and women, put them together in a cabin so's they raise him some more husky children." Herself the product of one of these unions, Elsey credited her robust constitution to her master's selection of parents—"That's the kind of a child I is, and that's why I is so big and so healthy at my old age." But she also noted that, in pairing slaves to mate, Tom Smith "treated his slaves like animals."[57]

Other ex-slaves who recalled such incidents often echoed Elsey's sentiments, describing breeding as one of the great horrors of slavery precisely because it reduced African-Americans to the status of barnyard animals. Arkansas ex-slave William Henry Rooks testified that "the very worse thing I ever knowed about [slavery] was some white men raised hands to sell like they raise stock now."[58] Likewise, black Texan Sarah Ford recalled that her mother, who had been a slave and told her all about slavery, "say de white folks don't let de slaves what works in de field marry none, dey jus' puts a man and breedin' woman together like mules."[59]

Moreover, even in the absence of deliberate attempts at breeding, ex-slaves clearly thought that their past owners had viewed the reproduction of their chattel in the same light as that of their livestock. Asked by a patronizing interviewer, "What sort of treatment did you have, Aunt Lula," the Alabama freedwoman Lula Cottonham Walker replied "de bes'," but her explanation undercut some of the enthusiasm in her answer. Walker, who had eight children as a slave (and twenty after emancipation), explained that her master treated her well because he valued her for her reproductive capacities. "If de massa had a good sow that wuz a givin' birth to a lot of pigs eve'y year, you don't think he goin' to take a stick an' beat her do you? Dat's de way he wuz wid his niggers."[60]

Not all slaveowners were as forbearing with the whip as Walker's master, and many ex-slaves who talked about whippings did not agree with Walker's proposition that masters would have no cause to beat productive work animals. Relatively well treated herself during her slave days, Lizzie Grant was owned by a man who rarely beat his slaves. But she remembered seeing other slaves brutally punished and beaten "all the time" in her youth, sometimes without "any cause." As she struggled to account for the unwarranted brutality she witnessed, Grant could only suggest that slaveowners who brutalized their slaves were behaving much like people who abused domestic animals. With slaves and animals alike, she explained, "some people mistreat their stock by not feeding them and their poor old mules get poor and give out on them then they grab a pole and nearly beat them poor old things to death, when the mules are not to blame."[61]

Other slaves were less philosophical about why whippings occurred, but they also noted parallels between the abuse of slaves and the abuse of animals. Oklahoma freedman Joe Ray, who spent his childhood on an Arkansas plantation, remembered, "Dere was two overseers on the place and dey carried a bull whip all the time. . . . I saw a slave man whipped until his shirt was cut to pieces! Dey were whipped like horses." Ray further observed that the only thing that limited the overseers' brutality was that, like horses, the slaves were too valuable to kill. "The master didn't want dem beat to death. If dey whip 'em too hard the old master shake his head and say, "Dat's too much money to kill."[62] Another slave who was "treated bad, knocked and kicked arount like I was a mule," suggested that whippings made the slaves like animals in yet another respect: the very fact that slave owners had it in their power to use physical discipline reduced the slaves to the level of animals. "We had to stand in fear of them, we had no protection," he explained. "They would take your clothes off and whip you like you was no more than mules."[63]

Freedpeople saw similar parallels between black slaves and animals in almost every detail of slave punishment. A number of ex-slaves recalled that under slavery they not only were punished like animals, but also were treated as animals under the law. Missourian Peter Cork noted that as a slave he could have killed fifty men without ever going to jail because slaves were "stock," and whipping was their only punishment. Harre Quarles also observed that, like animals, slaves were not subject to human law. Even for serious offenses, masters would only "run us out of the country and sell us because we were too valuable. They treated us just about like you [would] a good mule if he kick another mule and kills him."[64]

Not surprisingly, the slave sale provided these black Americans with some of their most powerful memories of being treated like animals. Only two years old when the Civil War began, freedwoman Mollie Barber grew up hearing vivid accounts of slave sales from her mother. Her mother's enduring preoccupation with slave sales is not surprising. Sold two or three times herself during her slave years, Barber's mother must have feared being sold again, or losing her young child to sale, for on the Turner plantation, where Barber and her mother lived, every time the Turners "need[ed] some money, off dey sell a slave, jest like now dey sell cows and hogs at de auction places."[65]

The resemblance between slave sales and livestock auctions only grew more pronounced closer to the point of sale. Slaves were usually driven to auction on foot by mounted white men. "You have drove cattle to a pasture or market haven't you" one ex-slave asked, remembering this spectacle; another explained, "Speclators uster buy up niggers jest lak dey was animals, and dey would travel around over de country and sell an' sell 'em. I've seen 'em come through there in droves lak cattle."[66] Once at auction, the slaves were scrutinized by prospective buyers. "A large crowd of masters gathered 'round," one slave witness recalled, "and dey would put de slaves on the block and roll de sleeves and pantlegs up and say, 'Dis is good stock; got good muscles, and he's a good hardworking nigger.' Why dey sold 'em jus like you see 'em sell stock now. If de woman was a good breeder she would sell for big money, 'cause she could raise children. They felt all over the woman folks."[67]

Moreover, the parallels to the animal auction did not stop with such indignities. Like the bodies of animals at auction, the slaves' bodies were scrutinized inside and out for physical evidence of their age and previous condition. During these auctions, ex-slave Ann Ladly explained, since the white folks did not "keep track of colored folks births . . . dey 'xamine 'em like dey was a hoss er a mule, and guess how old dey was." Mom Genia Woodberry remembered that her grandmother refused to reveal her teeth to a prospective buyer who "wanna know effen dey wuz sound 'fore he buy her. Dat de way dey do when dey sell hosses." In addition to assessing the age and soundness of the slaves, white examiners hoped to detect whether they had been beaten. As physical evidence of a mistreated or rebellious slave, a backful of scars was of great interest to purchasers. Recognizing such concerns, freedman Thomas Johns noted, "Course whippin' made a slave hard to sell, maybe couldn' be sold, 'cause when a man went to buy a slave he would make him strip naked and look him over for whip marks and other blemish, jus' like dey would a horse."[68]

The drama of the slave up on the block struck black and white observers alike as a spectacle in which African-American men and women were treated like livestock. White abolitionists complained that Southerners sold the slaves at auction "like beasts in the field."[69] And even nonabolitionist whites described the domestic slave trade as akin to the buying and selling of cattle.[70] This resemblance was recalled with great bitterness by African-Americans who witnessed slave auctions. "They used to stand slaves up on a platform down on the public square," one Alabama ex-slave testified, "and sell them like they was dogs or horses—women and men. It was awful."[71] Likewise, Martha

King was sold in Tuscaloosa, Alabama, by "a white man" who "'cried' me off just like I was a animal or varmit or something. He said, 'Here's a little nigger, who will give me a bid on her. She will make a good house gal someday.'"[72] Evidence that the obvious likeness between slave auctions and cattle auctions was recognized by African-Americans even as they underwent the indignity and heartbreak of being sold is seen in the recollections of Texas freedwoman Mariah Snyder. Snyder witnessed the sale of one woman who defiantly raised her hands and "hollered 'Weigh 'em cattle'; 'Weigh 'em cattle' while she was on the block."[73]

Given such experiences, it is not surprising that black Americans likened their status as slaves to that of animals. African-American slaves lived out their bondage in an agrarian society, and the overwhelming majority of them performed agricultural labor. As a people who worked alongside domestic animals, and supplemented their slave rations by hunting, they were intimately familiar with the animal world. Animal characters occupied a central place in their folklore, in the Brer Rabbit tales and other beast fables. But while the animals in such tales were "thoroughly humanized," in referring to themselves under slavery as like animals under authority of white people, ex-slaves clearly did not mean to anthropomorphize animals.[74] On the contrary, they maintained that as slaves they were treated like animals rather than human beings.

"Man-like Beasts and Beast-like Men": Animals, Slavery, and Race in the Antebellum South

Comparisons between slaves and animals are probably as old as slavery itself. According to the sociologist Orlando Patterson, one of the constitutive elements of slavery in all societies where it has been practiced is the "natal alienation" of the enslaved. Slavery, Patterson argues, is "social death," because slaves are by their condition denied any legitimate claim to their offspring and are formally alienated from their ancestors. Bondage bars slaves from the rights and responsibilities natural to free men and women, such as nurturing and protecting their kin.[75] This natal alienation from both their parents and their offspring robs slaves of any legitimate claim to a personal and familial identity, assigning them a property status akin to that of domestic animals. Indeed, David Brion Davis suggests, "the original model for such alienation was probably the domestication of animals, as may be indicated in the practice of pricing slaves according to their equivalent in cows, horses, camels, pigs and chickens."[76] Whether or not the origins of slavery can be established in the model of animal husbandry, such pricing practices certainly illustrate that the comparison of slaves to animals is an old one. So, too, does the fact that one of the words for slave in ancient Greek was *andrapodon*, "man-footed creature."[77]

With the development of racial slavery in the New World, this Western tradition of likening slaves to beasts acquired new potency. In Africa, Europeans were confronted with a people whose physical appearance differed dramatically from their own, whose status in the human family they questioned from the outset. "It was a strange and eventually tragic happenstance of nature," Winthrop Jordan observes, "that the Negro's homeland was the habitat of the animal which in appearance most resembles man." The parallel made a strong impression on early English visitors to Africa, who were previously unfamiliar with both black people and anthropoid apes. Given that the English had long imagined strange creatures with a disturbing resemblance to men in their bestiaries, they soon speculated that the apes might be demonic half men. At the same time, they pondered the alien color and customs of the African race. Under this convergence of circumstances, Jordan suggests, "it was virtually inevitable that Englishmen should discern similarity between the man-like beasts and beast-like men of Africa."[78] Similarly, Jan Nederveen Pieterse points out that the European "prehistory of racial thinking in natural science, in which blacks were compared with animals, has a lasting echo in attitudes towards blacks in the west."[79]

Antebellum Southerners drew on Western ideas about similarities between blacks and animals to fashion a proslavery racial ideology that came close to defending slavery on the grounds that black people were beasts of a sort: for black bestiality was one implication of the doctrine of polygenesis. Pluralists did not explicitly describe blacks as beasts, but they nonetheless classified people of African descent as human beasts of a kind when they claimed that the black race did not descend from Adam.[80] Indeed, this conflation of blacks with beasts was one of the most heretical features of the doctrine of polygenesis. The doctrine's implicit equation between blacks and animals troubled even proslavery apologists, who worried that Southerners who adopted this sacrilegious view of the Negro gave the antislavery movement legitimate cause to question Southern Christianity. Holding his ground against the American school of ethnology, one God-fearing Southern cleric proclaimed: "We will not even tacitly allow our enemies the moral advantage of representing that we hold our slaves only as a higher race of Ourangs, not really contemplated in the authoritative precepts on which the morality of Christendom is founded."[81]

Of course, polygenesis was by no means universally accepted in the South, and even the most rabidly polygenist white Southerners were never literally convinced that their black bondspeople were animals. Instead, white Southerners grappled with what David Brion Davis has called "the inherent contradiction of chattel slavery—the impossible attempt to bestialize human beings." Their failure to resolve this contradiction can be seen in the fact that alongside polygenesis, the South also produced the doctrine of paternalism, a political ideology that cast blacks as children rather than animals.

Characterized by some historians as the dominant political ideology of the old South, slaveowner paternalism envisioned the ideal social order as an organic hierarchy held together by relations of dependence, obligation, and protection—the family writ large. Eugene Genovese, the most influential modern-day student of Southern paternalism, argues that the relations between slaves and masters in the antebellum South were shaped by a historically unique paternalistic doctrine of reciprocal obligations that defined the involuntary labor of the slaves as a legitimate return on the masters' "protection and direction." This paternalistic doctrine had something to offer the slave as well, Genovese maintains. "In its insistence on mutual obligations —duties, responsibilities, and ultimately even rights," paternalism implicitly recognized the slaves' humanity, and thereby offered African-American slaves a powerful defense against the dehumanization implicit in slavery.[82]

Self-styled patriarchs, many Southern planters would have appreciated this characterization: in both their personal and public correspondence, Southern slaveowners often presented themselves as the benevolent masters of their black families. Among historians, however, Genovese's ideas about paternalism and class relations in the antebellum South have been widely contested. In particular, his characterization of Southern slaveholders as a paternalistic master class has been especially controversial. Historians such as James Oakes have sought to show that Southern slaveholders were agribusinessmen who—although they felt considerable doubts about the morality of slavery—viewed their slaves as profitable commercial property rather than as charges under their protection and direction.[83]

The slave testimony under consideration here cannot shed a great deal of light on whether the Southern slaveholders saw themselves as patriarchs or businessmen, for there is no reason to assume that planters and slaves understood racial slavery in the same way. But the wealth of comparisons between slaves and animals in testimony of ex-slaves does call into question another aspect of Genovese's argument: namely, whether the enslaved African-Americans found any recognition of their humanity, implicit or otherwise, in the reciprocal obligations of the master-slave relation. Here the slave testimony presents a striking contrast to the historian's argument. When they looked at the relations between black and white in the antebellum South, most ex-slaves seemed to recall not an organic paternalistic relationship of mutual obligations but the absolute dominance of man over animals.

They looked to the barnyard, rather than to the patriarchal family, to find other living creatures in their plantation world whose subjugation resembled their own.

The parallels the slaves saw between their own status and that of animals are thus significant for a number of reasons. They suggest that, however paternalistic the master class in the old South may have imagined itself to be, the slave labor system that prevailed there was frequently understood by the slaves as an arrangement that did not fully differentiate between black slaves and plantation work animals. Moreover, all evidence suggests that this understanding took on far-reaching implications among African-Americans enslaved within the racially divided slave system that developed in the American South. For the condition of being regarded as an animal by white people was associated, in the ex-slaves' minds, at least as much with race as with slavery.

The fundamentally racial character that social status held for African-Americans in the antebellum South is seen in the fact that ex-slaves who had been treated well often described their experiences in racial terms, saying they were treated like white people. Donaville Broussard, who grew up in Louisiana and "never worked hard" as a child, explained his good treatment in racial terms rather than attributing it to the benevolence of plantation paternalism. "The ladies and my mama, too," he recalled, "petted me as if I was the white child."[84] Similarly, Richard Kimmons, who in his youth was owned by a white family who fed their slaves the same food and drink as they served at their own table, observed, "Our white folks was good to us an' treated us like we was w'ite as dey was."[85] Ellen Butler, who served as a slave in Louisiana, did not enjoy such good treatment herself, but she described the lot of some slaves on a neighboring plantation in like terms. She said of the rich slaveowners who lived down the road from her childhood home, "They treated the slaves like white folks."[86] The equation ex-slaves drew between race and status could go both ways. To one ex-slave, white people who were treated poorly likewise became "niggers." Adaline Johnson described some very poor white people—probably indentured servants of some kind—who had been brought in to work at a hat shop near her childhood home in North Carolina as "white free niggers."[87]

Moreover, those fortunate ex-slaves who had been treated "like white folks," when they delineated their privileged status more precisely, would go on to explain that they had been treated like white people rather than "niggers"; or like human beings rather than animals—metaphors they sometimes used interchangeably. Ellis Ken Kannon, a Tennessee freedman, recalled of his life both before and after slavery: "Hab neber had any trubble wid white peeple en you'd be sprized how good dey ez ter me. Dey don't treat me lak a nigger."[88] "Aunt" Nina Scot of South Carolina described her slave experience in identically racial terms. "My Marster and his folks did not treat me like a nigger. . . . they treated me like they did other white folks."[89] The equation between race and being treated like human beings in the minds of ex-slaves comes across even more clearly in the recollections of Mississippi freedwoman Jane McLeod Wilburn. As a child, Wilburn testified, "All I had ter do wuz help 'round ther house and nuss ther baby—when I wuzn't playing wid ther white chillun; I thought I wuz jus' ez white ez they wuz. I sho didn't have no hard time an' I ain't never been slapped 'round lak I wuz a cat."[90]

Indeed, the highest compliment ex-slaves had for former owners who had been good to them was often simply that these owners had recognized that their black bondspeople were humans, not animals. These compliments were usually reserved for owners who refrained from some of the more dehumanizing practices of antebellum slavery, such as feeding slaves from a common trough or administering whippings. For instance, one Texas freedman recalled, "Us had a good marster and I 'speck us was pretty lucky. . . . we didn' sit down at no trough for to eat. Dey had tables in de slaves houses. Us sit down to us meals like human bein's."[91] Another ex-slave said of his master, "Massa Turner am de bestest man he could be and taken good care of us, for sho'. He treat us like humans. There am no whuppin's like some other places."[92] Likewise, Charlie Bowen of Texas, who counted himself both well fed and gently treated in his slave days, testified, "I ain't got a scar on me put there in slavery time. I allus had my bread and milk twixt meals when I was coming up. My white folks treated us as people and not as beasts."[93]

Whatever their experience, the issue for ex-slaves who assessed how they fared in the hands of their former owners seems to have remained the same. Had they been accorded status as human beings? Just as slaves who considered themselves relatively well off during slavery defined their good treatment as being treated like white people or human beings, less fortunate slaves reported that they were treated like animals rather than human beings. As we have seen, such complaints abound in slave testimony on the day-to-day life under the peculiar institution. Moreover, in assessing their experience as a whole, ex-slaves frequently invoked the same metaphor. Under slavery "de bes' treatment wuz far fum bein' good," was how freedwoman Phoebe Lyons summed up the black experience under slavery. "Dey nebber care effen us wuz tired, en dey doan treat us slaves like humans."[94] The wording of these bitter recollections is significant because it suggests that the slaves' perception that whites saw them as "no more than animals" was what many ex-slaves abhorred most about enslavement.[95]

"Dey Doan Treat Us Slaves Like Humans:"
The Slaves' Critique of Slavery

Open expressions of strong antislavery sentiment do not abound in the WPA interviews. As noted previously, the vast majority of these interviews were conducted in the South by white interviewers who were, in some cases, the descendants of slaveowners. The black respondents were elderly freedpeople who, for the most part, answered their white interrogators' questions with great caution and diplomacy. Whatever their actual sentiments on the subject, these witnesses of slavery were clearly ill at ease criticizing the slaveholding practice so recently abandoned by some of their interviewers' ancestors. But ex-slaves such as Phoebe Lyons, who did speak out to denounce slavery, often located the essential overriding wrong of the slaveholding whites in their failure to recognize the humanity of their black bondspeople. And many more ex-slaves simply recalled that they were treated like animals, without expressly condemning the institution of slavery.

Unlike their abolitionist contemporaries, black and white, whose arguments against slavery drew on history, economics, Enlightenment political philosophy, and antislavery interpretations of biblical doctrine, enslaved African-Americans could marshal few formal arguments against the institution of slavery. Revolutionary ideology, as a number of historians have pointed out, made some inroads into the slave community.[96] By the beginning of the nineteenth century, Gerald Mullin suggests in his study *Flight and Rebellion: Slave Resistance in Eighteenth-Century Virginia*, many urban slave artisans had come "to believe that the values and 'rights' of the Revolutionary era were also theirs." However, there is little reason to believe that these political ideas ever fully penetrated the parochial world of the plantation slave. Indeed, according to Mullin, one reason that Gabriel's Rebellion—an unsuccessful slave artisan conspiracy to attack Richmond in 1800—failed was that the "political and secular terms" in which the slave artisans sought to incite their bondspeople to revolt were alien to most plantation slaves.[97]

Mullin suggests that what was lacking in Gabriel's Rebellion, and in the free black Denmark Vesey's abortive plot to take Charleston in 1822, was a "sacred dimension" that would appeal to the religious and eschatological convictions of the plantation slaves. He argues that, among the antebellum slave insurrectionists, only Nat Turner, "a seer and a holy man" whose plans for revolt were charged "with supernatural signs, and sacred, poetic language that inspired action . . . led a 'sustained' insurrection."[98] The success or failure of these three insurrections is difficult to assess—certainly, none of them realized the goals of their organizers. But Mullin's discussion of these events does raise some rarely asked questions about the character and content of antislavery ideology among the slaves themselves.

African-American slaves did not need revolutionary ideology to desire freedom. As Orlando Patterson argues in a recent book, freedom has been the cherished ideal of the enslaved throughout human history.[99] In the antebellum South, this ideal found expression in slave religion. In Christianity's message of universal brotherhood and salvation, as well as in the stories of Moses and Christ, "the twin deliverers,"[100] African-American slaves found hope that they would ultimately be delivered from bondage.[101] Moreover, in addition to hoping that slavery would end, many African-American slaves quite evidently believed that slavery was wrong—a belief that is recorded in their testimony on the institution, as well as in the actions taken by many individual slaves to resist and escape. As scholarship on slave religion reveals, African-American slaves found evidence on the wrongness of slavery in the precepts of the Judeo-Christian tradition and in the message of the Scriptures. But they also expressed a somewhat more secular objection when they likened their treatment under slavery to that of animals: an objection based on their simple but unshakable conviction that black as well as white people were easily distinguishable from beasts and therefore should not be treated like animals.

The freedman Charlie Moses made this distinction in an interview in which he expressed his hope that blacks would never again have to endure bondage:

> Slavery days wuz bitter, bitter, an' I shall never fo'git the sufferin'. The young 'uns now a'days is happy an' don' know 'bout wah' times, but I does, an' I want to tell you now I pray the Lord to let us be free always. God Almighty nevah ment human beings to be lak animals. Us niggahs has a soul, an' a heart, an' a mine an we is'nt lak a dawg or a horse.[102]

Tom Windham, an Arkansas freedman, recalled his slave experience without bitterness but nevertheless shared Moses's conviction that black slaves ought to have been entitled to liberty by virtue of their humanity: "Us folks was treated well," he said of his slave days, but he then went on in his next breath to say, "I think we should have our liberty cause us ain't hogs or horses—us is human flesh."[103] Such sentiments are the implicit message of many of the comparisons between black slaves and brute creatures freedpeople employed to describe their experiences under slavery. Equally important, these comparisons offer us insight into how uneducated black Americans understood the racist ideology that vilified them.

In their testimony, some ex-slaves expressed a belief that their white owners quite literally did not understand that their black laborers were people, with human abilities similar to their own. When asked whether he had received any schooling as a slave, John McAdams answered: "No sir, our white people did not teach us how to read or write, said we were too thick headed to learn how to read or write and said they could come just as near learning their horses how to read as they could us." McAdams seemed to take these statements to be his owner's sincere beliefs, for he continued: "I think they were fooled when we were set free and we began to go to school and learn how to read and write."[104] McAdams's experience was shared by Mississippi freedwoman Sally Neely, who recalled that "the white people did not learn me how to read and write as they thought about us like we do mules and horses today. They did not ever think they could learn us anything."[105]

On the whole, though, slave testimony contains limited evidence on whether African-American slaves commonly believed that the white people who lorded over them truly thought slaves had no human capacities, or simply assumed that whites found it most profitable and convenient to treat their human chattel as livestock. Allen Manning described his master, a preacher, as kind to the slaves unless they disobeyed his orders. If disobeyed, this man of the cloth would whip his slaves without compunction because "he been taught that they was jest like his work hosses. . . . people do like they been taught to do."[106] Such explanations of white behavior are rare in slave testimony. Despite their frequent references to being treated like livestock by whites, most ex-slaves did not address the issue of whether whites really saw no difference between slaves and animals. A few reported, however, that individual whites had actually told them they that were just like animals, such as Fannie Moore, who said of her old master's mother: "She shore was a rip-jack. She say niggers didn't need nothin' to eat. Dey jes like animals, not like other folks."[107] Likewise, another ex-slave remembered an "old Democrat what didn't like colored people. . . . Said a nigger a dog and alligator was all alike to him."[108]

Whatever the prevalence of such comments, it seems likely that most slaves did not have to be told they were just like animals by whites before they thought to compare their condition to that of the domestic animals around them. As we have seen, African-American slaves took their understanding that white people saw them as animals far more from the actions of the white society that oppressed them than from anything anybody said. They observed that "slaves was about de same things as mules or cattle . . . and dey wasn't supposed ter be treated lak people anyway," because the slaves were in fact often treated like animals.[109] They could be bought and sold, had no claims to their offspring, and had few rights or responsibilities under the law. In addition, as so many of the freedpeople emphasized, enslaved African-Americans suffered from countless other indignities that served to make them feel as if they were regarded as more brute than human. They could be beaten and worked in the same manner as their masters' livestock, and many no more knew their own ages than did these beasts of burden. As we have seen, ex-slaves found further comparisons between the treatment of slaves and the treatment of animals in almost every aspect of slave life.

Fannie Moore, formerly a slave in South
Carolina (Library of Congress).

Wherever slavery has existed, slaves have struggled against their
"peculiarly inhuman condition," and throughout its history "slavery
has always raised certain fundamental problems that originated in the
simple fact that the slave is a man."[110] But confinement under a system of racial slavery in an otherwise fairly democratic society made
the problem of this inhuman condition particularly acute for African-
American slaves. Aware that they had been captured and brought to
America to serve under another race, black Americans could not look
upon themselves as "a normal class within the body politic"—a status
accorded to many slave populations in earlier slave societies. In the
Americas, as David Brion Davis notes, "the traditional dualism between the world of the slaves and the world of the free, which had always been encompassed within a single state, was made both geographical and racial."[111] Moreover, this dualism gained a special
meaning within the democratic social structure of the United States,
where social inequalities were deemed neither permanent nor divinely ordained.

The racial dualism of American slavery was attacked by Frederick
Douglass, who wrote of the Constitution:

Its language is "we the people"; not we the white people, not even we the citizens, not we the privileged class, not we the high, not we the low, but we the people, not we the horses, the sheep, the swine, and wheel barrows, we the people, we the human inhabitants; and, if negroes are people, they are included in the benefits for which the constitution of America was established and ordained.[112]

Douglass's black countrymen in the slave South were, for the most part, not familiar with the Constitution, but they too understood the institution of racial slavery to pose the question of whether "negroes are people." These African-Americans could not help but see the slave status held by most black people as a negative judgment against the humanity of their race. And it was a judgment that received plentiful reinforcement in racist ideology, which, while it did not actually posit that blacks were animals, certainly claimed that as an inferior race of humans, black people were far closer to animals than were whites.

It is virtually impossible to map exactly how white racist ideology trickled down to the slaves, although common sense alone suggests that they heard it in insult and epithet rather than in pseudoscientific speculations about the races of man. But above all, slaves took the imputation of racial inferiority from the treatment they received in bondage, and our evidence suggests that they may have missed the fine distinctions racist thinkers made between the animal-like inferiority of black people and the animal-like qualities of animals.

The imputation of animality contained within both racist ideology and the racial caste structure of American slavery was a heavy burden for African-Americans to bear. Even blacks who fled slavery could not escape it, as the Reverend James W. C. Pennington, a onetime slave from Maryland, explained in his autobiography. Attempting to communicate the indignity of slavery, Pennington wrote that among the great evils of the institution was that it cast the slave's "family history into utter confusion." In the background of anyone born into slavery, whether well or ill treated, "nowhere does he find any record of himself *as a man.*"

> On looking at the family record of his old, kind Christian master, there he finds his name in a catalogue with the horse, cows, hogs, and dogs. However humiliating and degrading it may be to find his name written down among the beasts of the field, that is the place, and the only place assigned to it by the chattel relations. I beg our Anglo-Saxon brethren to accustom themselves to think we need something more than mere kindness. We ask for justice, truth, and honour as other men do.[113]

The intellectual weapons that ordinary antebellum African-Americans, who did not escape slavery, could bring to bear against being classed among the beasts of the field differed considerably from Pennington's. Pennington was taught to read and write by a Pennsylvania Quaker family who sheltered him after he escaped. After settling in New England, he furthered his education, pursuing a career as a minister, educator, and writer (Pennington published one of the ethnological works discussed in earlier chapters). As a result of his education, Pennington was able to draw on the Scriptures and science to defend the unblemished origins, honorable ancestry, and inherent human abilities of his race. African-Americans who remained in bondage, however, for the most part could summon little formal evidence against the low estate of their race. Indeed, one ex-slave interviewed for the WPA appeared to concede racial slavery's implication that blacks were animals: "Preacher he teach us about the child that was born in the stable," Jack Harrison recalled, "but boss, I'se don't believe that negro has sole. He more like mule, they might be mule heaven for all I'se know."[114]

Among the freedpeople who recorded their experiences, however, Harrison is alone in this speculation. Most ex-slaves cited the fact that racial slavery assigned black people a status similar to that of animals as evidence that Southern slavery was a great wrong—an argument they supported both on religious grounds and with their conviction that "us is human flesh." As recorded by ex-slave Mollie Dawson, this conviction was to the slaves a source of both strength and frustration. Although she and other slaves were treated like animals rather than people, Dawson said, "We all knew dat we was only a race of people as our master was and dat we had a certain amount of rights but we was jest property and had ter be loyal ter our masers."[115]

"Turned Loose Like a Bunch of Stray Dogs": The Freedpeople Describe Emancipation

"I liked living in slave time better than in these days because people do not know the value of a good negro now," a Louisiana ex-slave named Prince Haas told a WPA interviewer. "A good negro was worth a thousand or twelve hundred dollars in slave time, but white folks would just soon take a shotgun and shoot him now-days."[116] Born in 1861, Haas was all of four years old when slavery ended, so his statement cannot be taken very seriously as a recollection of slavery. But it provides a more accurate assessment of the hardships that black Southerners faced after emancipation, and of the alteration in race relations that emancipation wrought. When the South finally surrendered after a long and bloody struggle, slavery gave way, but not the racism and racial caste structure that had emerged around it. And although most of the freedpeople who spoke of being treated like animals by whites did so in reference to the slave-master relationship, black Americans continued to find that they were regarded as less than human by their white countrymen after slavery ended. On the plantation where George G. King grew up, when emancipation came, his master had to finally release his slave runaways from the plantation's log cabin "jail" where he kept them during the war. But he warned them and his other former slaves not to expect too much of freedom. As King remembered it, " 'The Master he says we are all free, but it don't mean we is white. And it don't mean we is equal. Just equal for to work and earn our own living and not depend on him for no more meats and clothes.' "[117]

Still not equal, still not white, many ex-slaves found the experience of emancipation itself to be another instance in which whites did not recognize black humanity. In so doing, they turned once again to animal metaphors to describe their dilemmas after emancipation, this time comparing themselves to stray animals turned out to fend for themselves without provisions or protection.

As the Civil War came to an end, the newly freed black folk of the South celebrated emancipation as their much-prayed-for day of jubilee, on which they—like the long-suffering children of Israel—were finally released from enslavement by a wise and just God. However, emancipation was a bittersweet victory for the freedpeople, for they, as the Confederate general Robert V. Richardson observed at the time, received "nothing but freedom."[118] Landless and at the mercy of Southern landowners who sought to compel them to work for next to nothing, many of the freedpeople found themselves virtually reenslaved by the "Black Codes" enacted during presidential Reconstruction. Radical Reconstruction brought new hope and, for a brief time political rights, but in the new South that emerged after Reconstruction, African-Americans ultimately found themselves caught in a "seamless web of oppression, whose interwoven economic, political, and social strands all reinforced one another."[119]

Many ex-slaves remembered the hardships they experienced after slavery as vividly as those they had suffered under it. "Folks say dat slavery was wrong and I 'spose it was," reflected a South Carolina ex-slave, "but to be poor, like a heap of niggers is now, is de worse thing dat has ever come upon them."[120] And in describing the disappointments and difficulties of a freedom that both then and later in the nineteenth century would not bring African-Americans equal rights and equal opportunities in the country of their birth, a good number of ex-slaves once again had recourse to metaphors of animals. Looking back to the postwar period, ex-slaves compared their condition to that of stray animals as a means of explaining that after emancipation Southern slaveholders turned their bondspeople loose without even the minimal possessions required for human existence. Like stray animals, they recalled, they had nothing. When freedom came to the Louisiana plantation where he spent his youth, William Mathews testified, "Dey ain' had no time for no celebration for dey make us git right off de place. Jes' like you take an old horse an' turn it loose. You see a lot of cattle in de field eating de grass wit' a fence 'round dem, den somebody open de gate an' say, 'Git!'. Dat's how we was. No money, no nothin'. Jes' turn loose wit'out nothin'."[121] Likewise, on being asked whether the slaves had received any possessions with their freedom, one ex-slave replied "No, sir, we were not given a thing but a hard deal, turned loose with no clothes to wear on our backs, just like wild beasts to roam over the country."[122]

The freedpeople also likened their condition after the war to that of animals to emphasize that being freed with nothing forced them to remain subservient long after slavery ended. "Well son, we got hell if we did not do just like the white people told us to do," William Coleman remembered, "as we had been turned out like a bunch of cattle to live and that was sure hard on our race of people."[123] A Texas freedwoman, Mary Gaffney, shared his sentiment: "No sir, we was not given a thing but freedom. Yes we got hell if we were not careful what we done." She explained, "Instead of being free, slavery had just begun among the negroes and the poor white people, if we were not careful after we were supposed to be free, and went anywhere we were not to go, hell was to pay. In other words we was a people turned loose like a bunch of stray dogs."[124]

A couple of ex-slaves further observed that their people might as well have been stray animals after freedom insofar as slavery had left them unacquainted with the basic skills they needed to thrive as free human beings. "After the war between the states the negro didn't know anything," one woman recalled. "They was not much more than a bunch of cattle because they couldnt read and write. They couldnt make crop themselves, and much less hold office and good jobs like they do now." Another woman complained that "instead of giving us anything" after the war, the government "just turned us a lose like a bunch of wild hogs. That was about the only way they could class us in those days, as we did not have any book learning, nor could we hold jobs of any kind, only knew how to farm."[125]

Historian Eric Foner notes that although many postbellum era whites claimed that the newly freed slaves did not grasp the meaning of emancipation, blacks "carried out of bondage an understanding of their new condition shaped by both their experience as slaves and by observation of free society around them."[126] In their complaints about being set loose like animals, one thing the ex-slaves appear to have understood was that human freedom could not be fully achieved by a people turned "loose like animals wid nothin'."[127] And, in discussing their emancipation, these African-Americans expressed the same indignation about being treated like beasts rather than men as when they used animal metaphors to describe their slave experiences. After freedom, however, the metaphor was consistently distinguished by a poignant new twist: whereas the freedpeople had likened themselves to work animals during slavery, they now characterized themselves as

domestic animals cast loose. With this new refinement of their metaphor, these African-Americans expressed their belief that although
white Americans had freed their black slaves, emancipation did not
represent a white recognition of black humanity.

Few, if any, of the freedpeople who testified for the WPA seem to
have held any expectation of receiving the apocryphal freedom dues
of forty acres and a mule.[128] But a number of them did say that they
expected to be freed with more consideration of their needs as human
beings. The Texas freedman Eli Coleman said:

> I'se thought the Government would give us a home when they freed us
> but no sir, it looks like the Government would have give us part of our
> Masers' land cause everything he had or owned slaves made it for him,
> but we never got anything, just turned us out like a bunch of stray cat-
> tle. Had nothing—not even clothes 'cept what we had on our back the
> day we was freed.[129]

Another ex-slave, Louis Cain, thought the slaveowners "could have
give us enough land to make [a] living on and let us have some money
to build us a house and get us some mules to work the land. Instead
of that, they turned us out and turned us loose just like a stray bunch
of cattle to starve."[130] Other ex-slaves expressed much lower expecta-
tions but the same sentiment. "I didn't exactly expect a farm bed,"
said Harriet Barrett, but "I didn't expect to be put out or turned out
like cattle, and they did not give us anything until long after we were
freed. Then what they gave us wasn't much, just some cast off
clothes."[131] John McAdams could only recall that he expected something quite different from freedom than what he got. "I knows one
thing, I was not expecting to be turned loose like a bunch of stray cattle, but that is exactly what they done to us."[132]

"We could root hog or die, for all they cared," the Texas freedman
Frank Bell said of his people's Yankee emancipators.[133] Indeed, this
sentiment toward the freedpeople after the war was expressed by
both Northern and Southern whites who feared the newly freed
slaves would not work. As economist Gerald Jaynes has shown in his
recent work on the black Southern working class in the postbellum
period, economic concerns were at the heart of these white fears
about black productivity. Both Southern planters and Northern businessmen wanted to see the South return to producing cotton for ex-
port, and both feared that free black laborers would favor the cultivation of staples for their own subsistence over the cultivation of
cotton. However, as has so often happened in this nation's history,
these economic concerns were transformed by racial ideology into
questions about the racial character of black people. White Southerners maintained that blacks were innately lazy and would not work
unless compelled to do so, and even the staunch Republicans who
formed the Freedman's Bureau were prepared to force unwilling

black laborers to work. According to Jaynes, the possibilities for any kind of agrarian reform in the South were severely curtailed by "a national propensity to accept the thesis of black inferiority and the extreme fiscal conservatism of a ruling party facing a large public debt."[134] The economic and political interests at play in the reorganization of labor in the postwar South may not have always been entirely clear to the freedpeople. But few could lose sight of the fact that their white countrymen continued to believe in black inferiority. It is therefore not surprising that many of the ex-slaves viewed their release from bondage into a poverty that ensured their continued subordination as a race as further evidence that whites viewed them as less than human.

Thus, while freedom itself provided the ex-slaves with a long-sought-after recognition of their humanity, there is little reason to doubt that the freedpeople continued to encounter challenges to their status as human beings in the white racist ideology that endured unabated through emancipation, Reconstruction, and beyond. For not only did African-Americans find themselves subject to continuing racial discrimination, but the idea that black people were physically and mentally very close to animals was widely disseminated among whites in late nineteenth- and early twentieth-century America. During these years blacks were routinely depicted as ape-like figures in political cartoons, popular art, and advertising. The turn of the century saw a proliferation of ephemera now collected as racist memorabilia. Images of animal-like black children being menaced by crocodiles and black men and women grinning like monkeys graced postcards, souvenirs, and advertisements produced for the nation's fast-emerging consumer market. Particularly popular in the South, such images put a happy face on segregation, while at the same time reinforcing the idea of black inferiority.[135] Meanwhile, these animalistic presentations of African-Americans were themselves reinforced by popular discussions of a new subject, evolution. As articulated in the nineteenth century, Darwinism usually assigned blacks a very low place on the ladder of evolution—often midway between man and beast.

Admittedly, both popular and scientific representations of blacks as bestial creatures were directed primarily toward white rather than black audiences, and it is difficult to know how familiar the freedpeople were with this written and visual antiblack propaganda. In the interviews conducted by the WPA, ex-slaves make no reference to these kinds of written and visual depictions. And since the vast majority of freedpeople were not literate and lived in rural areas, it is possible that many of them never encountered these kinds of racist materials. The limited evidence contained in the WPA narratives, however, does suggest that the antiblack thought that cast blacks as animals continued to reach African-Americans long after emancipation.

"Us Ain't Dogs or Horses—Us Is Human Flesh"

For ordinary black Americans who experienced the degradation of slavery and continuing racial subordination in the segregated and severely discriminatory society that ultimately emerged in the postbellum South, the issue at stake in the antislavery movement's rallying cry—"Am I not a man?"—was not the character and descent of the black race, nor even the masculinity of black men. Rather, the character of the racial subordination experienced by the men and women who testified for the WPA project made them question whether white society even viewed them as human beings. When they defended their humanity, these ex-slaves were responding not to the polygenesists' attempt to classify blacks as a lower species of human beings, nor to interpretations of Darwinism that grouped the Negro with the apes. In their testimony, African-American ex-slaves recalled time and again the experience of being treated like animals. So when they defended their humanity, they defended it first and foremost against the actions and racist spirit of the white society that treated them as more animal than human.

In doing so, they rejected the repudiation of black humanity that they found in slavery and racist ideology and classed themselves as "human flesh." Does this mean, however, that these African-Americans rejected race altogether as a significant category of human difference? Historian Barbara Fields seems to suggest as much in one of her influential articles on American racial thought. In "Slavery, Race, and Ideology in the United States of America," she asserts that "Afro-Americans invented themselves, not as a race but as a nation. They were not troubled, as modern scholars often are, by the use of racial vocabulary to express their sense of nationality." After all, she continues, "it was not Afro-Americans who invented themselves as a race" or dreamed up racist "theories purporting to prove their biological inferiority."[136] The evidence presented in this chapter suggests that, to the contrary, racism and the material conditions of slavery and racial domination made it impossible for nineteenth-century Americans to ignore racial categories—regardless of who invented them. Moreover, the slave testimony presented here also suggests that African-Americans were profoundly troubled by the ways in which the white society around them used a racial vocabulary to assigned them as a group to a rank below other humans. Accordingly, when they rejected the repudiation of their humanity as found in racial slavery and racist ideology, they did so not as individuals, nor as African nationals or ex-slaves, but on behalf of their race. In asserting that "us is human flesh," African-Americans claimed a place alongside other human beings in Christianity's universal family.

What remains to be seen at this point is the position they assigned to the white race within this universal family: for while the ex-slaves clung to their conviction that blacks and whites shared a common humanity, they did not necessarily believe the races were identical. Indeed, their own experience suggested otherwise. As Paul Escott points out, the WPA narratives "make clear that masters and slaves lived in different worlds, indeed. The evil of enslavement and the strength of cultural differences set these two groups apart from each other and gave the slaves a fundamental sense of themselves as an oppressed racial group."[137] Still an open question remains: How did ordinary African-Americans interpret the immense differences in class, culture, and civil status that divided most black and white Americans during the nineteenth and early twentieth centuries? How did this oppressed racial group see its oppressors, as a race? These questions will be central to the next chapter, which examines the ex-slaves' ideas about white people.

FIVE

❧

"Devils and Good People Walking de Road at de Same Time"

White People in Black Folk Thought

One of the more contentious ex-slave interviews conducted by the WPA illustrates some of the difficulties entailed in exploring African-American views about white people. This interview took place in 1937 in the Cactus Cafe, a black saloon and restaurant in Texas. There a white male interviewer employed by the Texas WPA spoke with Millie Manuel, an elderly freedwoman well-known for her vow to never again speak to a white man on "dis side or de t'other of de Judgment Gate." Disregarding warnings about this vow, the zealous researcher tracked down Manuel, finding her in the Cactus Cafe, where a boisterous African-American crowd had gathered to celebrate the exploits of the new world boxing champion, Joe Louis. Sitting quietly in the back of the room was the ninety-year-old Manuel, whom the interviewer described as "the embodiment of peace, frail and thin with a kind expression on her wrinkled old face." Despite her pleasant appearance, this serene little old lady lost her composure when the WPA worker approached her. She became angry and agitated, shouting, "You get away from me white man!" Her protest was so loud that it drew the attention of the crowd and sent both the bartender and Manuel's granddaughter rushing to her defense, "elbowing their way through a gathering black semicircle."[1] After much explanation and persuasion (possibly from several quarters), Manuel reluctantly agreed to answer some questions, giving a brief and truculent account of her life.

She "got beat most to death" was her response when questioned about her life under slavery, "put up again' a post and layed onto with a cowhide." Evidently answering an ill-considered follow-up inquiry about her good times as a slave, Manuel snorted, "Christmas and biscuits? We never had any. We didn't have food of no account—no meat or nothin', just milk, and we would get a-hold of a egg once in a while.

Us and the hogs got what milk they couldn't eat. We never had nothin' that was happy." Manuel laid the blame for her sorrows squarely on the white race, which she condemned as a group. Her owners, she noted happily, were "all dead now and I's a-livin' and waitin' for Glory; and when I go I won't be seein' any of them. . . . the Lord has spared me and he didn't spare them—They is gone where the Good Shepard has sent them to be slaves for the devil."[2]

As can be seen in her response to the white interviewer, Manuel clearly thought that most whites were cut from the same cloth as her former owners. Prodded by the indefatigable interviewer to say something good about whites, she conceded, "Some whites is good maybe. . . . Some of the time white chillens was kind to me." But she also warned him that "the Good Shepherd will give the best white man a heaben that is hotter than the worstest nigger's hell."[3] Manuel's interview ended abruptly when the hapless interviewer asked her to pose for a photograph. She refused angrily, telling him, "Ain't goin' to trust yo' to take my picture, or no white man. . . . I wouldn't trust a white man no more than a rattler. I was given unto suffer. I got betrayed."[4]

Like most slave testimony, Millie Manuel's interview provides a fragmented and unsatisfying account of its subject's views of white people. Since Manuel sent the interviewer off without so much as a good-bye when he got out his camera, we will never know the full story behind this black woman's animus toward white people, nor her talk of suffering and betrayal. In her rage, however, Manuel was far more communicative on the subject of white people than were most ex-slaves, whether they spoke long after slavery or while the institution still flourished.

By their own acknowledgment, ex-slaves spoke with great caution and reticence on the subject of white people, especially when talking with whites. "These white folks here don't like to hear about how they fathers and mothers done these colored folks," one ex-slave told a black interviewer from Fisk.[5] In conversation with white interviewers, ex-slaves would often disclose only that they had no intention of speaking freely about white behavior. "The white fo'ks don't always treat you right," said Ed Jackson of his slavery days. "You can't tell now—iffen I tell you 'bout it—you might turn and use it agin' me."[6] Even when their interlocutor was black, many of the slaves interviewed by the WPA were still reluctant to tell the whole story of their relations with white people before or after slavery. Mrs. Jennie Patterson confessed to a black interviewer from the Hampton Institute, "Some of us slaves had ole mean an' wicked marsters an' mistess dat would beat 'em unmerciful," but she immediately added, "I don' tole you I was feared to tell all I done seen in my lifetime, an' I ain' tellin' white folks but so much even now in dis new day an' time."[7]

There can be little doubt that a similar reticence clouds much of nineteenth- and twentieth-century African-American testimony on white people. Slave fugitives, such as Frederick Douglass and Harriet Jacobs, who penned their antebellum memoirs hoping to woo the antislavery sympathies of Northern whites, were in no position to speak with absolute candor about whites as a group. As literary critic Jennifer Fleischner observes:

> African American slave narrators were compelled to put their grievances against the portion of the dominant white world in which they had been enslaved (the South) before the authority of those ruling whites into whose dominion they had fled (the North). Consequently, they had to marshal in their narratives these strategies of compromise, adaptation, resistance, and defense that they had learned as survival tactics for growing up as subordinated, oppressed, and abused members of hierarchical slavery households.[8]

Chief among these survival tactics, and most salient here, was a discretion that pervades both slave narratives and other black testimony on slavery.

One of the lessons that African-Americans learned under slavery was the necessity for reticence and caution in all forms of public self-expression. This lesson, as Lawrence Levine comments, "was repeated endlessly in black aphorisms" such as "A smart redbird don't have much to say" and "Everything good to hear is not good to talk."[9] The need for discretion in all dealings with white people was given special emphasis in the common saying "Got one mind for white folk to see / 'Nother I know that is me."[10] Such wisdom remained relevant long after slavery ended. Throughout the latter half of the nineteenth century and well into the twentieth, white folklorists who attempted to collect material on black culture commonly encountered great difficulty in persuading blacks to reveal their folklore and beliefs. Joel Chandler Harris complained in 1880 that he "found few Negroes who would acknowledge anything" of the legends he sought.[11] Not surprisingly, black reticence seems to have been particularly profound and enduring on the subject of white people. The problems that white folklorist William Ferris Jr. encountered while collecting oral lore in Mississippi in 1968 led him to conclude that "blacks rarely speak openly with whites because of their vulnerability as an oppressed minority. As the group in power, whites can afford to openly express their thoughts about blacks, whereas the latter conceal their feelings towards whites as a means of self-preservation."[12]

Mediated by white voices, constrained by the cultural imperatives of caution and reticence, slave testimony on white people is filled with silences, ruptures, and contradictions. The rage that Millie Manuel expressed against the white race is rarely echoed in the WPA narratives or elsewhere—perhaps only a very old woman in an all-black bar could speak so freely. And other things may be missing as well. In attempting to assess ideas about white racial character in black folk thought, we have to be ready to encounter dissemblance and ellipses—to heed the words of an ex-slave who warned that since African-Americans had learned to speak only indirectly about white people under slavery, "you can't 'pend on nothing colored folks tells you to this good day. They learned to be so deceivable when they was young."[13]

Such warnings, however, should not discourage us from scouring slave testimony for African-American ideas and beliefs about white people. As this chapter will illustrate, amid the ellipses and evasions there is a rich and complex commentary on white people in black folk thought. "The ways of white folks," to borrow Langston Hughes's phrase, shaped African-American life in ways that ex-slaves could not expunge from their testimony, despite the cultural imperatives of caution and discretion. Moreover, when it came to analyzing the behavior of white people, enslaved African-Americans felt the weight of other imperatives as well. As a powerless people, they were forced to be keen students of white behavior, and they frequently pondered the mysterious and malign powers of the dominant race. Like Millie Manuel, many contemplated the future of whites, anticipating an unpleasant afterlife for many members of this sinful race. And while many kept their conclusions to themselves, ex-slaves sometimes chose self-expression over discretion in recalling their slave experience, as can be seen in Manuel's recollections. Self-expression could be more satisfying than discretion, explained freedman Jack Maddox, who told his interviewer that he loved white folks "like a dog loves [a] hickory [stick]." "I can say these things now," Maddox proclaimed, "I'd say them anywhere—in the court house—before the judges, before God. 'Cause they done done all to me that they can do."[14]

"We Knowed Dey Was White and We Was Black": Racial Divisions in Black Folk Thought

"White folks 'jes naturally different from darkies," freedwoman Katie Sutton told a WPA worker. "We's different in color, in talk and in ligion and beliefs. We's different in every way and can never be spected to think or live alike."[15] Unfortunately, we cannot know more about what this particular black woman found so naturally different about white people: her interview is brief and devoted largely to the recitation of a slave song. But Sutton was far from the only African-American of the slavery generation to suggest that there were important differences between the races. What were they? The ideas that these enslaved African-Americans held about racial differences defy any easy summary or explanation.

In this respect the racial thought of the slaves is profoundly different from that of whites of the same era for whom race served, to use Henry Louis Gates's phrase, as "the ultimate trope of difference."[16] A social construction that helped "produce and maintain relations of power and subordination," race provided most white Americans with a useful and powerful explanation for the existing racial hierarchy in their society.[17] Racial ideology, as historian David Roediger has shown, had something to offer even to those white Americans whose material interests were not always well served by the oppression of black labor. Although the exploitation and enslavement of black workers rarely enriched working-class white Americans—whose attempts to raise their own wages were frequently undercut by the presence of low-priced black labor—white supremacy provided white workers with an important source of status and positive self-definition.[18] By contrast, racial explanations for the power relations in American society would seem to offer little to African-Americans of any class, slave or free.

Nonetheless, they could not escape from race. Regardless of their educational attainments, economic status, or condition of servitude, all nineteenth-century African-Americans lived in a society where important cultural and social differences divided most black people from most white people. Moreover, these differences received further reinforcement from a variety of inescapable forms of legal, civil, and political discrimination that set black Americans apart from white Americans throughout this era. As described in previous chapters, educated blacks in the North were outraged by both racial inequities perpetrated by the dominant group and the racial ideology that whites invoked to justify their treatment of black people. Confronted with the ever more demeaning theories about the debased origins and inborn inferiority of black people, educated blacks did not try to ignore or dismiss white American ideas about race. Instead, they fought for access to print culture and sought to vindicate their race by creating alternative readings of race that celebrated the humanity and historical achievements of black people—often at the expense of white history and humanity. By contrast, the unlettered African-Americans who formed the vast majority of nineteenth-century America's black population had very little access to racist doctrines or to the writings of the black intellectuals who debated them. But they understood slavery and the Southern caste system as a repudiation of the humanity of black people.

Moreover, ex-slaves attributed such inequities to whites as a race rather than to the slaveholding elite. In the antebellum South, as Peter Kolchin observes,

> The vast predominance of slaves in the black population, together with the ease of somatic identification, and the fact that whites seemed united to oppress them, led to the same widespread confusion of race and class among the slaves as existed among their masters. Slaves referred to themselves in racial terms—as in "colored" or "niggers" rather than slaves—and saw their oppressors as whites in general rather than slave owners in particular.[19]

Kolchin's observation, which is fully supported by the evidence in slave testimony, bears some elaboration because this "confusion of race and class" helped shaped the slaves' understanding of white people.

Contrary to historian Barbara Fields's suggestion that African-Americans viewed themselves as a nation rather than a race, racial categories rather than national identities loom large in slave testimony.[20] Indeed, the evidence in slave testimony suggests that race defined not only the way the slaves saw themselves but also the way they saw white people; as Kolchin notes, ex-slaves almost invariably referred to themselves in racial terms and frequently spoke of white people in the same way, designating their former owners as "our white folks" or "the white folks." Such racial terminology is ubiquitous in the WPA interviews, right down to the language the ex-slaves used to speak to white interviewers, whom they addressed as "white folks" when they assigned them any title other than "Sir" or "Ma'am."[21]

More evidence on how the bifurcated black-white character of the slave worldview led slavery-generation African-Americans to conflate race and class can be seen in their discussions of lower-class whites. The WPA interviews reveal that the freedpeople made only limited distinction between various kinds of white people. To be sure, ex-slaves were well aware of class distinctions among whites. They knew, as one said, that "all de white folks wasn' equal," and that the white "buckra" class—as the slaves sometimes termed rich whites—looked down on lower-class whites.[22] A few ex-slaves even expressed sympathy and solidarity toward lower-class whites. "Poor white folks never had a chance," observed Oklahoma freedman Tom Woods. "De slave holders had most of de money and de land and dey wouldn't let de poor white folks have a chance to own any land or anything else to speak of. Dese white folks wasn't much better off dan we was. Dey had to work hard and dey had to worry 'bout food, clothes and shelter."[23] Such sentiments were rare, however, because enslaved African-Americans tended to encounter propertyless whites under the worst of circumstances. Lower-class whites were often employed to oversee the slaves and patrol the plantations, which made them authorities who the slaves abhorred. Bad experiences in the hands of brutal overseers and patrollers led many slaves to despise poor whites—a sentiment that was often encouraged by slaveowners, who looked down on poor whites themselves. Recalling white overseers with a mixture of fear and contempt, Hannah MacFarland said: "The overseer was sho' nothing but poor white trash, the kind who didn't lak niggers and dey still don't, old devils. Don't let 'em fool you; dey don't lak a nigger a'tall."[24]

In singling out "poor white trash" as an especially mean segment of that race, some ex-slaves evidently divorced lower-class whites from the upper-class whites who employed them. "Why de good white folks put up wid them poor white trash patarollers I never can see or understand," commented South Carolina freedwoman Mauda Walker. "You never see classy white buckra men patarollin'! It was always some low-down white men, dat never owned a nigger in deir life, doin' de patarollin' and a strippin' de clothes off men, lak pappy, right befo' de wives and chillun and beatin' de blood out of him. No sir, good white man never dirty deir hands and souls in sich work of de devil as dat." Such distinctions were also popular among upper-class white Southerners who often prided themselves on their gentility. Slaveowner gentility, however, could not withstand close scrutiny. "A rich man wouldn't ever whip a slave," one shrewd freedwoman observed, explaining why poor whites were more brutal than their affluent counterparts. "They [the rich men] always hire someone to do this."[25]

Character differences between lower- and upper-class whites, however, were not much debated among the slaves for a simple reason: neither the slaves' disdain for whites who were nearly as propertyless as themselves, nor their bad experiences at the hands of white overseers and patrollers led them to make any kind of unvarying distinction between slaveholding and nonslaveholding, or poor and rich, whites. A great many of the ex-slaves interviewed by WPA workers made no distinction whatsoever between whites of different classes. Others spoke ill of "white trash" men, who acted as patrollers or had been cruel overseers. But they usually linked these men's oppressive authority to the jobs they performed rather than singling them out as a special kind of white people. And even the ex-slaves who held poor white trash in contempt noted that their whiteness had to be recognized all the same. Tom W. Woods, who was a slave in Alabama in his youth, recalled: "Us Darkies was taught dat poor white folks didn't amount to much. Course we knowed dey was white and we was black and dey was to be respected for dat, but dat was about all."[26]

Such respect toward whites, as well as feelings of fear and mistrust toward whites as a group, were undoubtedly fostered among the slaves by Southern law, which required black Americans to defer to all whites, rich and poor. By the antebellum era, the legal codes of all the slave states included "pass laws," which gave whites the power to detain, question, and punish any black person encountered outside the supervision of his or her owner—including free blacks who could not produce their papers. Moreover, both slaves and free blacks had virtually no recourse against whites who abused this authority, since Southern courts did not admit black testimony. Such laws, as the fugitive slave couple William and Ellen Craft emphasized in their narrative, "gave the lowest villain in the country, should he be a white man," broad powers over all African-Americans.[27] Likewise, they gave black Southerners every incentive to distrust whites as a class.

"A Rising to Kill the Whites": The Racial Politics of American Slave Revolts

The racial division of allegiance that shaped the slave world may have emerged most decisively in those rare moments when the power relations that sustained the slave system came under attack: when the slaves organized armed resistance to their condition. Fragmentary evidence on this subject can be found in the limited slave testimony available from the most notable episodes of organized slave resistance in the nineteenth century: Gabriel's, Vesey's, and Nat Turner's rebellions of 1800, 1822, and 1831, respectively, and a lesser known but equally important incident at Second Creek in Mississippi in 1861, which has recently been chronicled by Winthrop Jordan.[28] These incidents of slave resistance merit some attention here, for as atypical as their participants were in organizing armed resistance to slavery, the racial hostility they brought into their struggles provides us with a rare glimpse into how deep the feelings of racial difference ran in nineteenth-century African-American culture. The four incidents took place in different temporal and geographic settings and involved diverse groups of slave and free black participants, but the historical transcripts reveal that in every one of these episodes the goals of the black insurrectionists were expressed in strikingly similar terms. In all four rebellions the common enemy the conspirators banded together to fight was defined in simple racial terms as "white people," and the insurrectionists appealed to the racial enmity their fellow slaves felt toward whites to enlist their participation.

The leaders of Gabriel's Rebellion, an abortive slave plot to take Richmond organized in 1800 by a slave blacksmith named Gabriel Prosser, set their plan in motion by recruiting enlistees willing to join "a society to fight the white people for freedom." Potential conspirators were asked whether they "could kill white people stoutly," and the enlistees responded by affirming their hatred of white people and their willingness to kill them without hesitation or compunction. One such enlistee, challenged by a recruiter who told him that "he looked so poor and weakly that he could not kill a man," shot back the fiery response "Do not take me at my looks, I could kill a white man as free as eat."[29] Another recruit boasted, "I could slay white people like sheep."[30]

Twenty years later, a West Indian–born free black named Denmark Vesey induced slaves in the Charleston area into a similar conspiracy to attack that city, using identical appeals to his enslaved brethrens' feelings of racial difference and enmity toward white people. Inspired by the black revolt that took place in St. Domingue in 1791, Vesey enlisted slave supporters into what he called a "rising to kill the whites." Rolla, one of Vesey's main recruiters, even sought to sway potential participants with visions of a global race war, predicting that "Santa Domingo and Africa would come over and cut up the white people if we only made the motion here first."[31] Rolla's hopes were never fulfilled: like Gabriel's Rebellion, Vesey's plot was discovered before it could be enacted.

Similarly, the insurgents who participated in Nat Turner's famous revolt planned to pit race against race. The slaves who followed the visionary slave preacher Nat Turner on a bloody rampage through Southampton, Virginia, in 1831 "intended to rise and kill all the white people." When one conspirator worried that "their number was too few," another assured him, correctly as it turned out, "that as they went on and killed the whites the blacks would join them."[32] Turner himself was inspired to lead the revolt by a series of religious visions, including one that seemed to prophesy the same kind of race war contemplated by Gabriel and Vesey. "I saw white and black spirits engaged in battle," Turner told Thomas Gray in his *Confessions*, "and the sun was darkened—the thunder rolled in the Heavens, and blood flowed in streams—and I heard a voice saying, 'Such is your luck, such are you called to see, and let it come rough or smooth, you must surely bare [*sic*] it.'"[33]

The only large-scale antebellum era slave plot that went undetected long enough to be carried out, Nat Turner's Rebellion lasted for two days, during which Turner and his small band of men attacked over a dozen white farms, enlisting new recruits as they traveled. Originally composed of just seven men, Turner's force grew as large as sixty. The slave rebels killed at least fifty-seven white men, women, and children before they were apprehended by the slow-moving Virginia militia.[34]

Finally, in the incident at Second Creek, a plantation district ten miles south of Natchez, Mississippi, discontented slaves once again plotted to "kill the white folks." The plan took shape at the beginning of the Civil War, when a group of slave men heard about the bombardment of Fort Sumter and decided to revolt. An able and well-informed group, many of the conspirators worked as coachmen for the wealthy planters whose estates surrounded Second Creek. They planned to kill their masters and march onward to Natchez, where they expected to join the victorious Union Army. Their plans were never realized because the plot was discovered before it could be carried out. Moreover, it would have had little chance of succeeding even if it had remained secret, since the Union Army reached Natchez more than six months later than the conspirators had anticipated. But the racial terminology these hapless Second Creek rebels used to the describe their plans after they were caught is particularly interesting. When apprehended, the rebels, who were questioned by an extralegal "examination committee" of slaveholding whites before being put to death, used a racial language to describe their aims even though the details of their plan did not pit race against race. Those involved in planning the Second Creek Rebellion may have included one or more white conspirators, and the rebels' intent to join the Northern army certainly envisioned a biracial alliance against Southern whites. Yet, in their testimony, these black conspirators, like the participants in the earlier rebellions, defined their enemy simply as white people. In language that, if taken at face value, would make their plans very confusing indeed, the rebels spoke of joining the Northerners, or abolitionists, to kill the white folks. "Our folks join the Northerners," one of the conspirators recalled telling another. "I will join them too to help them kill the white folks."[35] Another expressed his aims this way: "Be a soldier. Kill all the damn white people."[36]

The Second Creek rebels and their predecessors who planned Gabriel's, Vesey's, and Turner's rebellions cannot be taken to be representative slaves because the vast majority of enslaved African-Americans did not plot organized resistance against their bondage. Complex motives specific to their time, place, and circumstances drove these particular slaves to embark on their dangerous undertakings. But there is no reason to assume that racial distinctions made by these slave rebels in plotting their differently situated rebellions were specific only to their desperate plans. Across time and place, slaves who participated in each of these attempts at resistance brought their individual grievances and experiences to their struggles. Yet their specific histories did not prevent them from defining the target of any organized black resistance in a remarkably similar way. And the way they defined this target provides us with a rare glimpse into a racial worldview they probably shared not only with other slave rebels but also with many slaves who did not rebel.

The slave rebels' plans bear out the sense of racial difference that we can see less distinctly in the testimony of other enslaved African-Americans. The slave rebels made no distinction between rich and poor planters, between slaveholding whites and the slaveless, and they spoke of all white people as their common enemy even when their plans included the possibility of incorporating white allies. In Gabriel's Rebellion the conspirators considered exempting Frenchmen because "they had understood," as one of the leaders testified, "that the French were at war with this Country . . . & that an army had landed at South Key which they hoped would assist them."[37] But in the case of Gabriel's Rebellion and the South Creek episode as well, the pragmatic allegiances that slave rebels hoped to form with their enemy's enemies did not keep them from viewing their struggle as a racial one.

Only gender and piety mitigated the starkly racial slave worldview that emerged during the slave rebellions. In the Vesey and Gabriel rebellions the conspirators considered exempting certain whites on religious grounds: some of Denmark Vesey's followers did not want to kill the ministers, while one of Gabriel's lieutenants understood that Quakers and Methodists would be spared along with their potential allies, the French.[38] And in all these planned struggles except the actual conflict that came to fruition in Nat Turner's Rebellion, in which the slave rebels slaughtered white men, women, and children alike without compunction, the participants debated whether white women would be treated differently from white men.[39] One participant in Gabriel's Rebellion said that the insurrectionists intended "to spare all poor white women who had no slaves"—although others testified that "whites were to [be] murdered and killed indiscriminately."[40] Likewise, in both Vesey's Rebellion and the Second Creek plot, the conspirators considered exempting white women from the carnage, sometimes with the aim of seizing them for sexual purposes. "*When we have done with the fellows,*" one of Vesey's followers reportedly told another, "*we know what to do with the wenches.*" Similarly, some of the South Creek drivers spoke of either "ravishing" the ladies or taking them for wives. "I will kill the old master and ride the ladies," one defiant Second Creek conspirator testified; another said that "the blacks were to kill all the men and take young ladies and women for wives."[41]

There is not enough evidence to establish the exact motives governing the slave conspirators' talk of treating white women differently from the men. At least one Second Creek rebel certainly did not plan to spare white women by exempting them from the killings: Nelson planned to "take . . . Miss Mary, because she had poured water upon his daughter."[42] While the slave insurrectionists' unresolved discussions about how white women would have been treated in their planned revolts do reveal that sexual difference further complicated the black rebels' sense of racial difference, the evidence they provide on this subject is scanty at best. At the same time, other available evidence on the slave experience suggests that sex or religion rarely superseded racial difference when African-Americans looked at white people.

Indeed, it is revealing that the slave rebels' qualms about killing white women and men of the cloth, like the plans of some of these rebels to enlist white allies, were often lost in the racial language used by the rebels. As we have seen, the slaves involved in all four revolts defined their aims as killing white people, despite the negotiations some of them had over who would be killed and the plans among two groups of rebels to enlist the aid of white allies. The racial goals formulated by the participants of all these antebellum slave conspiracies reveal, as Winthrop Jordan notes in relation to the testimony of the Second Creek rebels, that "the feeling of racial difference ran deep within" both blacks and whites in the slave South, and that for the slaves "whiteness had became synonymous with authority and oppression."[43]

This understanding of whiteness can be seen elsewhere in slave testimony and is perhaps best summarized in a passage that appears in the *Narrative of the Life and Adventures of Henry Bibb*, an autobiography written by a Kentucky slave who fled to freedom in Ohio. Bibb recounts that when he first escaped the South and arrived in Cincinnati he met a black man who told him he should seek aid from white abolitionists who would convey him to Canada. Bibb was astounded. "This was the first time in my life," he writes, "I had ever heard of such people being in existence as Abolitionists. I supposed that they were a different race of people."[44] Bibb's assumption that white people were so radically different from and naturally opposed to black people that the abolitionists could not belong to the white race, like the simple black-white distinctions made by the slave rebels, suggests that enslaved African-Americans understood both the character and the class interests of white people in racial terms. As historian Thomas Webber notes, in the slave quarters,

> Although specific white men and women were judged individually — some respected, some detested — the interests of whites as a group were seen to be inimical to those of the quarter community. More importantly, whites in general, and members of the slave holding class in particular, were held to be responsible for most of the sorrow that blacks experienced under slavery.[45]

It should come as no surprise that enslaved African-Americans resented whites and associated them with authority and oppression. Yet this point cannot be dismissed as obvious, for, as we shall see, white people in black folk thought are defined above all by the superior economic and social power that accompanied their whiteness rather than by their color or any special racial characteristics. The associations that slaves made between whiteness and power and authority, and the hostility that some of them expressed toward all white people as a consequence, are the strongest elements of a coherent racial ideology that can be found in black folk thought.

The Color and Character of White People in Black Folk Thought

The power and authority that nineteenth-century African-Americans saw in white people were in a sense the inverse of the qualities their white contemporaries associated with black people: namely, inferiority and degradation. But the inversion of white racial ideology in black folk thought had distinct limits. As emphasized in earlier chapters, by the nineteenth century white ideas about the inferiority and degradation of black people had become inextricably bound up with negative assessments of the Negro's color and human capabilities. White Americans were entitled to deal with black Americans as their inferiors under the laws of the land; whites confronted blacks as an exploited, degraded, and largely unfree class, but they understood black inferiority as more natural than political. To borrow James Campbell and James Oakes's elegant phrase, white Americans saw in black people "a vision of innate, ineradicable inferiority, rooted in the body."[46] By contrast, although African-Americans associated white people with power, authority, and oppression, there is little evidence that they developed a constellation of racial ideas about the innate corporeal, intellectual, and personal character of white people.

African-Americans of the antebellum period accepted race as an important distinction between human beings and spoke of race as a matter of color. Yet, unlike most white Americans who found the color of the black race to be the very badge of its members' inferiority, black Americans do not seem to have made strong associations between the power and authority of white people and their physical characteristics. Like black intellectuals, ordinary African-Americans did not share the white world's preoccupation with color as an important racial difference.

Previous chapters have noted that, while many white Americans throughout the nineteenth century and beyond found the dark complexions of black people to be among their most distinctive and distasteful characteristics, their emphasis on color distinctions was not echoed in the racial thought of black intellectuals. Color differences likewise received scant attention from the African-Americans who lived under slavery in the nineteenth century. Admittedly, the African ancestors of these slaves may well have shared in their unfamiliar-looking white captors' preoccupation with color. We know, for example, that when the kidnapped African Olaudah Equiano first encountered white men aboard the slave ship that carried him to the Americas, he was horrified by his new masters' pale complexions and long hair. One reason he was so taken aback by the appearance of these white men was that their coloring made him think they might be evil spirits, for among his Ibo countrymen a white complexion was regarded as a deformity.[47] The Ibo's distaste for the appearance of white people was widely shared in Africa, whose black inhabitants, one fifteenth-century writer reported, "in their native beauty most delight, / And in contempt doe paint the Divell white."[48] But there is no evidence in slave testimony to suggest that African color preferences lived on among nineteenth-century African-Americans. Like the black intellectuals whose ideas about color have already been examined, the uneducated blacks who served as slaves had little to say about the color of white people.

Ex-slaves frequently denigrated the temperament and conduct of their white masters but rarely mentioned their color. WPA workers in Arkansas did interview one black woman, born long after the Civil War, who reported that she had seen her grandmother's former master, and "He look like an old possum. He had a long beard down to his waist and he had long side burns too."[49] But the freeborn Victoria McMullen's comment on the appearance of a white person is noteworthy only for its rarity in the WPA testimony. Not only did the African-Americans interviewed by the WPA express no distaste for the complexion and physiognomy of their white oppressors; they rarely discussed the physical appearance of their former owners and overseers, or other familiar whites, at all. White people in the WPA testimony are all described by the ex-slaves simply as white with no elaboration regarding skin color, eye color, or any vagaries of complexion that more color-conscious observers might note.

On the subject of their own color and appearance, ex-slaves occasionally expressed an awareness that white people found the appearance of black people unlovely. A South Carolina ex-slave reacted with amazement when a white interviewer asked him whether his wife had been pretty. "You ask me if she was pretty?" Ed Barber exclaimed. "Dat's a strange thing. Do you ever hear a white person say a colored woman is pretty?"[50] Other freedpeople recalled that their former owners had routinely addressed them in derogatory terms that referred to their color, such as "black devils."[51] But the ex-slaves interviewed by the WPA did not dwell on the issue of color even to defend their own appearance.

Indeed, the absence of slave testimony on the subject makes it difficult to establish the significance of color in black folk thought. It is clear that both slave and free African-Americans commonly used black and white color imagery in their religious practice in a manner similar to that of white Americans, identifying black with evil and sin, and white with purity and holiness. "Remember *Christians*," wrote the early black poet Phillis Wheatley, "Negros, black as *Cain*, / May be refin'd, and join th' angelic train."[52] Uneducated slaves speaking many years later used identical color imagery, predicting a white future for themselves in the afterlife. "Some day I'ze gwine to be with my ole frien's an' if our skins here are black dey won't be no colors in Heaven," predicted Oklahoma freedman Frances Banks. "Our souls will all be white."[53] Likewise, an "old-time Negro house servant" described heaven to her white charges as a place with "golden streets and sparkling waters and . . . glorious noontide—where everyone was happy and had wings and a crown and a golden harp, and yet, still more glorious than all, where white folks and niggers were all white alike!"[54]

In ex-slave religious visions the newly white souls of black folk often joined a white God in an all-white heaven. Black Baptists in Tennessee who spoke of their religious conversion experiences to WPA interviewers from Fisk University recorded visions of a white God, who was often dressed in white and surrounded by light. "I saw the Lord in the east part of the world, and he looked like a white man. His hair was parted in the middle, and he looked like he had been dipped in snow, and he was talking to me," one reported.[55] Jesus, likewise, appeared in slave visions as "a man, pure white and shining."[56] These visions of white divinity were commonplace enough to attract the ire of one ex-slave preacher, who complained, "I don't believe in all that what the people say about having to see a little white man. That is all fogieism. What was it for them to see? Always a little *white* man. . . . Don't believe nothing like that."[57]

Some of the color imagery in slave religion may have been fostered by white slaveowners, such as the mistress who assured her slave maid that "if she worked hard and behaved herself, she would eventually turn white."[58] If so, predictions of a white afterlife for black people were nonetheless taken to heart by some slaves, such as the former mammy who rebuked her white interrogator for questioning her on the subject: "What's dat honey? How I knows I'se gwine ter be white? Why, honey, I'se s'prised! Do you 'spose 'cause Mammy's face is brack, her soul is brack too? Whar's yo' larnin' gone to?"[59] But, as Mechal Sobel points out, the religious imagery the slaves used may have had African roots that antedated their experiences in America. According to Sobel, in African religions "white was symbolic of goodness, purity, and holiness, while black symbolized evil. This color consciousness runs throughout the West African world view." Enslaved Africans brought this religious color code to America with them, Sobel suggests, where it became "mixed up with the complex self-perception of a black slave in a white slave-owning society. The black Baptist put on robes at his baptism and sang: 'Whitah dan snow; yes, whita dan snow, / Wash me, an' I shall be whitah dan snow.'"[60]

Whatever the origin and exact character of black color preferences, we may safely argue that the black discussion of color in the nineteenth and early twentieth centuries never focused on the color of white people as a central topic. More important, it is clear that for black Americans white power and authority never became linked to the physical being of white people. The freedmen and freedwomen interviewed by the WPA had virtually nothing to say about the appearance of white people, and they said little more about their own complexions. More abundant evidence on African-American color preferences can be found in black secular songs from the early twentieth century, as Lawrence Levine has shown. A few of these do denigrate white people, such as a Mississippi song that asserted, "Then white folks look like monkeys, / when dey gits old, old an' gray." But most of the secular songs about color described what complexion the singer preferred in a mate ("Some say give me a high yaller / I say give me a teasin' brown") and never mentioned white people, "except to warn blacks away from having affairs with them." As Levine notes, these songs of color preference demonstrate above all that "black culture

did not envision color as a simple polarity between white and black.
. . . the three colors most commonly referred to in these songs were
black, brown and yellow."[61]

The fact that African-Americans eventually came to see the color of
white people as an integral mark of their power and authority may be
less of a conundrum than the question of why the color of black people was so important to nineteenth-century white Americans. For the
lack of emphasis on color in the racial thought of both unlettered and
educated black Americans suggests that the preoccupation with the
corporeal character of black people that so distinguishes the racial
ideology of white Americans was not the inevitable response of one
physically different population to another, as scholarship on white
American racial thought sometimes seems to suggest. Rather than being
a natural response to racial difference, the disdain white Americans
expressed toward the color and physical being of black people reflects
one of the ways in which this dominant group's racial ideology served
to explain the subordination of black people as the natural condition
of the black race.

By contrast, the evidence concerning white people in black thought
suggests that racial ideology did not prove as useful to African-
Americans as an explanation for white domination and black subjugation. Not only do they not seem to have either demonized or val-
orized the physical characteristics of white people as a mark of this
dominant race's power and authority; they never crafted any unified
set of ideas about the racial character of white people to explain the
status and power of the white race. Although the testimony of African-
Americans reveals that they confronted white power as a reality that
took on almost natural dimensions, it presents little evidence to suggest that these black Americans found the source of white power and
authority in the innate racial character of white people.

Unlike black intellectuals, who often attributed the status and
wealth of white people to the rapacious, acquisitive character of the
Anglo-Saxon race, unlettered African-Americans confronted the power
and privilege of the white world as a mysterious and troubling phenomenon. "God created us all free and equal," an Oklahoma freedman told one WPA interviewer. "Somewhere along de road we lost
out."[62] In relating their life experiences both before and after emancipation, the freedpeople interviewed by the WPA workers described
white power, privilege, and hostility toward people of color as both
ubiquitous and unchanging. "People had a terrible time [in slavery],"
one ex-slave said, summing up American race relations over the
course of his life. "White folks had it all. When I come along they had
it and they had it ever since I been here."[63]

In contrast to white Americans who crafted powerful biological and
religious explanations for the Negroes' low estate that rendered black
inferiority both natural and divinely ordained, slavery-generation

African-Americans had few explanations for how white people had attained their tremendous power and authority. Only a few ex-slaves who spoke to interviewers from the WPA told their questioners that black subjugation was in fact natural and divinely ordained. Frank Hughes, for example, said, "I jes don't know Miss, but it looks like our color needs somebody over dem. Look at de leaders in de world, all white nearly. If de Lawd willed it otherwise dey would be mixed. . . . No mam, its God's will."[64] Likewise, Nettie Henry, a freedwoman who held a decidedly low opinion of her own race, complained, "I don know how come things got so unnatchel after de Surrender. 'Niggers' got to doin' all kin' of things what de Lord didn' intend 'em for, lak bein' policemen an' all lak dat."[65] But these kinds of explanations of white domination do not prevail in slave testimony. Far more ex-slaves describe the power of whites over blacks without any elaboration of its causes, as an inescapable reality. "You want to know what they did in slavery times!" Alice Johnson exclaimed to an interviewer from the Arkansas WPA. "They were doin' jus' what they do now. The white folks was beatin' the niggers, burning 'em and boilin' 'em, workin' 'em and doin' any other thing they wanted to do with them."[66]

The virtually limitless power that African-Americans such as Alice Johnson saw in white people was of course very real, and very much in evidence, both during the slave era and after. In the antebellum South, as Thomas L. Webber emphasizes, enslaved blacks could not avoid being aware of the implications of white power. "Most slaves, if they had not experienced severe abuse themselves, had witnessed enough abuse of other blacks, both free and slave, to agree with [fugitive slave author Moses] Grandy: 'There is nothing which a white man may not do against a black one if only he takes care that no other white man can give evidence against him.'"[67] Moreover, the legal and disciplinary powers that Southern whites wielded over their slaves were only the beginning of their resources: from the perspective of many slaves, "white folks had ebery thing fine an' ebery thing dey wanted."[68] Yet, aside from the relatively few ex-slaves who understood the subjection of black people under white domination to be God's will, the freedpeople identified no special qualities or personal traits distinctive to the white race that would explain white people's privileged position or oppressive behavior.

Thus white people are an omnipresent and yet curiously shadowy presence in ex-slave testimony as a whole. Slavery, as Eugene Genovese suggests, may have tied black people to white "in an organic and complex relationship so complex that neither could express the simplest human feelings in reference to each other."[69] But in the testimony of the thousands of freedpeople who spoke to interviewers from the WPA, white people are described in relatively one-dimensional terms as authority figures who were either kindhearted and good to their slaves or "mean." In both African-American folklore and ex-slave testimony, white people are defined more by their powerful position vis-à-vis black people than by any distinctive set of personal characteristics.

Nineteenth-century African-American songs, folklore, and humor all acknowledge the power and privilege white people held under the American racial system. "Massa in the grate house countin' all his money. . . . Mistress in de parler eatin' bread and an' honey. . . . Oh, shuck dat co'nan trow't in de ba'n," the slaves sang while they shucked corn, contrasting the daily lives of their owners with their own labors.[70] And many of the other African-American work songs from both the slave era and long after likewise contrasted the status of whites and blacks. "White man goes to college / Nigger to the field," began a lyric that was widely sung by African-American laborers at the turn of the century, "White man learns to read and write / Poor Nigger learn to steal, Honey Babe." In comparing the lot of black people with that of whites, the black folk who sang these songs, as Levine notes, expressed "a deep feeling of injustice and enduring sense of being used unfairly."[71] This sentiment is perhaps most explicit in the various versions of an enduring rhyme black workers sang from the antebellum era to the Great Depression, first transcribed by William Wells Brown as follows:

> The bee flies high,
> The little bee makes honey;
> The black folks makes the cotton
> And the white folks gets the money.[72]

In such songs African-Americans both depicted and expressed their resentment toward white power and privilege. One song from the 1920s ran, "White man in a starched shirt settin' in the shade, / Laziest man that God ever made."[73] But the contrast between these words and those of many other black songs that simply described the advantages of whites over blacks without linking them to inborn white characteristics serves to illustrate how rare assertions about the racial character of white people were in black folk culture.

Similarly, in African-American jokes from the nineteenth and early twentieth centuries, white people typically appear as authority figures whose pretensions and hypocrisy are lampooned, rather than their racial temperament. According to Levine, much of nineteenth-century black humor created laughter by carrying American racial codes to "their logical and absurd conclusion." For instance, the often-told joke about a slave who, when it was discovered he had killed and eaten one of his master's pigs, said, "Yes, suh, Master, you got less pig now but you sho' got mo nigger," mocked white claims to ownership in human beings. This subversive humor challenged white authority by exposing the absurdities inherent in the American racial system. The many comic anecdotes blacks told about having to treat white animals with respect—"you say, Mr. Mule; don't you come callin' no white mule just another mule"—carried the implication that the color line whites held to be so important was ludicrous: color distinctions might just as well be applied to barnyard animals as to people.[74]

In short, if African-Americans assigned any set of racial personality traits to white people, it has remained largely unrecorded. Black folk culture challenged racial stereotypes rather than revising them. In recounting their life experiences, ex-slaves assigned no personal characteristics to white folks that they did not also see in themselves. Individual ex-slaves described whites as "greedy" or "lazy," but other individuals were equally likely to define blacks in the same way. To be sure, a theme of African-American superiority runs through black culture.[75] As we have seen, this theme is very much in evidence in nineteenth-century black work songs, which contrasted the labor of black workers with the indolence of white folks. Many African-Americans also took pride in the ability of lowly black slaves to outwit white folks, as the slave tales often reveal. However, such pride rarely led to claims that blacks were naturally stronger or smarter than whites.

Indeed, most slave tales offered a moral far more complex than black superiority. Trickster tales frequently featured weak animals outsmarting more powerful beasts; a plot also featured in the John tales, a set of stories in which a slave named John matches wits with his owner. Yet, as Lawrence Levine cautions, the slave tales should not be read as thinly veiled comparisons of the races. Tales about "the nature of the world and the beings who inhabited it," they had no single message: Sometimes the strong triumphed over the weak, and some tales called on the slaves "to empathize with the trickster as well as the tricked."[76]

Likewise, the freedpeople interviewed by the WPA did not insist that the slaves could consistently outwit their masters. Neither intellectual nor physical, the superiority that ex-slaves claimed over white people lay outside the brain and body. It was almost invariably moral and behavioral rather than innate.

Many WPA informants described whites as "mean," but even this white meanness was something the freedpeople described as a matter of power and privilege, rather than of white disposition. "I been whipped from sunup till sundown," the Arkansas freedwoman Sallie Crane stated. "They jus' whipped me 'cause they could—'cause they had the privilege." Likewise, another freedwoman explained that she thought the slaves "wuz whipped mostly cause de Marsters *could* whip 'em."[77] The son of a Louisiana freedwoman offered the same interpretation of why his white grandfather sold his mother. "The man who owned and sold my mother was her father. . . . And why? . . . The power—just because he had the power and the thirst for money."[78] Speaking of disenfranchisement, Mary Gaffney interpreted white behavior the same way: "I guess . . . the reason they do us like they do is because they can."[79] Surprisingly, for all her bitter hatred of whites, even Texas freedwoman Millie Manuel could come up with no other explanation for white cruelty. When asked "Why did they whip you?" she answered, "Jes 'cose they could, I guess."[80]

"All Kind of White Folks": White Power and White Character

Although black folk crafted no racial explanations for the power of white people, this power remained a force to be reckoned with. As children, some slaves were so impressed by white power and privilege that they assumed white people were divine. During his boyhood on a Louisiana plantation, Oklahoma freedman Charley Williams was convinced that God and his master were one and the same. He got the heavenly and earthly powers mixed up, Williams explained, because he "never heard much about [Jesus] until I was grown." What little doctrine he did hear led to the misunderstanding. "Nobody could read de Bible when I was a boy, and dey wasn't no white preachers who talked to de niggers. We had meeting sometimes, but de nigger preacher jest talk about being a good nigger and 'doing to please de Master,' and I allus thought he meant to please old Master, and I allus wanted to do dat anyways." Similarly, Arkansas freedman Charles Hinton testified that as a young boy he thought his white master was God until "he took sick and died."[81] Other ex-slaves remembered looking for white protection from the natural world—as if the white people controlled that too. One night when the stars appeared to fall from the heavens, Edward Taylor was confident that even falling stars posed no danger to anyone under white protection. "I thought in dem days white folks was God, didn't know no better," he said in his vivid description of that night.

> I 'member well when de stars fell, I saw 'em twixt midnight and day and tried to ketch some of 'em. I was grown, too, most. I wasn't scared 'cause I thought long as I staid where de white folks was, dey would protect me from all harm, even de stars in de elements, storms, or what not, just stay near de white folks and I had nothing to worry about. I thought white folks made de stars, sun and everything on earth. I knowed nothing but to be driven and beat all de time. . . . when de stars fell people all runin' and hollerin' judgment done come. I didn't see no need in all dat citement, as long as de white folks livin' I thought they could keep us niggers livin'.[82]

Such youthful overestimations of white power, however, tended to give way in the face of opposing evidence. Charles Williams learned more about Jesus eventually and saw his master die a broken man after losing his money and his health during the Civil War; while other slaves told Charles Hinton that, far from being God, his late master had "committed suicide because he had lost all his money."[83]

Only in combating the wiles of slave conjure did some freedpeople credit the white race with having special natural powers. White power frequently defied the wiles of slave magic, compromising the cultural authority of the powerful slave conjurers to whom the slaves turned for help in their struggles with individual whites. Magical roots and powders, Henry Bibb found out through hard trial and error, could not prevent his master's floggings. Armed with "conjuration" and confident that his master could not punish him "while I had this root and dust," Bibb left his master's plantation without permission one weekend and returned to confront his aggrieved owner. After Bibb "commenced talking saucy," his master soon disabused him of this conviction. "He became so enraged at me for saucing him, that he grasped a handful of switches and punished me severely, in spite of all my roots and powders." One more failed attempt at conjuring his white owners convinced Bibb that running away, rather than magic, "was the most effectual way by which a slave could escape cruel punishment."[84] Other African-Americans took a different lesson from failed attempts by conjurers to control the behavior of white people. "The funny thing" about slavery days' "congerations," Mississippi freedman Julius Jones recalled, was that "they could hoo-doo each other but they sure couldn't hoo-doo the white folks."[85] Likewise, another ex-slave testified, "They had in those days a Hoo-doo nigger who could hoodoo niggers, but couldn't hoodoo masters. He couldn't make ole master stop whipping him, with the hoodooism, but they could make Negroes crawl."[86] The slaves who doubted that conjure could affect their masters and mistresses appear to have assumed that white people had a natural and racially distinct immunity to the powers of black conjurers. When Hattie Matthews, a slave woman's granddaughter, asked her grandmother why the slaves "didn't hoodoo de white folks ta get dem out ob dey way. She said de negroes couldn't hoodoo de white peoples cause dey had strait hair. It wuz somethin' bout de oil in de hair. White people habe ta wash dere hair ta get de oil out, but negroes habe ta put oil in deir hair."[87]

As Levine cautions, however, such beliefs should not be "blown out of proportion as further evidence of the slaves' recognition of their ultimate impotence in the face of white authority." For not many slaves duplicated Bibb's experiments with the impact of conjure on whites, and, unlike Bibb, many slaves did in fact believe that whites were susceptible to the power of slave magic. Moreover, as Levine notes, "The slaves recognized different loci of power and dealt with them pragmatically as they had to, but there is no indication that they ranked these various sources of power in terms of the neat secular hierarchy that governs modern Western Man, with temporal power standing at its apex."[88] In the slaves' deeply religious worldview, there were many kinds of power, and whites did not control all of them.

Notably, neither the WPA testimony nor black folklore contains racial stereotypes about white people akin to the racial stereotypes about the character of the Negro that were so pervasive in antebellum white Southern literature and public culture. White Southerners described their slaves so frequently in terms of stereotypical personality traits that some historians have studied slave stereotypes such as "Sambo" (the good-natured and docile slave) and "Nat" (the rebellious troublemaker) for evidence on the black personality under slavery.[89] These stereotypes, which also included female images such as the devoted black "mammy" and the lascivious "Jezebel," allowed whites to think about black people in contradictory ways as both docile and dangerous, childlike and savage, sexless and seductive.[90] Like white ideas about color, the stereotypes about black people in white American racial thought reflected the dominant culture's need and ability to impose a multipurpose set of negative images on an exploited racial class, rather than the inevitable response of one racial group to another. These stereotypes have few parallels in the nineteenth-century black discussion of white people.

The shadowy racial character of white people in black folk thought is all the more striking because, like other Americans of their generation, the ex-slaves do appear to have assigned a distinctive racial character to Native Americans. With the exception of a small number of Oklahoma blacks whose former owners had been members of the Five Civilized Tribes, few of the freedpeople interviewed by the WPA discussed Native Americans at any length. American Indians were a diminishing and retreating population in the Southern states where the majority of these freedpeople spent their lives, and most ex-slaves may well have had little personal experience with Indians. But the Southern ex-slaves who did mention Native American peoples almost invariably spoke of them as a naturally fierce and independent race. In particular, the freedpeople often claimed that black people with Indian heritage were especially hot tempered and defiant because of their "Indian blood." "My mother never did whip me over twice and I would mind her," said one freedwoman. "I was 'fraid of her, and I always did what she told me. She was part Indian, you know."[91] Likewise, Rachael Goings described her half-Cherokee mother with a revealing turn of phrase: "She wuz always mad and had a mean look in her eye. When she got her Indian up de white folks let her alone."[92] One Virginia man explained that he was "proud, fearless, and full of the devil" because his mother was "part Red Indian which is one of the fiercest tribes of Indians that lived as you probably know."[93]

The character African-Americans assigned to blacks with Indian blood is similar to the character white Americans assigned to the Native American race as a whole. As Brian Dippie notes, in American popular culture Native Americans "were invariably described as ferociously independent and proud."[94] This racial stereotype appears to have crossed the color line, for in addition to attributing a fierce and independent character to people with Indian blood, ex-slaves extended this characterization to Indians themselves. Anna Baker, whose Indian grandfather successfully escaped slavery and "never been seen again," noted, "I is heared since den dat white folks larnt dat if dey start to whip an Injun dey had better kill him right den or else he might get dem."[95] Susan Hamlin was convinced that the racial character of Native Americans had saved them from the black race's fate. She explained early American race relations: "De white race is so brazen. Dey come here an' run de Indians frum dere own lan', but dey couldn't make dem slaves 'cause dey wouldn't stan' for it. Indians use to git up in trees an' shoot dem with poison arrow. W'en dey couln't make dem slaves den dey gone to Africa an' bring dere black brother an' sister."[96]

In characterizing American Indians as a naturally fierce people, the ex-slaves spoke of this group quite differently than they did of whites: no comparable racial stereotypes about white character emerge in black folk thought.[97] Moreover, despite the substantial admixture of white blood among the slave population, surprisingly few slaves attributed any personal characteristics possessed by individuals of mixed black and white ancestry to the influence of white blood. Moreover, it is difficult to draw any general conclusions from such rare comments about white blood as can be found in the WPA testimony, for the white characteristics named by the handful of slaves who did mention white blood differed in each account. For example, Jim Henry, who had "three bloods in my veins, white folks, Indian folks, and Negro folks," believed his racial ancestry made him "thrifty like de white man, crafty like de Indians, and hard-workin' like de Negroes." But, Dora Franks's white blood made her thoughtful rather than thrifty. "I is sorter restless most of de time and has to keep busy to keep from thinkin' too much," she reflected. "I guess dat is because of de white blood I has in me."[98]

The difference between the way freedpeople spoke of Indians and the way they spoke of whites is difficult to explain. The rarity with which ex-slaves attributed any personal characteristics to the influence of white blood may be partly accounted for by a certain reticence among mixed-race individuals when it came to speaking of their white ancestry. On the basis of his quantitative analysis of the WPA interviews, Stephen Crawford suggests that "the ex-slaves seemed to have been reluctant to claim white parentage to white interviewers and especially reluctant to report that their master was their father."[99] Ex-slave reticence on the subject of white parents, however, was clearly not the only reason that these African-Americans did not read personal characteristics into their white ancestry. Even ex-slaves who spoke frankly to black interviewers about their white ancestry did not invoke any such characteristics, and specifically white personal characteristics are not defined elsewhere in slave testimony.

Another reason that ex-slaves subscribed to common American stereotypes about Indians but did not develop such well-defined stereotypes about whites may well have to do with proximity. Since many African-Americans had little contact with Native Americans, they took much of their information about this "vanishing people" from white stereotypes about the Indian. Reconfiguring these stereotypes to suit their own needs, ex-slaves associated Indians and Indian blood with "cherished traits of rebelliousness, ferocity and fortitude" —imagining an Indian well suited to the psychological needs of an enslaved people. The ephemeral quality of most slave assessments of the Indians is borne out by the fact that the one place where ex-slave stereotypes about Indians break down is *The WPA Oklahoma Slave Narratives*. WPA informants in Oklahoma had far more knowledge of actual Indians than did most other ex-slaves, for many belonged to slaveholding Indian families relocated there in the 1830s when the federal government expelled the Cherokees, Creeks, Chickasaws, and Chocktaws from their traditional homes in the Southwest. Products of a world where power was red as well as white, Oklahoma ex-slaves expressed little admiration for Indian ferocity. Instead, they debated the merits of Indian versus white slaveholders, with many concluding that Indian masters were preferable. Such assessments were based on personal experience rather than racial stereotypes. For instance, the good treatment that she received made Polly Colbert suspect that her Indian masters were "naturally kinder," but she also reckoned that "it was on account of de [Indians'] rich land dat us niggers dat was owned by Indians didn't have to work so hard as dey did in de old states."[100]

Like Indian slaveowners, whites as a group defied stereotypes. Outside of Oklahoma, African-Americans encountered white people on very different terms than they did Native Americans: terms that defined the character of their discourse about white people. Proximity and power shaped black Southerners' relationships with whites in ways that discouraged the former from making loose generalizations about white people or discussing whites in terms of a set of racial stereotypes. Rather than reducing white people to stereotypes, enslaved African-Americans had every incentive to take a very pragmatic interest in the individual characteristics of the white people with whom they interacted. As a subordinate group, African-Americans needed to be able to read white behavior accurately and well to survive in a white-dominated world.

Accordingly, one point that many WPA informants stressed was that the personalities of individual white people defied simple generalizations. In discussing the varying behavior of white Southerners toward black people both before and after emancipation, many informants emphasized that whites were not all alike. In doing so, they revealed that the immense power of white people over blacks in the worldly context of the American South significantly shaped the parameters of black folk thought about whites. For one thing, although blacks were set apart from whites in so many ways, their unequal power required them to be keen students of white behavior. In particular, they had to be able to recognize the differing characters of individual whites. One of the first things Olaudah Equiano realized about white people after surviving his passage to the New World was that they were not all alike. After being purchased from his Virginia owner by an English naval lieutenant who took him aboard his ship, Equiano found his "condition much mended; I had sails to lie on and plenty of good victuals to eat; and everybody aboard treated me very kindly, quite contrary to what I had seen of white people before; I therefore began to think that they were not all of the same disposition."[101]

American-born slaves grew up well aware of this fact. As Thomas Webber writes:

> To counteract white power, blacks became students of white mood and personality. They learned to be sensitive to the nuances of white behavior: to detect shifting moods, to anticipate anger, to play on fear, and to sense by a word or expression the fine line between what would be tolerated and what would be punished. Blacks learned that the proper stance to assume when dealing with any individual white differed not only from personality to personality but from mood to mood and circumstance to circumstance.

Accordingly, one ex-slave reported that during his slave years he trained himself "to watch the changes in my master's physiognomy, as well as those of the parties he associated with, so as to frame my conduct in accordance with what I had reason to believe was their prevailing mood at the time."[102]

Under slavery, Isaac Green noted, "Yo' actual treatment depended on de kind o' marster you had."[103] Ample evidence for Green's assertion is found in slave testimony, which records a variety of slaveholder behavior toward slaves, ranging from sadistic to loving. Slave testimony also reveals that enslaved African-Americans were highly aware of these variations. Ex-slaves who spoke to interviewers from the WPA often placed their own experience, good or bad, within the context of the range of possible experiences. "I don't know much about the meanness of slavery," one noted. "There was so many degrees in slavery, and I belonged to a very nice man."[104] Freedwoman Dora Richard could not say the same, but she also emphasized that there was nothing uniform about the African-American experience at the hands of white people under slavery: "Here's the way I want to tell you. Some of the white people are as good to the colored people as they could be and some of em are mean. My own folks do so bad I'm ashamed of em."[105]

A similar awareness of the variability of white behavior can be seen even in the testimony of ex-slaves who recalled their ex-owners with nostalgia and extravagant affection. Such ex-slaves, whose testimony, as Eugene Genovese notes, "taken at face value" might appear to endorse "the moonlight light-and-magnolias interpretation of slavery," gave witness disproportionately in the WPA interviews collected in states such as South Carolina, where rules of caste etiquette between the informants and the all-white interviewing staff led to particularly rosy reports.[106] However, these contented slaves often reserved their nostalgia for their former masters and recalled horrible owners on other plantations.[107] For instance, "Aunt" Charlotte Foster, asked if she would rather live now or in the old days, said she would gladly be a slave again to her former master. But she also spoke of beatings on a neighboring plantation and said flatly that white people beat their slaves "just because they wanted to beat 'em; they could do it, and they did."[108] Thus even ex-slaves who experienced (or claimed to have experienced) only kindness from white people under slavery often revealed that even well-treated slaves were entirely aware that not all white people were kind.

The freedpeople's observations about the mixed character of whites applied to their behavior after emancipation as well. Indeed, several ex-slaves observed that the varying behavior of whites during slavery was identical to that of contemporary whites. "Dey was all kinds of white folks just like dey is now," said 105-year-old Oklahoma freedman Anthony Dawson, who had been a slave in North Carolina:

> One man in Secesh [Confederate] clothes would shoot you if you tried to run away. Maybe another Secesh would help slip you out to the underground and say "God bless you poor black devil" and some of dem dat was poor would help you if you could bring 'em sumpin you stole, lak a silver dish, or spoons or a couple big hams. . . . But now and then they was a devil on earth, walking in the sight of God and spreading iniquity before him. He was de low-down Secesh dat would take what a poor runaway nigger had to give for his chance to git away, and den give him 'structions dat would lead him right into de hands of de patrollers and git him caught or shot!
>
> Yes dat's de way it was. Devils and good people walking in de road at de same time, and nobody could tell one from t'other.[109]

Other ex-slaves made the same point in less vivid detail. Charlie Bowen recalled telling a fellow ex-slave who maintained that some white people should pay for how they used to treat the slaves, "Folks is no different today than in slavery time. Some of them is good and some of them is bad."[110] "All the white folks warn't alike," said Hannah Jameson. "There was good and bad like today."[111] Arkansas freedman James Gill made a similar observation: "It was den, boss, just same wid white men as 'tis in dis day and time. Dere is a heap of good white folks now and dere is a heap of dem what ain't so good."[112]

Ex-slave Anthony Dawson in Tulsa, summer 1937 (Library of Congress).

Other African-Americans of the slavery generation emphasized the dissimilar character of individual whites as a feature of white racial character that, while not always apparent, must be understood. "I have heard a heap of colored people say that all white folks was just alike," explained one man. "That ain't so, 'cause there is some white folks will treat you right, and some will take everything away from you. They ain't all just alike."[113] For ex-slave Jordon Smith, the realization that all whites were not alike was a difficult one due to the hard experiences he had as a slave in Georgia and Texas. "I heared some slaves say they white folks was good to 'em, but it was a tight fight where us was," Stone recalled. "I's thought over the case a thousand times and figured it was 'cause all men ain't made alike. Some are bad and some are good. It's like that now. Some folks you works for got no heart and some treat you white. I guess it allus will be that way."[114]

Even individuals whose experiences had left them with the bitterest feeling toward the white race were curiously unwilling to tar all white people with same brush. A Fisk informant who was fathered by his white master, whom he called a "God damn son-of-a bitch," wanted to see where his father's grave was so he could spit on it. He also said that if he had his way with all white people, "I would like to have . . . a chopping block and chop every one of their heads off." As bloodthirsty as he was, however, he added this caveat: "Of course I don't hate them that is good. There are some good white folks. Mighty few, though."[115]

Slaves could not afford to obscure the differences among individual whites by thinking of them in terms of simple stereotypes, nor did they have the cultural power to impose stereotypical images on white people. Instead, their careful observation of white people taught them that white people were not all alike. It also made some black folk aware that whites were not unlike blacks in this regard. "I say I don't put all white folks in one sack," Steve Douglas cautioned. "God made lots of good white men, same as the nigger. He made lots of good niggers —but you can't put all of them in one sack."[116]

In recognizing that white people were as varied in individual character as black people, Steve Douglas and other African-Americans of his generation may well have put distinct limits on the racialism of their thought. For their emphasis on the mixture of good and bad individuals in the white race was quite unlike the racial stereotypes white Americans imposed on black people—which served to distance whites from individual blacks through negative imagery that divided the racial character of all blacks into a few superficial personality types. By refusing to "put all white folks in one sack," these African-Americans questioned whether race was a reliable measure of a person's character. Cal Woods put the matter explicitly, stating, "It is lack it is now, some folks good no matter what dey color, other folks bad."[117]

Ex-slaves found this message in Christian universalism, as well as in their day-to-day interactions with individual whites. For when African-Americans resisted slavery and racial discrimination as an injustice to black humanity and claimed "us is human flesh," they asserted their fundamental kinship with white people. And this sense of kinship is evident in the words of African-Americans who believed that the races shared the same fundamental moral character. Anthony Dawson, for instance, proclaimed, "There's a difference in the color of the skin, but the souls is all white, or all black, 'pending on man's life and not on his skin."[118] In a similar spirit, the magnanimous Fanny Johnson recalled that life under slavery was pretty "awful" and then went on: "But I don't hold no grudge against anybody. White or black, there's good folks in all kinds. . . . the good Lord knows what he is about."[119] Dawson and Johnson expressed the same conviction that W.E.B. DuBois found to pervade black spirituals. As DuBois wrote in *The Souls of Black Folk*:

Through all the sorrow of the Sorrow Songs there breathes a hope—a faith in the ultimate justice of things. The minor cadences of despair often change to triumph and calm confidence. Sometimes it is faith in life, sometimes a faith in death, sometimes assurance of boundless justice in some fair world beyond. But, whichever it is, the meaning is always clear: that sometime, somewhere, men will judge men by their souls and not their skins.[120]

The Color of Heaven

"I never saw a negro Universalist," wrote Emily Burke, a white observer, commenting on slave life in Georgia. "They all believe in the future retribution for their masters, from the hand of a just God."[121] Burke's observation was acute: for it was religion, rather than racial ideology, that African-Americans ultimately turned to for judgment on white people. By the late antebellum period, Christianity pervaded the American slave community. Moreover, it provided the interpretive framework through which African-Americans understood their lives and the peculiar world of slavery. As we have seen, religion helped the slaves understand the potential for good and bad in white individuals and to see the races as kin. Similarly, the religion of the slaves informed their attempts to come to terms with white power and cruelty. Rather than passing their own earthly judgments on the white race, African-Americans looked to the Lord to pass judgment on white people in the next world.

No one religious interpretation of the unequal status of the races emerges in ex-slave testimony, but there is a great deal of discussion about the status of the races in the next life. The slaves and their masters shared a Protestant religious faith that promised them that death would bring an end to the earthly distinctions that divided the living. The commingling of the races in the hereafter, however, was a prospect that troubled both blacks and whites. Although their Bible told them that all souls would meet as equals in heaven, masters and slaves alike found such an afterlife hard to imagine. Both wondered how the races would be divided after death.

Evangelical slaveholders feared death "as the moment when all earthly distinctions vanished, when the inequities that slaveholders perpetrated throughout life were scrutinized and judged."[122] Less pious Southern whites, however, were clearly not convinced that death would mitigate racial distinctions. A British actress named Fanny Kemble, who lived on a Georgia plantation during her brief marriage to a Southerner, was startled to overhear a white chambermaid question a slave's suggestion that bondage might be limited to "this world." The chambermaid clearly believed that even death would not alter the slaves' servitude, and that their lowly status would bar them from entering heaven. "I am afraid," Kemble commented sarcastically in her journal, "this woman actually imagines there will be no slaves in heaven; isn't that preposterous, now, when, by the account of most southerners, slavery itself must be heaven, or something uncommonly like it."[123]

Kemble's white servant was by no means alone in her conviction that heaven would be open to whites only. A surprising number of slaves heard the same thing from their white owners. Ex-slave Jennie Proctor was warned, "Nigger obey your marster and your mistress 'cause what you git from dem here in dis world am all you ev'r goin' to git, 'cause you jes' like de hogs and de other animals, when you dies you aint no more."[124] Likewise, "Uncle" George G. King was told that Negroes did not need religion because "there wasn't a Heaven for Negroes anyhow." Other slaves reported that they "were not told about heaven."[125]

Rather than excluding slaves from heaven altogether, some Southern whites promised their slaves a separate heaven of their own. Harriet Barrett's master made his slaves "go to church every Sunday and he taught us to always tell de truth, then the Saviour he save us. He said we would go to negro heaven."[126] Another slave heard the same message from a white preacher who enjoined the slaves "to always tell the truth and not to hurt our own race, if we was going to negro heaven." This Negro heaven, according to the religious instruction ex-slave Frank Robinson received was adjacent to but strictly segregated from the heaven where the slaves' owners would go. His minister told him:

> You slaves will go to heaven, but don't ever think that you will be close to your master and mistress. No! No! There will be a wall between you; but there will be holes in it that will permit you to look out and see your mistress as she passes by.[127]

Not all Southern whites, however, were content to envision blacks in a separate heaven of their own, adjacent or otherwise. There were also white Southerners who were unwilling to part with their slaves even after death. "De white folks what owned slaves," said Tennessee freedman Andrew Moss, "thought that when dey go to Heaven de colored folks would be dar to wait on em."[128] This hope was cherished by a slave mistress who told Eliza Washington, "I would give anything if I could have Maria in heaven with me to do little things for me."[129] Envisioning a heaven where they could continue to enjoy the services of their slaves, such whites sometimes promised the slaves a place in heaven's kitchen. Washington further reported that "Reverend Winfield used to preach to the colored people that if they be good niggers and not steal their master's eggs and things that they might go to the kitchen of heaven when they died." Likewise, Jack Jones testified "that the white preacher enjoined the Negro to be obedient to their masters and make good slaves. As a result they would go to Negro heaven, or kitchen heaven when they died." On hearing this generous promise, Jones's Uncle Sack laughed and said that at least the slaves "would get plenty to eat" in kitchen heaven—a prospect that clearly struck some Southern whites as the only heavenly reward to which African-Americans aspired.[130]

This vision of a servile heaven occasionally even crossed the color line, as can be seen in the testimony of one ex-slave who proclaimed himself willing to serve his master in heaven. Interviewed at the age of ninety-four, freedman Charley Williams lived in a ramshackle house in Tulsa, Oklahoma. Living in poverty, with "rain trickling through de holes in de roof" above him and "planks all fell out'n de flo' on de gallery," Williams was nostalgic about his slave childhood in Louisiana and Arkansas and had especially fond memories of his late master, who had always been kind to him. Confident of his salvation and ready to meet his maker, Williams was anxious to be reunited with his old master. Willing to resume his duties as a slave in return for his owner's renewed support and protection, Williams envisioned a plantation heaven:

When he saw his master in heaven, Williams said: "I reckon maybe I'll jest go up and ask what he want me to do, and he'll tell me, and iffen I don't know how he'll sho me how, and I'll try to do it to please him. And when I get done I wants to hear him grumble like he used to and say, 'Charley, you ain't got no sense but you is a good boy. . . . Git yourself a little piece o' dat brown sugar, but don't let no niggers see you eating it—if you do I'll whup your black behind!' For all his fantasies, however, Williams suspected that heaven would be nothing like earth. He concluded his reverie by saying, "Dat ain't de way it going be in Heaven, I reckon, but I can't set here on dis old rottendy gallery and think of no way I better like to have it!"[131]

Williams's vision of a plantation heaven was not widely shared among his fellow slaves, however. To the contrary, most slaves cherished the idea of achieving freedom in the next world. On one plantation the older slaves led the rest of the slave community in praying "that God don't think no different of the blacks and the whites"; while on another, Beverly Jones's Uncle Silas interrupted the white preacher's sermon to ask "Is God gonna free us slaves when we git to heaven?"[132] The slaves also commemorated their hopes of achieving freedom in the next world in a wide variety of songs, one of which proclaimed: "Masse sleeps in de feathah bed, / Nigger sleeps on de flooah / Whin we'ns all git to Heaven / Dey'll be no slaves no mo'."[133]

The prospect of encountering their former owners in the hereafter, moreover, was not always welcomed by ex-slaves. "I'se done got ready to see God when I'se die," declared elderly freedman Ben Simpson. "But boss, I hopes my old master is not up there to torment this old negro again."[134] Another man said of his white folks, "I was settin' here thinking the other night 'bout the talk of them kind of white folks going to Heaven. Lord God, they'd turn the Heaven wrong side out and have the angels working to make something they could take away from them."[135]

Such concerns, along with the emphasis on heaven in much of black religious worship, made the fate of the races in the hereafter an even greater preoccupation among Southern blacks than it was among their white counterparts. "Jordan's stream is wide and deep," African-American slaves sang as they worked, mulling over this question all the while. "Jesus stand on t'oder side. . . . I wonder if my maussa deh."[136] Not surprisingly, African-Americans' visions of heaven were ultimately quite different from those of their white contemporaries. In their religious worship, slavery-generation African-Americans invariably emphasized that they were children of God who possessed human souls. As such, they expected to receive the recognition denied them in this world in the next. Moreover, they hoped and prayed to encounter whites only on very different terms in the afterlife.

Some slaves hoped to leave white people behind altogether once they had attained salvation. "No white people went to Heaven," wrote a correspondent to the *Southern Workman* in 1897, describing the religious beliefs of his fellow slaves. "Many believe the same until this day."[137] Such ideas were echoed by Millie Manuel, the fiery Texas freedwoman who was convinced that "the Good Shepherd will give the best white man a heaben that is hotter than the worstest nigger's hell."[138] And fugitive slave Charles Ball likewise maintained that the enslaved African-Americans abhorred the idea of an eternity spent in "a state of perfect equality, and boundless affection, with the white people." Heaven would be no heaven to the slaves, Ball insisted, if their enemies went unavenged. "The idea of a revolution in the condition of the whites and the blacks," Ball wrote, "is the cornerstone of the religion of the latter." According to Ball, in the slaves' Negro heaven few whites would be admitted. "As a matter of favor," the slaves might occasionally open up the pearly gates to masters and mistresses who had been particularly kind and good, but even these favored white souls would, "by no means, be of equal rank with those who shall be raised from the depths of misery, in this world."[139] Emily Burke recorded that slaves in Georgia looked forward to an even more dramatic reversal of fortune: "They believe, and I have myself heard them assert the same, that in the life to come there will also be white and black people. But the white people will be slaves, and *they* shall have dominion over them!"[140]

Burke may have embellished the beliefs she recorded, for there is little other evidence to suggest that African-Americans foresaw any kind of slavery in the life to come.[141] But many of them certainly hoped for a dramatic reversal of the status of blacks and whites in the afterlife. "When the white folks would die," one ex-slave told an interviewer from Fisk, "the slaves would all stand around and 'tend like they was crying, but after that they would get outside and say, 'They are all going to hell like a damn barrel full of nails.'" Moreover, ex-slaves continued to express such sentiments long after slavery. Oklahoma freedman Robert Burns said, "Now, dat slavery is over I wish and hope dat God would treat all dem slave owners as dey did us when dey get in hell."[142] Indeed, the confidence and pleasure many ex-slaves expressed at the thought of certain whites burning in hell are among the strongest emotions about white people expressed in all ex-slave testimony.

"My Marster was mean an' cruel an' I hates him, hates him," said Mississippi freedman Charles Moss. "The God Almighty has condemned him to eternal fiah', of that I is certain."[143] Mary Reynolds spoke with similar venom about her former overseer: "I know that Solomon is burnin' in hell today and it pleasures me to know it."[144] Ellen Rogers, who was over one hundred years old when she was interviewed, also contemplated with relish the fate of whites she had known. "I hears voices from Hebben ev'ry day," she stated. "Some of dem voices say, 'Ol' man Austin he bu'nin' (burning) in hell right now cause he was so mean to he niggers.' Den dey say, 'Ol' Mistus Austin she in hell dis minnit cause she was mean to de niggers.'"[145]

Other slavery-generation African-Americans did not condemn particular whites but clearly enjoyed anticipating how the unsuspecting whites would fare under a just God. "Oh, heaven, heaven," ran the lines of one slave work song. "Everybody talking 'bout heaven ain't going there."[146] This point was elaborated with great eloquence by freedwoman Maria Bracey. "Hebben?" she replied, when asked about the afterlife. "De tree ob life in Hebben, an' honey an' milk for eat. Dey no houses, dere be no rain an' cold dere. Dey be no black an' w'ite; we be all alike den, an' hab wings an' play de harp. De fine w'ite folks ob Charleston gonna be surprise', w'en dey miss an' go down dere, where de black an' w'ite folks burn togedder."[147]

In addition to anticipating the eternal damnation of particularly cruel whites, ex-slaves expressed confidence that all whites would ultimately have to account for the sins of their race. White Southerners, one freedwoman observed, "can't beat up us people and jump up on a bed and close their eyes and die and expect to go to heaven."[148] The slaveowners, some of the ex-slaves suggested, had brought down a judgment against their whole race that would not soon end. "Don't ya kno' God gwine keep er punishin' white folks," predicted the Reverend Ishrael Massie. "Keep er sendin' dem floods, win' storms an' lettin' 'asters [disasters] come to deir chillun an' deir chillun's chillun in dis day an' time."[149]

For most ex-slaves, however, "Negro heaven" was not ultimately a segregated place. The serene confidence in the ultimate justice of

God that so impressed W.E.B. DuBois in African-American spirituals reflected a certainty that in heaven people will be received according to the judgment of their souls rather than their skins, white or black. For instance, even though he claimed that slave religion foresaw a complete revolution in the condition of blacks and whites, Charles Ball allowed that at least some good whites would be admitted to heaven. And the possibility of white salvation was one that many slaves did not seem to rule out altogether. Mary Reynolds, who had terrible experiences in slavery, nonetheless did not think all whites would burn; "they was good white folks that I heard tell of," although "they is plenty mo' of them in hell too" was her conclusion.[150] Freedpeople who spoke about their former owners in highly favorable terms expressed more confidence on this point: they often said that they expected to see their white folks again in heaven. Anticipating the Lord's judgment on her former owners with some precision, Texas freedwoman Penny Thompson predicted that her kindhearted master would be in heaven "fo' sho! But de Missy mus' be in hell fo' she sho was a devil."[151]

III

✍ ✍

NEW NEGROES, NEW WHITES

Black Racial Thought in the Twentieth Century

> If God is white,
>   Why should I pray?
> If I called him,
>   He'd turn away.
>
> T. Thomas Fortune Fletcher,
> "White God" (1927)[1]

SIX

☙

"A New Negro for a New Century"

Black Racial Ideology, 1900–1925

The early decades of this century ushered in the slow demise of scientific racism in the American academy. Led by a German-born anthropologist named Franz Boas, turn-of-the-century scientists investigated the biological basis of race for the first time, initiating an inquiry that ultimately led to the conclusion that culture and environment— rather than racial characteristics—were the main arbiters of human differences. This scientific revolution did not take place overnight. Boas's arguments against the innate inferiority of black people did not achieve a large following even among his peers until after 1910. Moreover, liberal environmentalism's ultimate triumph over nineteenth-century racial determinism would not be decisive until after World War II. Only in the late 1940s and the 1950s, in the wake of a war that pitted American democracy against Nazi fascism and racism, would the social science community finally prove ready to embrace the new racial liberalism presented in *An American Dilemma* (1944), the landmark study by Swedish economist Gunnar Myrdal.[1]

This scientific revolution was less revolutionary among black thinkers, who had long attributed most racial differences to culture and environment. "Negro writings from around the turn of the century," wrote Myrdal, commenting on this black environmentalist tradition, "sound so much more modern than white writings":

> The Negro writers constantly have proceeded on the assumption, later formulated by DuBois in *Black Reconstruction*: " . . . that the Negro in America and in general is an average and ordinary human being, who in a given environment develops like other human beings. . . ." This assumption is now, but was not a couple of decades ago, also the assumption of white writers."[2]

Yet the early twentieth-century upheaval in American racial thought embraced black as well as white thinkers. Early fans of Boas, whose ideas converged with the environmentalist tradition in black thought, African-Americans thinkers were among the first to embrace and publicize Boas's work. In so doing, many of these thinkers had to reconsider some of their own ideas, including the very concept of ethnology—for if there were no meaningful scientific distinctions between the races, as Boas argued, there could be no science of the races. Moreover, among blacks, shifts in the scientific understanding of race both coincided with and contributed to important changes in African-American racial thought taking place outside of the academy in the same period.

During the first quarter of the twentieth century, African-American ideas about race were profoundly shaken up by black disillusionment over the worsening race relations that followed World War I. This dislocation was compounded by the forces of black migration and European immigration, which reconfigured the nation's demography and democracy. Of all Americans, African-Americans had the most at stake in what W.E.B. DuBois foresaw in 1903 as "the problem of the twentieth century": the problem of the color line.[3] And during the first quarter of the century, this color line was the most pressing problem they faced.

The turn of the century has been justly called the nadir of American race relations. By the 1890s the North had abandoned black Americans to discrimination, disfranchisement, and "cast-iron" segregation in the New South.[4] With racial violence and racist invective against the Negro scaling new heights throughout the nation, the black future in America looked grimmer than it had since the end of slavery. As black historian Rayford Logan, who lived through these years, wrote, "The superstructure of the Terminal [which African-Americans reached] at the end of the Road to Reunion, was massive and apparently indestructible. It was also ugly. On the pediments of the separate wing reserved for Negroes were carved Exploitation, Disenfranchisement, Segregation, Discrimination, Lynching, Contempt."[5]

Yet this terminal, as Logan also noted, would not prove as sturdy as it looked. It began to crumble even as it was being completed during the first twenty-five years of the twentieth century, when racism began to lose the authority of science and African-Americans began to organize themselves for the long, hard struggle that would ultimately lead to the civil rights movement. These years also saw the end of an era in black racial thought. By 1925 black intellectuals had largely abandoned the nineteenth-century science of the races—ethnology—for social science. And in the larger black community, a generation of "new Negroes" who were products of segregation, but not of slavery, began to confront the white world with an overt racial hostility rarely seen in the nineteenth century.

Thus, just as ideas about race underwent profound transformations in American science during the early years of this century, racial ideology entered a period of flux in the black community between 1900 and 1925. Although Boasian arguments for racial equality were welcomed by many black intellectuals, African-American thinkers such as W.E.B. DuBois and Kelly Miller had to reformulate their ideas about race to accommodate Boas's attacks on the scientific significance of race. Meanwhile, the early decades of the twentieth century also saw the emergence of a variety of cultural revitalization movements in the black community, which embraced rather than repudiated the organic metaphor of race. These movements included Marcus Garvey's Universal Improvement Association (UNIA), along with a number of other separatist sects that emerged in the 1920s, such as the Moorish Science Temple Muslim sect. Although very different, both the Garvey movement and the various sects all celebrated black America's African heritage and glorious racial destiny. Ironically, then, just as the white scientific establishment was finally beginning to dismantle the racial edifice built by nineteenth-century science, racial essentialism was achieving unprecedented popularity in some quarters of the American black community.

The black community, unlike the white scientific community, emerged with no broadly accepted new paradigm on race as black racial thought entered the twentieth century. Although the environmental theory of racial development that ultimately emerged in the American social sciences was welcomed with great enthusiasm by black intellectuals, older ideas about race died hard among some black thinkers. Indeed, messianic black nationalism flourished as never before in the Garvey movement and the new black sects that sprang up during the 1920s. These groups popularized a religious racialism that had a widespread appeal in the black community—particularly among the newly urban black populations of many Northern cities. Such contradictory developments complicated African-American ideas about race in general, and white people in particular, as the black community entered the new century.

The End of Black Ethnology

As the twentieth century opened, the racialism that colored much of nineteenth-century black writing on race was at its height. At the inaugural meeting of the first major black learned society, the American Negro Academy, which took place in 1897, W.E.B. DuBois presented a speech entitled "The Conservation of Races." Describing race as "the central thought of all history," he defined the races as vast families "of human beings, generally of common blood and language, always of common history, tradition and impulses." American black people, he maintained, must cultivate their racial gifts in order to deliver "the full complete Negro message of the whole Negro race" to the world. DuBois embraced race as an organic distinction between human beings in order to call for the cultural uplift of the black race, which he conceded from "the dawn of creation has slept, but half awakening in the dark forests of its African fatherland." He predicted, "We are the first fruits of the new nation, the harbinger of that black tomorrow which is yet destined to soften the Teutonic whiteness of today."[6]

The romantic racialism that runs through DuBois's speech, along with his characterization of blacks as an "unawakened" race that had yet to find its own destiny, illustrate the profound impact of social Darwinism on the racial thought of DuBois and other turn-of-the-century black intellectuals. An interpretation of evolution formulated by Herbert Spencer, one of Darwin's countrymen and contemporaries, social Darwinism assumed that the status quo in human society evolved out of the same evolutionary struggle that shaped the species: the survival of the fittest. Social Darwinism lent itself readily to a variety of racist interpretations and in the hands of white writers was invariably employed to arrange the races in a racial hierarchy that placed black people on the bottom as perennial losers in the evolutionary struggle. As the black educator William H. Crogman complained, white social Darwinists "persist in holding us up to this country as that abnormal baby which never grows, which never can grow, and which American people must nurse for all time."[7] Despite such racist usages, social Darwinism appealed to black thinkers because, unlike polygenesis, it did not bar blacks from the human family; and although it placed blacks on the bottom of the evolutionary scale, it did not rule out the possibility that they might ultimately rise to a higher rank.

A malleable theory, social Darwinism appealed to a number of constituencies in the black community. Black intellectuals such as Alexander Crummell and W.E.B. DuBois embraced it as a social theory of black uplift that promised the racial redemption of the uneducated black freedmen and freedwomen who formed the majority of the black population. Crummell, who founded the American Negro Academy, shared DuBois's turn-of-the-century conviction that black Americans must pursue a racial destiny. He hoped that the academy would "provide leaders who could convince the freedmen of their unique destiny as a people and their moral superiority to whites."[8] At the same time, social Darwinism also appealed to black leaders who held out less hope for racial renaissance than Crummell and DuBois. An implicit social Darwinism is readily identifiable in the doctrine of industrial education preached by Booker T. Washington, who sought to provide black laborers with the skills and discipline needed to compete more successfully in the Darwinian struggle.

Moreover, social Darwinism had important implications for black women as well. As popularly understood during the nadir, evolutionary theory assigned women a more clearly defined role in racial uplift than had previous theories of racial difference such as polygenesis. If the races advanced by a process of sexual selection, as Darwin had

W.E.B. DuBois (courtesy of the Photographs and Prints Division, Schomburg Center for Research in Black Culture, The New York Public Library, Astor, Lenox, and Tilden Foundations).

argued, then women could make or break a race.[9] With this theory in mind, some late nineteenth-century commentators insisted that the depravity of black woman was the root cause of the failings of her race. "It is her hand that rocks the cradle in which the little pickaninny sleeps," wrote Eleanor Tayleur in an *Outlook Magazine* article on the "social and moral decadence" of black women. No longer required to perform the "honest work" they had performed during slavery, and no longer under the uplifting influence of white women, Taylor argued, black women had degenerated since emancipation. The "Frankenstein monster of civilization," black women had become "a great dark, helpless, hopeless mass . . . leading lawless and purposeless lives in the cane and cotton fields."[10] Similar sentiments were also expressed by William Hannibal Thomas, perhaps the only African-American writer of the nadir to adopt the antiblack hostility of that period. In *The American Negro*, a book-length diatribe on the degeneracy of African-Americans, Thomas predicted that black women might well kill off the race. Lascivious at a young age, and prone to aborting their own children, "American negro women are likely to become as infertile as the Greek courtesan, and it is needless to say that the people of any race is doomed to extinction when the women cease to become mothers."[11]

In turn, black women countered such racist invective by insisting that the defense and improvement of African-American womanhood were essential to racial uplift. Women were a vital element in the "regeneration and progress of a race," Anna Julia Cooper wrote in *A Voice from the South*, making the evolutionary importance of black women into an argument for "the protection and elevation of our girls." "Every attempt to elevate the Negro," she predicted, "whether undertaken by himself or through the philanthropy of others, cannot but prove abortive unless so directed as to utilize the indispensable agency of an elevated and trained womanhood."[12]

Other black women evidently agreed with Cooper. The turn of the century saw a new level of activism among black women, who organized to the National Association of Colored Women to defend themselves and their race against "unjust and unholy charges."[13] One black activist of that period, journalist and novelist Pauline E. Hopkins, even undertook an ethnological defense of black people. A review of the origins and history of the races, her *Primer of Facts Pertaining to the Early Greatness of the African Race and the Possibility of Restoration by its Descendants . . . Compiled and Arranged from the Works of the best known Ethnologists and Historians*, rehearsed arguments long traditional to black ethnology. The races descended from the same parent stock, she argued, and owed their distinctive complexions to the different environments that had nurtured their biblical ancestors, Ham, Shem, and Japhet. The first work of ethnology by a black woman, most of Hopkins's *Primer* was similar to ethnological works written by her male counterparts. Interestingly, however, it broke from the all-male world of black ethnology by closing with a lengthy attack on the political writings of a white Southern woman named Mrs. Jeanette Robinson Murphy, who bemoaned the end of slavery and described the abolitionists as "emissaries of Satan."[14]

The 1920s would see the publication of another female-authored work of black ethnology: Druscilla Dunjee Houston's *The Wonderful Ethiopians of the Cushite Empire* (1926).[15] For the most part, however, twentieth-century black women had little incentive to take up ethnology. During the years that elapsed between the publication of Hopkins's *Primer* and Houston's book, black ethnology became outmoded. Its traditional themes were gradually replaced by new evolutionary discourses on race, which discussed racial differences as a matter of heredity, selection, and evolution, rather than of scriptural history. A handful of African-American thinkers continued to publish scriptural defenses of the origins and lineage of the black race well past the 1920s, but such works would sound increasingly amateurish and outdated as the twentieth century progressed.[16]

As early as 1903, DuBois, who was then attempting to make his name as an academic at Atlanta University, had little patience with scriptural accounts of the history of the races. Calling for a more scientific approach to racial subjects, he relegated ethnology to the nursery school, lamenting, "We print in the opening of children's histories theories of the origins of the races that make the gravest of us smile."[17] Meanwhile, other academic writers cited the scriptural arguments for racial unity, but only in passing. For example, *The Progress of a Race* (1897), by W. H. Crogman, who taught classics at Clark University, and his associate H. F. Kletzing, began like much of nineteenth-century black writing on race, with sections entitled "The Unity of the Races," and "Of One Blood." But Crogman and Kletzing's arguments on these subjects were much shorter than those of earlier black writers, and they emphasized that these defenses of the Negro's status in the human family barely needed articulation anymore. "Attempts had been made in the past to prove that the Negro is not a human being," Crogman and Kletzing stated at the opening of their book, going on immediately to issue a brief but emphatic dismissal of this antiquated notion: "In this age of the world such a preposterous idea does not receive countenance. The remarkable progress of the Negro and the rapid disappearing of race prejudice and malice, have made this theory so absurd that to-day no one can be found to advocate it."[18]

As they replaced scriptural defenses of the status of black people in the human family with more secular discussions of their race's evolution, black writers of the nadir often put less emphasis on the similarities between the races than had previous black thinkers. Nineteenth-century authors who sought to defend black people against proslavery accusations that the black race was the product of a separate creation often insisted that differences between the races were inconsequential. They stressed the common origins of the races and attributed any shortcomings in the black race to the evil effects of slavery rather than a slower pace of racial development. Their turn-of-the-century successors, by contrast, were somewhat more open to the possibility of significant distinctions between the races. "That there are differences between the white and black races is certain," DuBois wrote in an 1898 study calling for more rigorous scientific work on "Negro Problems," adding, "just what those differences are is known to none with any approach to accuracy."[19]

Other black scholars went one step further and conceded that the black race lagged behind the white race in its development. Taking comfort in the notion that "under the influence of civilized customs and habits" blacks would ultimately come to equal whites, Crogman and Kletzing freely admitted that present-day blacks were both different than and inferior to whites. "From naked barbarians they have become civilized Christians," they said of African-Americans.

From groveling and stupid savages they have become intelligent and industrious workers, skilled in many of the arts of civilized life. By this vast progress in so short a period, the Negroes have demonstrated a capacity, an aptitude for improvement, which should make us hesitate to predict that they cannot finally ascend to the highest heights of human development.[20]

Such rhetoric, obviously, made smaller claims for black equality than can be seen in antebellum black writing on race. But black descriptions of their own race as backward expressed an understanding of human development that was pervasive in late nineteenth-century social science. As Hamilton Cravens notes, anthropologists of the period shared an "evolutionary or Neo-Lamarckian point of view [that] reduced culture to nature and assumed certain fixed stages of 'progress' through which all peoples must develop if they were to rise to the high plateau of white civilization."[21]

In addition to testifying to the impact of social Darwinism on black thinkers, the increasingly conservative tone of turn-of-the-century African-American racial thought also reflected the conservative political climate of the nadir. Comparing the fiery Frederick Douglass with the more accommodating Booker T. Washington, an educator who was the premier black leader of the nadir in 1908, Kelly Miller characterized both as men of their times:

> Douglass lived in the day of moral giants; Washington lives in the era of merchant princes. The contemporaries of Douglass emphasized the rights of man; those of Washington, his productive capacity. The age of Douglass acknowledged the sanction of the Golden Rule; that of Washington worships the Rule of *Gold*. The equality of men was constantly dinned into Douglass' ears; Washington hears nothing but the inferiority of the Negro and the dominance of the Saxon. Douglass could hardly receive a hearing today; Washington would have been hooted off the stage a generation ago.[22]

Thus, the turn of the century saw black racial thought at a crossroads. The new evolutionary understanding of blacks as an undeveloped race could not be easily reconciled with the traditional scriptural and historical defenses of black equality that emphasized the identical origins of the races and the ancient glories achieved by the African race: for the evolutionary model was progressive rather than cyclical in its orientation and provided no explanation of why the black race had fallen so far behind.[23] Moreover, the new evolutionary conception of the black race as backward was at odds with the egalitarian assessment of the capabilities of races long defended by black writers.

Black social Darwinism, however, did not develop sufficiently or last long enough to require its adherents to wrestle with its conservative implications. Even as DuBois preached the conservation of the races in 1897, he admitted that "essential difference of races" was hard to identify. A year later, when he encouraged American social scientists to scrutinize "the backward development of Negroes," he noted that "we do not know . . . whether the present difficulties arise more largely from ignorance than from prejudice, or *vice versa*."[24] DuBois's diffidence on the subject of innate racial differences even as he advocated the conservation of the races suggests that the Enlightenment environmentalism nurtured in black thought throughout the nineteenth century still retained life during the segregationist "age of merchant princes." And this environmentalism would soon receive powerful reinforcement from the egalitarian ideas about human development then emerging out of early twentieth-century cultural anthropology.

Indeed, the racial essentialism that marked DuBois's 1897 address already may have been on its way out among the new generation of educated black men who attended the American Negro Academy's first meeting. For DuBois's speech received a mixed response from the academy's members, who questioned his "emphasis on preserving racial identity." Kelly Miller, whose "Review of Hoffman's Race Traits and Tendencies of the American Negro" followed DuBois's address, received more universal acclaim from the academy's members for his carefully researched rebuttal of the statistician Frederick L. Hoffman's argument that the African-American race was deteriorating and on the verge of extinction. Miller's paper, which ended on an environmentalist note, concluding that American blacks confronted a "condition" rather than a predetermined racial destiny, was selected for publication at the meeting as the academy's first occasional paper. Moreover, it easily outsold DuBois's "Conservation of the Races," which the academy published the following year.[25]

The reception of Miller's spirited rebuttal to Hoffman reveals that the conservative racialism in turn-of-the-century black racial thought did not represent a complete capitulation to the racist scientific dogma of the day.[26] As described in earlier chapters, black racial ideology sought to recast the ethnographic image of the races to favor the black race and thus embraced a racial essentialism of its own, which can be seen in the romantic racialism and Spencerian notions of racial development that colored DuBois's "Conservation of the Races." Yet the fundamentally defensive character of black racial ideology always put distinct limits on its racial essentialism. Black writers who argued that their race had unique gifts that would enrich American society usually also maintained that the black race was essentially similar and equal to other races. Consequently, social Darwinism, which even in the hands of black thinkers placed the black race behind the white in evolutionary development, occupied an uneasy place in black racial thought.

Accordingly, social Darwinism was readily abandoned by many of its black adherents when Franz Boas began to question whether any significant differences divided the races of the world. Boas, the

founder of modern anthropology, launched his critique of evolutionary racism in the 1890s by arguing that science had established no
fixed equation between race and intellect.[27] The researches performed by Boas and his followers over the next several decades
broadened this critique by assembling an impressive body of evidence
to disprove the existence of any significant innate differences between
the peoples of the world. As historian Carl Degler writes, Boas's war
on "the idea that differences in culture were derived from differences
in innate capacity . . . proved to be revolutionary for the development
of anthropology and eventually of the social sciences in general."[28]

In the white scientific community, Boas's war would be hard
fought, but his new ideas about race and culture found far swifter acceptance among black intellectuals. The German-Jewish social scientist's arguments made a particularly profound impression on DuBois,
who later recalled, "When the matter of race became a question of
comparative culture, I was in revolt. I began to see that the cultural
equipment attributed to any people depended largely on who estimated it; and conviction came later in a rush as I realized what in my
education had been suppressed concerning Asiatic and African culture."[29] DuBois first encountered Boas at Atlanta University in 1906,
and one year later he was using Boas's findings at a meeting of the
American Sociological Society to critique the segregationist racial theories espoused by the prominent Southern sociologist Alfred Holt
Stone. Sounding very different in his review of a paper by Stone than
he had a decade earlier when he had called for the conservation of
the races, DuBois cited the authority of Boas to argue that there was
no scientific evidence for significant differences between the races. He
concluded, "What we ought to do in America is to seek to bind the
races together rather than . . . accentuate differences."[30]

Over the next couple of decades, Boas's research into human development led him to separate physical from mental characteristics
with increasing confidence, and his research on African cultures documented the complexity and achievement of these cultures to show
that "the mind of primitive man" was no different from the minds of
other men.[31] During this time Boas's views on both these subjects
were eagerly absorbed by a great number of educated blacks. Boas
himself was frequently invited to lecture at black universities, and he
published articles in black publications such as the *Crisis* and *Southern
Workman*.[32] And Boas's work on Africa was widely publicized by black
authors from DuBois to Booker T. Washington, who published popular works on black history that drew on his research.[33]

But it was Boas's arguments against innate racial differences that
had the most influence on black intellectuals, who declared an early
victory for his culture concept, proclaiming from about 1910 onward
that modern science found no evidence that "one race is inferior or
superior to another."[34] Black librarian Daniel Murray, who worked at

the Library of Congress, named 1908 as the point in time when "years of observation had established beyond successful refutation that the brain power of the African was equal to that of any European and that the difference in condition was irrefutably owing to the difference of environment."[35] Likewise, DuBois stated in *The Negro* in 1915: "It is generally recognized to-day that no scientific definition of race is possible. Differences, and striking differences, there are between men, and groups of men, but they fade into each other so insensibly that we can only indicate the main divisions of men in broad outline. . . . Today we realize there are no hard and fast racial types among men."[36] The same year the aging Booker T. Washington—never an energetic public proponent of Negro equality—invoked the authority of Boas on the same subject in a private letter to Iowa congressman T. E. Taylor. Responding to an inquiry from Taylor, who had attended a lecture in which it was claimed that the mental development of the black race stopped at the age of puberty, Washington referred him to Boas as "the leading authority on the question of the mental ability of the races" and cited a lengthy passage on the equal endowments of the races written by Boas.[37]

The new scientific conclusions in favor of human equality were explored at greater length by C. V. Roman, a black physician, in a work entitled *American Civilization and the Negro* (1916). Roman's book drew on the authority of progressive white social scientists to argue that "racial differences are not innate and permanent; but are superficial, environmental and transitory." He reviewed the human form, presenting sections on the skull, the face, the nose, the ears, the body, and argued that none of these physiological features distinguished human beings along racial lines.[38]

Roman extended his defense of human equality to embrace Native Americans and European immigrants, attacking the racist sentiments about these groups expressed by the prominent sociologist Edward Ross. Ross had recently stated, in reference to a gathering of European immigrants, "There were so many sugar-loaf heads, slit mouths, lantern-jaws, and goose bill noses . . . that one might imagine that a malicious jinni had amused himself by casting human beings in a set of skew molds." Roman argued that such antiquated racism ill befitted a contemporary man of science "with access to the learning of the world," and he chalked up Ross's opinions to a "pride of race" that left him poorly equipped to pass judgment on "a problem as intricate as that of immigration." "Professor Ross," he wrote, "has come from the Middle West, looked upon man made in the image of God, and proclaimed that except as produced in America he does not justify the Divine craftsmanship."[39]

In its scientific orientation, thoroughgoing environmentalism, and championship of the racial equality of all the diverse peoples of the world, *American Civilization and the Negro* represented a significant departure from the scripturally based, vindicationist defenses of the Negro race typical of nineteenth-century black ethnology.

The ease with which black leaders and thinkers converted to Boas's culture concept, however, should not be exaggerated. Like most paradigm shifts, Boas's scientific defense of racial equality was assimilated somewhat gradually and inconsistently by even its most receptive audiences. In particular, black thinkers were slow to embrace the anthropologist's complete rejection of the notion that any organic essence distinguished the races. Radical even to black thinkers, Boas's complete break with nineteenth-century racial determinism posed a problem for African-American leaders and thinkers because it called into question the very basis of black unity. Without race, could black people still have a special racial destiny? Long used to laying claim to special and redemptive black characteristics, black thinkers found certain aspects of racial determinism difficult to give up.

Accordingly, black intellectuals of the early twentieth century were frequently inconsistent in their racial thinking, mixing the language of racial essentialism with the environmentalism of cultural anthropology. For example, in an open letter to President Warren G. Harding entitled "Race Differences" (1921), Kelly Miller noted, "The Negro possesses patience, meekness, forgiveness of spirit which surpasses that yet manifested by other races." He went on to proclaim a few pages later: "Your doctrine of eternal difference is contrary to the scientific, ethical, and social tendencies of the age. . . . The varieties of gifts, talents, and attainments of different individuals, races, and nations of mankind are easily interchangeable and modifiable by culture and contact."[40]

The difficulties that the new scientific thinking about race created for black intellectuals are particularly evident in a lecture series entitled "The Theory and Practice of Race," given by African-American philosopher Alain Locke at Howard University in 1916. In these lectures the Harvard- and Oxford-educated Locke, who at age thirty was just beginning his professional career after years of study abroad, relied heavily on Boas to argue that race had no biological significance. A "pure science of race," he told the audience at his first lecture, "must be admitted to be impossible. That seems to be the frank conclusion of the most recent scholars in this field, particularly Professor [Franz] Boas in America, and Dr. [Friedrich] Hertz and Dr. [Felix] von Luschan in Germany, [all of whom] have come to this conclusion after a very long attempt to pursue this subject upon a very rigid scientific basis."[41] Yet, in the course of his five lectures, Locke ultimately proved resistant to abandoning the concept of race entirely. Unlike Boas, who came to see race largely as an iniquitous and pernicious scientific fallacy that retarded the assimilation of American ethnic groups into the dominant culture, Locke believed the concept of race had a great deal to offer—if properly understood.

Blending social Darwinism and Boas's culture concept, Locke argued that "any true history of race must be a sociological theory of race":

> [It] must be a theory of culture stages and of social evolution[,] and must interpret in terms of one and the same principle[, the accomplishments of all ethnic groups and civilizations,] so that the superiorities and inferiorities, or let us say to be really more scientific, [the] successes and failures of one ethnic group or another ethnic group, one type of civilization as contrasted with another type of civilization, one stage of civilization as contrasted with another stage civilization [, will be explained consistently.][42]

Locke sought to replace biological theories of race with a sociological theory in order to preserve racial consciousness, which he saw as an all-important stimulus for cultural and political development. Yet, in so doing, he also preserved racial essentialism in his own racial thought. For Locke undercut his own arguments about the fictive nature of racial categories with theories about race contacts that gave race a central role in all of human history. Moreover, his theories also ascribed rather familiar nineteenth-century notions about racial temperament to the various races. African-Americans and the Japanese were both "biologically and socially highly assimilative," while an "imperialistic temper" was common to all Anglo-Saxons "whether they practice[d] empire or not."[43]

One of the consequences of the inconsistent assimilation of liberal environmentalism into black thought was that the nineteenth-century black critique of whites as an especially predatory and brutal race survived even in the writing of black thinkers like Locke who were well-informed on the new scientific evidence against the idea that race could determine human character. Thus the battle over who had the better racial character continued in black thought, even alongside arguments against the significance of race.

In addition to critiquing Anglo-Saxons for their imperialistic temper, Locke suggested, by analogy, that the success of this dominant race did not preclude the possibility that their imperialistic civilization was in fact inferior to that of the race(s) it dominated. The "actual practical dominance" of this group would naturally lead it to "notions of superiority and also a very firm belief in superiority," he observed. But they could be wrong, "as the Romans were when they succeeded in sapping and undermining Greek civilization [, to consider] their own civilization superior, when[,] in fact, [as in the case of the Romans,] we know that it was relatively inferior [to that of the conquered Greeks,] from the point of view of general civilization and culture."[44]

C. V. Roman called one chapter of his book "Dark Pages in the White Man's Civilization." In it he exclaimed, "The savagery of Africa! Aye! And the savagery of Europe! Even as I write this, Europe is engaged in murder on a scale that Africa never knew." After chronicling English brutality in the Middle Ages as well as more recent white offenses against African-Americans in gory detail, however, he did go on to add this qualification: "This is the truth, but not the whole truth. 'The devil still left in the white man' is in the black man and in the red man and in the brown and in the yellow man. Civilization is the only thing which will eventually eradicate it."[45]

Likewise, DuBois, who, as several scholars have noted, never fully abandoned racial essentialism during his long career, still exhibited an ambivalent black chauvinism long after he embraced Boas's theories. In a book entitled *The Negro* (1915), he wrote, "[In] disposition the Negro is among the most lovable of men." On the next page he qualified this implicit assertion that black people were better natured than other races, adding:

> All this does not mean that the African Negro is not human with the all-too-well-known foibles of humanity. Primitive life among them is, after all, as bare and cruel as among the primitive Germans or Chinese, but it is not more so, and the more we study the Negro the more we realize that we are dealing with a normal human stock which under reasonable conditions had developed and will develop along the same lines as other men.[46]

Meanwhile, in nonscientific black thought of the early twentieth century, the traditional African-American critique of the brutal white man took on renewed vitality when America and the European nations fought among each other in World War I. That vitality was further renewed after the war ended, when black American soldiers returned to face race riots and an increase in lynching at home. "Whites are nothing but savages themselves; . . . they are still on a very low plane in point of moral development," wrote black minister Frances Grimké in 1918, mocking the white Americans who asked in reference to the Germans, "SHALL HUMANITY RULE OR THE SAVAGE?"[47] To Grimké, who was embittered by "ever-worsening relations between the races" in the United States, "Germany hardly equaled the United States in savagery."[48]

Grimké's disillusionment with white Americans and his hostility toward white people as a race were widely shared among black Americans across the country in the early twentieth century. In the postwar period, especially, many black Americans channeled their grievances against the white world into a variety of religious and cultural movements that emphasized racial distinctions and often promised African-Americans a racial redemption that would not be shared by the less-deserving white race. This period saw a race-conscious black cultural revitalization in the form of the Harlem Renaissance, as well as the rise of a variety of messianic black nationalist movements such as the Garvey movement, the Black Muslim sect, black Judaism, and the African

Orthodox Church. The 1920s also saw the emergence of new religious sects led by charismatic black leaders such as Daddy Grace and Father Divine. Race was a central concern in all these developments, and the new black religions of the 1920s, especially, all drew on the religious racialism of nineteenth-century black ethnology in their interpretations of black history and destiny.

Unlike the revisionist racial ideology of the nineteenth century, however, the racial doctrine of Marcus Garvey and other messianic black nationalists of the early twentieth century was not widely shared among black intellectuals. Among academically trained black thinkers in particular, the black ethnological tradition gave way with the rise of liberal environmentalism in American social science. To be sure, the destabilization of race as a scientific concept ushered in by liberal environmentalism was understood only gradually by both black and white social scientists and caught on even more slowly outside the academy. But liberal environmentalism was met with special enthusiasm among turn-of-the-century black intellectuals whose racial thought had always been more environmentalistic than that of their white contemporaries. By the 1920s, black intellectuals and scholars were active publicists for liberal environmentalism. They attacked the findings of racist social scientists in the pages of *Opportunity, The Crisis,* and other black publications.[49] Ethnologists no longer, the new generation of academically trained black social scientists that emerged during the 1920s often employed their scientific training in research aimed at showing the primacy of environmental factors in determining human capacity.

In particular, black academics such as Horace Mann Bond, Francis C. Sumner, Charles Johnson, and E. Franklin Frazier worked to construct a vigorous environmentalist critique of mental testing in the 1920s. Intelligence testing had been popularized during World War I when the U.S. Army began administering tests to its draftees. Poorly administered and riddled with biases, these tests set the average mental age of white draftees at thirteen, while African-Americans hovered even closer to the "edge of moronity."[50] Despite their manifestly absurd results, the army tests provided great impetus for further intelligence testing while "publicizing the conclusion of many social scientists that mental differences between the races and ethnic groups were biologically based."[51] Moreover, the racial differentials in the army test scores were understood by both popular thinkers such as the Nordic supremacist Madison Grant and a great number of white psychologists to represent conclusive evidence for the intellectual inferiority of black people. Both the findings of the tests and the scientific assumptions they employed were hotly contested by 1920s black intellectuals who, as William B. Thomas has shown, "launched a concentrated intellectual assault upon the racist conclusions which white psychologists extrapolated from mental test data."[52]

The aim of both black and white adherents of liberal environmentalism was to ultimately eradicate race distinctions, which became the goal of mainstream black protest organizations such as the NAACP and the Urban League that emerged during the early twentieth century. The environmentalist orientation and increasingly assimilationist goals of the twentieth century black elite could not support a racialist critique of white people that had obtained among nineteenth-century black intellectuals. With the rise of liberal environmentalism, black intellectuals no longer had to fight racism with revisionist racial ideologies of their own; now they had science on their side. Thus, although nineteenth-century ethnological ideas survived in black popular thought, environmentalist black intellectuals were eager to abandon the nineteenth-century "science of the races" to the past—and note only that it had been a white man's game all along. "*The science of inequality is emphatically a science of white people*," wrote C. V. Roman.

> It is they who invented it and set it a-going, who have maintained, cherished, and propagated it, thanks to *their* observations and *their* deductions. Deeming themselves greater than men of other colors, they have elevated into superior qualities all the traits which are peculiar to themselves, commencing with the whiteness of the skin and the pliancy of the hair. But nothing proves that these vaunted traits are traits of real superiority.[53]

Antiwhite Sentiment in the Post–World War I Era

In the second decade of the twentieth century, tribalism was on the rise among both black and white Americans. Although progressive white social scientists of the day had begun to publish arguments for the equality of the races, outside the academy influential white racial theorists such as Madison Grant and Lothrop Stoddard popularized a blend of antiblack, anti-Semitic, and anti-Catholic sentiment among Americans of Anglo-Saxon ancestry. These guardians of "Nordic" civilization urged Americans of northern and western European ancestry not to intermix with the more lowly "Alpines" and "Mediterraneans" of eastern and southern Europe, let alone fraternize with the Negro. They also warned against the "rising tide of color," predicting that white solidarity would be needed to protect civilization from being overcome by the ever-increasing hordes of non-Aryans whose high birthrates and "imperious urge[s]" threatened "the supreme fact of white world-political domination."[54] Meanwhile, in the black community, cultural critics and religious leaders spoke out against white supremacy with a new frankness.

"The colored races never welcomed white predominance," Stoddard noted mournfully, "and were always restive under white control."⁵⁵ Stoddard saw signs of a dangerous restlessness among the colored races throughout the world. But his initial awareness of trouble brewing among nonwhites may well have come from home, where racial conflict was rife, and African-Americans were posing new challenges to the color caste system. In the period immediately following World War I, economic and social stresses created by an enormous migration of Southern blacks to the urban North combined with heightening racial discrimination to spur aggressive protest and an enhanced sense of racial consciousness among American blacks. The black veterans who returned home to face economic discrimination, racial slurs, and a spate of race riots culminating in the bloody Red Summer of 1919 were part of a new generation of freeborn African-Americans, and this generation of "new Negroes" would prove very restive indeed.

Like most migrants, the many thousands of black migrants who arrived in Northern cities between 1910 and 1920 sought a different life from that of their parents. Spurred by tough economic times and the blight of the boll weevil, they fled the life of sharecropping and tenant farming that had become the fate of most Southern blacks after emancipation. They were drawn north by the prospect of industrial jobs—work that became available to large numbers of black laborers only during World War I, when wartime labor shortages overcame the color bar that had traditionally kept African-Americans out of Northern industry. Yet in traveling north, the black migrants sought not just these economic opportunities. They also aimed to escape from the indignities of the Southern caste system and had high hopes that these indignities would not be found in the North. Poignant rumors reported that the "northern people had said that southern people were not treating the colored folks right and wanted to move them all North." As James R. Grossman explains, "Images rooted in the days of the underground railroad and fertilized by continuing sectional debate and interregional communication led many black southerners to expect that northern whites would not share the racist attitudes that dominated the white South."⁵⁶ These hopes gave the North a powerful allure among young black Southerners, for the region's etiquette of racial deference and subordination was no longer enforced by slavery and did not sit well with a new generation of blacks who had never known slavery. As one migrant explained to a Labor Department investigator in 1916, a tolerance for the old-time caste system was not nurtured in black families:

> My father was born and brought up a slave. He never knew anything else until after I was born. He was taught his place and was content to keep it. But when he brought me up he let some of the old customs slip by. But I know there are certain things that I must do and I do them, and it doesn't worry me; yet in bringing up my own son, I let some more of the old customs slip by. For a year I have been keeping him

from going to Chicago; but he tells me this is his last crop; that in the fall he's going. He says, "When a young white man talks rough to me I can't talk rough to him. You can stand that; I can't. I have some education, and inside I has the feelings of a white man. I'm going."[57]

Moreover, the new Negro spirit of the postwar period was not confined to these Southern migrants. As Wilson Jeremiah Moses points out, the new black confidence and assertiveness celebrated during the Harlem Renaissance "was viewed as a result of social and cultural change deriving from, but not limited to, the migration of black peasants out of the South and into Harlem."[58] In part, this new confidence and assertiveness among black people were no doubt derived in complex ways from a half century of emancipation itself. With freedom came new kinds of interactions with whites. For instance, ex-slave Joanna Thompson Isom learned that "niggers ain't the onliest fools in the world" when she applied for government aid alongside impoverished whites. "I goes up to de office an' sees so many ole white folks what can't read an' write—dey don't know a single letter; I ses to myself; white folks all born free how cum dey can't read an' write; hit looks like sum body woul'd hav learned dem sumthin'."[59]

In the postwar period this new boldness in the black community was reinforced by a surge of resentment against white Americans that arose as worsening American race relations dashed the hopes for racial equality so cherished by the Southern migrants. The antiblack hostility of the post–World War I years also disappointed and angered the many black Americans who had expected that the black contributions to a war to protect democracy abroad would entitle African-Americans to share more fully in democracy's benefits at home. Indeed, Lawrence Levine has suggested that the disillusionment black America experienced when the armistice brought only continuing discrimination, race riots, and lynching was so severe that it triggered what one anthropologist has called a "revitalization moment: 'a deliberate, organized conscious effort by members of a society to construct a more satisfying culture.'"[60] Such a revitalization certainly took place in black America after the war, although, as Nathan Irvin Huggins points out, it did not take its inspiration from dashed hopes only. Speaking in reference to 1920s Harlem, Huggins observes that, like "others whose collective experience was World War I," black Americans "were caught up in its wake."

> Surely the ethnocentrism that generated self-determination as an Allied aim in that war informed a new racial awareness among blacks throughout the world. The war also forced a reevaluation of Western civilization and encouraged non-Europeans to esteem their own cultures as being as valid and civilized as Europe's.[61]

Whatever its exact origins, this new racial consciousness manifested itself in the activities of a wide variety of black Americans. "New Negroes were not only bohemian artists, but staid intellectuals, rugged labor leaders, tough-minded preachers, and conservative pan-Africanists," writes Moses. He further notes that their activities were not wholly new: "Most of them did not see themselves as breaking with past literary and intellectual traditions. During the twenties, they simply continued to engage in the same sort of activities that had always interested them."[62] Yet the militant mood of the American black community in the postwar era, together with the challenges the war and modern science had posed to nineteenth-century black ideas about race, combined to create a variety of new forms of discourse about both race and white people in black thought.

In the wake of the war, African-Americans from all walks of life expressed their hostility toward the white world with a new frankness. As a teenager in Jackson, Mississippi, following World War I, Richard Wright recalled that to win acceptance among the older boys he had to subscribe "to certain racial sentiments. The touchstone of my fraternity was my feeling toward white people, how much hostility I held toward them, what degrees of value and honor I assigned to race." Together the boys would ponder the subject of white folks in conversations that Wright remembered as a litany of boasts, insults, and uncertainty:

"Man them white folks sure is mean." Complaining.
"That's how come so many colored folks leaving the South." Informational. . . .
"The first white sonofabitch that bothers me is gonna get a hole knocked in his head." Naïve rebellion.
"That ain't gonna do you no good. Hell they'll catch you." Rejection of naive rebellion. . . .
"Man, what makes white folks so mean?" Returning to grapple with an old problem.
"Whenever I see one I spit." Emotional rejection of whites.
"Man, ain't they ugly?" Increased emotional rejection.[63]

Among other things, the discussions among these black youths expressed the mood of their times, for frank expressions of antiwhite sentiment were also widespread among the boys' elders. As previously mentioned, antiwhite sentiment colored the pronouncements of black ministers such as Frances Grimké and ran high in an uncharacteristically emotional poem W.E.B. DuBois wrote in 1920. "Valiant spoilers of women," he began his outburst against the white race.

And conquerors of unarmed men;
Shameless breeders of bastards,
Drunk with the greed of gold,
Bating their blood-stained hooks
With cant for the souls of the simple;
Bearing the white man's burden
Of liquor and lust and lies . . .

I hate them, Oh!
I hate them, well. . . .[64]

Similar outbursts were also penned by the writers of the Harlem Renaissance, who expressed their hostility toward whites in a defiant tone that "alarmed conservative whites."[65] In the most famous of these works, "If We Must Die" (1919), Jamaican-born Claude McKay called for black resistance to white violence: "If we must die, let it not be like hogs / Hunted and penned in an inglorious sport." McKay likened whites to "monsters" and "mad and hungry dogs / Making mock of our accursed lot."[66]

The new mood was also seen in the radical black press that emerged in Harlem after World War I, which preached African-American resistance and solidarity. Newspapers and magazines such as the *Messenger*, *The Challenge*, the *Voice*, *The Crusader*, *The Crisis*, the *Emancipator*, and the *Negro World* occupied a variety of positions on the political spectrum, but they all took on the white world with a new hostility that, in its strongest expressions, shaped into racialism. As the contemporary observer James Weldon Johnson noted, the "radicalism of these publications ranged from left center to extreme left; at the extreme it was submerged in what might be called racialism." According to Johnson, *The Challenge*, in particular, "assaulted, not the class line, but the color line."[67] Its editor, William Bridges, ran editorials arguing that white oppression would never end unless blacks resisted "like a raging tempest Wind, furious as a curse of hell." "White men expect to keep you in eternal slavery through superstitions they have long cast off," Bridges warned. "They delight in seeing you on your knees. They mean to remain on their feet. They want your eyes kept on the gold in heaven. They mean to keep their eyes on the gold of the world. They want you to seek rest beyond the grave. They mean to have all the rest this side [of] it."[68]

Nowhere, however, did the antiwhite sentiment of the postwar era flower more fully than in black religion, where nineteenth-century ideas about the racial families of man were elaborated into a variety of separatist ideologies that embraced race as a divinely ordained distinction between human beings, often promising their adherents retribution for their racial suffering. The Garvey movement, although nonsectarian, must be understood as one such separatist religion, for, as Randall Burkett has shown, religion structured the UNIA's Pan-Africanist vision. The UNIA—whose motto was "One God! One Aim! One Destiny!"—had a distinctive theology and liturgy.[69] Garvey's "civil religion" and the black sects that emerged in the early twentieth century, which included the "Moorish Temple of Science" and "Abyssinian" sects (both forerunners of the modern-day Nation of Islam), black Jewish groups, and the Spiritual Israel Church, did not share the same doctrines or even, in the case of the Muslim groups, the same God, but all glorified blackness and venerated Africa as the fount of human civilization. Moreover, to varying degrees, the racial theology in all these religious movements defined the white race (or, in the case of the black Jews, the gentiles) as the black race's enemy or competitor and prophesied a racial redemption in which black folk would ultimately triumph over their white oppressors.

As Howard Brotz has observed, the racial doctrine of the black sects that emerged in the early twentieth century drew on a "total pattern of mythology" that was already familiar to most black Americans.[70] As indicated in earlier chapters, the civilizations of Ethiopia and Egypt had long been celebrated by black Americans. However, while earlier black authors who sang the praises of ancient African civilizations often defended the antiquity and accomplishments of black people in assimilationist arguments for human equality, both the doctrine of the black sects and the racial Christianity of the Garvey movement took their racial self-defenses considerably further down the road to black chauvinism.

As shall be seen in the next section, the racial redemptionists also produced a more purely racial case against white people than did the many other black critics of the white race who spoke out in the 1920s. For although DuBois espoused Pan-Africanism and proclaimed his hatred of white men in verse, by the 1920s his Boasian understanding of race as a scientific fallacy, merging with his conversion to socialism, had mitigated the romantic racism so evident in his turn-of-the-century critiques of white people. He extolled socialism as "the Will to human Brotherhood of all Colors, Races, and Creeds; the Wanting of Wants of All."[71]

Meanwhile, younger black critics of the white race, such as the Harlem Renaissance writers, assailed white culture rather than the white race itself. As S. P. Fullinwinder points out, although Renaissance spokesman Alain Locke sought to present the movement's contributors as exemplars of the Negro's racial "folk-gift," the "Renaissance writers of the postwar decade scoffed at, and made merry of, the idea of a racial soul." Their "reaction to Locke tended to be a muffled snicker. The Renaissance was in revolt against myths, it had enough of 'racial souls' and 'geniuses.'"[72] Renaissance authors such as Claude McKay and Langston Hughes celebrated the "human and vital black man" as a healthy primitive, quite "alien to sterile mechanized European civilization."[73] But, to a large degree, the Harlem Renaissance critique of European civilization was cultural rather than racial, and it partook of the general disillusionment with Western civilization and search for authentic, primal experience that took place among both American and European intellectuals in the wake of World War I.

Moreover, to the extent that it asserted any kind of black chauvinism, the counterculture primitivism of Harlem Renaissance writers such as Hughes and McKay had little in common with the civilizationist doctrine preached by the religious racialists of their era. For instance, Garvey's black chauvinism looked to the race's past and future for its glories: when speaking of the present day, he classed his people among the "backward races."[74] Like most apostles of racial uplift, Garvey had a deep concern for black respectability, which made him quite unresponsive to any celebration of primitivism. "The white people have Negroes to write [this] kind of stuff," he wrote of Claude McKay's risqué novel of black working-class life, *Home to Harlem*, "so that the Negro can still be regarded as a monkey or some imbecile creature."[75] Indeed, this civilizationism was widely shared in the early twentieth-century black religions of racial redemption. As Wilson Jeremiah Moses points out:

> Black religion—whether of the Muslim, Hebrew, or Christian variety—tended to assume there was something wrong with being a black African. The program for uplift even among the sects, however, usually involved a renunciation of certain values, historically associated with the values of the Afro-American masses. The cult leaders often attempted to stamp out those aspects of black mass culture that did not conform to mainstream culture, justifying their position by incorrectly attributing all Africanistic behaviors, of which traits they disapproved, to the heritage of slavery.[76]

Antiwhite Mythologies of Cultural Redemption

The black religious racialists of the early twentieth century incorporated the antiwhite sentiment of the postwar era into theologies that were as racial as they were religious. Their primary impulse was to uplift the black race rather than vilify the white race. But their doctrines tended to raise the black race at the expense of the white race, which in some of the black sect's eschatologies was in fact deemed to be villainous by nature. However, if the religious racism of the Garvey movement and the other black nationalist religions that emerged in the 1920s and 1930s was more explicitly antiwhite than the romantic racism of nineteenth-century black intellectuals, it still owed a great deal to the racial thought of these earlier black thinkers. In particular, in building their doctrine around racial interpretations of human history, which often included gendered critiques of the white race as predatory and brutal, the new black nationalist religions took the romantic racialism invented by black and white intellectuals during the nineteenth century to its outer limits.

Before moving on to discuss the racial doctrines of the new black religions, however, it is important to note that the origins of their racial eschatologies were twofold. The nationalist religions were by no means purely intellectual movements. Indeed, sects such as the Muslims "mainly attracted the poorest and least-educated Negroes in the North, many of them born in the South."[77] And while Garveyism had a more diverse clientele, including, as Randall Burkett has shown, educated black churchmen of many denominational affiliations, the size of the Garvey movement testified to its appeal among the uneducated black masses.[78] Drawing supporters estimated to number over a million in the United States alone, Marcus Garvey had a following that outnumbered the more educated following of the NAACP many times over.[79] The doctrines of Marcus Garvey and other black sectarians were able to appeal to the black masses because their religious racialism addressed concerns about religion and race that had a long history in the black South. These "black gods of the metropolis," as anthropologist Arthur Huff Fauset called them, combined the revisionist racial ideology of black intellectuals with ideas from slave religion to forge racial doctrines that must have presented an intriguing mixture of old and new eschatology to the Southern migrants who increasingly predominated in the black populations of the cities.

The most successful of these gods—until his incarceration and subsequent deportation on charges of mail fraud—Garvey infused his nationalism with a religious imagery that spoke directly to the traditionally voiced hopes of the black masses. E. Franklin Frazier, writing after Garvey's imprisonment in Atlanta, observed that, unlike Garvey's steamships, the religious appeal of his movement could not be treated in a "cavalier fashion." "The writer recalls that when he was a child one could still hear Negroes express the hope that some Moses would appear among them and lead them to the promised land of freedom and equality," Frazier noted, adding that Booker T. Washington was initially greeted as such a Moses. After Washington's uninspiring message discouraged this image, Frazier explained, "Garvey re-introduced the idea of a Moses, who was incarnate in himself, and with his masterly technic [*sic*] for dealing with crowds, he welded Negroes into a mass movement."[80]

Both the black sects and the Garvey movement also addressed time-honored African-American questions about the color of God and his disposition toward the races that are evident in the ex-slaves' discussions of the fate of white people in the afterlife. For instance, the charismatic leaders, such as Daddy Grace and Father Divine, were understood by their followers as living gods, who by their very being confirmed the divinity of black people. According to black anthropologist Arthur Huff Fauset, who studied the Father Divine sect in the 1940s, Divine's followers believed that "Father Divine had come in his present form because the Negro is one of the lowliest creatures on earth. God prefers to bring salvation to the lowly."[81] The black Jewish followers of the Church of God held that both God and Jesus—whom they accepted into their Judaic doctrine—were black, as were the original inhabitants of the earth.[82] And the Muslims believed that the races were meant to have their own gods: "Christianity is for the European (paleface); Muslimism is for the Asiatic (olive-skinned). When each group has its own peculiar religion there will be peace on earth."[83]

Marcus Garvey resolved the issue of God's color and racial affiliation by arguing that God had no color. "There is a God and we believe in Him. He is not a person nor a physical being. He is a spirit and He is universal intelligence." However, this understanding of God as a spiritual force did not put the issue of color to rest in Garvey's civil religion. He frequently told his black audiences that they must renounce any conceptualization of God as white and start "to see God through our own spectacles." "'God is not white or black,' he told a Cincinnati audience in 1921, 'angels have no color, and they are not white peaches from Georgia. But if [whites] say that God is white, this organization says that God is black; if they are going to make the angels beautiful white peaches from Georgia; we are going to make them beautiful black peaches from Africa."[84] The same year, the UNIA's *Universal Negro Catechism* laid out Garvey's doctrine on this subject for all to memorize:

Q. What is the color of God?

A. A spirit has neither color, nor natural parts, nor qualities.

Q. But do we not speak of His Hands, His eyes, His arms, and other parts?

A. Yes; it is because we are able to speak of Him only in human and figurative terms.

Q. If, then, you had to speak of the color of God, how would you describe it?

A. As black, since we are created in His image and likeness.

Q. On what would you base your assumption that God was black?

A. On the same basis as that taken by white people when they assume God is their color.[85]

The color of God's more corporeal representatives, in particular Jesus and Mary, proved a more complex issue for Garvey. His followers scandalized some New Yorkers by parading through the city with paintings of an Ethiopian Christ and a black Madonna and child to celebrate Garvey's Fourth International Convention of Negroes. Their parade met a crotchety reception even from black journalists, who complained, "The black Ku Kluxer now wanted Colored folk to worship a colored God."[86] In his own writings, however, Garvey held to a more universalistic vision of Christ. He exhorted his followers to "never admit that Jesus Christ was a white man, otherwise he could not be the Son of God and God to redeem all mankind." But he went on to explain, "Jesus Christ had the blood of all races in his veins, and tracing the Jewish race back to Abraham and to Moses, from which Jesus sprang through the line of Jesse, you will find Negro blood everywhere, so Jesus had much of Negro blood in him."[87]

At the same time Garvey also told his black readers to

lay a special claim to your association with Jesus and the son of God. Show that whilst the white and yellow worlds, that is to say—the worlds of Europe and Asia Minor persecuted and crucified Jesus son of God, it was the black race through Simon the black Circenian [*sic*] who be-friended the Son of God and took up the Cross and bore it alongside of Him up to the heights of Calvary.

And as Randall Burkett observes, "the overall impact" of Garvey's discussion of Jesus "was to reinforce a particularist interpretation of Christ's significance." Garvey not only emphasized the virtues of Simon the African but also contrasted them at length with the behavior of whites. "Oh Jesus the Christ, Oh Jesus the redeemer, when white man scorned you, when white men spat upon you, when white men pierced your side out of which blood and water gushed forth, it was a black man in the person of Simon the Cyrenian who took the cross and bore it on the heights of Calvary."[88]

The racial particularism of Garvey's "civil religion" was a feature of many of the new black sects that emerged in the 1920s and 1930s, and it provided fertile ground for racial interpretations of human history in which the white race fared most unfavorably against the illustrious record of the black race. Father Hurley, who in 1923 founded one of the earliest black spiritual associations in the United States, Universal Hagar's Spiritual Church, believed that white people were "the offspring of Cain, who had been cursed with a pale color because of leprosy."[89] Whites forced the Ethiopian people to adopt their "fake religion," during "slavery times a white God, a white Jesus, white prophets and white prophetesses."[90] Whites were also deemed the villains of history by an Abyssinian sect member who was interviewed in the wake of the Chicago race riot of 1919. This black shopkeeper told representatives from the Chicago Commission on Race Relations,

I hate and despise the white man. They will always be against the Ethiopian. . . . White men stole the black man from Africa and counseled each other as to what to do with him and what to call him, for when the Negro learned that he was the first civilized human on earth he would rise up and rebel against the white man. To keep him from doing this it was decided to call him Negro after the Niger river in Africa. This was to keep him from having a knowledge of the Bible, for his right name was Ethiopian. This was done so we could always be ruled by the white man.[91]

By far the most radical of the antiwhite mythologies was the story of Yakub, which came out of the Black Muslim movement. It is difficult to date the origin of this story. The Moorish "back-to-Islam" movements that began in the 1920s under the leadership of a black Carolinian who called himself Noble Drew Ali regarded their religion as secret and guarded their teachings so zealously that it took the black anthropologist Arthur Huff Fauset two years to find an ex-member who would let him look inside Ali's *Holy Koran*.[92] But the story of Yakub clearly goes back at least to Prophet W. D. Fard, who rose to prominence in 1930, shortly after Ali's death, and then vanished abruptly a few years later.[93] Fard, who would be anointed God of the Muslims by the Nation of Islam after his disappearance in 1933, "spoke in mysterious metaphors—referring to the Black Nation as his 'Uncle' and its white oppressors as the 'Cave Man,' 'Satan,' and the 'blue-eyed devils.'"[94]

Fard claimed that the white race originated from Yakub, a black scientist who selectively bred black babies to create a mutant white race. The "big-head scientist," who was a God of the Black Nation, made this race of devils to plague the peaceable Black Nation that then covered the earth. Employing "the ugliest colors, as everyone knows," he colored them "pale white with blue eyes . . . and he called them 'Caucasians.'"[95] The white devils Yakub created were aggressive troublemakers who were inferior to black people in every way. In *Black Nationalism*, E. U. Essien-Udom explains that, according to the Muslims,

> contrasted with the original Man (the so-called Negroes), the white is inferior physically and mentally. He is also weak because he is grafted from the black. He is the real "colored" man, i.e., the deviant from the black color norm. His brain capacity is smaller than that of the black man. The original man is handsomer and his women are more beautiful. The mixing of blood must not be allowed because it will further deteriorate the strength and beauty of black people.[96]

Yet all was not lost when Yakub inflicted this race of people on the world. For Yakub's devilish experiments were performed according to the will of God, "who wanted the 'devils' to rule for 6000 years in order to test the mettle of the black nation."[97] And with the rise of the Black Muslims, the white race's tenure was almost up, and a great conflict between Allah and the white race loomed which would end in a "total, apocryphal victory" for the Black Nation.[98]

Despite the strangeness of this story, and its rejection of the Judeo-Christian tradition, the revisionist racist ideology in the Muslim prophets' teachings shared some of the central themes of Garveyism and the black messianic sects. All posited that the black race had an especially close relationship with God, and a lineage superior to that of the white race. Like the black intellectuals of the nineteenth century, the religious racialists compared the races against the vast panorama of history and found the white race overly aggressive and morally deficient. Indeed, the nineteenth-century origins of religious racialism can be seen most plainly in the Black Muslim and Garveyite critiques of white people, which were virtually identical to the attacks on Anglo-Saxon lineage and behavior that had been voiced by more mainstream black thinkers during the nineteenth century.

In addition to branding the white race "devils" created by science, the Muslims liked to emphasize that "when the black man was at the height of his civilization, white people were living in the caves of Europe after they had been thrown out of Asia. At that time they were crawling on their hands and knees like the beasts of the forest and living on raw meat."[99] With these references the Muslims replicated the images of European savagery in the Middle Ages that were so pervasive in nineteenth-century black racial thought. These images were also regularly employed by Garvey, who, as E. David Cronon observes, delighted in references to the greatness of colored civilization at a time when white men were barbarians and savages."[100] "They have sprung from the same family tree of obscurity as we have," Garvey said in one of his typical pronouncements on this subject.

> Their history is as rude in its primitiveness as ours; their ancestors ran wild and naked, lived in caves and on the branches of trees, like monkeys, as ours; they made human sacrifices, ate the flesh of their own dead and the raw meat of the wild beast for centuries even as they accuse us of doing; their cannibalism was more prolonged than ours; when we were embracing the arts and sciences on the banks of the Nile their ancestors were still drinking blood and eating out of the skulls of their conquered dead; when our civilization had reached the noonday of progress they were still running naked and sleeping in holes and caves with rats, bats, and other insects and animals. After we had already fathomed the mystery of the stars and reduced the heavenly constellations to minute and regular calculus they were still backswoodmen, living in ignorance and blatant darkness.[101]

Garvey presented his most extended critique of white character in an experimental composition entitled "The Tragedy of White Injustice" (1927), which he described as "not an attempt at poetry; just a peculiar style of using facts as they impress me as I go through the pages of history and as I look at and note the conduct of the white race." In this extended poem, which was by no means remarkable as literature, Garvey developed his contrast between the brutal predatory white man and the better-natured "backward races" in heavy-handed metaphors suggestive of a distinctly nineteenth-century view of race and racial development.[102] "American Indian tribes were free," he wrote of the halcyon days before white civilization:

> Sporting, dancing, and as happy as could be;
> Asia's hordes then lived a life of their own;
> To a civilization they would have grown;
> Africa's millions laughed with the sun,
> In a cycle of man a course run;

> In stepped the white man, bloody and grim,
> The light of these people to dim.[103]

Like the black intellectuals in the nineteenth century, Garvey and the other religious racialists of his era fashioned a distinctly male image of the white race as overly brutal and predatory. In the Garvey movement, in particular, this gender emphasis was far from accidental. For, as Barbara Bair argues, the Garvey movement emphasized separate spheres for black men and women in a direct "reaction against the racist attribution of stereotypical 'feminine' qualities (passivity, subordination, exclusion from skilled and professional employment) to black males and of stereotypical 'masculine' qualities (strength, authority, and physicality) to black females." In particular, in describing the goals of the UNIA, Garvey and his followers characterized the organization a "new manhood" movement, making "race manhood" the black ideal.[104] Likewise, the Muslims contrasted a revisionary black male ideal, which cast the black man as the "Original Man," with the white man whom they claimed was an inferior copy. White men, they asserted, were weaker and less intelligent than black men, lacking even these conventional male virtues. At the same time, the "pale-faced" race had an excess of masculine aggression: whites were a brutal and predatory race, whereas blacks were "good by nature and 'very religiously inclined.'"[105]

Thus, in important respects, the racial ideology of these messianic black nationalists looked backward rather than forward. Their revisionist interpretations of human history harked back to nineteenth-century racial thought. Like both the black and white thinkers of an earlier century, the nationalists characteristically invested racial distinctions with a transhistorical permanence that put the races perpetually at odds. Accordingly, for all their militance, their attacks on white supremacy challenged neither its racial essentialism nor its masculine race ideals. What was new in the racial religions of the early twentieth century was the intensity of their antiwhite sentiment and the explicitly antiwhite mythologies they constructed, which included attacks on the white race's color and status in the human family as well as its character.

In attributing the color of the white race to Gehazi, who was cursed for sin (II Kings 5:27), as did the black Jews of the Church of God, or in attributing it to the machinations of Yakub, as did the Muslims, these messianic black nationalists sound suspiciously similar to white racists who placed black people under the curse of Ham or deemed them Cain's children.[106] With their antiwhite mythologies of cultural redemption, the nationalists proceeded further down the path to racist ideological construction than their more assimilationist forebears had been prepared to go. "The first white man, that we have an account of, became white for forging a falsehood," wrote "Euthymus" in the *Liberator* in 1831, quickly adding, "Not that I would cast a stigma on any of our fairer brethren; no, I would rather have my arm amputated."[107] Euthymus's unwillingness to stigmatize the white race's origins was evidently shared by other black thinkers of the nineteenth century, for none made an attempt to locate the origins of the white complexion in anything unsavory. As we have seen, black racial thought remained staunchly environmentalist on the subject of color throughout the nineteenth century.

Mainstream black thought would remain environmentalist in the twentieth century, when the authority of science would come to its side at last. At the same time, however, the social dislocation experienced by black Americans in the 1920s, as migration reshaped their communities and the racial climate after the armistice defeated their hopes, tested some black Americans' faith in the potential unity of the races. It is not surprising that many listened when Marcus Garvey warned "those who would believe that the black minority would win a share of the white majorities' economic and political power that 'nothing of the kind had happened in all of human history.'"[108] Moreover, the religious framework in which the black nationalists placed their antiwhite mythologies of cultural redemption no doubt exerted a strong appeal for Southern-born blacks who long after slavery still found it necessary to sing songs affirming that black people were God's children, "Jes' de same as if yo' white."[109]

A New Negro for a New Century?

In their 1900 compendium, *A New Negro for a New Century*, Booker T. Washington, Fannie Barrier Williams, and N. B. Wood chronicled the "upward struggles of the Negro race." As Henry Louis Gates notes, their emphasis on the race's "'capacity' for 'elevation' . . . along with the myriad versions of [the] folk phrase 'We is risin'" echoed "the eighteenth-century terminology related to the idea of a great vertical chain upon which the races 'rose' from the animal kingdom to the most sublime instances of humanity." Intent on rebutting claims against the racial fitness of black men to military command made by Theodore Roosevelt in *Scribner's Magazine* in 1899, *A New Negro* dwelled at length on the black contributions to every American war.[110] Humble yet manly, their "new negro for a new century" pursued a racial destiny subtly distinct from that of the white race.

Over the next twenty-five years the new Negro predicted by Washington, Williams, and Wood would become a dated racial ideal. As American science began to repudiate the significance of racial differences, the idea of separate racial destinies would increasingly lose its appeal among African-Americans. To be sure, the messianic black nationalism of the 1920s lives on even now. The Black Muslims have flourished in the Nation of Islam, and Garvey has been rescued from the obscurity into which he fell after his death to become one of black America's heroes. Moreover, in recent years radical advocates of Afrocentrism have surpassed the racial essentialism of the Garvey movement by maintaining that the races are distinguished by more than their histories, destinies, and complexions. Proponents of extreme Afrocentrism argue that Africans and Europeans are fundamentally different by nature, the products of different creations—a position that would have found more favor with rabid segregationists of Garvey's era than with Garvey himself.

But the racialist black nationalism of the 1920s did not triumph as the mainstream racial ideology of black America. Instead, the integrationist goals of less militant organizations such as the NAACP shaped black struggles leading up to the civil rights movement. In the context of such struggles, black Americans criticized the politics and culture of white Americans quite bitterly, but they no longer traded insults with white supremacists by attacking the innate racial character of white people. Indeed, by the 1920s the racialist critiques of white people in black nationalism struck some black contemporaries as amusing. In 1925 black journalist George Schuyler lampooned the graphic images of Anglo-Saxon barbarity so beloved by Garvey in an article that spoofed civilizationist arrogance in both black and white racial thought. "No, we should not despair of our black brothers," Schuyler wrote.

> Remember the Caucasians were once in almost the same boat. Tacitus said he didn't think the Germans would ever be civilized (and during the late annoyance many of our educators and statesmen said the same thing). All Europe at one time was inhabited by tribes of Nordics who did little else than lie around and enjoy life. Frivolity and indolence had Europe in their dastardly grip, and there was no John H. Sumner, Lord's Day Alliance or Anti-Saloon League to say them nay. . . . The country wasn't developed at all. People wasted an immense amount of time on cathedrals, stained glass, poetry, tournaments and fairs. For a time it looked as if the white race was destined to be a failure. Jongleurs, troubadours, fat priests, hungry bandits, and lean knights wandered around the country from place to place. A peaceful citizen was often held up in broad daylight. There was never the feeling of security that one experiences in cities free from outlawry, such as Memphis and Pittsburgh. . . . In the midst of this slothfulness the white people of that day are reported to have actually been happy. What a sorry picture![111]

The distinctly twentieth-century cultural relativism that colors this article by Schuyler indicates how quickly Boas's culture concept caught on among educated blacks, who were eager to abandon the nineteenth-century hierarchy of racial civilizations—which always seemed to locate blacks at the bottom. By the 1930s these old ideas could be confidently dismissed by a new generation of academically trained black intellectuals such as E. Franklin Frazier, Abram Harris, and Ralph Bunche, who came of age at a time when the liberal environmentalist understanding of race poineered by Franz Boas was beginning to gain broad acceptance in American social science. To these young black intellectuals race was "a useful myth which had been perpetuated by powerful whites and manipulated by the black leadership class for its own selfish interests." This new generation of black intellectuals, James O. Young notes, so scorned the notion of race that "although in their private correspondence and memoranda they often saw the value of intraracial unity, in their published work they practically ignored the idea, and even sometimes treated it with contempt."[112]

Just how racial ideology fared among the great mass of ordinary blacks who did not work in the academy, publish articles, join one of the militant black sects, or participate in the UNIA is more difficult to say. Certainly, more African-Americans participated, directly and indirectly, in the twentieth-century black struggle for integration and assimilation than have ever supported black separatist movements to date. And these assimilationist goals have long placed certain constraints on the degree to which many black Americans have chosen to differentiate themselves from their white countrymen. In a discussion entitled "Our White Folks" (1927) in the *American Mercury*, George Schuyler argued that African-Americans looked upon themselves as Americans, as an "integral part" of the nation's "black and white civilization." Barred from enjoying the full benefits of citizenship, black Americans hoped that white people could be educated to see the need for change in American race relations. In explaining this hope, Schuyler maintained that the average black American was capable of seeing white people as individuals despite their race. With characteristic sarcasm, Schuyler noted that,

> The AfraAmerican, being more tolerant than the Caucasian, is ready to admit that white people are not all the same, and it is not unusual to read or hear a warning from a Negro orator or editor against condemning all crackers as prejudiced asses, although agreeing that such a description fits a majority of them. The Ethiop is given to pointing out individual pinks who are exceptionally honorable, tolerant and unprejudiced. In this respect, I venture to say, he rises several notches higher than the gentility of the ofays, to whom, even in this day and time, all coons look alike.[113]

Conclusion

When Frantz Fanon, who would become one of the great black thinkers of the twentieth century, left his native Martinique as a young man, he found that racial identity was not the same everywhere. In white majority societies, being black meant something different than it did in the largely black and mixed-race world of the Antilles. In Europe and America, Fanon discovered, "not only must a black man be black; he must be black in relation to the white man."[1] So it always was for the black Americans considered in this study. Whether free or slave, educated or unlettered, African-Americans of the nineteenth and early twentieth centuries grew up in a society where both social reality and the relentless influence of racist ideology forced all of its members to define both themselves and others around them in racial terms. These African-Americans confronted their white fellow Americans across a racial divide structured by class, codified by law, and dignified by a white supremacist ideology that deemed the low status of black people to be a reflection of the inferior character and abilities of their race.

Moreover, they did so at a time when the white supremacist ideology that rationalized their low estate went virtually uncontested outside the black community. A significant minority of whites supported black causes throughout the nineteenth century, but during this era even the black race's allies almost never questioned the importance of racial determinism in the synthesis of physical, biological, and historical knowledge that their era's science employed to explain human affairs.

Previous scholarship on American racial thought has considered the racist ideology embedded in this synthesis in great detail, but it has neglected to consider the particular dilemmas it imposed on black Americans, who were forced to redefine both themselves and their white fellow Americans against social realities and scientific knowledge that relegated their race to the lowest rank in the human family. Modern historians have recognized that nineteenth-century African-Americans resisted the social, political, and legal proscriptions against them and have chronicled these struggles with great eloquence. Yet, by and large, they have not mapped the understanding of race that informed nineteenth-century black struggles for freedom and equality. As a consequence, they have left open a huge question, for there is no reason to assume the African-American struggle for equality was informed by a conviction in the fallacy of innate distinctions between the races. Likewise, a related question remains unanswered: If such a conviction existed, on what premises would it be based? Twentieth-century science has rejected the notion of biological distinctions between the races, but in the nineteenth century African-Americans could not turn to this authority for any affirmation of their claims to the same freedom and rights accorded to white Americans.

In examining African-American ideas about white people between 1830 and 1925, this book has sought to identify the ideas and images that shaped black perceptions of white Americans during these years, while also assessing the status of innate racial differences within African-American thought. African-American ideas about white people can be examined only with simultaneous attention to the ways in which nineteenth-century black Americans understood race as a concept: for the story of black racial thought in the nineteenth century is in a sense a story defining the limits of what a people can be made to believe about themselves. Told that they were a people of dubious origins, whose complexion marked them wholly inferior by nature to all Caucasians, black Americans did not always argue that complexion was the only distinction between the races. But they certainly argued against the white doctrine of black racial inferiority, and in doing so they redefined the character of both races.

However, neither their arguments nor their assumptions about race are easily summarized, for nineteenth-century African-Americans in different walks of life approached their revisions of the dominant culture's racial ideology in different ways. A great cultural gulf divided the educated blacks who recorded their thoughts on race in writing from the unlettered black majority whose racial ideas must be sought in other kinds of testimony, such as folklore and interviews. Indeed, the distance between the racial thought of black intellectuals and that of uneducated African-Americans is so great that this project has considered their thought separately.

Black intellectuals, who were well versed in racist doctrine, crafted an informed rebuttal to white racial ideology by creating their own version of ethnology—the nineteenth-century science of the races. Drawing on the environmentalist theories of human development propounded by the great European thinkers of the Enlightenment, they argued that different environments rather than different origins were what distinguished the races of man. In their ethnological arguments, black thinkers traced the ancestry of their race back to Adam by maintaining that the races originated from Noah's three sons, Ham, Japhet, and Shem, whose far-flung progeny came to look different because they settled different parts of the world. The black race, they emphasized, had a glorious past because it descended from

Ham, whose children had created great civilizations in ancient Ethiopia and Egypt. Like white ethnology, black ethnology blended scriptural interpretation and scientific speculation in its study of race. But whereas white ethnologists often suggested that the black race was the product of a separate creation, black ethnologists stressed shared origins and the equal human capacities of all human beings.

Although these black thinkers devoted themselves to defending the equal status of black people in the human family, they did not always argue that the races were identical. African-American ethnology contains some of the most ringing denunciations of race as fallacy heard in nineteenth-century America. However, even the incisive black critics who voiced such denunciations, such as James McCune Smith and Frederick Douglass, never entirely rejected the idea of innate racial differences in their own thinking. The environmentalist theories of human development that such thinkers employed to defend the common origins and capacities of all men did not rule out the possibility of racial differences but instead sought to explain such differences by attributing them to the influence of environmental factors. Likewise, these environmentalist theories did not preclude the possibility that there might be superior and inferior races, providing such distinctions were not held to be permanent. For environmentalism claimed only that racial distinctions had developed over time and were subject to further change.

With their arguments against black inferiority thus resting on the slippery slope of eighteenth-century environmentalism, black thinkers did not insist that there was no difference between the races. Instead, they offered revisionist assessments of both races that frequently went beyond upholding the equity of the races to argue that the character of Anglo-Saxon's compared unfavorably with the better nature of their own race. In arguments that assumed the racial families had long been divided by different God-given attributes, black writers challenged the historical accomplishments of the white race by emphasizing its barbarous Anglo-Saxon lineage. Their attacks on the history of the white race sought to recast the ethnographic image of the proud Anglo-Saxon race, so celebrated in white American culture.

Rejecting the white image of the Anglo-Saxon race as the ideal against which all other races fell short, black intellectuals portrayed white people as a predatory race whose brutality spanned all of human history. In doing so, they contested both the proclaimed superiority of the Anglo-Saxon race and the gender ideals embedded in the white racial ideal. For in the virtually all-male discourse of white nineteenth-century racial thought, the Anglo-Saxon ideal was defined by male characteristics. White racists contrasted the power, intellect, courage, independence, and manliness that they attributed to their own race against the more feminine characteristics they attributed to women and black people alike. Black ethnology was also a male endeavor, and its practitioners did not question the idea that any race should be defined by its men. But they held up their own race's religious and moral virtues—characteristics also credited to the black race by white friends of the Negro—as essential qualities lacking in the white race. By defining whites as a brutal and predatory race that took all of its celebrated masculine virtues too far, black intellectuals sought to create a revisionist racial ideal in which the masculinity of African-American men could be recognized.

Meanwhile, race raised different questions for the last generation of African-American slaves, whose testimony was considered in the second half of this study. At issue for these black men and women, in defining their own racial character, was the question of humanity, pure and simple. These uneducated people were unversed in the specific claims of white racist doctrine and wholly unfamiliar with the biological understanding of the family of man that underlay white claims of innate superiority. But African-American slaves nevertheless understood racism as an attack on the status of their own race. Indeed, their experiences under slavery, and their continuing subordination after emancipation, led them to believe that whites considered them less than human. Throughout their written and oral testimony, these African-Americans expressed the same complaint. They maintained that white people did not see blacks as human beings, with human natures and souls. They resisted this crushing evaluation with a vibrant religious culture that took as its central theme: "We are the people of God."[2]

In claiming a place for themselves in the human family, the unlettered African-Americans who formed the majority of nineteenth-century America's black population asserted that they shared a common humanity with their white oppressors. But the idea of racial differences nonetheless held meaning for a people who found themselves in every way subordinate to a white ruling class. The realities of slavery and racial subordination led these African-Americans to understand the class structure of American society in distinctly racial terms. They understood the interests and allegiances of blacks and whites to be quite distinct, and they saw white people as distinguished, above all, by the superior social and economic power that accompanied their whiteness.

Yet, unlike the more educated black Americans who wrote ethnology, slaves did not attribute any set of distinctive racial characteristics to white people. Slavery required them to observe white behavior closely, and the lesson they learned was that all whites were not alike. They described many whites as "mean." Indeed, in the testimony collected by Federal Works Project interviews, ex-slave men and women bore witness to their sufferings at the hands of cruel white overseers and owners. But these witnesses of slavery ultimately emphasized that, like the black race, the white race was made up of a mixture of good and bad individuals. Their refusal to generalize about white racial character left them with little explanation for white power and privilege—a phenomenon they found mysterious and troubling. However, they took comfort in their abiding faith in what W.E.B. DuBois described as "the ultimate justice of things."[3] These men and women had every confidence that the power and privilege of the white race would not save white people from divine judgment; and they were equally confident that blacks would not always be slighted on account of their race. "Dey be no black an' white in heaven," as one South Carolina freedwoman put it.[4]

Although race raised different questions for uneducated and educated black Americans, some of the basic issues that defined their perceptions of white people were the same. Slave or free, schooled or otherwise, all of these nineteenth-century African-Americans redefined the character of the races in response to a racist ideology that, as they understood it, deemed black people as less than human. African-Americans who grew up under slavery complained that their white owners mistook them for animals, while black intellectuals saw the idea of polygenesis as an allegation that black people were like monkeys rather than men.

The common impulse that united blacks' struggles against white racial ideology should not surprise us, for it reflects the common ideological context in which they took place. All these African-Americans fought the definitions imposed on them by a racist white majority. Moreover, although the mass of unlettered blacks who traveled from slavery to freedom over the course of the nineteenth century had life experiences a world apart from those of the literate and sophisticated black men who practiced ethnology, the cultural gulf between these two groups should not be overstated. For black ethnology's practitioners included a great number of ex-slaves. Men such as Frederick Douglass, James W. C. Pennington, Harvey Johnson, and Bishop Henry MacNeal Turner brought something of their early experiences in slavery into their eloquent attacks of white racial ideology. For instance, Pennington, a fugitive blacksmith from Maryland who published one of the earliest black attacks on white ethnology, no doubt spoke from personal experience when he wrote of the slave-master relationship: "The proud and selfish Anglo-Saxon found to his great surprise, that *his mind* had to devise ways and means, not to hold in check brutes only, as a man would halter and break a horse into harness, but that he had to deal with a mind possessing all the natural attributes for which [*sic*] himself is peculiar." Pennington described slavery as "A WAR OF THE MINDS," a phrase that might also be applied to the contest between black and white racial thought in the nineteenth century.[5] Black Americans were drawn into this contest from the late eighteenth century onward as racist ideology began to be mistaken for biological reality by their white fellow Americans. In a contest made unequal by the white majority's vastly superior cultural and political power, black Americans were, to some degree, ensnared by the fallacy of race even as they sought to refute racism's insult against their humanity.

For the idea of racial differences acquired a certain reality for nineteenth-century black Americans. Black intellectuals often shared in their white countrymen's tendency to discuss the races as being divided by natural characteristics. Moreover, uneducated and educated black Americans often shared in the confusion of race and class that prevailed in their society as a whole and characterized themselves as a distinct people united by their common coloring. Many of these African-Americans echoed abolitionist David Walker's suspicions about whether white people were "*as good by nature*" as black people.[6] Such suspicions are evident in the testimony of the slaves who believed that there would be "plenty mo'" white folks in hell than in heaven.[7] And these suspicions were elaborated into a revisionist racial ideology in the writings of black intellectuals who derided the brutal character of the "proud and selfish Anglo-Saxon."[8]

Yet the antiwhite sentiments in black racial thought cannot be understood simply as white racism reversed, since a racial ideology that arises in self-defense is necessarily quite distinct from one that serves as a rationalization for a discriminatory social order. If nothing else, the context that shaped African-American attempts to redefine the character of the races in their own favor put distinct limits to the development of racial essentialism in nineteenth-century black thought as a whole. Although African-Americans made claims for the superiority of their own race, these ideas about racial difference were most often articulated in a literature largely devoted to defending the equal, if not identical, status of black people in the human family. Furthermore, their attacks on the racial characteristics of white people centered on white morality rather than on the appearance, abilities, or humanity of white people—and these attacks took place during a period when the morality of white Americans was by no means above reproach.

Nonetheless, the black chauvinism in African-American thought still bears analysis as racial ideology, precisely because few categories have been established, other than reverse racism, for the interpretation of the racial thought of nondominant groups. Jean-Paul Sartre described the literature of African writers who celebrated "negritude" in the 1940s as an "anti-racist racism," and his phrase might well be applied to the racial thought of nineteenth-century African-American intellectuals. For these African-Americans, like later African writers such as Léopold Senghor, criticized the racial character of white people while ultimately seeking the "abolition of all ethnic privileges." Sartre believed that the African writers' idea of negritude must be understood as part of a dialectical progression toward the "exact idea of *proletariat*." "In fact," he explained, negritude appears as the minor term of a dialectical progression: The theoretical and practical assertion of the supremacy of the white man is its thesis; the position of negritude as an antithetical value is the moment of negativity. But this negative moment is insufficient by itself, and the Negroes who employ it know this very well; they know that it is intended to prepare the synthesis or realization of the human in a society without races. Thus negritude is the root of its own destruction, it is a transition and not a conclusion, a means not an ultimate end.[9]

However, Sartre's analysis of negritude is not easily applied to nineteenth-century African-American thinkers. For unlike the Marxist African writers of whom he spoke, these African-Americans were too anxious to see their people achieve middle-class goals, and too caught up in what Sartre eloquently described as the "psychobiological syncretism" of race, to dream of a raceless proletariat.[10] Yet his insight that black chauvinism emerges in a dialectical relationship with white supremacy cannot be denied. Moreover, it helps explain why the black chauvinism in nineteenth-century black racial thought always went hand in hand with arguments emphasizing the unity of the races.

What remains to be seen in the American context, however, is whether the negritude in African-American racial thought really contains the roots of its own destruction. One lesson that the study of African-American racial thought teaches about the character of racial ideology—even when applied to egalitarian ends—is that the concept of race is virtually inseparable from the idea of a hierarchy among the races. Across the color line, black American and white American alike, once they allowed for the possibility of differences between the races, tended to make comparisons that favored their own race at the expense of others. Lamenting this tendency, John Stephens Durham, a prominent black teacher, lawyer, and diplomat, wrote in 1897: "On the one hand, the Negro has been ignorantly denounced by historians and ethnologists. . . . On the other hand, colored historians in a spirit of resentment quite natural, all things considered, have written books to excite what they call race pride."[11]

Durham voiced this complaint in a pamphlet entitled *To Teach the Negro History: A Suggestion*, and he went on to admonish: "Teach your boy that nature did not make one special creation and color it white, and another special creation, and paint it black." However, Durham did not explain how blacks could afford to abandon race pride in a society where they felt compelled to teach that their race did not descend from a separate Creation. Durham himself was content to believe "that each variety of the human species is in the place that it has earned," an idea that may have informed his plea for teachers of Negro history to instruct their pupils in the unity of the races without embellishing on the black race's achievements.[12] Yet Durham's strictures against race pride in the teaching of black history ignored the fact that so long as the human species was seen as divided, arguments for the common origins of black and white people would not suffice to prove their equal worth. And therein lay the crucial dilemma faced by black Americans who sought to use race pride as a weapon against racism.

The nineteenth-century black intellectuals who defended their own race by portraying white people as brutal and predatory by nature addressed the realities of an era in which, particularly in the American South, the exploitation and subordination of black Americans was indeed sustained by force and intimidation. Yet their discourse on white people was more than social criticism couched in the language of race. With their graphic descriptions of the white race's Anglo-Saxon past, and glowing accounts of their own race's ancient glories, these writers sought to establish that the racial character of black people more than equaled that of white people; and they frequently predicted a racial redemption in which "the destined superiority of the Negro" would at long last be recognized.[13] Their arguments fit the category that Sartre called negritude, but, contrary to his predictions, these arguments may have undercut rather than sustained any aspirations they had toward a raceless society. For the danger that lay in race pride during the nineteenth century was that it only partly challenged the racial essentialism on which the doctrine of black racial inferiority was based.

As we have seen, black thinkers such as Frederick Douglass and Harvey Johnson seem to have been aware of these dangers, for they questioned race as a concept. Yet these writers lacked both the cultural authority and the scientific engagement to create an entirely alternative discourse about race. Moreover, as Nancy Leys Stepan and Sander L. Gilman point out, although both black and Jewish intellectuals resisted being stereotyped as inferior by nineteenth-century science, members of both these groups ultimately found it difficult to step "'outside of'" science "in the era of the successful establishment of science as an epistemologically neutral and instrumentally successful form of knowledge."[14] Thus, for black intellectuals, race pride was necessary despite its dangers.

By contrast, the mass of uneducated African-Americans had no difficulties stepping outside of science, for they never entered the learned discourse on race that nineteenth-century science informed. Indeed, one reason that the racial character of white people is so hazy in the testimony of ex-slaves may well have something to do with the fact that while these men and women had intimate experience with racism's practice, they knew little of its discourse. In attempting to determine what strategies minority group members could have employed to successfully oppose the dominant discourse of race in nineteenth-century America, Stepan and Gilman speculate that the optimal strategy might have been to create an "'alternative ideology.'" This ideology would serve to place its adherents "outside the discourse of scientific racism ... by positing a radically different worldview, with different perceptions of reality, goals, and points of reference." Having made this suggestion, Stepan and Gilman go on to make the shrewd observation that such an alternative was not really possible for the educated blacks and Jews who grappled with scientific racism—for they could not step outside the scientific discourse of the culture.

This "alternative ideology," however, seems to have proved more attainable for the mass of black folks, who had never stepped inside this discourse to begin with. To be sure, ex-slaves frequently confused race and class and expressed hope that all "mean" white people would roast in hell. Yet ex-slaves' association of whiteness with power and their religious hopes for racial justice did not ultimately cohere into a fully developed racial ideology. These African-Americans saw great differences between the power and position of white people and black people, and also commented on a variety of distinctions in culture, beliefs, and behavior which they saw as distinguishing the two groups. But essentialist explanations for any of these differences are hard to find in slave culture. "Dere ain't no differunce twixt niggers an' white folks cept dey color," Joanna Thompson Isom commented in one of the very few recorded ex-slave remarks concerning the physical differences between the races. "White folks stay out of de sun, but ef you cuts dey finger, dey both bleeds alike; nationality wont let dem be de same; if hit wuzn't fer station in de worl' w'ud be better off; dats what makes dem have to stay on dey own side of de street."[15]

Beginning at the turn of the century, new developments in the sciences would ultimately confirm Isom's belief in the physical identity of the races—if not her assertion that white people achieved their color by staying out of the sun. However, the demise of scientific racism would prove instructive for black intellectuals, who had been better acquainted with its tenets. Indeed, the rise of cultural anthropology would reconfigure the racial thought of these thinkers by offering them a highly desirable alternative to racial determinism. Over the first quarter of the twentieth century, Franz Boas's arguments for culture as the arbiter of human differences resolved much of the tension between racial determinism and environmentalism that had long existed in the thought of black intellectuals: for they ultimately abandoned racial determinism in favor of Boas's liberal environmentalism. Indeed, by the midcentury, black intellectuals would greet the negritude of African writers such as Senghor with some dismay. "American Negro intellectuals," the black historian St. Clair Drake notes, ultimately "declined the invitation" to a shared negritude extended by these Africans, for it reminded them of the bad old days.

> It evokes unpleasant memories of Southern orators warning against the powerfulness of Negro blood that "always tells." It is a reminder of all preachers—black and white (including Arnold Toynbee)—who es-

pouse a peculiar kind of black messianism in which Negroes are said to have a mission to teach white men how to abjure materialistic goals and demonstrate that patience and long suffering are higher virtues than the iniquitous struggle for power. . . . It rejects those values of the Western world which they have learned to prize—critical rationality, success in controlling the natural environment, Aristotle's Law of Measure, and, above all, individuality. It confuses race and culture, cause and effect, in a fashion they have learned to avoid.[16]

Yet not all African-Americans would learn such lessons. As discussed in chapter 6, the early decades of the twentieth century saw a new generation of academically trained black intellectuals abandon older ideas about race in favor of liberal environmentalism. But liberal environmentalism was not accepted by all of their fellow African-Americans. The same period also gave rise to a variety of new black separatist ideologies that embraced race as an organic and divinely ordained distinction between human beings. The Garvey movement and a variety of new black nationalist religions preserved both the negritude of nineteenth-century black racial thought and its attendant attack on the racial character of white people. Like African-American intellectuals of the nineteenth century, these religious racialists compared the races against the vast panorama of history, finding their own race's lineage superior and deeming whites overly aggressive and morally deficient.

A similar constellation of arguments remains alive today in the form of Afrocentrism, whose proponents tend to assume that black people everywhere are united by a common culture, which is in many ways superior to the organically distinct Eurocentric culture possessed by white people. Like the writings of nineteenth-century black intellectuals, Afrocentrists stress the ancient glories achieved by the African race, tracing human civilization back to the Nile valley to demonstrate "African transcendance."[17] As interpreted by some black Americans, Afrocentrism is less of a racial ideology than it is a call for the dissemination of knowledge about black history and culture to combat the negative racial stereotypes that still plague African-Americans. As such, Afrocentrism has value, for as St. Clair Drake noted with reference to African negritude:

> The myth of negritude—the belief that black men have developed cultures of worth and that although these cultures may be different from those of the West they have values which all can appreciate and share— has important morale-building functions. It can give confidence to the masses in the West Indies and America, as well as in Africa, who smart under the stigma of their blackness and of being of African descent.[18]

However, Afrocentric writers frequently make far more essentialist uses of black history than the morale-building functions described by Drake. Proponents of a certain kind of Afrocentrism even argue that

Africans and Europeans are forever distinguished by separate geographic origins, which shaped the character of the two races into white "ice people" and black "sun people."[19] This is a rich irony indeed, for Afrocentrism's glorification of the African and Egyptian origins of the black race has its own origin in the racial thought of nineteenth-century black intellectuals, who in many cases took pen to paper for the primary purpose of defending the common ancestry of the human family against white racists who sought to argue that blacks descended from a separate Creation.

Indeed, the irony is many-layered, for early black celebrations of the African-American's glorious racial past frequently drew on white colonizationists' celebrations of the Negro's African heritage, which were originally forwarded by members of the all-white American Colonizationist Society as a rationale for returning free blacks to Africa, where their race had once done so well. As mentioned in chapter 1, David Walker, one of the first black writers to emphasize his people's glorious history in ancient times, first had to inform his black readers, whom he suspected would know the Egyptians largely for their oppression of the Jews, "that the Egyptians, were Africans or coloured people, such as we are."[20]

Yet nineteenth-century black Americans cannot be held responsible for the ironies their ideas engendered in the hands of later writers. And while we must analyze the racialism in their thought and assess the degree to which their racial critiques of white people successfully opposed white racial ideology, we cannot judge their success by modern standards. We must keep in mind that African-American arguments for the equal status of black people in the human family were radically revisionist in an era when racism colored the general understanding of both social reality and the laws of human development held by virtually all of their white fellow Americans. Moreover, their intellectual resistance to racism's relentless ideological assault was in many ways as heroic and difficult as the protest actions they took against slavery and racial subordination—and it certainly informed these actions. African-American struggles to understand, and sometimes redefine, the racial character of the white race, while defending the character of their own, tell the story of that intellectual resistance.

Notes

Introduction

1. Olaudah Equiano, *Equiano's Travels: The Interesting Narrative of the Life of Olaudah Equiano or Gustavus Vassa, The African*, 4th ed. (Dublin: by the author, 1791), 50.

2. Philip D. Curtin, ed., *Africa Remembered: Narratives by West Africans from the Era of the Slave Trade* (Madison: University of Wisconsin Press, 1967), 215 n. 49. See also, William D. Piersen, "White Cannibals, Black Martyrs: Fear, Depression, and Religious Faith as Causes of Suicide among New Slaves," *Journal of Negro History* 62, no. 2 (April 1977): 147–158.

3. See Winthrop D. Jordan, *White Over Black: American Attitudes toward the Negro, 1550–1812* (Chapel Hill: University of North Carolina Press, 1968; repr., New York: Norton, 1977), 28–29.

4. Piersen, "White Cannibals, Black Martyrs," 148.

5. Ayuba Suleimen Ibrahima Diallo, "The Capture and Travels of Ayuba Suleimen Ibrahima" (1734), in Curtin, *Africa Remembered*, 57.

6. Classic studies of American racial thought, such as Jordan's *White Over Black* and George Fredrickson's *The Black Image in the White Mind*, chart the course of white racism virtually without reference to black thinking on racial questions. Jordan prefaces *White Over Black* with the explanation that "this is not a book about Negroes, except as they were the object of white men's attitudes," and Fredrickson likewise acknowledges at the outset that his book focuses, "almost exclusively, on what whites thought about blacks." Jordan, *White Over Black*, viii; George Fredrickson, "Introduction to the Wesleyan Edition" of *The Black Image in the White Mind: The Debate on Afro-American Character and Destiny, 1817–1914* (New York: Harper and Row, 1977; repr., Middletown, Conn.: Wesleyan University Press, 1987), xiii.

7. In recent years, scholars have begun to study whiteness, although still largely from the perspective of whites. Studies include David R. Roediger, *The Wages of Whiteness: Race and the Making of the American Working Class* (New York: Verso, 1991); Vron Ware, *Beyond the Pale: White Women, Racism, and History* (London: Verso, 1992); Matt Wray and Annalee Newitz, *White Trash: Race and Class in America* (New York: Routledge, 1997); and Ruth Frankenberg, *White Women, Race Matters: The Social Construction of Whiteness* (Minneapolis: University of Minnesota Press, 1993). Among the few places where firsthand African-American perspectives on whiteness can be found are in David R. Roediger's anthology, *Black on White: Black Writers on What It Means to Be White* (New York: Schocken Books, 1998), and in some of the essays contained in the "white issues" of two recent journals: *Minnesota Review* 47 (1996) and *Transition* 73 (1998). One writer who has written several interesting essays about black perceptions of whiteness is bell hooks. See bell hooks, "Representing Whiteness in the Black Imagination," in *Cultural Studies*, ed. Lawrence Grossberg, Cary Nelson, and Paula A. Treichlin (New York: Routledge, 1992); 338–346, and *Black Looks: Race and Representation* (Boston: South End Press, 1992).

8. Sarah Parker Remond in a letter published in the *National Antislavery Standard*, 3 November 1866.

9. Toni Morrison, *Playing in the Dark: Whiteness and the Literary Imagination* (Cambridge, Mass.: Harvard University Press, 1992), 38.

10. Black writers, James Weldon Johnson noted in 1928, typically address a double and "divided . . . audience made up of two elements with differing and often opposite and antagonistic points of view." James Weldon Johnson, "The Dilemma of the Negro Author," *American Mercury* 15 (December 1928): 477.

11. Anna Julia Cooper, *A Voice from the South* (New York: Oxford University Press, 1988), i.

12. Ibid., iii. Maria Stewart's writings are contained in *Maria W. Stewart, America's First Black Woman Political Writer: Essays and Speeches*, ed. Marilyn Richardson (Bloomington: Indiana University Press, 1987).

13. James C. Scott, *Domination and the Arts of Resistance: The Hidden Transcripts* (New Haven, Conn.: Yale University Press, 1990). On African-American hidden transcripts, see Robin D. G. Kelley, *Race Rebels: Culture, Politics, and the Black Working Class* (New York: Free Press, 1994), esp. chapter 2.

14. Quoted in David R. Roediger, "And Die in Dixie: Funerals, Death, and Heaven in Slavery," *Massachusetts Review* 22 (Spring 1981): 180.

15. James W. C. Pennington, *A Lecture Delivered Before the Glasgow Young Men's Christian Association* (Edinburgh: H. Armour, printer, [1850]), 2.

16. James Baldwin, *Notes of a Native Son*, in *Collected Essays* (New York: Library of America, 1998), 123.

17. Purvis to J. Miller McKim, 2 December 1860 (J. M. McKim Papers, Cornell University Library), in James MacPherson, *The Negro's Civil War: How American Negroes Felt and Acted during the War for the Union* (New York: Vintage Books, 1965), 99–100.

18. Fannie Moore in *The American Slave: A Composite Autobiography*, ed. George Rawick (Westport, Conn.: Greenwood Press, 1972–1973), North Carolina Narratives, v. 15. pt. 2, 128.

19. Jacques Barzun, *Race: A Study in Superstition* (1937; rev. 2d ed., New York: Harper and Row, 1965), xi.

Chapter 1

1. "Petitions of New England Slaves for Freedom (1773–1779)," reprinted in Gary B. Nash, *Race and Revolution* (Madison, Wis.: Madison House, 1990), 175.

2. For an overview of this debate, see Alden T. Vaughan, "The Origins Debate: Slavery and Racism in Seventeenth-Century Virginia," *Virginia Magazine of History and Biography* 97 (July 1989): 311–354.

3. George Fredrickson, "Towards a Social Interpretation of American Racism," in *Key Issues in the Afro-American Experience*, vol. 1, ed. Martin Kilson, Nathan Huggins, and Daniel Fox (New York: Harcourt, Brace, Jovanovich, 1971), 256.

4. George Fredrickson, *The Black Image in the White Mind: The Debate on Afro-American Character and Destiny, 1817–1914* (New York: Harper and Row, 1972; repr., Middletown, Conn.: Wesleyan University Press, 1987), 1.

5. James Forten, "An Address Delivered Before the American Moral Reform Society," 17 August 1837, *Minutes and Proceedings of the American Moral Reform Society held at Philadelphia . . . from the 14th to 19th of August, 1837* (Philadelphia: Historic Publications, 1969), 36.

6. Alexander Saxton, *The Rise and Fall of the White Republic: Class Politics and Mass Culture in Nineteenth-Century America* (London: Verso, 1990), 15.

7. Thomas Jefferson, *Notes on Virginia*, in *The Life and Selected Writings of Thomas Jefferson*, ed. Adrienne Koch and William Peden (New York: Modern American Library, 1944), 262, 261.

8. Winthrop D. Jordan, *White Over Black: American Attitudes toward the Negro, 1550–1812* (Chapel Hill: University of North Carolina Press, 1968; repr., New York: Norton, 1977), 455.

9. Petition of the New Hampshire Slaves, 12 November 1779, in "Slavery in New Hampshire," *Magazine of American History* 21 (January 1889): 63–64.

10. Absalom Jones and Richard Allen, *Narrative of the Proceedings of the Black People, During the Late Awful Calamity in Philadelphia* (1793), in *Negro Protest Pamphlets: A Compendium* (New York: Arno Press, 1969), 19–20.

11. "Letter on Slavery. By a Negro" (1789), in *Racial Thought in America: A Documentary History*, vol. 1, *From the Puritans to Abraham Lincoln*, ed. Louis Ruchames (Amherst: University of Massachusetts Press, 1969), 201.

12. Letter from Benjamin Banneker to the Secretary of State (Philadephia, 1792), in Nash, *Race and Revolution*, 178.

13. Henri Gregoire, *De la litterature des negres* (Paris: Chez Maradan, 1808).

14. Thomas Jefferson, *The Works of Thomas Jefferson*, ed. Paul Leicester Ford (New York: Putnam, 1905). Letter to Banneker, 30 August 1791, 6:310; letter to Joel Barlow, 8 October 1809, 11:121.

15. Reverend Griffith Hughes, *Natural History of Barbados* (1750), quoted in Jordan, *White Over Black*, 188.

16. Smith's *Essay* begins: "The unity of the human race, notwithstanding the diversity of colour, and form under which it appears in different portions of the globe, is a doctrine, independently of the authority of divine revelation, much more consistent with the principles of sound philosophy, than any of the numerous hypotheses which have referred its varieties to a radical and original diversity of species." Samuel Stanhope Smith, *An Essay on the Causes of the Variety of Complexion and Figure in the Human Species* (1787; repr., Cambridge, Mass.: Belknap Press of Harvard University, 1965), 7.

17. David Brion Davis, *The Problem of Slavery in Western Culture* (New York: Oxford University Press, 1966), 455.

18. Fredrickson, "Towards a Social Interpretation of American Racism," 251.

19. Jordan, *White Over Black*, 287.

20. William Stanton, *The Leopard's Spots: Scientific Attitudes towards Race in America, 1815–1859* (Chicago: University of Chicago Press, 1960), 3.

21. Winthrop Jordan, Introduction to Smith, *An Essay on the Causes of the Variety of Complexion and Figure in the Human Figure*, xxxii.

22. James Forten, "Letters From a Man of Color on the Late Bill before the Senate of Pennsylvania" (Philadelphia, 1813), reprinted in Nash, *Race and Revolution*, 192.

23. George Lawrence, "Oration on the Abolition of the Slave Trade" (New York, 1813), reprinted in Nash, *Race and Revolution*, 200.

24. David Brion Davis, *The Problem of Slavery in the Age of Revolution* (Ithaca, N.Y.: Cornell University Press, 1975), 303.

25. Jones and Allen, *Narrative of the Proceedings of the Black People*, 21.

26. Adam Carman, *An Oration Delivered at the Fourth Anniversary of Abolition of the Slave Trade in the Methodist Episcopal Church* (New York: John C. Totten, 1811), 19.

27. William B. Gravely, "The Dialectic of Double Consciousness in Black American Freedom Celebrations, 1808–1863," *Journal of Negro History* 67 (1982), 309; William Hamilton, "An Address to the New York African Society," (1809), quoted in Gravely, "The Dialectic of Double Consciousness," 309.

28. Benjamin Quarles, "The Revolutionary War as a Black Declaration of Independence," in *Slavery and Freedom in the Age of the American Revolution*, ed. Ira Berlin and Ronald Hoffman (Charlotteville: University Press of Virginia, 1983), 297.

29. For a review of the complex issues involved in this philosophy, see George A. Levine, "Interpreting Early Black Ideology: A Reappraisal of the Historical Consensus" *Journal of the Early Republic* 1 (Fall 1981): 269–287. For a more detailed history of antebellum black activism, see James Horton and Lois Horton's *In Hope of Liberty: Culture, Community, and Protest among Northern Free Blacks, 1700–1860* (New York: Oxford University Press, 1997).

30. *Liberator*, 3 December 1831, quoted in Linda Perkins, "Black Women and Racial 'Uplift' Prior to Emancipation," in *The Black Woman Cross-Culturally Considered*, ed. Filomina Chioma Steady (Cambridge, Mass.: Schenkeman, 1981), 325.

31. Petition presented by Philadephia blacks "To the Humane and Benevolent Inhabitants of the City and County of Philadelphia," in *Early Negro Writing, 1730–1837*, ed. Dorothy Porter (Boston: Beacon Press, 1971), 265.

32. Leonard I. Sweet, *Black Images of America, 1784–1870* (New York: Norton, 1976), 40.

33. Fredrickson, *The Black Image in the White Mind*, 18.

34. Robert Goodloe Harper, "A Letter from General Harper of Maryland to Elias Caldwell, Secretary of the American Society for Colonizing Free People of Colour in the United States with their own Consent" (Baltimore, 1918), quoted in Fredrickson, *The Black Image in the White Mind*, 14.

35. The first mass meeting against colonization occurred in Philadelphia just weeks after the ACS's first meeting in December 1817. P. J. Staudenraus, *The African Colonization Movement, 1816–1865* (New York: Columbia University Press, 1961), 32.

36. On Paul Cuffe, see Lamont D. Thomas, *Rise to Be a People: A Biography of Paul Cuffe* (Urbana: University of Illinois Press, 1986); and Floyd J. Miller, *The Search for a Black Nationality: Black Colonization and Emigration, 1787–1863* (Urbana: University of Illinois Press, 1975).

37. "Resolutions of the People of Color, at a Meeting held on 25th of January, 1831. With an Address to the Citizens of New York, 1831. In Answer to Those of the New York Colonization Society," in *Early Negro Writing, 1730–1837*, ed. Dorothy Porter (Boston: Beacon Press, 1971), 283.

38. William Hamilton in "Minutes of the Fourth Annual Convention for the Improvement of the Free People of Color in the United States" (1834), in *Minutes of the Proceedings of the National Negro Conventions*, ed. Howard Holman Bell (New York: Arno Press and the New York Times, 1969), 5.

39. Theodore Wright, "Address before the Convention of the New York State Anti-Slavery Society," *Colored American*, 14 October 1837.

40. *Freedom's Journal*, 13 April 1827.

41. *Freedom's Journal*, 6 April, 20 July, 27 July 1827.

42. *Freedom's Journal*, 13 April 1827.

43. C. F. Volney, *Volney's Ruins: or, Meditation on the Revolutions of Empires; translated under the immediate inspection of the author from the Sixth Paris Edition* (Boston: C. Gaylord, 1835), 33–35. According to Martin Bernal's controversial book *Black Athena*, Egypt was considered the fount of ancient civilization by educated Europeans until the mid-nineteenth century, when German romantic scholars rewrote history to move the origins of Western civilization to Greece, so that the development of learning and culture could be attributed to an Aryan people. Similarly, Egypt's debt to Ethiopia was obscured by European thinkers "concerned to keep black Africans as far as possible from European civilization." Martin Bernal, *Black Athena: The Afroasiatic Roots of Classical Civilization* (New Brunswick, N.J.: Rutgers University Press, 1987), 30.

44. More extended discussions of the history of the story of Ham include Benjamin Braude, "The Sons of Noah and the Construction of Ethnic and Geographical Identities in the Medieval and Early Modern Periods," *William and Mary Quarterly* 54 (January 1997):103–142; Edith R. Saunders, "The Hamitic Hypothesis: Its Origin and Functions in Time Perspective," *Journal of African History* 10 (1969): 521–532; and William McKee Evans, "From the Land of Guinea: The Strange Odyssey of the 'Sons of Ham,'" *American Historical Review* 85 (1980): 15–43.

45. The first issue of the American Colonization Society's *African Repository and Colonial Journal*, published in 1825, contains the article "On the Early History of the Negro Race," which makes arguments very similar to Russwurm's on the Egyptian origins and Cushite character of the black race. Written by an author named only as "T.R.," this article also refers to "the mutability of human affairs" and conceivably could have served as a model for Russwurm's series—although Russwurm's pieces seem to reflect a far closer reading of

Volney and a greater interest in presenting evidence to counter color prejudice. Either way, the colonizationist article differs markedly from Russwurm's in its overall argument: whereas Russwurm discusses the Egyptian history of the black race to condemn slavery and color prejudice, the *African Repository* suggests that American civilization can help Egypt rise again by sending her descendants back "by *colonies* to Africa."

46. Fredrickson, *The Black Image in the White Mind*, 2.

47. *Freedom's Journal*, 6 April 1827.

48. While black people remained Ham's accursed children in the minds of many white Americans, the recoloring of Ham and his descendants resolved the troubling questions the "Hamitic hypothesis" posed for nineteenth-century theologians. As Edith R. Saunders notes, nineteenth-century clergy faced a conundrum: "If the Negro was a descendent of Ham, and Ham was cursed, how could he be the creator of a great civilization?" Saunders, "The Hamitic Hypothesis," 526.

49. *Freedom's Journal*, 6 April 1827.

50. Fredrickson's *Black Image in the White Mind*, chapter 3, contains an unsurpassed discussion of the American school of ethnology. Also useful is Robert J. C. Young, *Colonial Desire: Hybridity in Theory, Culture and Race* (New York: Routledge, 1995), chapter 5.

51. *Freedom's Journal*, 13 April 1827.

52. Russwurm's reasons for leaving, and free black responses to his departure, are discussed in Phil Samuel Sigler, "The Attitudes of Free Blacks towards Emigration to Liberia" (Ph.D. diss., Boston University, 1969).

53. On the American and English antislavery movements, see Davis, *The Problem of Slavery in the Age of Revolution*. Several useful essays on the tactics and strategies used by American abolitionists are also contained in Jeanne Fagin Yellin and John C. Van Horne, *The Abolitionist Sisterhood: Woman's Political Culture in Antebellum America* (Ithaca, N.Y.: Cornell University Press, 1994).

54. On the status of Northern free blacks, see Horton and Horton, *In Hope of Liberty*; James Oliver Horton, *Free People of Color: Inside the African-American Community* (Washington, D.C.: Smithsonian Institution, 1993); Leonard P. Curry, *The Free Black in Urban America, 1800–1850: The Shadow of the Dream* (Chicago: University of Chicago Press, 1981); Shane White, *Somewhat More Independent: The End of Slavery in New York City, 1770–1810* (Athens: University of Georgia Press, 1991); and Jane H. Pease and William H. Pease, *They Who Would Be Free: Blacks' Search for Freedom, 1830–1861* (1974; repr., Urbana: University of Illinois Press, 1990).

55. While the society's constitution did not explicitly bar African-American women, the organization's high membership fees made it off-limits for most free blacks (and working-class white women as well). Moreover, the organization was unofficially understood to exclude black members. One Boston abolitionist criticized the group's leadership in 1836, writing that "they do not allow coloured women to join their society." Shirley J. Yee, *Black Women Abolitionists: A Study in Activism, 1828–1860* (Knoxville: University of Tennessee Press, 1992), 91–92.

56. The conflicts between white and black abolitionists are described in Pease and Pease, *They Who Would Be Free*, esp. chapter 5. Other useful studies of blacks in the abolitionist movement include John H. Bracey, Jr., August Meier, and Elliot Rudwick, eds., *Blacks in the Abolitionist Movement* (Belmont, Calif.: Wadsworth, 1971); Benjamin Quarles, *Black Abolitionists* (New York: Oxford University Press, 1969); and Yee, *Black Women Abolitionists*.

57. Theodore S. Wright, *The Colored American*, 14 October 1837.

58. Samuel Cornish, *Colored American*, 25 March 1837, quoted in Pease and Pease, *They Who Would Be Free*, 83.

59. David Walker, *"One Continual Cry": David Walker's "Appeal to the Colored Citizens of the World" (1829–1830)*, ed. Herbert Aptheker (New York: Humanities Press, 1965), 67.

60. The most detailed account of Walker's life and thought is Peter Hinks's *To Awaken My Afflicted Brethren: David Walker and the Problem of Antebellum Slave Resistance* (University Park: Pennsylvania State University Press, 1997).

61. Walker, *"One Continual Cry,"* 126, 127, 128.
62. Ibid., 82.
63. Ibid., 69–70.
64. Ibid., 78.
65. Ibid., Walker, 79–80.
66. Walker, *"One Continual Cry,"* 80.
67. Ibid., 79.
68. Pompée-Valentin Vastey quoted in Robert Benjamin Lewis, *Light and Truth: Collected from the Bible and Ancient and Modern History, Containing the Universal History of the Colored and the Indian Race, from the Creation of the World to the Present Time* (1836; repr., Boston: Committee of Colored Men, 1851), 326. I have been unable to locate the original source of this quote, although it is also cited by early black scholar Daniel Murray, who prepared an entry on Vastey for his never-published "Encyclopedia of the Negro Race." Daniel Murray Papers, State Historical Society of Wisconsin, 1977, reel 24. For more of Vastey's always fascinating opinions, see Pompée-Valentin Vastey, *Reflexions on the Blacks and Whites, Remarks Upon a Letter addressed by M. Mazeres, a French Colonist, to J. C. L. Sismonde de Sismonde* (London: J. Hatchard, 1817).
69. David Ruggles, *"The Extinguisher" Extinguished, or David M. Reese "Used up by David Ruggles a Man of Color" together with some remarks on a late Production entitled "An Address on Slavery and Against the Immediate Emancipation with a plan of their Being Gradually Emancipated and Colonized in 32 Years"* (New York: by the author, 1834), 41.
70. Anna Julia Cooper, "Angry Saxons and Negro Education" (1938), reprinted in *The Voice of Anna Julia Cooper*, ed. Charles Lemert and Esme Bhan (Lanham, Md.: Rowan and Littlefield, 1998), 259–261.

Chapter 2

1. Edmund Morgan, *Inventing the People: The Rise of Popular Sovereignty in England and America* (New York: Norton, 1988), 13.
2. Plato's *Republic*, quoted in Stephen Jay Gould, *The Mismeasure of Man* (New York: Norton, 1981), 19.
3. Paul Finkelman, *Dred Scott v. Sanford: A Brief History with Documents* (Boston: Bedford Books, 1997), 61.
4. David Walker, *"One Continual Cry": David Walker's "Appeal to the Colored Citizens of the World" (1829–1830)*, ed. Herbert Aptheker (New York: Humanities Press, 1965), 72.
5. This quote is from ex-slave Tom Windham, whose testimony is contained in *The American Slave: A Composite Autobiography*, ed. George Rawick (Westport, Conn.: Greenwood Press, 1972–73), Arkansas Narratives, v. 11, pt. 7, 211.
6. Gail Bederman, *Manliness and Civilization: A Cultural History of Gender and Race in the United States, 1880–1917* (Chicago: University of Chicago Press, 1995), 20.
7. Maria W. Stewart, *America's First Black Woman Political Writer: Essays and Speeches*, ed. Marilyn Richardson (Bloomington: Indiana University Press, 1987), 46.
8. Ibid., 57, 37, 48.
9. Walker, *"One Continual Cry,"* 79.
10. Thomas Jefferson, *Notes on Virginia*, in *The Life and Selected Writings of Thomas Jefferson*, ed. Adrienne Koch and William Peden (New York: Modern American Library, 1944), 262.
11. On Morton's reception, see Gould, *The Mismeasure of Man*, chapter 2. On Morton and the American school of ethnology, see George Fredrickson *The Black Image in the White Mind: The Debate on Afro-American Character and Destiny, 1817–1914* (Middletown, Conn.: Wesleyan University Press, 1987), chapter 3; William R. Stanton, *The Leopard's Spots: Scientific Attitudes towards Race in America, 1815–1859* (Chicago: University of Chicago Press, 1960); and Robert J. C. Young, *Colonial Desire: Hybridity in Theory, Culture, and Race* (New York: Routledge, 1995), chapter 5.

12. Samuel Morton, *Crania Aegyptiaca: or, Observations on Eygptian Ethnography, derived from Anatomy, History, and the Monuments* (Philadelphia: J. Penington, 1844).

13. For a more detailed discussion of the whitening of Egypt, see Young, *Colonial Desire*, 118–141.

14. George Fitzhugh, *Sociology for the South; or the Failure of Free Society* (Richmond, 1854), quoted in Fredrickson, *The Black Image in the White Mind*, 84.

15. See Thomas Virgil Peterson, *Ham and Japheth: The Mythic World of Whites in the Antebellum South* (Metuchen, N.J.: Scarecrow Press, 1978).

16. Gould, *The Mismeasure of Man*, 53.

17. Ibid., 54.

18. *Colored American*, 26 January 1839.

19. Frederick Douglass, "The Claims of the Negro Ethnologically Considered," speech delivered to the Philozetian and Phi Delta Societies of Western Reserve College in Hudson Ohio, 12 July 1854, in *The Frederick Douglass Papers, Series One: Speeches, Debates, and Interviews*, vol. 2 (1847–1854), ed. John W. Blassingame (New Haven, Conn.: Yale University Press, 1982), 506.

20. A biographical sketch of Lewis based on information supplied by his daughter can be found in the Daniel Murray Papers (microfilm edition), State Historical Society of Wisconsin, 1977, reel 6.

21. Robert Benjamin Lewis, *Light and Truth: Collected from the Bible and Ancient and Modern History, Containing the Universal History of the Colored and the Indian Race, from the Creation of the World to the Present Time* (1836; repr., Boston: by a "Committee of Colored Men," 1851), 10.

22. Ibid., 123.

23. Ibid., 114.

24. See ibid., chapter 11.

25. Martin Robinson Delany, *The Condition, Elevation, Emigration, and Destiny of the Colored People of the United States* (Philadelphia: by the author, 1852; repr., New York: Arno Press and the New York Times, 1968), 129.

26. David E. Swift, *Black Prophets of Justice: Activist Clergy before the Civil War* (Baton Rouge: Louisiana State University Press, 1989), 176–177.

27. Hosea Easton, *A Treatise on the Intellectual Character, and Civil and Political Condition of the Colored People of the United States; and the Prejudice Exercised Towards Them: with a Sermon on the Duty of the Church To Them* (Boston: Isaac Knapp, 1837), 5.

28. Ibid., 42.

29. Ibid., 9, 10, 19, 14.

30. Ibid., 23, 24.

31. Ibid., 20.

32. Easton, *Treatise on the Intellectual Character*, 52, 53.

33. At first glance, the cast of characters in Exodus and Psalms 68:31 do not mix: the Israelites are redeemed in Exodus, whereas it is their oppressors, the Egyptians, who along with the Ethiopians appear to be the chosen people in the Psalms. According to historian of black religion Albert J. Raboteau, however, these discrepancies did not trouble nineteenth-century black clergy and laity. "In black religious thought and ritual," he writes, the book of Exodus and Psalms 68:31 "were complementary." Albert J. Raboteau, *A Fire in the Bones: Reflections on African-American Religious History* (Boston: Beacon Press, 1995), 42.

34. For a detailed discussion of messianic themes in African-American culture, see Wilson Jeremiah Moses, *Black Messiahs and Uncle Toms: The Social and Literary Manipulations of a Religious Myth* (University Park: Pennsylvania State University Press, 1982); Moses also discusses African-American Ethiopianism in a collection of essays entitled *The Wings of Ethiopia: Studies in African-American Life and Letters* (Ames: Iowa State University Press, 1990).

35. Easton, *Treatise on the Intellectual Character*, 10, 11.

36. Ibid., 12.

37. James W. C. Pennington, *A Text Book of the Origin and History &c. &c. of the Colored People* (Hartford, Conn.: L. Skinner, 1841; repr., Detroit: Negro History Press, 1969).

38. Swift, *Black Prophets of Justice*, 177.

39. Pennington, *Text Book*, 3, 7, 12, 14, 18, 39.

40. Ibid., *Text Book*, 47.

41. Easton, 18; Pennington, *Text Book*, 54

42. Pennington, *Text Book*, 91, 94.

43. Ibid., 89.

44. Letter by James W. C. Pennington to the *American Missionary* 3 (December, 1848), 22.

45. James W. C. Pennington, *A Lecture Delivered Before the Glasgow Young Men's Christian Association* (Edinburgh: H. Armour, printer, [1850]), 20.

46. Henry Highland Garnet, "An Address to the Slaves of North America (Rejected by the National Convention, 1843)," reprinted in *Walker's Appeal and Garnet's Address* (1843; repr. New York: Arno Press, 1969).

47. Henry Highland Garnet, *The Past and the Present Condition, and the Destiny of the Colored Race: A Discourse Delivered on the Fifteenth Anniversary of the Female Benevolent Society of Troy, New York* (Troy, N.Y.: Steam Press of J. C. Kneeland and Co., 1848), 6, 26.

48. Ibid., 28.

49. Ibid., 25.

50. Ibid., 27, 12.

51. George Frederick Holmes, quoted in Drew Gilpin Faust, *A Sacred Circle: The Dilemma of the Intellectual in the Old South, 1840–1860* (Baltimore, Md.: Johns Hopkins University Press, 1977), 46.

52. Edmund Ruffin, quoted in Faust, *A Sacred Circle*, 122.

53. George Frederick Holmes, quoted in Faust, *A Sacred Circle*, 121.

54. The two most prominent proslavery collections were *The Pro-slavery Argument; as Maintained . . . by Chancellor Harper, Governor Hammond, Dr. Simms, and Professor Dew* (1852; repr., New York: Greenwood Publishing, 1968); and E. N. Elliot, ed., *Cotton is King, and Pro-slavery Arguments; Comprising the Writing of Hammond, Harper, Christy, Stringfellow, Hodge, Bledsoe, and Cartwright . . .* (Augusta, Ga.: Pritchard, Abbot and Loomis, 1860).

55. James Henry Hammond, "Hammond's Letters on Slavery," in *The Pro-slavery Argument*, 144–145.

56. Pennington, *Text Book*, 3.

57. Daniel Murray Papers, State Historical Society of Wisconsin, reel 6.

58. The first three titles are cited in George A. Levesque, "Boston's Black Brahmim: Dr John S. Rock," *Civil War History* 26 (1980): 329. The last title is announced in the *Liberator*, 5 December 1856.

59. On responses to Rock's lectures, see Levesque, "Boston's Black Brahmin," 329–330.

60. George Washington Forbes, "Dr. John S. Rock" (typescript, Rare Book Room, Boston Public Library, n.d.), 3.

61. *Liberator*, 12 March 1858.

62. Ibid.

63. On Smith's medical training, see W. Montague Cobb, "James McCune Smith," *Journal of the National Medical Association* 44 (March 1952): 160.

64. James McCune Smith, *The Destiny of the People of Color, A Lecture Delivered Before the Philomathean Society and Hamilton Lyceum, in January 1841* (New York, 1843), 9.

65. James McCune Smith, "On the Fourteenth Query of Thomas Jefferson's Notes on Virginia," *Anglo-African Magazine* 1, no. 8 (August 1859): 225–238.

66. James McCune Smith, *A Dissertation on the Influence of Climate on Longevity* (New York: Office of the Merchant's Magazine, 1846), 26.

67. Delany, *The Condition, Elevation, Emigration, and Destiny of the Colored People*, 202.

68. James McCune Smith, "Civilization: Its Dependence on Physical Circumstances," *Anglo-African Magazine* 1 (January 1859): 5.

69. Ibid., 7.

70. Ibid., 6.

71. Ibid., 7.

72. Ibid.

73. Jefferson, *Notes on Virginia*, 256, 262.

74. Smith, "On the Fourteenth Query," 236.

75. Ibid., 231.

76. The idea that blacks had better resistance to heat and poorer tolerance for cold than whites arose from the observation of slave health and dates back to the colonial era. See Peter H. Wood, *Black Majority: Negroes in Colonial South Carolina from 1670 through the Stono Rebellion* (New York: W. W. Norton, 1974), 63–94. Most nineteenth-century explanations for this phenemonon sound preposterous today, but the basic observation has not been disproved. According to medical historian Todd L. Savitt, modern medical researchers find that "Negroes living in Africa and the United States are better equipped to tolerate humid heat than whites," although "both races possess the same capacity to become acclimatized to hot, humid conditions." Likewise, contemporary scientists hold that blacks do, in fact, "have a poorer adaptive response to cold than whites." Todd L. Savitt, "Slave Health and Southern Distinctiveness," in *Disease and Distinctiveness in the American South*, ed. Todd L. Savitt and James Harvey Young (Knoxville: University of Tennessee Press, 1988), 127, 128.

77. J. Hector St. John de Crèvecoeur, *Letters from an American Farmer* (1782; repr., New York: Penguin Books, 1981), 68.

78. Smith, "Civilization," 7.

79. Alexander Crummell, "The Destined Superiority of the Negro," in Crummell, *The Greatness of Christ and Other Sermons* (New York: Thomas Whittaker, 1882).

80. *North Star*, 13 June 1850, in *The Life and Writings of Frederick Douglass*, vol. 2, *Pre–Civil War Decade, 1850–1860*, ed. Philip S. Foner (New York: International Publishers, 1950), 130.

81. *Liberator*, 4 May 1865.

82. Robert S. Levine, *Martin Delany, Frederick Douglass, and the Politics of Representative Identity* (Chapel Hill: University of North Carolina Press, 1997), 2.

83. See Paul Gilroy, *The Black Atlantic: Modernity and Double-Consciousness* (Cambridge, Mass.: Harvard University Press, 1993), 22, for the story of Delany's brief stint at Harvard.

84. Delany, *The Condition, Elevation, Emigration, and Destiny of the Colored People*, 36.

85. Martin Robison Delany, "The Political Destiny of the Colored Race on the American Continent," in *Life and Public Services of Martin R. Delany*, ed. Frank E. Rollin [Mrs. Frances E. Rollin Whipper] (1868; repr., New York: Arno Press and the New York Times, 1968), 334.

86. Delany, "The Political Destiny of the Colored Race," 336.

87. Rollin [Mrs. Francis E. Rollin Whipper], *Life and Public Services of Martin R. Delany*, 19. On the differences between Delany and Douglass, see Levine, *Martin Delany, Frederick Douglass*.

88. This exchange between Delany and Douglass is quoted in Leonard T. Sweet, *Black Images of America, 1784–1870* (New York: Norton, 1976), 113–114 n. 98. Sweet lists Victor Ullman, *Martin R. Delany: The Beginnings of Black Nationalism* (Boston: Beacon Press, 1971), 169, and *Douglass' Monthly* (August 1862) as his sources.

89. Waldo E. Martin, *The Mind of Frederick Douglass* (Chapel Hill: University of North Carolina Press, 1984), 93.

90. Quoted in ibid., 97.

91. Frederick Douglass, "The Future of the Race," *A.M.E Church Review* 6 (October 1889): 230–231.

92. Frederick Douglass, "The Claims of the Negro Ethnologically Considered," speech delivered to the Philozetian and Phi Delta Societies of Western Reserve College in Hudson Ohio, 12 July 1854, in *The Frederick Douglass Papers, Series One*, 2:506, 510.

93. Douglass, "The Claims of the Negro Ethnologically Considered," 500.

94. See Martin, *The Mind of Fredrick Douglass*, 225.

95. Audrey McCluskey and John McCluskey, "Frederick Douglass on Ethnology: A Commencement Address at Western Reserve College, 1854," *Negro History Bulletin* 40 (July–August 1977): 747–749.

96. Douglass, "The Claims of the Negro Ethnologically Considered," 510; Douglass cites Smith on page 522.

97. Ibid., 510.

98. Ibid.

99. Ibid., 520.

100. Ibid., 521.

101. Douglass, "The Claims of the Negro Ethnologically Considered," 523, 524.

102. Ibid., 524.

103. Quoted in Martin, *The Mind of Frederick Douglass*, 218, 219.

104. Frederick Douglass, "The Douglass Institute: An Address Delivered in Baltimore, Maryland, on 29 September, 1865," in *The Frederick Douglass Papers* 4:93.

105. Martin, *The Mind of Frederick Douglass*, 198.

106. Fredrickson, *The Black Image in the White Mind*, 115.

107. For black opposition to such stereotyping, see the responses of the colored citizens of New Bedford to a speech by Horace Mann in which he characterized the African race as superior to the white race in sentiment and affection but inferior in intellect; *Liberator*, 22 October 1852.

108. On the gender crisis provoked by the Civil War, see Catherine Clinton, ed., *Divided Houses: Gender and the Civil War* (New York: Oxford University Press, 1992).

109. Ira Berlin, *Freedom: A Documentary History of Emancipation 1861–1867, Series II, The Black Military Experience* (New York: Cambridge University Press, 1985), 6.

110. Theodore Parker, quoted in the *Liberator*, 22 October 1852; Thomas Wentworth Higginson, "The Ordeal by Battle," *Atlantic Monthly*, July 1861, 94.

111. Thomas Wentworth Higginson, *Army Life in a Black Regiment* (1870; repr., East Lansing: Michigan State University Press, 1960), 190.

112. Joseph T. Glatthaar, *Forged in Battle: The Civil War Alliance of Black Soldiers and White Officers* (New York: Free Press, 1990), 251.

113. *Douglass' Monthly* (September 1861), in *The Life and Writings of Frederick Douglass*, vol. 3, *The Civil War, 1861–1865*, ed. Philip Foner (New York: International Publishers, 1952), 152.

Chapter 3

1. Ethiop, "What Shall We do with the White People?" *Anglo-African Magazine* 2 (February 1860): 41.

2. Ibid., 44, 45.

3. Ibid., 44, 43, 41.

4. Ibid., 45.

5. David Walker, *"One Continual Cry": David Walker's "Appeal to the Colored Citizens of the World" (1829–1830)*, ed. Herbert Aptheker (New York: Humanities Press, 1965), 80.

6. Thomas Jefferson, *The Life and Selected Writings of Thomas Jefferson*, ed. Adrienne Koch and William Peden (New York: New American Library), 256; Rush quoted in Winthrop D. Jordan, *White Over Black: American Attitudes toward the Negro, 1550–1812* (Chapel Hill: University of North Carolina Press, 1968; repr., New York: Norton, 1977), 458.

7. Jordan, *White Over Black*, 520.

8. Frank Clark, *Congressional Record*, 60th Cong. 1st sess. (22 February 1908) Appendix, 40, quoted in I. A. Newby, *Jim Crow's Defense: Anti-Negro Thought in American, 1900–1939* (Baton Rouge: Louisiana State University Press, 1965), 91.

9. Stephen Jay Gould, *The Mismeasure of Man* (New York: Norton, 1981), 32.

10. Jordan, *White Over Black*, 516.

11. Oliver Goldsmith, *History of the Earth II*, quoted in Jordan, *White Over Black*, 248. On the concept of racial degeneracy, see Stuart Gilman, "Degeneracy and Race in the Nineteenth Century," *Journal of Ethnic Studies* 10:4(1983):27–50.

12. J. F. Dyson, *A New and Simple Explanation of the Unity of the Human Race and the Origin of Color* (Nashville, Tenn.: Southern Methodist Publishing House, 1886), 20.

13. "Letter from Benjamin Banneker to the Secretary of State" (Philadephia, 1792), in Gary B. Nash, *Race and Revolution* (Madison, Wis.: Madison House, 1990), 178.

14. *Liberator*, 12 March 1858.

15. Letter from Sidney to the *Colored American*, 13 March 1841.

16. Walker, *"One Continual Cry,"* 74.

17. Blumenbach as paraphrased by Gould in *The Mismeasure of Man*, 32.

18. Harvey Newcombe, *The "Negro Pew" Being an Inquiry Concerning the Propriety of Distinctions in the House of God on Account of Color* (1837; repr., Freeport, N.Y.: Books for Libraries Press, 1971), 63.

19. David Ruggles said in reply to a pamphlet by colonizationist Davis M. Reese: "Has Dr. Reese never read of nations with a prejudice against white skin?" But Ruggles did not elaborate. David Ruggles, *"The Extinguisher" Extinguished, or David M. Reese "Used up by David Ruggles a Man of Color" together with some remarks on a late Production entitled "An Address on Slavery and Against the Immediate Emancipation with a plan of their Being Gradually Emancipated and Colonized in 32 Years* (New York: by the author, 1834), 13.

20. See, for example, "Extract from Bishop Heber's Indian Journal," *Freedom's Journal*, 16 May 1828, 60. The bishop writes of India's inhabitants: "It is well known that to them a fair complexion gives an idea of ill-health, and of that sort of deformity which in our eyes belongs to an Albino."

21. Pompée-Valentin Vastey, *Freedom's Journal*, 14 February 1829.

22. As if to show the tables could be turned, a black writer who used the psuedonym Euthymus noted in the *Liberator*: "The first white man that we have an account of, became white for forging a falsehood." But he then added, "Not that I would cast a stigma on our fairer brethren; no I would rather have my arm amputated." *Liberator*, 27 August 1831. I have found no other references to the story he mentions.

23. See, for example, Harmannaus Hoetink, *The Two Variants in Caribbean Race Relations*, trans. Eva M. Hooykaas (New York: Oxford University Press, 1967), 120–160. Hoetink argues that differences in the skin color and physical features of various groups constitute "somatic norm images," which shape the psychosocial relations between members of these groups. Hoetink's ideas have been criticized by, among others, Barbara Fields, who points out that while few other scholars are "as bald" as Hoetink in attaching great importance to "the fallacy of race as a physical fact[,] . . . in moments of mental relaxation, historians often accept it tacitly." Barbara J. Fields, "Ideology and Race in American History," in *Region, Race and Reconstruction: Essays in Honor of C. Vann Woodward*, ed. J. Morgan Kousser and James M. MacPherson (New York: Oxford University Press, 1982), 145.

24. *Liberator*, 27 August 1831. Euthymus's letter is reprinted in Carter G. Woodson, *The Mind of the Negro as Reflected in Letters Written During the Crisis* (Washington, D.C.: Association for the Study of Negro Life and History, 1926), 232–234.

25. S.S.N., "Anglo-Saxons and Anglo-Africans," *Anglo-African Magazine* 1 (August 1859): 250.

26. Henry MacNeal Turner, *The Negro in All Ages: A Lecture Delivered in the Second Baptist Church of Savannah, G.A.* (Savannah, Ga.: D. G. Patton, Steam Printer, 1873), 14–15.

27. *Liberator*, 12 March 1858.

28. Frederick Douglass, *Frederick Douglass' Paper* (22 July 1853), quoted in Jane H. Pease and William H. Pease, *They Who Would Be Free: Blacks' Search for Freedom, 1830–1861* (1974; repr., Urbana: University of Illinois Press, 1990), 104. For cites of other, similar observations, see Pease and Pease, *They Who Would Be Free*, n. 24, 104.

29. See Frederick Cooper, "Elevating the Race: The Social Thought of Black Leaders, 1827–1850," *American Quarterly* 24 (December 1972): 604–625; and Monroe Fordham, *Major Themes in Northern Black Religious Thought, 1800–1860* (Hicksville, N.Y.: Exposition Press, 1975).

30. Frederick Douglass "The Church and Prejudice" (1841), quoted in Waldo E. Martin Jr., *The Mind of Frederick Douglass* (Chapel Hill: University of North Carolina Press, 1984), 112.

31. George A. Levesque, "Interpreting Early Black Ideology: A Reappraisal of the Historical Consensus," *Journal of the Early Republic* 1 (1981): 286.

32. I. A. Newby, *Jim Crow's Defense: Anti-Negro Thought in America, 1900–1930* (Baton Rouge: Louisiana State University Press, 1973), 79–80.

33. Jordan, *White Over Black*, 505.

34. Bean argued that "the Neuro-muscular mechanism in the Black Race is less controlled, and when the nerve impulses, not so finely graded as in the White Race, reach the mimetic muscles, the latter are set into sudden strong contractions of the primitive type. The bulky lips are pulled upward and outward, the large white teeth are exposed in contrast with the black face, and instead of a graded smile or laugh we notice the broad grin characteristic of the Black Race." Robert Bennett Bean, *The Races of Man* (1932), quoted in Newby, *Jim Crow's Defense*, 43.

35. Martin Robinson Delany, *The Condition, Elevation, Emigration, and Destiny of the Colored People of the United States* (Philadelphia: by the author, 1852; repr., New York: Arno Press and the New York Times, 1968), 202. In an essay entitled "Political Destiny of the Colored Race on the American Continent," Delany took this argument further, arguing that the superior adaptation of Africans to a new country and a different climate had made black laborers preferable to both Indians and Europeans in the settlement of the New World, and that blacks would eventually prevail over whites in the Southern United States because they were better suited to life there. "Is it not worthy to notice here," Delany argued, "that while the ingress of foreign whites to this continent has been voluntary and constant, and that of blacks involuntary and occasional, yet the whites in the southern part have decreased in numbers, degenerated in character, and become mentally and physically enervated and imbecile; while the black and colored people have studiously increased in number, regenerated in character, and have grown mentally and physically vigorous and active, developing every function of their manhood, and are now, in their elementary character, decidedly superior to the white race." Martin Delany, "Political Destiny of the Colored Race in America," in *Life and Public Services of Martin R. Delany*, ed. Frank A. Rollin (Boston: Lee and Shepard, 1868; repr., New York: Arno Press, 1969), 353.

36. However, the Haitian Pompée-Valentin Vastey remarked that in Haiti's tropical climate whites deteriorated physically and were soon reduced to an alarming appearance. "The complexion, so late the pride, becomes haggard, wan, and discolored; their watery and tender eyes are unable to bear the solar rays; their bodies become feeble and emaciated, and their moral and physical powers destroyed; so that the White man appears, in the eyes of the black a mere walking skeleton, disgraced by nature." Pompée-Valentin Vastey, *Freedom's Journal*, 14 February 1829.

37. *Liberator*, 12 March 1858.

38. Hosea Easton, *A Treatise on the Intellectual Character, and Civil and Political Condition of the Colored People of the United States; and the Prejudice Exercised Towards Them: with a Sermon on the Duty of the Church To Them* (Boston: Isaac Knapp, 1837), 48.

39. Joseph E. Hayne, *The Amonian or Hamitic Origins of Ancient Greeks, Cretans, and all the Celtic Races*, rev. 2d ed. (Brooklyn: Guide Printing and Publishing Company, 1905).

40. Ethiop in "African-American Picture Gallery," *Anglo-African Magazine* 1, no. 6 (April 1859): 175.

41. William Wells Brown, *The Rising Son, or the Antecedents and Achievements of the Colored Race* (Boston: A. G. Brown, 1874), 87, 85–86.

42. Newby, *Jim Crow's Defense*, 37.

43. Brown, *The Rising Son*, 87–88.

44. Dyson, *A New and Simple Explanation*, 47.

45. Joseph E. Hayne, *The Negro in Sacred History* (Charleston, S.C.: Walker, Evans, Cogswell, 1887), 7.

46. Hayne's other works include *The Black Man, or, A Natural History of the Hamitic Race* (Raleigh, N.C.: Edwards Broughton Printers, 1893); *The Amonian or Hamitic Origins; and Ham and his Immediate Descendents, and their Wonderful Achievements* (New York: Weltz Press, 1909). Daniel Murray's bibliography lists an additional title by Hayne that I have yet to come across, *Of One Blood* (1905).

47. For a pathbreaking discussion of this subject, see Nancy Leys Stepan and Sander L. Gilman, "Appropriating the Idioms of Science: The Rejection of Scientific Racism," in *The Bounds of Race: Perspectives on Hegemony and Resistance*, ed. Dominick LaCapra (Ithaca, N.Y.: Cornell University Press, 1991), 72–103. Stepan and Gilman discuss the responses of African-Americans and Jews to scientific racism.

48. Newby, *Jim Crow's Defense*, 44.

49. Frederick Douglass, "Men of Color, to Arms" (21 March 1863), reprinted in *The Life and Writings of Frederick Douglass*, vol. 3, The Civil War, ed. Philip Foner (New York: International Publishers, 1952), 318.

50. David R. Roediger, *The Wages of Whiteness: Race and the Making of the American Working Class* (New York: Verso, 1991), 174, 172–173.

51. Jacob D. Cox, Letter to Aaron Perrym, 9 February 1863, quoted in George M. Fredrickson, *The Black Image in the White Mind: The Debate on Afro-American Character and Destiny, 1817–1914* (New York: Harper and Row, 1972; repr., Middletown, Conn.: Wesleyan University Press, 1987), 169.

52. Governor William Marlow of Florida, quoted in Joseph T. Glatthaar, *Forged in Battle: The Civil War Alliance of Black Soldiers and White Officers* (New York: Meridian, 1990), 250.

53. The Sanitary Commission's research is discussed in Jonathan S. Haller Jr. *Outcasts of Evolution: Scientific Attitudes of Racial Inferiority, 1859–1900* (New York: McGraw-Hill, 1979), 19–34.

54. Russ James, quoted in John David Smith, *An Old Creed for the New South: Proslavery Ideology and Historiography, 1865–1918* (Westport, Conn.: Greenwood Press, 1985), 20.

55. Francis P. Blair Jr., quoted in Eric Foner, *A Short History of Reconstruction, 1863–1877* (New York: Harper and Row, 1990), 145.

56. William C. Nell, *Services of the Colored Americans in the War of 1776 and 1812* (Boston: Prentiss and Sawyer, 1851); William Wells Brown, *The Negro in the American Rebellion; his heroism and his fidelity* (Boston: A. G. Brown, 1880); Peter Clark, *The Black Brigade of Cincinnati* (Cincinnati: J. B. Boyd, 1864); Edward A. Johnson, *History of the Negro Soldiers in the Spanish American War* (Raleigh, N.C.: Capital Printing, 1899; repr., New York: Johnson Reprint Corp., 1970); Joseph T. Wilson, *Black Phalanx* (1890; repr., New York: Arno Press and the New York Times, 1968); George Washington Williams, *History of the Negro Troops in the War of the Rebellion, Preceded By a Review of the Miltary Service of Negroes in Ancient and Modern Times* (New York: Harper and Brothers, 1888).

57. William Wells Brown, *The Black Man: His Antecedents, His Genius, and His Achievements* (Boston: James Redpath, 1863), 33–34.

58. Henry MacNeal Turner, *Respect Black: The Writings and Speeches of Henry MacNeal Turner*, ed. Edwin S. Redkey (New York: Arno Press and the New York Times, 1971), 22.

59. Turner, *The Negro in All Ages*, 23.

60. Rev. J. W. Beckwith, "The Descendents of Ham the Superior Race," *New National Era*, 17 and 24 February, 3 March 1870.

61. Brown, *The Rising Son*, 86.

62. Ibid.; Brown, *The Black Man*, 35–36.

63. John Stephens Durham, *To Teach the Negro History: A Suggestion* (Philadelphia: David McKay, 1897), 13.

64. Robert Levine, *Martin Delany, Frederick Douglass, and the Politics of Representative Identity* (Chapel Hill: University of North Carolina Press, 1997), 226.

65. Lt. Edward M. Stroeber, cited in Victor Ullman, *Martin R. Delany: The Beginnings of Black Nationalism* (Boston: Beacon Press, 1971), 330.

66. Martin Delany, "The International Policy of the World Toward Africa," in Rollin, *Life and Public Service of Martin R. Delaney*, 313, 315.

67. Ibid., 315, 317.

68. On the sexual politics of this period, see Glenda Gilmore, *Gender and Jim Crow* (Chapel Hill: University of North Carolinia Press, 1996).

69. Charles Carroll, *"The Negro is a Beast," or, "In the Image of God"; The Reasoner of the Age, The Revelation of the Century! The Bible as it is! The Negro and his Relationship to the Human Family . . . The Negro is Not the Son of Ham* (St. Louis: American Book and Bible House, 1900).

70. Hayne, *The Negro in Sacred History*, 18.

71. Ibid., 17.

72. See, for example, Alexander Crummell, *A Defense of the Negro Race in America From the Assaults and Charges of Reverend J. L. Tucker D.D. of Jackson, Mississippi* (Washington, D.C.: Judd and Detweiler, 1883); B. J. Bolding, *What of the Negro Race?* (Chambersberg, Pa.: published by the *Democratic News*, Chambersberg, Pa., 1906), which was a reply to a series of articles published in the Chambersberg *Democratic News* by a Reverend G.H.L. Hasskarl; and Harvey Johnson's *Question of Race: A Reply to W. Cabell Brice, esq.* (Baltimore, Md.: J. F. Weisenhampel, 1891).

73. Martin Delany, *Principia of Ethnology: The Origin of the Races and Color with an Archaeological Compendium of Ethiopian and Egyptian Civilization from Years of Careful Examination and Enquiry* (Philadelphia: Harper and Brothers, 1879), 9, 20.

74. Ibid., vii–viii.

75. Ibid., 23.

76. Ibid., 86.

77. Ibid., 94.

78. Alexander Crummell, "Destined Superiority of the Negro: A Thanksgiving Day Discourse, 1877," in *Destiny and Race: Selected Writings*, ed. Wilson Jeremiah Moses (Amherst: University of Massachusetts Press, 1992), 198.

79. On Crummell's life, see Wilson J. Moses, *Alexander Crummell: A Study of Civilization and Discontent* (New York: Oxford University Press, 1989).

80. Crummell actually quotes this maxim in "The Race-Problem in America," in *Africa and America: Addresses and Discourses* (Springfield, Mass.: Willey and Co., 1891; repr., Miami, Fla.: Mnemosyne Publishing, 1969), 47. Crummell's friend John E. Bruce, a militant black journalist, used the phrase also, writing in one article that "race, as Disraeli says, is the key to history." John Edward Bruce, *The Selected Writings of John Edward Bruce: Militant Black Journalist*, ed. Peter Gilbert (New York: Arno Press and the New York Times, 1971), 161.

81. Crummell, "Destined Superiority of the Negro," 194; Alexander Crummell, "God and the Nation" (1854), in *The Future of Africa* (New York: Scribner, 1862).

82. Crummell, "God and the Nation," 156.

83. Crummell, "Destined Superiority of the Negro," 198.

84. Ibid., 199, 203.

85. Alexander Crummell, "The English Language in Liberia, (1860, 1861)" and "The Progress and Prospects of Liberia" (1854), in *The Future of the Negro Race* (New York: Scribner, 1862), 24, 148.

86. Crummell, "Destined Superiority of the Negro," 203.

87. W.N.A., "Anglo-Saxon Brutality," *Southern Workman* 11 (November 1879): 108.

88. James Theodore Holly, "The Divine Plan of Human Redemption in Its Ethnological Development," *A.M.E. Church Review* 1 (1884): 82, 81.

89. Anna Julia Cooper, *A Voice from the South* (1892; repr., New York: Oxford University Press, 1988), 157, 173.

90. Gail Bederman, *Manliness and Civilization: A Cultural History of Gender and Race in the United States, 1880–1917* (Chicago: University of Chicago Press, 1995), 46.

91. Wells quoted in ibid., 61–62.

92. Bruce, *Selected Writings of John Edward Bruce*, 39, 43, 81.

93. W.E.B. DuBois, "Jefferson Davis as a Representative of Civilization," Commencement Address, Harvard University (1890), in *Writings* (New York: Library of America, 1986), 811.

94. Rufus Perry, *The Cushite: or The Descendants of Ham as Found in the Sacred Scriptures and in the Writings of Ancient Historians and Poets from Noah to the Christian Era* (Springfield, Mass.: Willey and Co., 1893), 11, 12, 146–147.

95. Harvey Johnson, *The Nations From a New Point of View* (Nashville, Tenn.: National Baptist Publishing Company, 1903), 238. This book contains three works that Johnson published earlier in pamphlet form, *The White Man's Failure in Government* (1900), along with *The Hamite* (1891) and *The Question of Race: A Reply to W. Cabell Brice, esq.* (1891).

96. See also Harvey Johnson, *Race Prejudice and Pride: On What are They Based? What Has the White Man Ever done to Equal the Tremendous Achievements of the Sons of Ham?* ([Baltimore, Md.?], n.d.)

97. Johnson, *The Nations From a New Point of View*, 142.

98. Ibid., 128.

99. Ibid., 60.

100. Ibid., 81, 71.

101. Ibid., 197–198.

102. Marcus Garvey, "The Tragedy of White Injustice," in *The Poetical Works of Marcus Garvey*, ed. Tony Martin (Dover, Mass.: Majority Press, 1983), 4.

103. Frederick Douglass, "The Claims of the Negro Ethnologically Considered," speech delivered to the Philozetian and Phi Delta Societies of Western Reserve College in Hudson, Ohio, 12 July 1854, in *The Frederick Douglass Papers, Series One: Speeches, Debates, and Interviews* vol. 2 (1847–1854), ed. John W. Blassingame (New Haven, Conn.: Yale University Press, 1982), 502.

104. Fredrickson, *The Black Image in the White Mind*, 98, 99.

105. Theodore Parker, "The Nebraska Question," sermon delivered on 12 February 1854, quoted in ibid., 100.

106. Letter to Miss Cobbe, 4 December 1857, in John Weiss, *Life and Correspondence of Theodore Parker* (New York, 1864), I, 463, quoted in Fredrickson, *The Black Image in the White Mind*, 100.

107. Fredrickson, *The Black Image in the White Mind*, 109.

108. Thomas Greathead Harper, *Contemporary Evolution of the Negro Race* (Washington, D.C.: American Negro Monographs, 1910), 5.

109. Theophilus Gould Steward, *The End of the World; or, Clearing the Way for the Fullness of the Gentiles* (Philadelpia: A.M.E. Book Room, 1888), 72–73.

110. Bruce, *Selected Writings of John Edward Bruce*, 84.

111. Toni Morrison, *Playing in the Dark: Whiteness and the Literary Imagination* (Cambridge, Mass.: Harvard University Press, 1992), xi.

112. Stepan and Gilman, "Appropriating the Idioms of Science," 103.

Part II

1. Historical works that employ such sources are too numerous to be listed in detail. Some fine recent studies of slave communities that make effective use of plantation records include Anne Patton Malone, *Sweet Chariot: Slave Family and Household Structure in Nineteenth-Century Louisiana* (Chapel Hill: University of North Carolina Press, 1992); Brenda Stevenson, *Life in Black and White: Family and Community in the Slave South* (New York: Oxford University Press, 1996); and William Dusinberre, *Them Dark Days: Slavery in the American Rice Swamps* (New York: Oxford University Press, 1996).

2. Most of the ex-slave narratives collected by the Federal Writers' Project appear in *The American Slave: A Composite Autobiography* [*AS*], ed. George Rawick (Westport, Conn.: Greenwood Press, 1972–1973, Supplement, Series I, 1977; Supplement, Series II, 1979), which presents forty volumes of interviews (in subsequent citations this collection will appear as AS). Largely constituted of interview collections from state Federal Writers' project offices, the *AS* collection also republishes two volumes of interviews collected ast Fisk University: *The Unwritten History of Slavery* (v. 18) and *God Struck Me Dead* (vol. 19). Additional WPA interviews are published in *Weevils in the Wheat: Interviews with Virginia Ex-Slaves*, ed. Charles L. Perdue Jr., Thomas E. Barden, and Robert K. Phillips (Charlottesville: University Press of Virginia, 1976); Georgia Writers' Project, *Drums and Shadows: Survival Studies among Georgia Coastal Negroes* (Athens: University Press of Georgia, 1940; repr., 1986); *Mother Wit: The Ex-Slave Narratives of the Louisiana Writers' Project*, ed. Ronnie W. Clayton (New York: Peter Lang, 1990); and *The WPA Oklahoma Slave Narratives*, ed. T. Lindsay Baker and Julie P. Baker (Norman: University of Oklahoma Press, 1996).

3. John Blassingame writes of the interviews in Rawick's first nineteen volumes of *The American Slave*: "They probably contain more religious and secular songs than any other single collection." John Blassingame, introduction to *Slave Testimony: Two Centuries of Letters, Speeches, Interviews, and Autobiographies*, ed. John Blassingame (Baton Rouge: Louisiana State University Press, 1977), lv.

4. Ibid., xliii. Blassingame makes a very negative assessment of the WPA interviews as a historical source, arguing that the evidence they provide is inferior to that of other slave sources such as fugitive slave narratives and newspaper accounts of slavery given by ex-slaves in the post–Civil War era. In addition to being distorted by influence of the 1930s caste etiquette, their accuracy, Blassingame believes, is compromised by the failure of many interviewers to record their informants' testimony verbatim, and the advanced age of the ex-slave informants, which made their memories of slavery unreliable. While the problems Blassingame identifies with the WPA evidence certainly exist, his animus toward the interviews as a historical source seems somewhat unaccountable given that virtually no ex-slave sources, including the fugitive slave sources and newspaper interviews with ex-slaves, present unmediated accounts of slave experiences (ibid., xl–lxv). For a discussion of Blassingame's comments on the WPA collection, as well as an in-depth assessment of the strengths and weaknesses of the historical evidence in the collection, see Rawick's introduction to *AS*, Supplement, Series I, v. 1, ix–li.

5. *AS*, South Carolina Narratives, v. 2, 298.

6. *AS*, Mississippi Narratives, Supplement, Series I, v. 9, pt. 4, 1607.

7. *AS*, Mississippi Narratives, Supplement, Series I, v. 10, pt. 5, 1956.

8. Melvina Johnson Young, "Exploring the WPA Narratives: Finding the Voices of Black Men and Women," in *Theorizing Black Feminisms: The Visionary Pragmatism of Black Women*, ed. Stanlie M. James and Abena P. A. Busia (New York: Routledge, 1993), 55. Young's article contains a thoughtful discussion of the interviewing process behind the WPA narratives. Other useful discussions of the narratives can be found in Charles Davis and Henry Louis Gates, *The Slave's Narrative* (New York: Oxford University Press, 1985).

9. See *AS*, The Unwritten History of Slavery (Fisk University), v. 18, and God Struck Me Dead (Fisk University), v. 19. There is some disagreement over how much impact the race of the interviewers in fact had on the ex-slaves' testimony. On the basis of a quantitative study of WPA interviews, Paul Escott argues that those conducted by black interviewers were measurably freer of deference, evasiveness, and tributes to planter benevolence. But Stephen Crawford, in his quantitative analysis of the interviews, finds that "controlling for plantation size seems to eliminate much of the difference between white and black interviewer samples." Crawford, however, does note that the ex-slaves tended to speak more freely about subjects such as whipping and white parentage to black interviewers, and that "the atmosphere seems to change when blacks interview blacks." This change in atmosphere can be observed by anyone who reads the

narratives closely, whether or not it can be documented in quantitative terms, and for the purposes of this study the interviews conducted by black interrogators are among the richest in the WPA collection. Paul D. Escott, *Slavery Remembered: A Record of the Twentieth-Century Slave Narratives* (Chapel Hill: University of North Carolina Press, 1979), 10; Stephen C. Crawford, "Quantified Memory: A Study of the WPA and Fisk University Slave Narrative Collection" (Ph.D. diss., University of Chicago, 1980), 40, 41, 37.

10. *AS*, Ohio Narratives, v. 16, 44.

11. Blassingame notes of the fugitive slave narratives that "many of the most reliable accounts contain elements that cannot be attributed to blacks," including long digressions on the duplicity of Northern whites for owning blacks. He further adds that "some of the most complicated philosophical, religious, and historical arguments were sometimes attributed to the slaves to show that bondage violated divine law and the natural rights of man." Unfortunately, such editorial work goes a long way toward obscuring ex-slave opinions on subjects such as race and white people in these narratives, since the ideological arguments presented in the narratives often raise suspicions about provenance. Blassingame, introduction, *Slave Testimony*, xxvii–xxviii.

Chapter 4

1. Charles Williams, "I'se Much a Man" (n.d.). Williams's previously unpublished manuscript is included in *The American Slave: A Composite Autobiography* [AS], ed. George Rawick (Westport, Conn.: Greenwood Press, 1972–1973), Supplement, Series II, v. 1, 181–249. This manuscript ended up in the WPA archives when it came to the attention of the director of the Arkansas Federal Writers' Project, Bernice Bancock, who tried unsuccessfully to get it published. The history of Williams's "I'se Much a Man" is discussed in Rawick's introduction to the Arkansas Narratives in *AS*, Supplement, Series II, v. 1, i–ii.

2. Charles Williams, *AS*, Arkansas Narratives, Supplement, Series II, v. 1, 224, 248. Williams's mother had been "a slave driver for her master" and evidently wielded a cowhide whip on Williams for most of his life (200).

3. Charles Williams, *AS*, Arkansas Narratives, Supplement, Series II, v. 1, 239.

4. Charles Williams, *AS*, Arkansas Narratives, Supplement, Series II, v. 1, 200, 244.

5. "Slaves Have No Souls," *AS*, The Unwritten History of Slavery (Fisk University), v. 18, 45–46.

6. Tom Windham, *AS*, Arkansas Narratives, v. 11, pt. 7, 211.

7. Katie Sutton, *AS*, v. 6, Indiana Narratives, 193–195, and *AS*, Indiana Narratives, Supplement, Series I, v. 5, 211; Patience M. Avery, in *Weevils in the Wheat: Interviews with Virginia Ex-Slaves*, ed. Charles L. Perdue Jr., Thomas E. Barden, and Robert K. Phillips (Charlottesville: University Press of Virginia, 1976), 15.

8. Lizzie Grant, *AS*, Texas Narratives, Supplement, Series II, v. 4, pt. 4, 1559.

9. Gus Rogers, *AS*, Alabama Narratives, v. 6, 335–336; *AS*, v. 18.

10. Alice Cole, *AS*, Texas Narratives, Supplement, Series II, v. 3, pt. 2, 763. See also Frank Hughes, *AS*, Texas Narratives, Supplement, Series I, v. 8, 1063.

11. Ann Perry, *AS*, South Carolina Narratives, v. 3, pt. 3, 255.

12. In his book *The Redemption of Africa and Black Religion* (Chicago: Third World Press, 1970), St. Clair Drake reports that the "illiterate Negro preachers" counterattacked the story of Ham's curse "by insisting that Noah was drunk when he pronounced the curse and therefore it was invalid" (47–48). However, he provides no evidence for this assertion, and I have been unable to find any documentation to support it in the books listed in his bibliography. This claim was made by some black intellectuals, but I have not been able to find similar arguments in the limited evidence available on the theological doctrine of illiterate African-Americans.

13. These are the words of a Union Army chaplain named W. G. Kephart, letter of 9 May 1864, quoted in Albert J. Raboteau, *A Fire in the Bones: Reflections on African-American Religious History* (Boston: Beacon Press, 1995), 33.

14. Lawrence W. Levine, *Black Culture, Black Consciousness: Afro-American Folk Thought from Slavery to Freedom* (New York: Oxford University Press, 1977), 84.

15. Charity More, *AS*, South Carolina Narratives, v. 3 , 206–207.

16. Levi Pollard, in *Weevils in the Wheat*, 233.

17. *Black Culture, Black Consciousness*, 85.

18. Ibid., 86.

19. Ibid., 33, 34.

20. Letter from KA-LE to John Quincy Adams, New Haven, 4 January 1841, in *Slave Testimony: Two Centuries of Letters, Speeches, Interviews, and Autobiographies*, ed. John Blassingame (Baton Rouge: Louisiana State University Press, 1977), 34.

21. "Slaves Have no Souls" *AS*, v. 18, Unwritten History of Slavery (Fisk University), 45.

22. Robert Burns, *AS*, Oklahoma Narratives, Supplement, Series I, v. 12, 80; see also Jennie Proctor, *AS*, Texas Narratives, vol. 5, pt. 3, 213.

23. Berry Smith, *AS*, Mississippi Narratives, Supplement, Series I, v. 10, pt. 5, 1984.

24. Raboteau, *A Fire in the Bones*, 19. On the relationship between slavery and religion, see also Mitchell Snay, *The Gospel of Disunion: Religion and Separatism in the Antebellum South* (Chapel Hill: University of North Carolina Press, 1997).

25. Blake Touchstone, "Planters and Slave Religion in the Deep South," in *Masters and Slaves in the House of the Lord: Race and Religion in the American South*, ed. John B. Boles (Lexington: University Press of Kentucky, 1988), 121.

26. Charles Colcock Jones, *A Catechism for Colored Persons* (Charleston, S.C.: Observer Office Press, 1834), esp. 82, 95.

27. This catechism is reported in Anson West, *A History of Methodism in Alabama* (1893), 605, quoted in Donald Mathews, *Slavery and Methodism: A Chapter in American Morality* (Princeton, N.J.: Princeton University Press, 1965), 87.

28. For more on slave religion, see Albert J. Raboteau, *Slave Religion: The "Invisible Institution" in the Antebellum South* (New York: Oxford University Press, 1978).

29. John White, in *The WPA Oklahoma Slave Narratives*, ed. T. Lindsay Baker and Julie P. Baker (Norman: University of Oklahoma Press, 1996), 469.

30. Wes Brady, *AS*, Texas Narratives, Supplement, Series II, v. 2, pt. 1, 401.

31. Margaret Nickerson, *AS*, Florida Narratives, v. 17, 252.

32. Anna Morgan, *AS*, South Carolina Narratives, Supplement, Series I, v. 11, 252.

33. Catherine Slim, *AS*, v. 16, Ohio Narratives, 79.

34. Baily Cunningham, in *Weevils in the Wheat*, 81.

35. Hal Hutson, in *The WPA Oklahoma Slave Narratives*, 205.

36. Aaron Carter, *AS*, Mississippi Narratives, v. 7, Supplement, Series I, pt. 2, 356.

37. Lizzie Williams, *AS*, Mississippi Narratives, Supplement, Series I, v. 10, pt. 5, 2335.

38. Mary Jane E? [last name is illegible] *AS*, Arkansas Narratives, v. 9, pt. 3, 157–158.

39. *AS, Unwritten History of Slavery* (Fisk University), v. 18, 43.

40. Frederick Douglass, *Narrative of the Life of Frederick Douglass, an American Slave* (1845), ed. Houston A. Baker Jr. (New York: Penguin Books, 1982), 47.

41. Lucie Ann Warfield, *AS*, Ohio Narratives, Supplement, Series I, v. 5, 455.

42. H. B. Holloway, *AS*, Arkansas Narratives, v. 9, pt. 3, 291.

43. Mary Estes Peters, *AS*, Arkansas Narratives, v. 10, pt. 4, 326.

44. Mrs. Sallie Johnson, *AS*, Texas Narratives, Supplement, Series II, v. 6, pt. 5, 2049.

45. Hal Hutson, in *The WPA Oklahoma Slave Narratives*, 205.

46. Richard Toler, *AS*, Ohio Narratives, v. 16, 100.

47. Cureton Milling, *AS*, South Carolina Narratives, v. 3, pt. 3, 194.

48. Thomas Cole, *AS*, Texas Narratives, v. 4, pt. 1, 225.

49. Foster Weathersby, *AS*, Mississippi Narratives, Supplement, Series I, v. 10, pt. 5, 2228.

50. Josephine Howard, *AS*, Texas Narratives, Supplement, Series II, v. 5, pt. 4, 1806.

51. Ben Lawson, in *The WPA Oklahoma Slave Narratives*, 245.

52. Richard Toler, *AS*, Ohio Narratives, v. 16, 100.

53. Rachel Cruze, *AS*, Ohio Narratives, Supplement, Series I, v. 5, 299.

54. Sallie Crane, *AS*, Arkansas Narratives, v. 8, pt. 2, 52.

55. Annie Boyd, *AS*, Kentucky Narratives, v. 16, 59.

56. On the infrequency of slave breeding, see Michael Tadman, *Speculators and Slaves: Masters, Traders, and Slaves in the Old South* (Madison: University of Wisconsin Press, 1989), 121–127

57. Eliza Elsey, in *The WPA Oklahoma Slave Narratives*, 140–141.

58. William Henry Rooks, *AS*, Arkansas Narratives, v. 10, pt. 6, 76.

59. Sarah Ford, *AS*, Texas Narratives, v. 4, pt. 2, 42.

60. Lula Cottonham Walker, *AS*, Alabama Narratives, Supplement, Series I, v. 1, 432.

61. Lizzie Grant, *AS*, Texas Narratives, Supplement, Series II, V. 5, pt. 4, 1557.

62. Joe Ray, in *The WPA Oklahoma Slave Narratives*, 344.

63. "Kicked Around Like a Mule," *AS*, Unwritten History of Slavery (Fisk University), v. 18, 105.

64. Peter Cork, *AS*, Missouri Narratives, v. 11, 86; Harre Quarles, *AS*, Texas Narratives, Supplement, Series II, v. 8, pt. 7, 3215.

65. Mollie Barber, in *The WPA Oklahoma Slave Narratives*, 43.

66. Toby Jones, *AS*, Texas Narratives, Supplement, Series II, v. 6, pt. 5, 2146; Mollie Watson, in *The WPA Oklahoma Slave Narratives*, 451.

67. Carrie E. Davis, in *The WPA Oklahoma Slave Narratives*, 102.

68. Ann Ladly, *AS*, Texas Narratives, Supplement, Series II, v. 6, pt. 5, 2256; Mom Genia Woodberry, *AS*, South Carolina Narratives, v. 3, pt. 4, 225; Thomas Johns, *AS*, Texas Narratives, v. 4, pt. 2, 204.

69. Elias Hicks, *Observations on the Slavery of the Africans and Their Descendants, and on the Use of their Produce of their Labor* (1861), excerpted in *The Antislavery Argument*, ed. William H. Pease and Jane H. Pease (Indianapolis: Bobbs-Merril, 1965), 146.

70. Marsh Cunningham, one of the few white informants interviewed by WPA workers in Oklahoma, recalled of slave sales he had witnessed: "They would strip them, put them on the auction block[,] and sell them—bid them off just like you would cattle." *AS*, Oklahoma Narratives, v. 7, 45.

71. "Massa's Slave Son," *AS*, Unwritten History of Slavery (Fisk University), v. 18, 81.

72. Martha King, in *The WPA Oklahoma Slave Narratives*, 240.

73. Mariah Snyder, *AS*, Texas Narratives, Supplement, Series II, v. 9, pt. 8, 3709.

74. Levine, *Black Culture, Black Consciousness*, 102, 103.

75. Orlando Patterson, *Slavery and Social Death: A Comparative Study* (Cambridge, Mass.: Harvard University Press, 1982), 5–9.

76. David Brion Davis, "Of Human Bondage," review of *Slavery and Social Death*, by Orlando Patterson, *New York Review of Books*, 17 February 1983, 20. For a more detailed argument of this point, see Karl Jacoby, "Slaves by Nature? Domestic Animals and Human Slaves," *Slavery and Abolition* 14 (April 1994): 89–97.

77. See F. D. Harvey, "Herodotus and the Man-Footed Creature," in *Slavery and Other Forms of Unfree Labor*, ed. Léonie J. Archer (London: Routledge, 1988), 42–52.

78. Winthrop D. Jordan, *White Over Black: American Attitudes toward the Negro, 1550–1812* (Chapel Hill: University of North Carolina Press, 1968; repr., New York: Norton, 1977), 29, 30.

79. Jan Nederveen Pieterse, *White on Black: Images of Africa and Blacks in Western Popular Culture* (New Haven, Conn.: Yale University Press, 1992), 43. Pieterse shows that blacks were often depicted either with animals or as animals in Western art. See esp. chapter 2.

80. Arguments for polygenesis were of course not limited to the American South. Pieterse cites the work of Jamaican planter and administrator Edward Long as an example of how closely blacks came to be associated with beasts in Western naturalism. In addition to describing blacks as bestial and contending that they far more closely re-

sembled orang-utangs than white people, Long argued that blacks were a different species than whites, dividing the *genus homo* into three categories, "Europeans and other humans, blacks, and orang-utans" (40).

81. "The Human Family," *Southern Quarterly Review* 27 (1855): 119, quoted in William Sumner Jenkins, *Proslavery Thought in the Old South* (Chapel Hill: University of North Carolina Press, 1935), 282. Partly on account of such objections, polygenesis never gained complete acceptance in the antebellum South. The polygenic account of the origin of the races could not be easily reconciled with the biblical account of the origins of man, and many Southerners were content to defend slavery on the basis of the "well established" fact that "the negro is now an inferior species, or at least variety of the human race." E. N. Elliott, ed., *Cotton is King and Pro-Slavery Arguments* (Augusta, Ga., 1860), quoted in George M. Fredrickson, *The Black Image in the White Mind: The Debate on Afro-American Character and Destiny, 1817–1914* (New York: Harper and Row, 1972; repr., Middletown, Conn.: Wesleyan University Press, 1987), 83.

82. Eugene D. Genovese, *Roll Jordan, Roll: The World the Slaves Made* (New York: Pantheon Books, 1974), 5.

83. James Oakes, *The Ruling Race: A History of American Slaveholders* (New York: Vintage Books, 1983).

84. Donaville Broussard, *AS*, Texas Narratives, v. 4, pt. 1, 151.

85. Richard Kimmons, *AS*, Texas Narratives, Supplement, Series II, v. 6, pt. 5, 2193.

86. Ellen Butler, *AS*, Texas Narratives, v. 4, pt. 1, 178.

87. Adaline Johnson recalled: "At the crossroads there was this hat shop. White man brought a lot of white free niggers to work in the hat shop. Way they come free niggers." I assume from her rather cryptic statement about how they became free niggers that the "white free niggers" she describes may well have been indentured servants of some kind. *AS*, Arkansas Narratives, v. 9, pt. 4, 56.

88. Ellis Ken Kannon, *AS*, Tennessee Narratives, v. 16, 39.

89. "Aunt" Nina Scot, *AS*, South Carolina Narratives, v. 3, pt. 4, 88.

90. Jane McLeod Wilburn, *AS*, Mississippi Narratives, Supplement, Series I, v. 10, pt. 5, 2284.

91. George Owens, *AS*, Texas Narratives, v. 5, pt. 3, 166.

92. Scott Hooper, *AS*, Texas Narratives, v. 4, pt. 2, 157.

93. Charlie Bowen, *AS*, Texas Narratives, Supplement, Series II, v. 2, pt. 1, 347.

94. Phoebe Lyons, *AS*, Ohio Narratives, Supplement, Series I, v. 5, 403.

95. Jack Maddox, *AS*, Texas Narratives, Supplement, Series II, v. 7, pt. 6, 2523.

96. See, especially, Benjamin Quarles, "The Revolutionary War as a Black Declaration of Independence," in *Slavery and Freedom in the Age of the American Revolution*, ed. Ira Berlin and Ronald Hoffman (Charlottesville: University Press of Virginia, 1983), 283–301; and Merton L. Dillon, *Slavery Attacked: Southern Slaves and Their Allies, 1619–1865* (Baton Rouge: Louisiana State University Press, 1990).

97. Gerald W. Mullin, *Flight and Rebellion: Slave Resistance in Eighteenth-Century Virginia* (New York: Oxford University Press, 1972), 157, 160.

98. Ibid., 160.

99. Orlando Patterson, Freedom, vol. 1, *Freedom in the Making of Western Culture* (New York: Basic Books, 1991), 1.

100. I borrow this phrase from David Brion Davis, who observes that the idea of America as a new Canaan could cut two ways: many white "Americans did consider themselves a chosen people, providentially appointed to rule Ham's children in order to build a new Jerusalem. Ham's children, however, also dreamed of a new Jerusalem as they flocked to camp meetings or heard their own preachers tell of Moses and Christ, the twin deliverers." David Brion Davis, *The Problem of Slavery in the Age of Revolution, 1770–1823* (Ithaca, N.Y.: Cornell University Press, 1975), 556.

101. The question of whether religion inspired African-American slaves to seek freedom in this world rather than the next is a controversial subject in the historiography of slavery. Eugene Genovese—whose arguments on slave religion are far too rich,

complex, and self-contradictory to summarize with any accuracy here—concludes his long section on religion in *Roll Jordan, Roll* with a negative assessment of slave religion as a liberatory theology. "The synthesis that became black Christianity offered profound spiritual strength to a people at bay; but it also imparted a political weakness, which dictated, however necessarily and realistically, acceptance of the hegemony of the oppressor." I find Genovese's arguments that the slaves accepted the hegemony of the oppressor to be among the weakest arguments in *Roll Jordan, Roll*, since the concept of hegemony, with the issues of legitimacy and consent it entails, is not ideally suited to map the power relations in a slave society. Moreover, in his conclusions on religion, Genovese fails to heed his own warning against "the mechanistic error of assuming that religion either sparked the slaves to rebellion or rendered them docile." Genovese, *Roll Jordan, Roll*, 284, 183. Albert J. Raboteau is more successful in heeding this important warning when he writes, "To describe slave religion as merely other worldly is inaccurate, for the slaves believed that God had acted, was acting, and would continue to act within human history and within their own particular history as a peculiar people just as long ago he had acted on behalf of another chosen people, biblical Israel. Moreover, slave religion had a this worldly impact, not only in leading some slaves to acts of external rebellion, but also in helping slaves assert and maintain a sense of personal value—even of ultimate worth." Raboteau, *Slave Religion*, 318. Other important discussions of slave religion can be found in John Blassingame, *The Slave Community: Plantation Life in the Antebellum South*, rev. ed. (New York: Oxford University Press, 1979); Mechal Sobel, *Trabelin' On: The Slave Journey to an Afro-Baptist Faith* (Princeton, N.J.: Princeton University Press, 1988); and Levine, *Black Culture, Black Conscuousness*, esp. 3–80.

102. Charlie Moses, *AS*, Mississippi Narratives, Supplement, Series I, v. 9, pt. 4, 1601.

103. Tom Windham, *AS*, Arkansas Narratives, v. 11, pt. 7, 211.

104. John McAdams, *AS*, Texas Narratives, Supplement, Series II, v. 7, pt. 6, 2465.

105. Sally Neely, *AS*, Texas Narratives, Supplement, Series II, v. 7, pt. 6, 2889.

106. Allen V. Manning, in *The WPA Oklahoma Slave Narratives*, 279.

107. Fannie Moore, *AS*, North Carolina Narratives, v. 15, pt. 2, 128

108. Cecile George in Louisiana Federal Writers' Project, *Gumbo Ya-Ya: A Collection of Louisiana Folktales* (Cambridge, Mass.: The Riverside Press, 1945); see also George's interview in *Mother Wit: The Ex-Slave Interviews of the Louisiana Writers' Project*, ed. Ronnie W. Clayton (New York: Peter Lang, 1990), 83–87.

109. Mollie Dawson, *AS*, Texas Narratives, Supplement, Series II, v. 4, pt. 3, 1132.

110. Patterson, *Freedom*, vol. 1, 9; Davis, *The Problem of Slavery in Western Culture*, 31.

111. Davis, *The Problem of Slavery in Western Culture*, 46.

112. Frederick Douglass, *The Constitution of the United States: Is it Pro-Slavery or Antislavery?* (Halifax: T. and W. Birtwhistle, [1860]), excerpted in *The Antislavery Argument*, 356.

113. James W. C. Pennington, *The Fugitive Blacksmith; or, Events in the History of James W. C. Pennington*, 3d ed. (1850; repr., Westport, Conn.: Negro Universities Press, 1971), xii.

114. Harrison's commitment to this opinion (if it is indeed his own), I should add, is called into question by his assertion later in the same interview that he thinks blacks should vote. Jack Harrison, *AS*, Texas Narratives, Supplement, Series II, v. 5, pt. 4, 1653, 1656.

115. Mollie Dawson, *AS*, Texas Narratives, Supplement, Series II, v. 4, pt. 3, 1132.

116. Prince Haas, in *Mother Wit*, 91. Haas was born in 1861.

117. "Uncle" George G. King, in *The WPA Oklahoma Slave Narratives*, 238.

118. In 1865 Richardson said, "The emancipated slaves own nothing because nothing but freedom has been given to them." Quoted in Eric Foner, *Nothing but Freedom: Emancipation and Its Legacy* (Baton Rouge: Louisiana State University Press, 1983), 6.

119. Eric Foner, *Reconstruction: America's Unfinished Revolution, 1863–1877* (New York: Harper and Row, 1988), 598.

120. Isom Roberts, *AS*, South Carolina Narratives, v. 3, pt. 4, 28.

121. William Mathews, *AS*, Texas Narratives, Supplement, Series II, v. 7, pt. 6, 2619.

122. I infer the question from its answer; Lizzie Grant, *AS*, Texas Narratives, Supplement, Series II, v. 5, pt. 4, 1567.

123. William Coleman, *AS*, Texas Narratives, Supplement, Series II, v. 3, pt. 2, 877.

124. Mary Gaffney, *AS*, Texas Narratives, Supplement, Series II, v. 5 , pt. 4, 1454.

125. Emma Simpson, *AS*, Texas Narratives, Supplement, Series II, v. 9, pt. 8, 3572; Lizzie Atkins, *AS*, Texas Narratives, Supplement, Series II, v. 2, pt. 1, 101.

126. Foner, *Reconstruction*, 78.

127. James Lucas, *AS*, Mississippi Narratives, v. 7, 97.

128. I did not come across any reference to forty acres and a mule in Rawick's collection other than John Davenport's dismissive "No, de slaves never expected anything when de war was over, dem in de neighborhood didn't. Some say something about gitting 40 acres of land and a mule, but we never expected it." *AS*, South Carolina Narratives, v. 2, pt. 1, 243.

129. Eli Coleman, *AS*, Texas Narratives, Supplement, Series II, v. 3, pt. 2, 853.

130. Louis Cain, *AS*, Texas Narratives, Supplement, Series II, v. 3, pt. 2, 596.

131. Harriet Barrett, *AS*, Texas Narratives, Supplement, Series II, v. 2, pt. 1, 202–203.

132. John McAdams, *AS*, Texas Narratives, Supplement, Series II, v. 7, pt. 6, 2474.

133. Frank Bell, *AS*, Texas Narratives, Supplement, Series II, v. 2, pt. 1, 240.

134. Gerald David Jaynes, *Branches without Roots: Genesis of the Black Working Class in the American South, 1862–1882* (New York: Oxford University Press, 1986), 14.

135. Jan Nederveen Pieterse, *White on Black: Images of Africa and Blacks in Popular Culture* (New Haven, Conn.: Yale University Press, 1992), 44–45.

136. Barbara Fields, "Slavery, Race, and Ideology in the United States of America," *New Left Review* 181 (1990): 114–115.

137. Escott, *Slavery Remembered*, 20.

Chapter 5

1. Millie Manuel, in *The American Slave: A Composite Autobiography* [AS], ed. George Rawick (Westport, Conn.: Greenwood Press, 1972–1973), Supplement, Series II, Texas Narratives, v. 7, pt. 6, 2568–2569.

2. Ibid., 2569–2571.

3. Ibid., 2571, 2568.

4. Ibid., 2571.

5. *AS*, Unwritten History of Slavery (Fisk Narratives), v. 18, 142.

6. Ed Jackson, *AS*, Texas Narratives, Supplement, Series II, v. 5, pt. 4, 1888.

7. Mrs. Jennie Patterson, in *Weevils in the Wheat: Interviews with Virginia Ex-Slaves*, ed. Charles L. Perdue Jr., Thomas E. Barden, and Robert K. Phillips (Charlottesville: University Press of Virginia, 1976), 219–20.

8. Jennifer Fleischner, *Mastering Slavery: Memory, Family and Identity in Women's Slave Narratives* (New York: New York University Press, 1996), 21–22.

9. Lawrence W. Levine, *Black Culture, Black Consciousness: Afro-American Folk Thought from Slavery to Freedom* (New York: Oxford University Press, 1977), 101.

10. Cited and discussed in Mel Watkins, *On the Real Side: Laughing, Lying, and Signifying —The Underground Tradition of African-American Humor That Transformed American Culture from Slavery to Richard Pryor* (New York: Simon and Schuster, 1994), 52.

11. Levine, *Black Culture, Black Consciousness*, 100.

12. William Ferris Jr., quoted in John Blassingame, "Using the Testimony of Ex-Slaves," in *The Slave's Narrative*, ed. Charles T. Davis and Henry Louis Gates, Jr. (New York: Oxford University Press, 1985), 85.

13. Edward Jones, *AS*, Mississippi Narratives, Supplement, Series I, v. 8, 1205.

14. Jack Maddox, *AS*, Texas Narratives, Supplement, Series II, v. 7, pt. 6, 2521.

15. Katie Sutton *AS*, Indiana and Alabama Narratives, v. 6, pt. 2, 193. There is another, shorter, version of Katie Sutton's interview in *AS*, Supplement, Series I, v. 5, 210–211, which does not include these statements.

16. Henry Louis Gates, Jr., ed., *"Race," Writing, and Difference* (Chicago: University of Chicago Press, 1986), 5.

17. Evelyn Brooks Higginbotham, "African-American Women's History and the Metalanguage of Race," *Signs* 17 (Winter 1992): 253.

18. David R. Roediger, *The Wages of Whiteness: Race and the Making of the American Working Class* (New York: Verso, 1991). Roediger shows that racial formation and class formation have been closely entwined processes in American history. He argues that by 1800 white workers had begun to forge their identities in opposition to blacks, constructing "whiteness" to defend their dignity and independence as workers.

19. Peter Kolchin, *Unfree Labor: American Slavery and Russian Serfdom* (Cambridge, Mass.: Harvard University Press, 1987), 330.

20. Barbara Jeanne Fields, "Slavery, Race and Ideology in the United States of America," *New Left Review* 181 (1990): 115.

21. Antebellum visitors to the Sea Islands commented on the slaves' use of this racial form of address, according to Bertram Wilbur Doyle, who finds evidence in the diaries of Fanny Kemble and Elisabeth Weare Pearsen to show that "the Negroes on the Sea Islands of South Carolina used 'buckra,' both formally and informally, to refer to white people." Bertram Wilbur Doyle, *The Etiquette of Race Relations in the South: A Study in Social Control* (Port Washington, N.Y.: Kennikat Press, 1937), 3.

22. Sallie Paul, *AS*, South Carolina Narratives, v. 3, pt. 3, 233; Dinah Cunningham talks about how her master and mistress and their "buckra" friends looked down on one of the overseers. The word "buckra" was also sometimes used to refer to all white people, or all white Southerners. Dinah Cunningham, *AS*, South Carolina Narratives, v. 2, pt. 1, 235.

23. Tom W. Woods, in *The WPA Oklahoma Slave Narratives*, ed. T. Lindsay Baker and Julie P. Baker (Norman: University of Oklahoma Press, 1996), 500.

24. Hannah MacFarland, in *The WPA Oklahoma Slave Narratives*, 274.

25. Mauda Walker, *AS*, South Carolina Narratives, v. 3, pt. 4, 171; Ella Johnson, *AS*, Georgia Narratives, Supplement, Series I, v. 4, pt. 2, 344.

26. Tom W. Woods, in *The WPA Oklahoma Slave Narratives*, 501.

27. Ellen Craft and William Craft, *Running a Thousand Miles for Freedom* (1860; repr. New York: Arno Press, 1969), 36.

28. Winthrop Jordan, *Tumult and Silence at Second Creek: An Inquiry into a Civil War Slave Conspiracy* (Baton Rouge: Louisiana State University Press, 1993).

29. State of Virginia, Executive Papers, September–December, 1800, quoted in Gerald Mullin, *Flight and Rebellion: Slave Resistance in Eighteenth-Century Virginia* (New York: Oxford University Press, 1972), 142, 145.

30. Testimony of Philip Nicholas at the trial of Nicholas King, Executive Papers, 25 September 1900, quoted in Douglass Egerton, *Gabriel's Rebellion: The Virginia Slave Conspiracies of 1800 and 1802* (Chapel Hill: University of North Carolina Press, 1993), 57.

31. *The Trial Record of Denmark Vesey*, ed. John Oliver Killens (Boston: Beacon Press, 1970), 61, 42.

32. "Verbatim Record of the Trials in the Court of Oyer and Terminer of Southampton County," reprinted in *The Southampton Slave Revolt of 1831: A Compilation of Source Material*, ed. Henry Irving Tragle (Amherst: University of Massachusetts Press, 1971), 196.

33. Thomas R. Gray, "The Confessions of Nat Turner" (1831), in Tragle, *The Southampton Slave Revolt of 1831*, 308–309.

34. I take these estimates on the death toll in Turner's Rebellion from the most thorough account of the event currently available: Tragle, *The Southampton Slave Revolt of 1831*, 4.

35. Jordan, *Tumult and Silence*, 283.

36. Ibid., 274.

37. Benjamin Woolfolk, "Woolfolk's Confessions," quoted in Mullin, *Flight and Rebellion*, 152.

38. *The Trial Record of Denmark Vesey*, 46; Mullin, *Flight and Rebellion*, 158.

39. In his confession to Thomas R. Gray, Turner reportedly said, "Until we had armed and equipped ourselves, and gathered sufficient force, neither age nor sex was to be spared (which was invariably adhered to)." Gray, "The Confessions of Nat Turner," in Tragle, *The Southampton Slave Revolt of 1831*, 310–311.

40. Benjamin Woolfolk, Prosser's Ben, quoted in Mullin, *Flight and Rebellion*, 158.

41. *The Trial Record of Denmark Vesey*, 42; Jordan, *Tumult and Silence*, 273, 272.

42. Jordan, *Tumult and Silence*, 298.

43. Ibid., 202.

44. Henry Bibb, *Narrative of the Life and Adventures of Henry Bibb, an American Slave* (1850; repr., New York: Negro Universities Press, 1969), 51.

45. Thomas L. Webber, *Deep Like Rivers: Education in the Slave Quarter Community, 1831–1865* (New York: Norton, 1978), 71.

46. James Campbell and James Oakes use this phrase in summarizing Winthrop Jordan's ideas in "The Invention of Race: Rereading *White Over Black*," *Reviews in American History* 21, no. 1 (March 1993): 174.

47. Olaudah Equiano, *The Interesting Narrative of Olaudah Equiano or Gustavus Vassa the African*, 4th ed. (Dublin: by the author, 1791), 50, 14.

48. P[eter] H[eylyn], *Microcosmus, or a Little Description of the Great World* (Oxford, 1621), quoted in Winthrop Jordan, *White Over Black: American Attitudes Towards the Negro, 1550–1812* (Chapel Hill: University of North Carolina Press, 1968; repr., New York: Norton, 1977), 9–10.

49. Victoria McMullen, *AS*, Arkansas Narratives, v. 10, pt. 5, 33.

50. Ed Barber, *AS*, South Carolina Narratives, v. 2, pt. 1, 35.

51. Jake Terrill, *AS*, Texas Narratives, Supplement, Series II, v. 9, pt. 8, 3774.

52. Phillis Wheatley, "On being brought from AFRICA to AMERICA," (written 1768; published 1773), in *The Collected Works of Phillis Wheatley*, ed. John C. Shields (New York: Oxford University Press, 1988), 18.

53. Frances Banks, *AS*, Oklahoma Narratives, Supplement, Series I, v. 12, 12.

54. Newspaper article by Sarah F. Babb, reprinted in *AS*, Mississippi Narratives, Supplement, Series I, v. 6, 69.

55. Ex-slave quoted in Mechal Sobel, *Trabelin' On: The Slave Journey to an Afro-Baptist Faith* (Westport, Conn.: Greenwood Press, 1979), 114.

56. Rebecca Jane Grant, *AS*, South Carolina Narratives, v. 2, pt. 2, 180.

57. *AS*, Unwritten History of Slavery (Fisk University), v. 18, 50.

58. Leon Litwack, *Been in the Storm So Long: The Aftermath of Slavery* (New York: Knopf, 1979), 120.

59. *AS*, Arkansas Narratives, v. 8, pt. 2, 75–76.

60. However, Sobel's account of the African origins of the color values in slave religious imagery is not easily reconciled with early European reports from Africa that, when it came to complexion, "the Negro's preference in color was the inverse to the European's" (Jordan, *White Over Black*, 10)—unless we assume that the black–white dichotomies in African religious thought did not apply to skin color, in which case they have little relevance here (Sobel, *Trabelin' On*, 115). On European ideas about color preferences in Africa, see Jordan, *White Over Black*, 10.

61. Levine, *Black Culture, Black Consciousness*, 289, 285, 286.

62. James Southall, in *The WPA Oklahoma Slave Narratives*, 407.

63. Cambell Armstrong, *AS*, Arkansas Narratives, v. 8, pt. 1, 68.

64. Frank Hughes, *AS*, Mississippi Narratives, Supplement, Series I, v. 8, pt. 3, 1064.

65. Nettie Henry, *AS*, Mississippi Narratives, Supplement, Series I, v. 8, pt. 3, 979.

66. Alice Johnson, *AS*, Arkansas Narratives, v. 9, pt. 4, 59.

67. Webber, *Deep Like Rivers*, 103.
68. Ed Williams, *AS*, Mississippi Narratives, Supplement, Series I, v. 10, pt. 5, 2308.
69. Eugene D. Genovese, *Roll Jordan, Roll: The World the Slaves Made* (New York: Pantheon Books, 1974), 3.
70. James Battle Avirett, *The Old Plantation* (New York: F. T. Neely, 1901), 144–145.
71. Levine, *Black Culture and Black Consciousness*, 250, 249.
72. William Wells Brown, *Clotel, or the President's Daughter* (1853; repr., New York, 1969), quoted in Levine, *Black Culture and Black Consciousness*.
73. Levine, *Black Culture and Black Consciousness*, 248.
74. Ibid., 309, 310.
75. See Herbert Aptheker, "Afro-American Superiority: A Neglected Theme in the Literature," *Phylon* 31, no. 4 (1970), 336–343; and Webber, *Deep Like Rivers*, chapter 7 ("Black Superiority"), 91–101.
76. Examples of the John tales can be found in J. Mason Brewer, "John Tales," *Publications of the Texas Folklore Society* 21 (1946): 81–104. They are also discussed by Lawrence W. Levine, whose *Black Culture, Black Consciousness* contains an excellent analysis of the meaning of these and other slave trickster tales. While such tales are sometimes read as allegorical accounts of Southern race relations, Levine argues that the slave trickster tales contain complex messages about the world, and human nature, that go well beyond any simple equation between the trickster and the slave (or between white people and the tricked). The slave trickster, he explains, cannot be seen as a stand-in for the slave, but instead functions "on several different symbolic levels—as black slave, as white master, as irrational force." Levine, *Black Culture, Black Consciousness*, 120–121.
77. Sallie Crane, *AS*, Arkansas Narratives, v. 8, pt. 2, 53; Nancy Settle, *AS*, Georgia Narratives, v. 13, pt. 3, 235.
78. Ronnie W. Clayton, ed., *Mother Wit: The Ex-Slave Narratives of the Louisiana Writers' Project* (New York: Peterlang, 1990), 95.
79. Mary Gaffney, *AS*, Texas Narratives, Supplement, Series II, v. 5, pt. 4, 1456.
80. Millie Manuel, *AS*, Texas Narratives, Supplement, Series II, v. 7, pt. 6, 2569.
81. Charley Williams, in *The WPA Oklahoma Narratives*, 482; Charles Hinton, *AS*, Arkansas Narratives, v. 9, pt. 4, 197.
82. Edward Taylor, *AS*, Missouri Narratives, v. 11, 339. Richard Caruthers reported that when the stars fell the slaves where he lived thought they fell at the command of their bad-tempered white overseer. *AS*, Texas Narratives, v. 4, pt. 1, 197.
83. Charles Hinton, *AS*, Arkansas Narratives, v. 9, pt. 3, 278.
84. Bibb, *Life and Adventures of Henry Bibb*, 27, 28.
85. Julius Jones, *AS*, Mississippi Narratives, Supplement, Series I, v. 8, pt. 3, 1219.
86. *AS*, Unwritten History of Slavery (Fisk University), v. 18, 100.
87. Hattie Matthews, *AS*, Missouri Narratives, v. 11, 250.
88. Levine, *Black Culture, Black Consciousness*, 73.
89. John Blassingame comments with special reference to Stanley Elkins's *Slavery: A Problem in American Institutional and Intellectual Life* (Chicago: University of Chicago Press, 1959): "The Sambo stereotype was so pervasive in antebellum Southern literature that many historians, without further research, argue that it was an accurate description of the dominant slave personality. According to historians of this stripe, the near unanimity of so many white observers of the slave cannot be discounted." John Blassingame, *The Slave Community: Plantation Life in the Antebellum South*, rev. ed. (New York: Oxford University Press, 1979), 226.
90. On stereotypes about female slaves, see Deborah Gray White, *Ar'n't I Woman: Female Slaves in the Plantation South* (New York: Norton, 1985), chapter 1.
91. *AS*, Unwritten History of Slavery (Fisk University), v. 18, 279.
92. Rachael [or Rachal; the spelling is inconsistent] Goings, *AS*, Missouri Narratives, v. 11, pt. 8, 121.
93. Robert Ellett, in *Weevils in the Wheat*, 84.

94. Brian W. Dippie, *The Vanishing American: White Americans and U.S. Indian Policy* (Middletown, Conn.: Wesleyan University Press, 1982), 89.

95. Anna Baker, *AS*, Mississippi Narratives, Supplement, Series I, v. 6, pt. 1, 99–100.

96. Unfortunately, Hamlin does not expand on her fascinating account of early American history. However, her testimony is notable because she gave two interviewers entirely different accounts of her life and views. She gave the statement quoted here to Augustus Ladson, an interviewer whom the internal evidence in the interview suggests was black. But Hamlin offered an entirely different discussion of racial history to Jessie A. Butler, a condescending white interviewer who did not correct Hamlin's impression that she was "from the Welfare office, from which she had received aid prior to its closing." Hamlin told Butler, "Dose black ignoramuses in Africa forgot God, and didn't have no religion and God blessed and prospered the white people dat did remember him and sent dem to teach de black people even if dey have to grab dem and bring dem into bondage till dey learned some sense. The Indians forgot God and dey had to be taught better so dey land was taken way from dem. God sure bless and prosper de white people and He put de red and de black people under dem so dey could teach dem and bring dem into sense wid God." Susan Hamlin, *AS*, South Carolina Narratives, v. 1, pt. 2, 235, 226, 230. Hamlin's differing narratives are discussed in James West Davidson and Mark Hamilton Lytle, *After the Fact: The Art of Historical Detection* (New York: Knopf, 1982), 159–168.

97. C. Vann Woodward comes to similar conclusions in his reading of the slave narratives. In the WPA narratives, he observes, "Indian blood is frequently invoked to account for cherished traits of rebelliousness, ferocity and fortitude. . . . White blood is never mentioned in such connections." "History from Slaves Sources," in *The Slave's Narrative*, ed. Charles T. Davis and Henry Louis Gates Jr. (New York: Oxford University Press, 1985), 57.

98. Jim Henry, *AS*, South Carolina Narratives, v. 2, pt. 2, 266; Dora Franks, *AS*, Mississippi Narratives, Supplement, Series I, v. 7, pt. 2, 787.

99. Stephen C. Crawford, "Quantified Memory: A Study of the WPA and Fisk University Slave Narrative Collections" (Ph.D. diss.: University of Chicago, 1980), 41.

100. Polly Colbert, in *The WPA Oklahoma Slave Narratives*, 86.

101. Equiano, *The Interesting Narrative of Olaudah Equiano*, 61.

102. Webber, *Deep Like Rivers*, 109–10.

103. Isaac [Isaiah] Green, *AS*, Georgia Narratives, v. 12, pt. 2, 59.

104. Richard Slaughter, in *Weevils in the Wheat*, 269.

105. Dora Richard, *AS*, Arkansas Narratives, v. 10, pt. 6, 35.

106. Genovese, *Roll Jordan, Roll*, 123.

107. In a guarded comment typical of the South Carolina narratives one ex-slave said, "I heared tell uv trouble 'tween de whites en de colored peoples, but dere wasn't none uv dat 'round whey I stay." Washington Desier, *AS*, South Carolina Narratives, v. 2, pt. 1, 333. The predominance of ex-slaves in certain regions who witnessed white cruelty only on neighboring plantations is no doubt related in some way to a reticence on the part of the elderly, poor, and dependent black informants who testified in the slave interviews. Many had apprehensions about saying anything at all against white people, and they may have been particularly reluctant to speak ill of white people they had actually known and whose kin they often still knew—as one said, "These white folks here don't like to hear about how they fathers and mothers done these colored folks." *AS*, Unwritten History of Slavery (Fisk University), v. 18, 142.

108. Charlotte Foster, *AS*, South Carolina Narratives, v. 2, pt. 2, 81.

109. Anthony Dawson, in *The WPA Oklahoma Slave Narratives*, 119.

110. Charlie Bowen, *AS*, Texas Narratives, Supplement, Series II, v. 2, pt. 1, 349.

111. Hannah Jameson, *AS*, Texas Narratives, Supplement, Series II, v. 6, pt. 5, 1935.

112. James Gill, *AS*, Arkansas Narratives, v. 9, pt. 3, 24.

113. *AS*, Unwritten History of Slavery (Fisk University), v. 18, 131.

114. Jordon Smith, *AS*, Texas Narratives, v. 5, pt. 4, 39.

115. *AS*, "Massa's Slave Son," Unwritten History of Slavery (Fisk University), v. 18, 84.

116. Steve Douglas, *AS*, Texas Narratives, Supplement, Series II, v. 4, pt. 3, 1228.

117. Cal Woods, *AS*, Arkansas Narratives, v. 11, pt. 7, 229.

118. Anthony Dawson, in *The WPA Oklahoma Slave Narratives*, 124.

119. Fanny Johnson, *AS*, Arkansas Narratives, v. 9, pt. 4, 85.

120. W.E.B. DuBois, *The Souls of Black Folk* (1903; repr., New York: New American Library, 1982), 274.

121. Emily P. Burke, *Pleasure and Pain: Reminiscences of Georgia in the 1840s* (Savannah, Ga.: Beehive Press, 1978), 15.

122. James Oakes, *The Ruling Race: A History of American Slaveholders* (New York: Vintage Books, 1983), 112.

123. Frances Anne Kemble. *Journal of a Residence on a Georgian Plantation in 1838–1839* ed. John A. Scott (Athens: University of Georgia Press, 1984), 60.

124. Jennie Proctor, *AS*, Texas Narratives, v. 5, pt. 1, 213.

125. "Uncle" George G. King, in *The WPA Oklahoma Slave Narratives*, 239; Dolla Bess Hilyard, *AS*, Florida Narratives, v. 17, 54.

126. Harriet Barret, *AS*, Texas Narratives, Supplement, Series II, v. 2, pt. 1, 200.

127. Jake Terrill, *AS*, Texas Narratives, Supplement, Series II, v. 9, pt. 8, 3774; Frank Robinson, quoted in David R. Roediger, "And Die in Dixie: Funerals, Death, and Heaven in Slavery," *Massachusetts Review* 22 (Spring 1981): 179.

128. Andrew Moss, *AS*, Tennessee Narratives, v. 16, 49.

129. Eliza Washington, *AS*, Arkansas Narratives, v. 11, pt. 7, 53.

130. Jack Jones, *AS*, Mississippi Narratives, Supplement, Series I, v. 8, pt. 3, 1212.

131. Charley Williams, in *The WPA Oklahoma Slave Narratives*, 473.

132. Mary Reynolds, *AS*, Texas Narratives, Supplement, Series II, v. 8, pt. 7, 3289; Mrs. Beverly Jones in *Weevils in the Wheat*, 184.

133. Millie Williams, *AS*, Texas Narratives, v. 10, pt. 9, 4113. For more on the presentation of heaven in slave songs, see Levine, *Black Culture, Black Consciousness*, 23, 34, 36–37.

134. Ben Simpson, *AS*, Texas Narratives, Supplement, Series II, v. 9, pt. 8, 3555.

135. Jack Maddox, *AS*, Texas Narratives, Supplement, Series II, v. 7, pt. 6, 2521.

136. Quoted in David Roediger, "And Die in Dixie," 180.

137. *Southern Workman* 26 (1897): 210.

138. Millie Manuel, *AS*, Texas Narratives, Supplement, Series II, v. 7, pt. 6, 2568.

139. Charles Ball, *Fifty Years in Chains; Or, The Life of an American Slave* (New York, 1858; repr. Miami, Fla.: Mnemosyne Publishing, 1969), 150.

140. Burke, *Pleasure and Pain*, 15.

141. The only reference of this kind I have found in WPA evidence is Millie Manuel's comment on her late owners: "They is gone where the Good Shepard has sent them to be slaves for the devil." *AS*, Texas Narratives, Supplement, Series II, v. 7, pt. 6, 2569.

142. *AS*, Unwritten History of Slavery (Fisk University), v. 18, 136; Robert Burns, *AS*, Oklahoma Narratives, Supplement, Series I, v. 12, 81.

143. Charles Moss, *AS*, Mississippi Narratives, Supplement, Series I, v. 9, pt. 4, 1597.

144. Mary Reynolds, *AS*, Texas Narratives, Supplement, Series II, v. 8, pt. 7, 3289.

145. Ellen Rogers, *AS*, Texas Narratives, Supplement, Series II, v. 8, pt. 7, 3359.

146. Harold Courlander, *Negro Folk Music, U.S.A.* (New York: Columbia University Press, 1963), 67.

147. Maria Bracey, *AS*, South Carolina Narratives, Supplement, Series I, v. 11, 66.

148. "Aunt" Rhody Halsell, *AS*, Missouri Narratives, v. 11, 198.

149. Reverend Ishrael Massie, in *Weevils in the Wheat*, 206.

150. Mary Reynolds, *AS*, Texas Narratives, Supplement, Series II, v. 8, pt. 7, 3289.

151. Penny Thompson, *AS*, Texas Narratives, v. 9, pt. 8, 3871.

Part III

1. The epigraph that prefaces this section is taken from the collection *Ebony and Topaz: A Collectanea*, ed. Charles S. Johnson (New York: Opportunity, National Urban League, 1927).

Chapter 6

1. Gunnar Myrdal, *An American Dilemma: The Negro Problem and American Democracy* (New York: Harper and Brothers, 1994 [1944]. For a discussion of the impact of *An American Dilemma*, see Walter Jackson, *Gunnar Myrdal and America's Conscience: Social Engineering and Racial Liberalism, 1938–1987* (Chapel Hill: University of North Carolina Press, 1990), chapter 8. Jackson quite rightly emphasizes that African-American protest activities such as Randolph's March on Washington movement, the Double-V campaign, and the Detroit race riot influenced how *An American Dilemma* was received by its American audience. One reason that the book was so influential, Jackson explains, was that it "offered to many whites a persuasive interpretation of the race issue at a critical juncture in Afro-American history" (318).

2. Myrdal, *An American Dilemma*, 96.

3. W.E.B. DuBois, *The Souls of Black Folk* (1903; repr., New York: New American Library, 1982), xi.

4. Rayford Logan, *The Negro in American Life and Thought: The Nadir, 1877–1901* (New York: Dial Press, 1945); Sean Dennis Cashman, *African-Americans and the Quest for Civil Rights, 1900–1990* (New York: New York University Press, 1991), 6.

5. Rayford Logan, *The Betrayal of the Negro: From Rutherford Hayes to Woodrow Wilson* (New York: Collier Books, 1965), 313.

6. W.E.B. DuBois, "The Conservation of the Races" (1897), in *Writings* (New York: Library of America, 1986), 817, 822.

7. William H. Crogman, "Negro Education: Its Helps and Hindrances," in National Education Association, *Journal of Proceedings and Addresses* 23 (Boston 1885), quoted in William Toll, "Free Men, Freedmen, and Race: Black Social Theory in the Gilded Age," *Journal of Southern History* 44 (November 1978): 578.

8. Toll, "Free Men, Freedmen, and Race," 595.

9. On women and evolutionary theory, see Louise Michele Newman, "Laying Claim to Difference: Ideologies of Race and Gender in the U.S. Women's Movement, 1870–1920" (Ph.D. diss., Brown University, 1992).

10. Eleanor Tayleur, "The Negro Woman: I. Social and Moral Decadence," *Outlook* 76 (January 10, 1904), 266, 267.

11. William Hannibal Thomas, *The American Negro: What He Was, What He Is, and What He May Become* (New York: Macmillan, 1901), 193.

12. Anna Julia Cooper, "Womanhood: A Vital Element in the Regeneration and Progress of a Race," in *A Voice from the South* (New York: Oxford University Press, 1988), 25–26.

13. Josephine Ruffin, "Address of Josephine Ruffin, President of the Conference," *The Women's Era* 2 (August 1895): 14; On black women's activism during the nadir and beyond, see Deborah Gray White, *Too Heavy a Load: Black Women in Defense of Themselves, 1894–1994* (New York: Norton, 1999.)

14. Murphy as quoted in Pauline E. Hopkins, *A Primer of Facts Pertaining to the Early Greatness of the African Race and the Possibility of Restoration by its Descendants . . . Compiled and Arranged from the Works of the best known Ethnologists and Historians*. (Cambridge: P. E. Hopkins and Co., 1905), 23.

15. Druscilla Dunjee Houston, *The Wonderful Ethiopians of the Cushite Empire* (Oklahoma City: Universal Publishing, 1926).

16. See, for example, A. L. Hall, *The Ancient, Medieval, and Modern Greatness of the Negro* (Memphis, Tenn.: Striker Print, 1907); James Morris Webb, *The Black Man: The Father of Civilization, Proven by Biblical History* (Chicago: Fraternal Press, 1924); and Edward A. Johnson, *Adam Vs. Ape-Man and Ethiopia* (New York: J. Little and Ives, 1931). The scriptural origins of the races are also discussed in a very strange and somewhat incoherent attack on modern science written by a slave-born preacher from North Carolina: see Napoleon Bonaparte Boyd, *Revised Search Light on the Seventh Day Bible and X-Ray, By Organic, Supernatural, and Artificial Science* (Greenville, N.C.: by the author, 1924).

17. W.E.B. DuBois, "The Laboratory in Sociology at Atlanta University," *Annals of the American Academy of Political and Social Science* 21 (May 1903): 503.

18. W. H. Crogman and H. F. Kletzing, *The Progress of a Race* (Atlanta: J. L. Nichols, 1897), 23.

19. W.E.B. DuBois, "The Study of Negro Problems," *Annals of the American Academy of Political and Social Science* 11 (January 1898), reprinted in *The Black Sociologists: The First Half Century*, ed. John H. Bracey Jr., August Meier, and Elliot Rudwick (Belmont, Calif.: Wadsworth, 1971), 25.

20. Crogman and Kletzing, *Progress of a Race*, 189.

21. Thomas Greathead Harper, *Contemporary Evolution of the Negro Race* (Washington, D.C.: American Negro Monographs, 1910). Other examples of black writing on race that show a strong social Darwinist influence are Sutton Griggs's works on "collective efficiency," which preached a self-help philosophy that laid out a set of principles that promised blacks a way to hasten along the evolutionary road. Griggs's work on this subject included *The Science of Collective Efficiency* (Memphis, Tenn.: National Public Welfare League, 1921), and *Guide to Racial Greatness, or the Science of Collective Efficiency* (Memphis, Tenn.: National Public Welfare League, 1923). See also William Ferris, *The African Abroad, Or, his Evolution in Western Civilization, Tracing His Development Under Caucasian Milieu* (New Haven, Conn.: Tuttle, Morehouse and Taylor Press, 1913); and Caesar Augustus Taylor, *The Conflict and Commingling of the Races* (New York: Broadway Publishing, 1913); Hamilton Cravens, *The Triumph of Evolution: The Heredity–Environment Controversy, 1900–1941* (Baltimore, Md.: Johns Hopkins University Press, 1988), 94.

22. Kelly Miller, *Race Adjustment [and] The Everlasting Stain* (New York: Arno Press and the New York Times, 1968), 17.

23. This problem was not, of course, insurmountable. Indeed, a neat resolution to the question of how blacks had fallen behind in the evolutionary struggle was provided in 1921 by Branstan S. Clark, who suggested the inhospitable environment of the European continent was the source of "the white man's superiority in wealth, power and intellectual achievement." This was in contrast to the Africans, who were so comfortable on the African continent that their ancient civilizations declined as "they became lethargic and started to retrograde." "Those who made their homes in Europe had to wage a daily ditch fight in order to exist. They had to struggle with snow and ice; they had to wrest their food form [*sic*] the very jaws of wild animals." Clark's 1921 attempt to reconcile evolution and Africa's ancient glory in his self-published *Is it the Color of Our Skin that is Responsible for Our Down Trodden Condition all over the World* (n.p.: by the author, 1921), 15, was already anachronistic when it first appeared.

24. DuBois, "The Conservation of the Races," 815; DuBois, "The Study of Negro Problems," 19.

25. Alfred A. Moss, *The American Negro Academy: Voice of the Talented Tenth* (Baton Rouge: Louisiana State University Press, 1981), 50, 51; Kelly Miller, "A Review of Hoffman's Race Traits and Tendencies of the American Negro" (Washington, D.C., 1897), reprinted in *The American Negro Academy Occasional Papers 1–22* (New York: Arno Press and the New York Times, 1969), 36; Moss, *The American Negro Academy*, 93–94, 96.

26. Elsewhere Miller combined black chauvinism with social Darwinism to attack Hoffman's predictions. In "The Land of Goshen" he questioned the ability of sociologists to predict the future, writing, "To the most casual observer it is clearly evident that

the white race cannot compete with the Negro industrially in a hot climate and among the miasmatic lowlands. Where the white man has to work in the burning sun, the cadaverous, emaciated body, drooping spirit and thin, nasal voice bespeak the rapid decline of this breed. On the other hand the Negro multiplies and makes merry. His body is vigorous and spirit bouyant. There can be no doubt that in many sections the Negro element is gradually driving out the whites. In the struggle for existence the fittest will survive." Miller, *Race Adjustment*, 161.

27. Franz Boas, "Human Faculty as Determined by Race," *Proceedings of the American Association for the Advancement of Science* 43 (1894): 301–327. On Boas, see Vernon J. Williams, *From a Caste to a Minority: Changing Attitudes of American Sociologists toward Afro-Americans* (Westport, Conn.: Greenwood Press: 1989); Vernon J. Williams, *Rethinking Race: Franz Boas and His Contemporaries* (Lexington: University of Kentucky Press, 1996); Marshall Hyatt, "Franz Boas and the Struggle for Black Equality: The Dynamics of Ethnicity," *Perspectives in American History*, n.s., 2 (1985): 269–295; and Carl N. Degler, *In Search of Human Nature: The Decline and Revival of Darwinism in American Social Thought* (New York: Oxford University Press, 1991).

28. Degler, *In Search of Human Nature*, 62.

29. W.E.B. DuBois, *Dusk of Dawn*, in *Writings*, 626–627.

30. Alfred Holt Stone, "Is Race Friction Between Whites and Blacks in the United States Growing and Inevitable?" *American Journal of Sociology* 13 (March 1908): 679–779; W.E.B. DuBois, "Discussion of Race Friction by Alfred F. Stone," *American Journal of Sociology* 13 (March 1908): 838.

31. Franz Boas, *The Mind of Primitive Man* (New York: Free Press, 1938).

32. Franz Boas, "The Industries of Southern Negroes," *Southern Workman* 38 (April 1909): 217–229; Boas, "The Real Race Problem," *Crisis* 1 (December 1910): 22–25.

33. W.E.B. DuBois, *The Negro* (1915; repr., Millhouse, N.Y.: Kraus Thomson, 1975); Booker T. Washington, *The Story of the Negro* (1909; repr., New York: Negro Universities Press, 1969). The influence that Boas had on DuBois's and Washington's works is discussed by John David Smith in *An Old Creed for the New South: Proslavery Ideology and Historiography, 1865–1918* (Westport, Conn.: Greenwood Press, 1985), 202–3, 214.

34. Monroe N. Work, "The Passing Tradition and African Civilization," *Journal of Negro History* 1, no. 1 (1916): 35.

35. Murray's note on this subject is from an undated entry under "anthropology" that he prepared for the never-completed "Murray's Historical and Biographical Encyclopedia of the Colored Race Throughout the World" sometime between 1895 and 1930. See the Daniel Murray Papers (microfilm edition), State Historical Society of Wisconsin, 1977, reel 9.

36. DuBois, *The Negro*, 13, 16.

37. Booker T. Washington, *The Booker T. Washington Papers*, ed. Louis R. Harlan and Raymond W. Smock (Urbana: University of Illinois Press, 1984), 352–353, 362.

38. C. V. Roman, *American Civilization and the Negro* (1916; repr., Northbrook Ill.: Metro Books, 1972), 322, 329–334, 135.

39. Ibid., 135.

40. Kelly Miller, "Race Differences: So to the Eternal Difference of Race, Open Letter to President Harding and Reply, Nov. 30, 1921," in Miller, *Race Adjustment*, 117, 125.

41. Alain LeRoy Locke, *Race Contacts and Interracial Relations: Lectures on the Theory and Practice of Race*, ed. Jeffrey C. Stewart (Washington, D.C.: Howard University Press, 1992), 7–8.

42. Ibid., 11. The amendments in the text are added by Stewart, who reconstructed Locke's lectures from his notes.

43. Ibid., 94, 32.

44. Ibid., 23.

45. Roman, *American Civilization and the Negro*, 102, 121.

46. DuBois, *The Negro*, 137, 138. On the racialism in DuBois's thought, see Harold Isaac, "Pan-Africanism as 'Romantic Racism,'" in *W.E.B. DuBois: A Profile*, ed. Rayford

Logan (New York: Hill and Wang, 1971), 210–248; and Anthony Appiah, "The Uncompleted Argument: DuBois and the Illusion of Race," in *"Race," Writing, and Difference*, ed. Henry Louis Gates, Jr. (Chicago: University of Chicago Press, 1968): 21–37.

47. Frances J. Grimké, quoted in S. P. Fullinwider, *The Mind and Mood of Black America* (Homewood, Ill.: Irwin-Dorsey, 1969), 17.

48. Ibid., 14, 15.

49. See, for example, Charles S. Johnson, "Mental Measurements of Negro Groups," *Opportunity* 1 (February 1923) 21–25; Alain LeRoy Locke, "The Problem of Race Classification" *Opportunity* 1 (September 1925): 261–265; Howard M. Long, "Race and Mental Tests," *Opportunity* 1 (March 1923): 27–28; Long, "On Mental Tests and Racial Psychology—A Critique," *Opportunity* (May 1925): 134–138; Horace Mann Bond, "Intelligence Tests and Propaganda," *The Crisis* 28 (1924): 61–64; and Bond, "Some Exceptional Negro Children," *The Crisis* (1927): 257–259.

50. Stephen Jay Gould, *The Mismeasure of Man* (New York: Norton, 1981), 196.

51. Degler, *In Search of Human Nature*, 50.

52. William B. Thomas, "Black Intellectuals' Critique of Early Mental Testing: A Little-Known Saga of the 1920s," *American Journal of Education* 90 (May 1982): 258–292.

53. Roman, *American Civilization and the Negro*, 350–51

54. Lothrop Stoddard, *The Rising Tide of Color Against White World-Supremacy* (New York: Scribner's, 1920), 9.

55. Ibid., 11.

56. James R. Grossman, *Land of Hope: Chicago, Black Southerners, and the Great Migration* (Chicago: University of Chicago Press, 1989), 161.

57. U.S. Department of Labor, *Negro Migration in 1916–1917*, quoted in Allan H. Spear, *Black Chicago: The Making of a Negro Ghetto, 1890–1920* (Chicago: University of Chicago Press, 1967), 137.

58. Wilson Jeremiah Moses, *The Wings of Ethiopia* (Ames: Iowa State University Press), 202; Alain LeRoy Locke, ed., *The New Negro: An Interpretation* (1925; repr., New York: Arno Press, 1968).

59. Isom reflected, "Since I been doin' dis beggin'—dats what I call dis here 'relief,' I goes up to de office an' sees so many ole white folks what can't read an' write—dey don't know a single letter; I ses to myself; white folks all born free how cum dey can't read an' write; hit looks like sum body woul'd hav learned dem sumthin'. I ses: Niggers aint de onliest fools in the world." Joanna Thompson Isom, in *The American Slave: A Composite Autobiography* [*AS*], ed. George Rawick, Mississippi Narratives, Supplement, Series I (Westport, Conn.: Greenwood Press, 1977) v. 8, pt. 3, 1101.

60. The anthropologist Levine cites is Anthony F. C. Wallace. Lawrence Levine, "Marcus Garvey and the Politics of Revitalization," in *Black Leaders of the Twentieth Century*, ed. John Hope Franklin and August Meier (Urbana: University of Illinois Press, 1982), 113.

61. Nathan Irvin Huggins, *Harlem Renaissance* (New York: Oxford University Press, 1971), 6–7.

62. Moses, *Wings of Ethiopia*, 203.

63. Richard Wright, *Black Boy: A Record of Childhood and Youth* (1937; repr., New York: Harper and Row, 1966), 90–91.

64. W.E.B. DuBois, *Darkwater: Voices From Within the Veil* (1920; repr., New York: Schocken Books, 1969), 53–54.

65. Huggins, *Harlem Renaissance*, 72.

66. Quoted in ibid., 71. McKay's poem was first published in Max Eastman's *Liberator* 2 (July 1919): 21.

67. James Weldon Johnson, *Black Manhattan* (1939; repr., New York: Atheneum, 1968), 246, 248.

68. Quoted in ibid., 250, 249.

69. Randall K. Burkett, *Garveyism as a Religious Movement: The Institutionalization of a Black Civil Religion* (Metuchen, N.J.: Scarecrow Press, 1978).

70. Howard Brotz, *The Black Jews of Harlem: Negro Nationalism and the Dilemma of Negro Leadership* (New York: Schocken Books, 1970), 82.

71. DuBois, *Darkwater*, 159.

72. Fullinwinder, *The Mind and Mood of Black America*, 122, 123, 122.

73. Huggins, *Harlem Renaissance*, 173.

74. For example, Garvey told his Jamaican countrymen in 1916: "It is true, that by accident and unfavorable circumstance, the Negro lost hold of the glorious civilization that he had once dispensed, and in the process of time reverted to savagery. . . . yet it does not follow that the Negro must always remain backward. . . . there is a great chance for the Negro to do something for himself on the same standard of established customs among the *advanced*." "A Talk with Afro-West Indians" (January 1916), in *Marcus Garvey and the Vision of Africa*, ed. John Henry Clarke (New York: Vintage Books, 1974), 84–85.

75. Marcus Garvey, "*Home to Harlem*: An Insult to the Race," *Negro World* 29 (September 1928), quoted in Moses, *Wings of Ethiopia*, 213.

76. Moses, *Wings of Ethiopia*, 102.

77. Theodore Draper, *The Rediscovery of Black Nationalism* (New York: Viking Press, 1969), 85.

78. Burkett reports that in the early twenties more than 250 clergymen were on record in Garvey's *Negro World* as active supporters of Garvey. His list of their denominational affiliations shows that Garvey drew supporters from virtually all the Protestant churches, with the largest numbers coming from predominantly black denominations such as the Baptists, A.M.E., and A.M.E. Zion. Randall K. Burkett, *Black Redemption: Churchmen Speak for the Garvey Movement* (Philadelphia: Temple University Press, 1978), 9.

79. Garvey himself claimed as many as 6 million followers, while W.E.B. DuBois put the number as low as 80,000, and Kelly Miller and William Pickens each credited Garvey with several million followers. For a discussion of these widely varying estimates, see David Cronon, *Black Moses: The Story of Marcus Garvey and the Universal Negro Improvement Association* (Madison: University of Wisconsin Press, 1955), 205.

80. E. Franklin Frazier, "The Garvey Movement," *Opportunity* 4 (November 1926): 346.

81. Arthur Huff Fauset, *Black Gods of the Metropolis: Negro Religious Cults in the Urban North* (1944; repr., New York: Octagon Books, 1970), 62.

82. This information on the doctrine of the Church of God is from Fauset, *Black Gods of the Metropolis*. Fauset researched this sect in the 1940s, but his information is relevant here because he notes that this sect was established many years earlier by its leader Prophet Cherry. As descibed by Fauset, the Church of God's Judaism sounds quite different from the black Judaism discussed by Howard Brotz in his study *The Black Jews of Harlem* (1964), possibly because it is an earlier variant. In contrast to the black Jews described by Brotz, the Church of God Jews maintained that they were "*the* Jews" and that "the so-called Jew was an interloper and a fraud" (34).

83. Fauset, *Black Gods of the Metropolis*, 47.

84. Levine, "Marcus Garvey and the Politics of Revitalization," 124.

85. George Alexander McGuire, comp., "Universal Negro Catechism" of the Univeral Negro Improvement Association, New York, March 1921, in *The Marcus Garvey and Universal Negro Improvment Papers*, vol. 3, ed. Robert Hill (Berkeley: University of California Press, 1984), 303.

86. Amy Jacques Garvey, *Garvey and Garveyism* (New York: Collier Books, 1970), 141.

87. Burkett, *Garveyism as a Religious Movement*, 54–55.

88. Ibid., 53, 54.

89. Hans Baer, *The Black Spiritual Movement: A Religious Response to Racism* (Knoxville: University of Tennessee Press, 1984), 95.

90. Hurley, quoted in ibid.

91. Chicago Commission on Race Relations, *The Negro in Chicago: A Study of Race Relations and a Riot in 1919* (1922; repr., New York: Arno Press and the New York Times, 1968), 480.

92. Fauset, *Black Gods of the Metropolis*, 45 n. 6.

93. See E. U. Essien-Udom, *Black Nationalism: The Search for Identity in America* (Chicago: University of Chicago Press, 1962), 134 n. 30. Essien-Udom notes that one of the lessons relating to Yakub in the Lost-Found Muslim Lesson is identified as being "given by our Prophet W. C. Fard." I have not been able to find any detailed history of early black Muslim activity.

94. Draper, *Rediscovery of Black Nationalism*, 73–74.

95. Ibid., 77.

96. Essien-Udom, *Black Nationalism*, 134.

97. Ibid., 134.

98. Draper, *Rediscovery of Black Nationalism*, 80.

99. Essien-Udom, *Black Nationalism*, 134.

100. Cronon, *Black Moses*, 47.

101. Marcus Garvey, "African Fundamentalism" (1925), in *Marcus Garvey and the Vision of Africa*, ed. John Henrik Clarke (New York: Vintage Books, 1974), 157.

102. On Garvey as a poet (whose literary gifts not even his most fervent admirers seem prepared to defend), see Caroline Cooper, "Unorthodox Prose: The Poetry of Marcus Garvey," in *Garvey: His Work and Impact*, ed. Rupert Lewis and Patrick Bryan (Trenton, N.J.: Africa World Press, 1991), 113–121; and Tony Martin, *Literary Garveyism* (Dover, Mass.: Majority Press, 1983), chapter 8 .

103. Marcus Garvey, *The Poetical Works of Marcus Garvey*, ed. Tony Martin (Dover, Mass.: Majority Press, 1983), 4.

104. Barbara Bair, "True Women, Real Men: Gender Ideology and Social Roles in the Garvey Movement," in *Gendered Domains: Rethinking Public and Private in Women's History*, ed. Dorothy O. Helly and Susan M. Reverby (Ithaca, N.Y.: Cornell University Press, 1992), 156.

105. Essien-Udom, *Black Nationalism*, 133.

106. On Gehazi's curse see the discussion of the Church of God, in Fauset, *Black Gods of the Metropolis*, 34.

107. Euthymus, in *The Mind of the Negro as Reflected in Letters Written During the Crisis, 1800–1860*, ed. Carter G. Woodson (Washington, D.C.: Association for the Study of Negro History, 1926), 233.

108. Quoted in Levine, "Marcus Garvey and the Politics of Revitalization," 113.

109. Newman I. White, *American Negro Folk Songs* (Cambridge, Mass.: Harvard University Press, 1928), 27. On early twentieth-century black folk culture, see Lawrence W. Levine, "The Concept of the New Negro and the Realities of Black Culture," in *Key Issues in the Afro-American Experience*, vol. 2, ed. Nathan Huggins, Martin Kilson, and Daniel M. Fox (New York: Harcourt Brace Jovanovich, 1971), 125–147.

110. Booker T. Washington, Fannie Barrier Williams, and N. B. Wood, *A New Negro for a New Century* (1900; repr., New York: Arno Press, 1969); Henry Lewis Gates Jr., "The Trope of the New Negro and the Reconstruction of the Image of the Black," *Representations* 24 (Fall 1988): 137, 138.

111. George S. Schuyler, "The Negro and Nordic Civilization," *Messenger* 7 (May 1925): 207.

112. James O. Young, *Black Writers of the Thirties* (Baton Rouge: Louisiana State University Press, 1973), 37.

113. George Schuyler, "Our White Folks" (1927), in *The Black Man and the American Dream: Negro Aspirations in America, 1900–1930*, ed. June Sochen (Chicago: Quadrangle Books, 1971), 310.

Conclusion

1. Frantz Fanon, *Black Skin, White Masks* [1952], trans. Charles Lam Markmann (New York: Grove Weidenfield, 1967), 110.

2. Lawrence W. Levine, *Black Culture, Black Consciousness: Afro-American Folk Thought from Slavery to Freedom* (New York: Oxford University Press, 1977), 33.

3. W.E.B. DuBois, *The Souls of Black Folk* (1903; repr., New York: New American Library, 1982), 274.

4. Maria Bracey in *The American Slave: A Composite Autobiography [AS]*, ed. George Rawick (Westport, Conn.: Greenwood Press, 1972), v. 2, South Carolina Narratives, 66.

5. James W. C. Pennington, *A Lecture Delivered Before the Glasgow Young Men's Christian Association* (Edinburgh: H. Armour, printer, [1850]), 2.

6. David Walker, *"One Continual Cry": David Walker's Appeal to the Colored Citizens of the World (1829–1830)*, ed. Herbert Aptheker (New York: Humanities Press, 1965), 79, 80, 77.

7. Mary Reynolds, *AS*, Texas Narratives, Supplement, Series II, v. 8, pt. 7, 3289.

8. Pennington, *Lecture*, 2.

9. Sartre's comment, originally from *Orphée Noir*, preface to *Anthologie de la nouvelle poésie nègro et malgache* (1948), is quoted in Fanon, *Black Skin, White Masks*, 132–133.

10. Ibid.

11. John S. Durham, *To Teach the Negro History: A Suggestion* (Philadelphia: David McKay, 1897), 9. The multitalented Durham, who served as United States counsel at Santo Domingo in 1890 and minister to Haiti from 1891 to 1895, was also an engineer and a journalist, according to Willard B. Gatewood's brief discussion of Durham's career in *Aristocrats of Color: The Black Elite, 1880–1920* (Bloomington: Indiana University Press, 1990), 99–100.

12. Durham, *To Teach the Negro History*, 9.

13. The phrase comes from Alexander Crummell, "The Destined Superiority of the Negro, A Thanksgiving Discourse," in *The Greatness of Christ and Other Sermons* (New York: Thomas Whittier, 1882).

14. Nancy Leys Stepan and Sander L. Gilman, "Appropriating the Idioms of Science: The Rejection of Scientific Racism," in *The Bounds of Race: Perspectives on Hegemony and Resistance*, ed. Dominick LaCapra (Ithaca, N.Y.: Cornell University Press, 1991), 101.

15. Joanna Thomson Isom, *AS*, Mississippi Narratives, Supplement, Series I, v. 8, pt. 3, 1101.

16. St. Clair Drake, "Hide My Face? On Pan-Africanism and Negritude," in *Soon, One Morning: New Writing by American Negroes 1940–1962*, ed. Herbert Hill (New York: Knopf, 1963), 88.

17. Molefi Kete Asante, *The Afrocentric Idea* (Philadelphia: Temple University Press, 1987), 181.

18. Drake, "Hide My Face?" 94.

19. Promoted by Afrocentric luminaries such as Leonard Jeffries, the idea of dividing whites and blacks into ice people and sun people may have originated in the writings of African writer Cheik Anta Diop. In a book entitled *The Cultural Unity of Black Africa* (1963; repr., London: Karnak House, 1989), Diop, who died in the mideighties, posits that human civilization had emerged from two cradles: a patriarchal Northern cradle that originated in Crete and a matriarchal southern cradle that began in Africa. Another book that seems to have influenced Afrocentric thought on this subject is Michael Bradley, *The Iceman Inheritance* (1978; repr., New York: Kayode Publications, 1991). In this book, Bradley (who is, ironically enough, a white Canadian) maintains that the deleterious effects of a cold climate over generations shaped the Europeans into an especially aggressive race, although one of the best-known advocates of the ice people/sun people thesis, Leonard Jeffries, himself does not appear to have published anything on this subject. For more on Jeffries, see Michael Eric Dyson's chapter "Leonard Jeffries and the Struggle for the Black Mind" in *Reflecting Black: African-American Cultural Criticism* (Minneapolis: University of Minnesota Press, 1993), 157–163.

20. Walker, *"One Continual Cry,"* 70.

Selected Bibliography

Primarily a record of cited works, this bibliography does not list every source used in the preparation of this book. Those who wish to examine a more extensive list of relevant sources should consult my doctoral dissertation, "The White Image in the Black Mind: African American Ideas about White People, 1830–1925" (Yale University, 1993).

Primary Sources

Allen, William F., et al. *Slave Songs of the United States.* New York: A. Simpson, 1867.

Avirett, James Battle. *The Old Plantation.* New York: F. T. Neely, 1901.

Baker, T. Lindsay, and Julie P. Baker, eds. *The WPA Oklahoma Slave Narratives.* Norman: University of Oklahoma Press, 1996.

Ball, Charles. *Fifty Years in Chains; Or, The Life of an American Slave.* Miami, Fla.: Mnemosyne Publishing, 1969 [1858].

Bell, Howard Holman, ed. *Minutes of the Proceedings of the National Negro Conventions.* New York: Arno Press, 1969.

Bibb, Henry. *Narrative of the Life and Adventures of Henry Bibb, an American Slave.* New York: Negro Universities Press, 1969 [1850].

John Blassingame, ed. *Slave Testimony: Two Centuries of Letters, Speeches, Interviews, and Autobiographies.* Baton Rouge: Louisiana State University Press, 1977.

Boas, Franz. "Human Faculty as Determined by Race." *Proceedings of the American Association for the Advancement of Science* 43 (1894): 301–327.

Boas, Franz. "The Industries of Southern Negroes." *Southern Workman* 38 (April 1909): 217–219.

Boas, Franz. *The Mind of Primitive Man.* New York: Free Press, 1938.

Boas, Franz. "The Real Race Problem." *Crisis* 1 (December 1910): 22–25.

Bolding, B. J. *What of the Negro Race?* Chambersberg, Pa.: by the *Democratic News*, 1906.

Boyd, Napoleon Bonaparte. *Revised Search Light on the Seventh Day Bible and X-Ray, By Organic, Supernatural and Artificial Science.* Greenville, N.C.: by the author, 1924.

Brown, William Wells. *The Black Man: His Antecedents, His Genius, and His Achievements.* Boston: James Redpath, 1863.

Brown, William Wells. *The Negro in the American Rebellion; his heroism and his fidelity.* Boston: A. G. Brown, 1880.

Brown, William Wells. *The Rising Son, or the Antecedents and Achievements of the Colored Race.* Boston: A. G. Brown, 1874.

Bruce, John Edward. *The Selected Writings of John Edward Bruce: Militant Black Journalist.* Ed. Peter Gilbert. New York: Arno Press and the New York Times, 1971.

Burke, Emily P. *Pleasure and Pain: Reminiscences of Georgia in the 1840s.* Savannah, Ga.: Beehive Press, 1978.

Carman, Adam. *An Oration Delivered at the Fourth Anniversary of Abolition of the Slave Trade in the Methodist Episcopal Church.* New York: John C. Totten, 1811.

Carroll, Charles. *"The Negro is a Beast," or, "In the Image of God"; The Reasoner of the Age, The Revelation of the Century! The Bible as it is! The Negro and his Relationship to the Human Family . . . The Negro is Not the Son of Ham.* St. Louis: American Book and Bible House, 1900.

Chicago Commission on Race Relations. *The Negro in Chicago: A Study of Race Relations and a Riot.* New York: Arno Press, 1968 [1922].

Clark, Branstan S. *Is it the Color of Our Skin that is Responsible for Our Down Trodden Condition all over The World?* N.p.: by the author, 1921.

Clark, Peter. *The Black Brigade of Cincinatti.* Cincinatti: J. B. Boyd, 1864.

Clayton, Ronnie W., ed. *Mother Wit: The Ex-Slave Narratives of the Louisiana Writers' Project.* New York: Peter Lang, 1990.

Cooper, Anna Julia. *A Voice from the South.* New York: Oxford University Press, 1988 [1892].

Cooper, Anna Julia. *The Voice of Anna Julia Cooper.* Ed. Charles Lemert and Esme Bhan. Lanham, Md.: Rowan and Littlefield, 1998.

Council, W. H. *Lamp of Wisdom, Or Race History Illuminated.* 1898.

Craft, Ellen, and William Craft. *Running a Thousand Miles for Freedom.* New York: Arno Press, 1969 [1860].

Crevecoeur, J. Hector St. John de. *Letters from an American Farmer.* New York: Penguin Books, 1981 [1782].

Crogman, W. H., and H. F. Kletzing. *The Progress of a Race.* Atlanta: J. L. Nichols, 1897.

Crummell, Alexander. *Africa and America: Addresses and Discourses.* Miami, Fla.: Mnemosyne Publishing, 1969 [1891].

Crummell, Alexander. *Civilization the Primal Need of the Race, The Inaugural Address, and The Attitude of the American Mind Toward the Negro Intellect.* Washington, D.C.: American Negro Academy, 1898.

Crummell, Alexander. *A Defense of the Negro Race in America From the Assaults and Charges of Reverend J. L. Tucker D.D. of Jackson, Mississippi.* Washington, D.C.: Judd and Detweiler, 1883.

Crummell, Alexander. *Destiny and Race: Selected Writings.* Ed. by Wilson Jeremiah Moses. Amherst: University of Massachusetts Press, 1992.

Crummell, Alexander. *The Future of Africa.* New York: Scribner, 1862.

Crummell, Alexander. *The Greatness of Christ and Other Sermons,* New York: Thomas Whittaker, 1882.

Delany, Martin Robinson. *The Condition, Elevation, Emigation, and Destiny of the Colored People of the United States.* New York: Arno Press and the New York Times, 1968 [1852].

Delany, Martin R. "Political Destiny of the Colored Race in America." In *Life and Public Services of Martin R. Delany,* ed. Frank A. Rollin [Mrs. Francis E. Rollin Whipper]. New York: Arno Press, 1969 [1868], 327–367.

Delany, Martin R. *Principia of Ethnology: The Origin of the Races and Color with an Archeological Compendium of Ethiopian and Egyptian Civilization from Years of Careful Examination and Enquiry.* Philadelphia: Harper and Brother, 1879.

Delany, Martin R. "Official Report of the Niger Valley Exploring Party." In *Search for a Place: Black Separatism and Africa, 1860,* M. R. Delany and Robert Campbell. Ann Arbor: University of Michigan Press, 1969.

Douglass, Frederick. "The Claims of the Negro Ethnologically Considered: A Speech delivered to the prestigious Philozetian and Phi Delta Societies of Western Reserve College in Hudson Ohio, 12, July, 1854." In *The Frederick Douglass Papers,* Series One: Speeches, Debates, and Interviews, vol. 2, ed. John W. Blassingame. New Haven, Conn.: Yale University Press, 1982, 497–525.

Douglass, Frederick. *The Constitution of the United States: Is It Pro-Slavery or Antislavery?* Halifax: T. and W. Birtwhistle, 1860.

Douglass, Frederick. "The Future of the Race." *A. M. E. Church Review* 6 (October 1889).

Douglass, Frederick. *The Life and Writings of Frederick Douglass*. Ed. Philip Foner. New York: International House Publishers, 1950.

Douglass, Frederick. *Narrative of the Life of Frederick Douglass, An American Slave*. Ed. Houston Baker, Jr. New York: Penguin Books, 1982 [1845].

DuBois, W.E.B. *Darkwater: Voices from within the Veil*. New York: Schocken Books, 1969 [1920].

DuBois, W.E.B. "'Discussion of Race Friction' by Alfred Holt Stone." *American Journal of Sociology* 13 (March 1908): 834–838.

DuBois, W.E.B. *The Gift of Black Folk, The Negroes in the Making of America*. Millwood, N.Y.: KTO Press, 1975 [1924].

DuBois, W.E.B. "The Laboratory in Sociology at Atlanta University." *Annals of the American Academy of Political Science* 21 (May 1903): 160–163.

DuBois, W.E.B. *The Negro*. Millwood, N.Y.: KTO Press, 1975 [1915].

DuBois, W.E.B. "Races of Men." In *Select Discussions of Race Problems*, ed. J. A. Bigham. Atlanta: Atlanta University Publications, 1916: 17–24.

DuBois, W.E.B. *The Souls of Black Folk*. New York: New American Library, 1982 [1903].

DuBois, W.E.B. "The Study of Negro Problems." In *The Black Sociologists: The First Half Century*, ed. John H. Bracey Jr., August Meier, and Elliot Rudwick. Belmont, Calif.: Wadsworth, 1971: 14–28.

DuBois, W.E.B. *Writings*. New York: Library of America, 1986.

Durham, John S. *To Teach the Negro History: A Suggestion*. Philadelphia: David McKay, 1897.

Dyson, J. F. *A New and Simple Explanation of the Unity of the Human Race and the Origin of Color*. Nashville, Tenn.: Southern Methodist Publishing House, 1886.

Easton, Hosea. *A Treatise on the Intellectual Character and Civil and Political Condition of the Colored People of the United States; and the Prejudice Exercised Towards Them: with a Sermon on the Duty of the Church to Them*. Boston: Isaac Knapp, 1837.

Elliott, E. N., ed. *Cotton is King, and Pro-slavery Arguments; Comprising the Writing of Hammond, Harper, Christy, Stringfellow, Hodge, Bledsoe, and Cartwright.* . . . Augusta, Ga.: Pritchard, Abbot and Loomis, 1860.

Equiano, Olaudah. *Equiano's Travels: The Interesting Narrative of the Life of Olaudah Equiano or Gustavus Vassa, The African*. 4th ed., Dublin: by the author, 1791.

Ethiop. "African-American Picture Gallery." *Anglo-African Magazine* 1, no. 6 (April 1859): 173–177.

Ethiop. "What Shall We do with the White People?" *Anglo-African Magazine* 2 (February 1860): 41–45.

Ferris, William. *The African Abroad, Or, his Evolution in Western Civilization, Tracing His Development Under Caucasian Mileau*. New Haven, Conn.: Tuttle, Morehouse and Taylor Press, 1913.

Forten, James. "An Address Delivered Before the American Moral Reform Society, August 17, 1837." *Minutes and Proceedings of the American Moral Reform Society held at Philadelphia . . . from the 14th to the 19th of August, 1837*. Philadelphia: Historic Publications, 1969.

Frazier, E. Franklin. "The Garvey Movement." *Opportunity* (November 1926): 347.

Garnet, Henry Highland. "An Address to the Slaves of North America (Rejected by the National Convention, 1843)." Reprinted in *Walker's Appeal and Garnet's Address*. New York: Arno Press, 1969 [1843].

Garnet, Henry Highland. *The Past and Present Condition, and the Destiny of the Colored Race: A Discourse Delivered on the Fifteenth Anniversary of the Female Benevolent Society of Troy, New York*. Troy, N.Y.: Steam Press of J. C. Kneeland and Co., 1848: 89–96.

Garvey, Marcus. *Marcus Garvey and the Vision of Africa*. Ed. John Henry Clarke. New York: Vintage Books, 1974.

Garvey, Marcus. *The Poetical Works of Marcus Garvey*. Ed. Tony Martin. Dover, Mass.: Majority Press, 1983.

Garvey, Marcus. *Marcus Garvey and Universal Negro Improvement Association Papers*. Ed. Robert Hill. Berkeley: University of California Press, 1984.

Georgia Writers' Project. *Drums and Shadows: Survival Studies among Georgia Coastal Negroes.* Athens: University Press of Georgia, 1986 [1940].

Gregoire, Henri. *De la litterature des negres.* Paris: Chez Maradan, 1808.

Griggs, Sutton E. *Science of Collective Efficiency.* Memphis, Tenn.: National Public Welfare League, 1921.

Hall, A. L. *The Ancient, Medieval, and Modern Greatness of the Negro.* Memphis, Tenn.: Striker Print, 1907.

Harper, Thomas Greathead. *Contemporary Evolution of the Negro Race.* Washington, D.C.: American Negro Monographs, 1910.

Hayne, Joseph E. *The Amonian or Hamitic Origins of Ancient Greeks, Cretans, and all the Celtic Races.* Rev. 2d ed. Brooklyn: Guide Printing and Publishing Company, 1905.

Hayne, Joseph E. *The Black Man, or, A Natural History of the Hamitic Race.* Raleigh, N.C.: Edwards and Broughton, Printers, 1893.

Hayne, Joseph E. *Ham and his Immediate Descendents, and their Wonderful Achievements.* New York: Welte Press, 1909.

Hayne, Joseph E. *The Negro in Sacred History.* Charleston, S.C.: Walker, Evans, Cogswell, 1887.

Higginson, Thomas W. *Army Life in a Black Regiment.* East Lansing: Michigan State University Press, 1960 [1870]: 88–95.

Higginson, Thomas W. "The Ordeal by Battle." *Atlantic Monthly* 8 (July 1961).

Hopkins, Pauline E. *A Primer of Facts Pertaining to the Early Greatness of the African Race and the Possibility of Restoration by its Descendants . . . Compiled and Arranged from the Works of the best known Ethnologists and Historians.* Cambridge: P. E. Hopkins and Co., 1905.

Houston, Druscilla Dunjee. *The Wonderful Ethiopians of the Cushite Empire.* Oklahoma City: Universal Publishing, 1926.

Jefferson, Thomas. *The Life and Selected Writings of Thomas Jefferson.* Ed. Adrienne Koch and William Peden. New York: Modern American Library, 1944.

Jefferson, Thomas. *The Works of Thomas Jefferson.* Ed. Paul Leicester Ford. New York: G. P. Putnam and Sons, 1905.

Johnson, Edward A. *Adam Vs. Ape-Man and Ethiopia.* New York: J. Little and Ives, 1931.

Johnson, Edward A. *History of the Negro Soldiers During the Spanish American War.* New York: Johnson Reprint, 1970 [1899].

Johnson, Harvey. *A Gross Theological Error Corrected: White Men Were the First Slaves, Ham, the Son of Noah not Cursed, but Canaan, Ham's Youngest Son.* Baltimore, Md.: J. B. Clarke, Printer, n.d.

Johnson, Harvey. *The Nations From a New Point of View.* Nashville, Tenn.: National Baptist Publishing Company, 1903.

Johnson, Harvey. *Race Prejudice and Pride: On What are They Based? What Has the White Man Ever Done to Equal the Tremendous Achievements of the Sons of Ham?* [Baltimore, Md.], n.d.

Johnson, Harvey. *The Question of Race: A Reply to W. Cabell Brice, esq.* Baltimore, Md.: J. F. Weishampel, 1891.

Johnson, James Weldon. *Black Manhattan.* New York: Athenaeum, 1968 [1939].

Johnson, James Weldon. "The Dilemma of the Negro Author." *American Mercury* 15 (December 1928): 477–481.

Jones, Absalom, and Richard Allen. "Narrative of the Proceedings of the Black People, During the Late Awful Calamity in Philadelphia" [1793]. In *Negro Protest Pamphlets: A Compendium.* New York: Arno Press, 1969.

Jones, Charles Colcock. *A Catechism for Colored Persons.* Charleston: Observer Office Press, 1834.

Kemble, Frances Anne. *Journal of a Residence on Georgia Plantation in 1838–1839.* Ed. John A. Scott. Athens: University of Georgia Press, 1984.

Killens, John Oliver, ed. *The Trial Record of Denmark Vesey.* Boston: Beacon Press, 1970.

Lewis, Robert Benjamin. *Light and Truth: Collected from the Bible and Ancient and Modern History, Containing the Universal History of the Colored and Indian Race, from the Creation of the World to the Present Time.* Boston: by a "Committee of Colored Men," 1851 [1836].

Locke, Alain LeRoy, ed. *The New Negro: An Interpretation.* New York: Arno Press, 1968 [1925].

Locke, Alain LeRoy. *Race Contacts and Interracial Relations: Lectures on the Theory and Practice of Race.* Ed. Jeffrey C. Stewart. Washington, D.C.: Howard University Press, 1992.

Louisiana Federal Writers' Project. *Gumbo Ya-Ya: A Collection of Louisiana Folktales.* Cambridge, Mass.: Riverside Press, 1945.

MacKay, Claude. *Home to Harlem.* New York: Harper and Bros, 1928.

Miller, Kelly. "The Artistic Gifts of the Negro." *Voice of the Negro* 3 (April 1906): 252–257.

Miller, Kelly. *Race Adjustment [and] The Everlasting Stain.* New York: Arno Press and the New York Times, 1968.

Miller, Kelly. *A Review of Hoffman's Race Traits and Tendencies of the American Negro.* Washington, D.C.: American Negro Academy, 1897.

Morton, Samuel. *Crania Aegyptiaca: or, Observations on Egyptian Ethnography derived from Anatomy, History, and the Monuments.* Philadelphia: J. Penington, 1844.

Nell, William C. *Services of the Colored Americans in the Wars of 1776 and 1812.* Boston: Prentiss and Sawyer, 1851.

Newcombe, Harvey. *The "Negro Pew" Being an Inquiry Concerning the Propriety of Distinctions in the House of God on Account of Color.* Freeport, N.Y.: Books for Libraries Press, 1971 [1837].

Park, Robert Ezra. *Race and Culture.* New York: Free Press, 1950.

Pease, William H., and Jane H. Pease, eds. *The Antislavery Argument.* New York: Bobbs-Merrill, 1965.

Pennington, J. W. C. *A Lecture Delivered Before the Glasgow Young Men's Christian Association.* Edinborough: H. Armour, printer, [1850].

Pennington, James W. C., *The Fugitive Blacksmith; or, Events in the History of James W.C. Pennington.* 3d ed. Westport, Conn.: Negro Universities Press, 1971 [1850].

Pennington, James W. C. *A Text Book on the Origins and History of the Colored People.* Detroit: Negro History Press, 1969 [1841].

Perdue, Charles L., Jr., Thomas E. Barden, and Robert K. Phillips, eds. *Weevils in the Wheat: Interviews with Virginia Ex-Slaves.* Charlottesville: University Press of Virginia, 1976.

Perry, Rufus. *The Cushite: or The Descendants of Ham as Found in the Sacred Scriptures and in the Writings of Ancient Historians and Poets from Noah to the Christian Era.* Springfield, Mass.: Willey and Co., 1893.

Porter, Dorothy. *Early Negro Writing, 1730–1837.* Boston: Beacon Press, 1971.

The Pro-slavery Argument; as Maintained . . . by Chancellor Harper, Governor Hammond, Dr. Simms, and Professor Dew. New York: Greenwood Publishing, 1968 [1852].

Rawick, George, ed. *The American Slave: A Composite Autobiography.* 19 vols. Westport, Conn.: Greenwood Press, 1972.

Rawick, George, ed. *The American Slave: A Composite Autobiography.* Supplement, Series I. 12 vols. Westport, Conn.: Greenwood Press, 1977.

Rawick, George, ed. *The American Slave: A Composite Autobiography.* Supplement, Series II. 11 vols. Westport, Conn.: Greenwood Press, 1979.

Rollin, Frank A. [Mrs. Francis E. Rollin Whipper], ed. *Life and Public Services of Martin R. Delany.* New York: Arno Press and the New York Times, 1969 [1868].

Roman, C. V. *American Civilization and the Negro.* Northbrook, Ill.: Metro Books, 1972 [1916].

Ruchames, Louis, ed. *Racial Thought in America: A Documentary History.* Amherst: University of Massachusetts Press, 1969.

Ruggles, David. *"The Extinguisher" Extinguished, or David M. Reese "Used up by David Ruggles a Man of Color" together with some remarks on a late Production entitled "An Address on*

Slavery and Against the Immediate Emancipation with a plan of their Being Gradually Emancipated and Colonized in 32 Years. New York: by the author, 1834.

S.S.N., "Anglo-Saxons and Anglo-Africans. *The Anglo-African Magazine* 1 (1859): 251–247.

Sampson, John P. *Mixed Races.* Hampton, Va.: by the author, 1881.

Schuyler, George. "Blessed are the Sons of Ham." *Nation* 3 (March 1927): 313–315.

Schuyler, George. "The Negro and Nordic Civilization." *Messenger* (May 1925): 198–201, 207.

Schuyler, George "Our White Folks." In *The Black Man and the American Dream: Negro Aspirations in America, 1900–1930,* ed. June Sochen. Chicago: Quadrangle Books, 1971, 299–310.

Simmons, William J. *Men of Mark: Eminent, Progressive and Rising.* Chicago: Johnson Publishing Company, 1970 [1887].

Smith, James McCune. *The Destiny of the People of Color, A Lecture Delivered Before the Philomathean Society and Hamilton Lyceum, in January 1841.* New York, 1843.

Smith, James McCune. *A Dissertation on the Influence of Climate on Longevity.* New York: Office of the Merchant's Magazine, 1846.

Smith, James McCune. "Civilization: Its Dependence on Physical Circumstances." *Anglo-African Magazine* 1 (January 1859): 5–17.

Smith, James McCune. "On the Fourteenth Query of Thomas Jefferson's Notes on Virginia." *Anglo-African Magazine* 1, no. 8 (August 1859): 225–238.

Smith, James McCune, "The German Invasion." *The Anglo-African Magazine* 1 (February 1859 and March 1859): 44–52, 83–86.

[Smith, Parker T.]. "Chapters on Ethnology." *Christian Recorder* (23 March, 13 April, 4 May, 23 May, and 1 June 1861).

Smith, Samuel Stanhope. *An Essay on the Causes of the Variety of Complexion and Figure in the Human Species.* Cambridge: Belknap Press of Harvard University, 1965 [1787].

Starobin, Robert S., ed. *Blacks in Bondage: Letters of American Slaves.* New York: Marcus Weiner Publishing, 1988.

Steward, Theophilus Gould. *The End of the World; or, Clearing the Way for the Fullness of the Gentiles.* Philadelphia: A.M.E. Bookrooms, 1888.

Steward, Theophilus Gould. *Genesis Reread; or The Latest Conclusions of the Physical Sciences viewed in Relation to the Mosaic Record, to which is added an important note on the Direct Evidence of Christianity by Bishop J.P. Campbell.* Philadelphia: A.M.E. Bookrooms, 1885.

Stewart, Maria W. *Maria W. Stewart, America's First Black Women Political Writer: Essays and Speeches.* Ed. Marilyn Richardson. Bloomington: Indiana University Press, 1987.

Stoddard, Lothrop. *The Rising Tide of Color Against White World Supremacy.* Introduction by Madison Grant. New York: Charles Scribner's Sons, 1920.

Stone, Alfred Holt. "Is Race Friction Between Whites and Blacks in the United States Growing and Inevitable?" *American Journal of Sociology* 13 (March 1908): 679–779.

Tanner, Benjamin Tucker. *The Color of Solomon—What? "My Beloved is White and Ruddy."* Philadelphia: A.M.E. Book Concern, 1895.

Tanner, Benjamin T. *The Negro's Origins.* Philadelphia, [1869].

Tayleur, Eleanor. "The Negro Woman: I. Social and Moral Decadence." *Outlook* 76 (January 10, 1904): 276–271.

Taylor, Caesar Augustus. *The Conflict and Commingling of the Races.* New York: Broadway Publishing, 1913.

Thomas, William Hannibal. *The American Negro: What He Was, What He Is, and What He May Become.* New York: Macmillan, 1901.

Tragle, Henry Irving, ed. *The Southampston Slave Revolt of 1831: A Compilation of Source Materials.* Amherst: University of Massachusetts Press, 1971.

Turner, Henry MacNeal. *The Negro in All Ages: A Lecture Delivered in the Second Baptist Church of Savannah, G.A.* Savannah, Ga.: D. G. Patton, Steam Printer, 1873.

Turner, Henry MacNeal. *Respect Black: The Writings and Speeches of Henry MacNeal Turner.* Ed. Edwin S. Redkey. New York: Arno Press, 1971.

Vastey, Pompée-Valentin. *Reflexions on the Blacks and Whites, Remarks Upon a Letter addressed by M. Mazeres, a French Colonist, to J. C. L. Sismonde de Sismonde*. London: J. Hatchard, 1817.

C. F. Volney. *Volney's Ruins: or, Meditation on the Revolutions of Empires; translated under the immediate inspection of the author from the Sixth Paris Edition*. Boston: C. Gaylord, 1935.

Walker, David. *"One Continual Cry": David Walker's "Appeal to the Colored Citizens of the World" (1829–1830)*. Ed. Herbert Aptheker. New York: Humanities Press, 1965.

Washington, Booker T., Fannie Barrier William, and N. B. Wood. *A New Negro for a New Century*. New York: Arno Press, 1969 [1900].

Washington, Booker T. *The Booker T. Washington Papers*. Ed. Louis R. Harlan and Raymond Spock. 13 vols. Urbana: University of Illinois Press, 1984.

Washington, Booker T. *The Story of the Negro: The Rise of the Race from Slavery*. New York: Negro Universities Press, 1969 [1909].

Webb, James Morris. *The Black Man: Father of Civilization, Proven by Biblical History*. Chicago: Fraternal Press, 1924.

Williams, George Washington. *History of the Negro Troups in the War of the Rebellion, Preceded by a Review of the Military Service of Negroes in Ancient and Modern Times*. New York: Harper and Brothers, 1888.

Wilson, Joseph T. *Black Phalanx*. New York: Arno Press and the New York Times, 1968 [1890].

Woodson, Carter Godwin. *The Mis-Education of the Negro*. Washington, D.C.: Associated Publishers, 1933.

Woodson, Carter G. *The Mind of the Negro as Reflected in Letters Written During the Crisis, 1800–1860*. Washington, D.C.: Association for the Study of Negro History, 1926.

Work, Monroe N., ed. *The Negro Brain*. Vol. 11, *The Health and Physique of Negro Americans*. Atlanta: Atlanta University Publications, 1906.

Work, Monroe N. "The Passing Tradition and African Civilization." *Journal of Negro History* 1, no. 1 (1916): 34–41.

Work, Monroe. "Some Parellisms in the Development of African and Other Races." *Southern Workman* 35 (November 1906): 614–631, and 36 (January–March 1907): 37–43, 105–111, 166–175.

Wright, Richard. *Black Boy: A Record of Childhood and Youth*. New York: Harper and Row, 1966 [1937].

Secondary Sources

Appiah, Anthony. "The Uncompleted Argument: DuBois and the Illusion of Race." In *"Race," Writing, and Difference*, ed. Henry Louis Gates Jr. Chicago: University of Chicago Press, 1968: 21–37.

Aptheker, Herbert. "Afro-American Superiority: A Neglected Theme in the Literature." *Phylon* 31 (Winter 1970): 336–342.

Asante, Molefi Kete. *The Afrocentric Idea*. Philadelphia: Temple University Press, 1987.

Baer, Hans. *The Black Spiritual Movement: A Religious Response to Racism*. Knoxville: University of Tennessee Press, 1984.

Bair, Barbara. "True Women, Real Men: Gender Ideology and Social Roles in the Garvey Movement." In *Gendered Domains: Rethinking Public and Private in Women's History*, ed. Dorothy O. Helly and Susan M. Reverby. Ithaca, N.Y.: Cornell University Press, 1992: 154–166.

Baldwin, James. *Collected Essays*. New York: Library of America, 1998.

Barzun, Jacques. *Race: A Study in Superstition*. Rev. ed. New York: Harper and Row, 1965 [1937].

Bederman, Gail. *Manliness and Civilization: A Cultural History of Gender and Race in the United States, 1880–1917*. Chicago: University of Chicago Press, 1995.

Bell, Howard H. *A Survey of the Negro Convention Movement*. New York: Arno Press and the New York Times, 1970.

Berlin, Ira, et al., eds. *Freedom: A Documentary History of Emancipation, 1861–1867*. New York: Cambridge University Press, 1982–1993.

Bernal, Martin. *Black Athena: The Afroasiatic Roots of Classical Civilization*. Vol. 1, *The Fabrication of Ancient Greece*. New Brunswick, N.J.: Rutgers University Press, 1987.

Blassingame, John. *The Slave Community: Plantation Life in the Antebellum South*. Rev. ed. New York: Oxford University Press, 1979 [1972].

Blassingame, John, ed. *Slave Testimony: Two Centuries of Letters, Speeches, Interviews, and Autobiographies*. Baton Rouge: Lousiana State University Press, 1977.

Blight, David W. "In Search of Learning, Liberty, and Self Definition: James McCune Smith." *Afro-Americans in New York History and Life* 9 (July 1985): 10–19.

Bracey, John H., Jr., August Meier, and Elliot Rudwick, eds. *Blacks in the Abolitionist Movement*, Belmont Calif.: Wadsworth, 1971.

Bradley, Michael. *The Iceman Inheritance*. New York: Kayode Publications, 1991 [1978].

Braude, Benjamin. "The Sons of Noah and the Construction of Ethnic and Geographical Identities in the Medieval and Early Modern Periods." *William and Mary Quarterly* 54 (January 1997): 103–142.

Brewer, J. Mason. "John Tales." *Publications of the Texas Folklore Society* 21 (1946): 81–104.

Brotz, Howard. *The Black Jews of Harlem: Negro Nationalism and the Dilemma of Negro Leadership*. New York: Schocken Books, 1970.

Bruce, Dickson, Jr. "Ancient Africa and Early Black American Historians," *American Quarterly* 36 (1984): 684–699.

Bruce, Dickson D. "The Ironic Conception of American History: The Early Black Historians, 1883–1915." *Journal of Negro History* 69 (Spring 1984): 53–62.

Burkett, Randall K. *Black Redemption: Churchmen Speak for the Garvey Movement*. Philadelphia: Temple University Press, 1978.

Burkett, Randall K. *Garveyism as a Religious Movement: The Institutionalization of a Black Civil Religion*. Metuchen, N.J.: Scarecrow Press, 1978.

Campbell, James, and James Oakes. "The Invention of Race: Rereading White Over Black." *Reviews in American History* 21 (March 1993): 172–183.

Cashman, Sean Dennis. *African-Americans and the Quest for Civil Rights, 1900–1990*. New York: New York University Press, 1991.

Clinton, Catherine, ed. *Divided Houses: Gender and the Civil War*. New York: Oxford University Press, 1992.

Cobb, W. Montague. "James McCune Smith." *Journal of the National Medical Association* 44 (March 1952): 160.

Collier-Thomas, Bettye. "Harvey Johnson and the Baltimore Mutual United Brotherhood of Liberty 1885–1910." In *Black Communities and Urban Development in America, 1720–1990*, vol. 4, pt. 1, ed. Kenneth L. Kusmer. New York: Garland Publishing, 1991: 214–228.

Cooper, Caroline. "Unorthodox Prose: The Poetry of Marcus Garvey." In *Garvey: His Work and Impact*, ed. Rubert Lewis and Patrick Bryan Lewis. Trenton, N.J.: Africa World Press, 1991: 113–121.

Cooper, Frederick. "'Elevating the Race: The Social Thought of Black Leaders, 1827–1850." *American Quarterly* 24 (December 1972): 604–625.

Courlander, Harold. *Negro Folk Music, U. S. A.* New York: Columbia University Press, 1963.

Cravens, Hamilton. *The Triumph of Evolution: The Heredity-Environment Controversy, 1900–1941*. Baltimore, Md.: Johns Hopkins University Press, 1988.

Crawford, Stephen C. "Quantified Memory: A Study of the WPA and Fisk University Slave Narrative Collections." Ph.D. diss., University of Chicago. 1980.

Cronon, David E. *Black Moses: The Story of Marcus Garvey and the Universal Negro Improvement Association*. Madison: University of Wisconsin Press, 1955.

Curry, Leonard P. *The Free Black in Urban America, 1800–1850: The Shadow of the Dream*. Chicago: University of Chicago Press, 1981.

Curtin, Philip D., ed. *Africa Remembered: Narratives by West Africans from the Era of the Slave Trade*. Madison: University of Wisconsin Press, 1967.

Curtin, Philip D. *The Image of Africa: British Ideas and Action, 1780–1850*. Madison: University of Wisconsin Press, 1964.

Dain, Bruce. "A Hideous Monster of the Mind: Afro-American Race Theory, 1787–1859." Ph.D. diss., Princeton University, 1996,.

Davidson, James West, and Mark Hamilton Lytle. *After the Fact: The Art of Historical Detection*. New York: Knopf, 1982.

Davis, Charles T., and Henry Louis Gates Jr., eds. *The Slave's Narrative*. New York: Oxford University Press, 1985.

Davis, David Brion. *The Problem of Slavery in the Age of Revolution, 1770–1823*. Ithaca, N.Y.: Cornell University Press, 1975.

Davis, David Brion. *The Problem of Slavery in Western Culture*. New York: Oxford University Press, 1988 [1966].

Degler, Carl N. *In Search of Human Nature: The Decline and Revival of Darwinism in American Social Thought*. New York: Oxford University Press, 1991.

Dillon, Merton L. *Slavery Attacked: Southern Slaves and Their Allies, 1619–1865*. Baton Rouge: Louisiana State University Press, 1990.

Diop, Cheik Anta. *The Cultural Unity of Black Africa*. London: Karnak House, 1989 [1963].

Dippie, Brian W. *The Vanishing American: White Attitudes and U.S. Indian Policy*. Middletown, Conn.: Wesleyan University Press, 1982.

Doyle, Bertram Wilbur. *The Etiquette of Race Relations in the South: A Study in Social Control*. Port Washington, N.Y.: Kennikat Press, 1937.

Drake, St. Clair. "Hide My Face?—On Pan-Africanism and Negritude." In *Soon, One Morning: New Writing by American Negroes, 1940–1966*, ed. Herbert Hill. New York: Alfred A. Knopf, 1963: 77–105.

Drake, St. Clair. *The Redemption of Africa and Black Religion*. Chicago: Third World Press, 1970.

Draper, Theodore. *The Rediscovery of Black Nationalism*. New York: Viking Press, 1969.

Dubinberre, William. *Them Dark Days: Slavery in the American Rice Swamps*. New York: Oxford University Press, 1996.

Dyson, Michael Eric. *Reflecting Black: African-American Cultural Criticism*. Minneapolis: University of Minnesota Press, 1993.

Egerton, Douglas R. *Gabriel's Rebellion: The Virginia Slave Conspiracies of 1800 and 1802*. Chapel Hill: University of North Carolina Press, 1993.

Elkins, Stanley. *Slavery: A Problem in American Institutional and Intellectual Life*. Chicago: University of Chicago Press, 1959.

Ellison, Ralph. *Shadow and Act*. New York: Vintage Books, 1972.

Escott, Paul. *Slavery Remembered: A Record of Twentieth-Century Slave Narratives*. Chapel Hill: University of North Carolina Press, 1979.

Essien-Udom, E. U. *Black Nationalism: A Search for Identity in America*. Chicago: University of Chicago Press, 1962.

Evans, William McKee. "From the Land of Canaan to the Land of Guinea: The Strange Odyssey of the 'Sons of Ham.'" *American Historical Review* 85 (1980): 15–43.

Falk, Leslie A. "Black Abolitionist Doctors and Healers." *Bulletin of the History of Medicine* 54 (1980): 258–272.

Fanon, Frantz. *Black Skin, White Masks*. Trans. Charles Lam Markmann. New York: Grove Weidenfeld, 1967 [1952].

Fauset, Arthur Huff. *Black Gods of the Metropolis: Negro Religious Cults in the Urban North*. New York: Octagon Books, 1970 [1944].

Faust, Drew Gilpin. *A Sacred Circle: The Dilemma of the Intellectual in the Old South, 1840–1860*. Baltimore, Md.: Johns Hopkins University Press, 1977.

Fields, Barbara Jeanne. "Ideology and Race in American History." In *Region, Race, and Reconstruction: Essays in Honor of C. Vann Woodward*, ed. J. Morgan Kousser and James M. McPherson. New York: Oxford University Press, 1982: 143–177.

Fields, Barbara Jeanne. "Slavery, Race and Idealogy in the United States of America." *New Left Review* 181 (1990): 95–118.

Finkelman, Paul. *Dred Scott v. Sanford: A Brief History with Documents*. Boston: Bedford Books, 1997.

Fleischner, Jennifer. *Mastering Slavery: Memory, Family, and Identity in Women's Slave Narratives*. New York: New York University Press, 1996.

Foner, Eric. *Nothing but Freedom: Emancipation and Its Legacy*. Baton Rouge: Louisiana State University Press, 1983.

Foner, Eric. *Reconstruction: American's Unfinished Revolution, 1863–1877*. New York: Harper and Row, 1988.

Foner, Eric. *A Short History of Reconstruction, 1863–1877*. New York: Harper and Row, 1990.

Fordham, Monroe. *Major Themes in Northern Black Religious Thought, 1800–1860*. Hicksville, N.Y.: Exposition Press, 1975.

Frankenberg, Ruth. *White Women, Race Matters: The Social Construction of Whiteness*. Minneapolis: University of Minnesota Press, 1993.

Franklin, John Hope. "The Dilemma of the American Negro Scholar." In *Soon, One Morning: New Writing by American Negroes, 1940–1962*, ed. Herbert Hill. New York: Alfred A. Knopf, 1963: 60–76.

Fredrickson, George M. *The Black Image in the White Mind: The Debate on Afro-American Character and Destiny, 1817–1914*. Middletown, Conn.: Wesleyan University Press, 1987 [1972].

Fredrickson, George M. "Towards a Social Interpretation of American Racism." In *Key Issues in the Afro-American Experience*, vol. 1, ed. Martin Kilson, Nathan Huggins, and Daniel Fox. New York: Harcourt, Brace, Jovanovich, 1971: 240–254.

Friedman, Lawrence. *The White Savage: Racial Fantasies in the Post-Bellum South*. Englewood Cliffs, N.J.: Prentice Hall, 1970.

Fullinwinder, S. P. *The Mind and Mood of Black America*. Homewood, Ill.: Irwin-Dorsey, 1969.

Garvey, Amy Jacques. *Garvey and Garveyism*. New York: Collier Books, 1970.

Gates, Henry Louis, Jr., ed. *"Race," Writing, and Difference*. Chicago: University of Chicago Press, 1986: 129–155.

Gates, Henry Louis, Jr. "The Trope of the New Negro and the Reconstruction of the Image of the Black." *Representations* 24 (Fall 1988).

Gatewood, Willard B. *Aristocrats of Color: The Black Elite, 1880–1920*. Bloomington: Indiana University Press, 1990.

Genovese, Eugene D. *Roll Jordan, Roll: The World the Slaves Made*. New York: Pantheon Books, 1974.

Gilmore, Glenda. *Gender and Jim Crow*. Chapel Hill: University of North Carolina Press, 1996.

Gilroy, Paul. *The Black Atlantic: Modernity and Double-Consciousness*. Cambridge, Mass.: Harvard University Press, 1993.

Glatthaar, Joseph T. *Forged in Battle: The Civil War Alliance of Black Soldiers and White Officers*. New York: Free Press, 1990.

Gossett, Thomas F. *Race: The History of an Idea in America*. Dallas, Tex.: Southern Methodist University Press, 1963.

Gould, Stephen Jay. *The Mismeasure of Man*. New York: Norton, 1981.

Gravely, William B. "The Dialectic of Double Consciousness in Black American Freedom Celebrations, 1808–1863." *Journal of Negro History* 67 (1982): 302–317.

Grossman, James R. *Land of Hope: Chicago, Black Southerners, and the Great Migration*. Chicago: University of Chicago Press, 1989.

Haller, Johnathan S. *Outcasts of Evolution: Scientific Attitudes of Racial Inferiority*. New York: McGraw-Hill, 1979.

Harlan, Louis. *Booker T. Washington, the Wizard of Tuskegee, 1901–1915*. New York: Oxford University Press, 1983.

Harvey, F. D. "Herodotus and the Man-Footed Creature." In *Slavery and Other Forms of Unfree Labor*, ed. Léonie J. Archer. London: Routledge, 1988: 42–52.

Higginbotham, Evelyn Brooks. "African-American Women's History and the MetaLanguage of Race." *Signs* 17 (Winter 1992): 251–274.

Hinks, Peter. *To Awaken My Afflicted Brethren: David Walker and the Problem of Antebellum Slave Resistance*. University Park: Pennsylvania State University Press, 1997.

Hoetink, Harmannaus. *The Two Variants in Caribbean Race Relations*. Trans. Eva M. Hooykaas. New York: Oxford University Press, 1967.

hooks, bell. *Black Looks: Race and Representation*. Boston: South End Press, 1992.

hooks, bell. "Representing Whiteness in the Black Imagination." In *Cultural Studies*, ed. Lawrence Grossberg, Cary Nelson, and Paula A. Treichlin. New York: Routledge, 1992: 338–346.

Horsman, Reginald. *Race and Manifest Destiny: The Origins of American Racial Anglo-Saxonism*. Cambridge, Mass.: Harvard University Press, 1981.

Horton, James Oliver. *Free People of Color: Inside the African-American Community*. Washington, D.C.: Smithsonian Institution, 1993.

Horton, James, and Lois Horton. *In Hope of Liberty: Culture, Community, and Protest among Northern Free Blacks, 1700–1860*. New York: Oxford University Press, 1997.

Huggins, Nathan Irvin, *The Harlem Renaissance*, New York: Oxford University Press, 1971.

Hyatt, Marshall. "Franz Boas and the Struggle for Black Equality: The Dynamics of Ethnicity." *Perspectives in American History*, n.s. 2 (1985): 269–295.

Isaac, Harold. "Pan-Africanism as 'Romantic Realism.'" In *W.E.B. DuBois: A Profile*, ed. Rayford Logan. New York: Hill and Wang, 1971: 210–248.

Jackson, Walter. *Gunnar Myrdal and America's Conscience: Social Engineering and Racial Liberalism, 1938–1987*. Chapel Hill: University of North Carolina Press, 1990.

Jacoby, Karl. "Slaves by Nature? Domestic Animals and Human Slaves." *Slavery and Abolition* (April 1994): 89–97.

Jaynes, Gerald David. *Branches without Roots: Genesis of the Black Working Class in the American South, 1862–1882*. New York: Oxford University Press, 1986.

Jenkins, William Sumner. *Pro-Slavery Thought in the Old South*. Chapel Hill: University of North Carolina Press, 1935.

Jordan, Winthrop D. *Tumult and Silence at Second Creek: An Inquiry into a Civil War Slave Conspiracy*. Baton Rouge: Louisiana State University Press, 1993.

Jordan, Winthrop D. *White Over Black: American Attitudes toward the Negro, 1550–1812*. New York: Norton, 1977 [1968].

Johnson, Walter Livezey. "Masters and Markey Slavery in the New Orleans Slave Trade, 1804–1864." Ph.D. diss., Princeton University, 1995.

Kelley, Robin D. G. *Race Rebels: Culture, Politics, and the Black Working Class*. New York: Free Press, 1994.

Kelley, Robin D. G. "'We Are Not What We Seem': Rethinking Black Working Class Opposition in the Jim Crow South." *Journal of American History* (June 1993): 75–112.

Kolchin, Peter. *Unfree Labor: American Slavery and Russian Serfdom*. Cambridge, Mass.: Harvard University Press, 1987.

Levesque, George A. "Boston's Black Brahmin: Dr. John S. Rock." *Civil War History* 26 (December 1972): 609–625.

Levine, George A. "Interpreting Early Black Ideology: A Reappraisal of the Historical Consensus." *Journal of the Early Republic* 1 (Fall 1981): 269–287.

Levine, Lawrence W. *Black Culture, Black Consciousness: Afro-American Folk Thought from Slavery to Freedom*. New York: Oxford University Press, 1977.

Levine, Lawrence W. "The Concept of the New Negro and the Realities of Black Culture." In *Key Issues in the Afro-American Experience*, vol. 2, ed. Nathan Huggins, Martin Kilson, and Daniel M. Fox. New York: Harcourt Brace Jovanovich, 1971: 125–147.

Levine, Lawrence. "Marcus Garvey and the Politics of Revitalization." In *Black Leaders of the Twentieth Century*, ed. John Hope Franklin and August Meier. Urbana: University of Illinois Press, 1982: 105–138.

Levine, Robert S. *Martin Delany, Frederick Douglass, and the Politics of Representative Identity*. Chapel Hill: University of North Carolina Press, 1997.

Lewis, David. *W.E.B. DuBois: The Biography of a Race*. New York: Henry Holt, 1993.

Lincoln, C. Eric. *The Black Muslims in America*. Boston: Beacon Press, 1973.

Litwack, Leon. *Been in the Storm So Long: The Aftermath of Slavery*. New York: Knopf, 1979.

Livingstone, David M. *Darwin's Forgotten Defenders*. Grand Rapids, Mich.: William B. Eerdman, 1987.

Logan, Rayford W. *The Betrayal of the Negro: From Rutherford B. Hayes to Woodrow Wilson*. New York: Collier Books, 1965.

Logan, Rayford. *The Negro in American Life and Thought: The Nadis, 1877–1901*. New York: Dial Press, 1945.

McCluskey, Audrey, and John McCluskey. "Frederick Douglass on Ethnology: A Commencement Address at the Wester Reserve College, 1854." *Negro History Bulletin* 40, no. 4 (July–August 1977): 747–749.

McGruder, Larry. "Kelly Miller: The Life and Thought of a Black Intellectual, 1863–1939." Ph.D. diss., Miami University, 1984.

MacPherson, James. *The Negro's Civil War: How American Negroes Felt and Acted during the War for the Union*. New York: Vintage Books, 1965.

Malone, Anne Patton. *Sweet Chariot: Slave Family and Household Structure in Nineteenth-Century Louisiana*. Chapel Hill: University of North Carolina Press, 1992.

Marable, Manning. *W.E.B. DuBois: Black Radical Democrat*. Boston: Twayne Publishers, 1986.

Martin, Tony. *Literary Garveyism*. Dover, Mass.: Majority Press, 1983.

Martin, Waldo E., Jr. *The Mind of Frederick Douglass*. Chapel Hill: University of North Carolina Press, 1984.

Mathews, Donald. *Slavery and Methodism: A Chapter in American Morality*. Princeton, N.J.: Princeton University Press, 1965.

Meier, August. *Negro Thought in America, 1880–1915: Racial Ideologies in the Age of Booker T. Washington*. Ann Arbor: University of Michigan Press, 1963.

Miller, Floyd J. *The Search for a Black Nationality: Black Emigration and Colonization, 1787–1863*. Urbana: University of Illinois Press, 1975.

Morgan, Edmund S. *American Slavery, American Freedom: The Ordeal of Colonial Virginia*. New York: Norton, 1975.

Morrison, Toni. *Playing in the Dark: Whiteness and the Literary Imagination*. Cambridge, Mass.: Harvard University Press, 1992.

Moses, Wilson Jeremiah. *Alexander Crummell: A Study in Civilization and Discontent*. New York: Oxford University Press, 1989.

Moses, Wilson Jeremiah. *Black Messiahs and Uncle Toms: The Social and Literary Manipulations of a Religious Myth*. University Park: Pennsylvania State University Press, 1982.

Moses, Wilson Jeremiah. *The Golden Age of Black Nationalism, 1850–1925*. New York: Oxford University Press, 1978.

Moses, Wilson Jeremiah. *The Wings of Ethiopia: Studies in African-American Life and Letters*. Ames: Iowa State University Press, 1990.

Moss, Alfred A., Jr. *The American Negro Academy: Voice of the Talented Tenth*. Baton Rouge: Louisiana State University Press, 1981.

Mullin, Gerald W. *Flight and Rebellion: Slave Resistance in Eighteenth-Century Virginia*. New York: Oxford University Press, 1972.

Myrdal, Gunnar. *An America Dilemma: The Negro Problem and America Democracy*. New York: Harper and Brothers, 1994 [1944].

Nash, Gary B. *Race and Revolution*. Madison Wis.: Madison House, 1990.

Newman, Louise Michele. "Laying Claim to Difference: Ideologies of Race and Gender in the U.S. Women's Movement, 1870–1920." Ph.D. diss., Brown University, 1992.

Newby, I. A. *Jim Crow's Defense: Anti-Negro Thought in America, 1900–1930*. Baton Rouge: Louisiana State University Press, 1973.

Patterson, Orlando. *Freedom*. Vol. 1, *Freedom in the Making of Western Culture*. New York: Basic Books, 1991.

Patterson, Orlando. *Slavery and Social Death: A Comparative Study*. Cambridge, Mass.: Harvard University Press, 1982.

Pease, William H., and Jane H. Pease. *They Who Would Be Free: Blacks' Search for Freedom, 1830–1861*. Urbana: University of Illinois Press, 1990 [1974].

Perkins, Linda. "Black Women and Raical 'Uplift' Prior to Emancipation." In *The Black Woman Cross-Culturally Considered*, ed. Filomina Chioma Steady. Cambridge, Mass.: Schenkeman, 1981: 317–334.

Peterson, Thomas Virgil. *Ham and Japheth: The Mythic World of Whites in the Antebellum South*. Metuchen, N.J.: Scarecrow Press, 1978.

Piersen, William D. "White Cannibals, Black Martyrs: Fear, Depression, and Religious Faith as Causes of Suicide among New Slaves." *Journal of Negro History* 62, no. 2 (April 1977): 147–158.

Pieterse, Jan Nederveen. *White on Black: Images of Africa and Blacks in Popular Culture*. New Haven, Conn.: Yale University Press, 1992.

Quarles, Benjamin. *Black Abolitionists*. New York: Oxford University Press, 1969.

Quarles, Benjamin. "The Revolutionary War as a Black Declaration of Independence." In *Slavery and Freedom in the Age of the American Revolution*, ed. Ira Berlin and Ronald Hoffman. Charlottesville: University Press of Virginia, 1983: 283–301.

Raboteau, Albert J. *A Fire in the Bones: Reflections on African-American Religious History*. Boston: Beacon Press, 1995.

Raboteau, Albert J. *Slave Religion: The "Invisible Institution" in the Antebellum South*. New York: Oxford University Press, 1978.

Rawick, George. "Self-Organization under Slavery." *Radical History Review* 4 (Spring/Summer 1977).

Rawick, George. *From Sundown to Sunup: The Making of the Black Community*. Westport, Conn.: Greenwood Press, 1978.

Redkey, Edwin S. *Black Exodus: Black Nationalism and Back-to-Africa Movements, 1980–1910*. New Haven, Conn.: Yale University Press, 1969.

Robinson, Armstead L. "The Difference That Freedom Made: The Emancipation of Afro-Americans." In *The State of Afro-American History: Past, Present, and Future*, ed. Darlene Clark Hine. Baton Rouge: Louisiana State University Press, 1986: 51–74.

Roediger, David R., ed. *Black on White: Black Writers on What It Means to Be White*. New York: Schocken Books, 1998.

Roediger, David R. "And Die in Dixie: Funerals, Death, and Heaven in Slavery." *Massachusetts Review* 22 (Spring 1981): 163–183.

Roediger, David R. *The Wages of Whiteness: Race and the Making of the American Working Class*. New York: Verso, 1991.

Russett, Cynthia Eagle. *Darwin in America: The Intellectual Response, 1865–1912*. San Francisco: W. H. Freeman, 1976.

Russett, Cynthia Eagle. *Sexual Science: The Victorian Construction of Womanhood*. Cambridge, Mass.: Harvard University Press, 1989.

Sanders, Roland. *Lost Tribes and Promised Lands: The Origins of American Racism*. Boston: Little Brown, 1978.

Satter, Beryl. "Marcus Garvey, Father Divine, and the Gender Politics of Race Difference and Race Neutrality." *American Quarterly* 48, no. 1 (March 1996): 43–76.

Saunders, Edith R. "The Hamitic Hypothesis: Its Origin and Function in Time Perspective." *Journal of African History* 10, no. 4 (1969): 521–532.

Savitt, Todd L. "Slave Health and Southern Distinctiveness." In *Disease and Distinctiveness in the American South*, ed. Todd L. Savitt and James Harvey Young. Knoxville: University of Tennessee Press, 1988.

Saxton, Alexander. *The Rise and Fall of the White Republic: Class Politics and Mass Culture in Nineteenth-Century America*. London: Verso, 1990.

Scott, James. *Domination and the Arts of Resistance: Hidden Transcripts*. New Haven, Conn.: Yale University Press, 1990.

Shack, William A. "Ethiopia and Afro-Americans: Some Historical Notes." *Phylon* 25 (1974): 142–55.

Smith, John David. *An Old Creed for the New South: ProSlavery Ideology and Historiography, 1865–1918*. Westport, Conn.: Greenwood Press, 1985.

Snay, Mitchell. *The Gospel of Disunion: Religion and Separatism in the Antebellum South*. Chapel Hill: University of North Carolina Press, 1997.

Sobel, Mechal. *Trabelin' On: The Slave Journey to an Afro-Baptist Religious Faith*. Westport, Conn.: Greenwood Press, 1979.

Sochen, June, ed. *The Black Man and the American Dream: Negro Aspirations in America, 1900–1930*. Chicago: Quadrangle Books, 1971.

Sochen, June. *The Unbridgeable Gap: Blacks and the American Dream, 1900–1930*, Chicago: Rand McNally, 1972.

Spear, Allen H. *Black Chicago: The Making of a Negro Ghetto, 1890–1920*. Chicago: University of Chicago Press, 1967.

Stanton William. *The Leopard's Spots: Scientific Attitudes towards Race in America, 1815–1859*. Chicago: University of Chicago Press, 1960.

Staudenraus, P. J. *The African Colonization Movement*. New York: Columbia University Press, 1961.

Stein, Judith. *The World of Marcus Garvey*. Baton Rouge: Louisiana State University Press, 1986.

Stephan, Nancy Leys, and Sander L. Gilman. "Appropriating the Idioms of Science: The Rejection of Scientific Racism." In *The Bounds of Race: Perspectives of Hegemony and Resistence*, ed. Dominic La Capra. Ithaca, N.Y.: Cornell University Press, 1991: 73–103.

Stevenson, Brenda. *Life in Black and White: Family and Community in the Slave South*. New York: Oxford University Press, 1996.

Stocking, George W. *Race, Culture, and Evolution: Essays in the History of Anthropology*. New York: Collier Macmillan, 1968.

Stuckey, Sterling. *Slave Culture: Nationalist Theory and the Foundations of Black America*. New York: Oxford University Press, 1987.

Sweet, Leonard I. *Black Images of America, 1784–1870*. New York: W. W. Norton, 1976.

Swift, David E. *Black Prophets of Justice: Activist Clergy before the Civil War*. Baton Rouge: Lousiana State University Press, 1989.

Tadman, Michael. *Speculators and Slaves: Masters, Traders, and Slaves in the Old South*. Madison: University of Wisconsin Press, 1989.

Thomas, Lamont D. *Rise to Be a People: A Biography of Paul Cuffe*. Urbana: University of Illinois Press, 1986.

Thomas, William B. "Black Intellectuals' Critique of Early Mental Testing: A Little-Known Saga of the 1920s." *American Journal of Education* 90 (May 1982): 258–292.

Toll, William. "Free Men, Freedmen, and Race: Black Social Theory in the Gilded Age." *Journal of Southern History* 44 (November 1978): 571–596.

Touchstone, Blake. "Planters and Slave Religion in the Deep South." In *Masters and Slaves in the House of the Lord: Race and Religion in the American South*, ed. John B. Boles. Lexington: University Press of Kentucky, 1988.

Ullman, Victor. *Martin R. Delany: The Beginnings of Black Nationalism*. Boston: Beacon Press, 1971.

Van Horne, John C. *The Abolitionist Sisterhood: Woman's Political Culture in Antebellum America*. Ithaca, N.Y.: Cornell University Press, 1994.

Vaughan, Alden T. "The Origins Debate: Slavery and Racism in Seventeenth-Century Virginia." *Virginia Magazine of History and Biography* 97 (July 1989): 311–354.

Vincent, Theodore G. *Voices of a Black Nation: Political Journalism in the Harlem Renaissance Era*. San Francisco: Ramparts Press, 1974.

Walker, Clarence E. "The American Negro as Historical Outsider." *Canadian Review of American Studies* 17 (Summer 1986): 137–154.

Walker, Clarence, E. *Deromanticizing Black History: Critical Essays and Reappraisals.* Knoxville: University of Tennessee Press, 1991.

Ware, Vron. *Beyond the Pale: White Women, Racism, and History.* London and New York: Verso, 1992.

Watkins, Mel. *On the Real Side: Laughing, Lying, and Signifying—The Underground Tradition of African-American Humor that Transformed American Culture from Slavery to Richard Pryor.* New York: Simon and Schuster, 1994.

Webber, Thomas L. *Deep Like Rivers: Education in the Slave Quarter Community, 1831–1865.* New York: W. W. Norton, 1978.

White, Deborah Gray. *Ar'n't I a Woman? Female Slaves in the Plantation South.* New York: W.W. Norton, 1985.

White, Deborah Gray. *Too Heavy a Load: Black Women in Defense of Themselves, 1894–1994.* New York: W. W. Norton, 1999.

White, Shane. *Somewhat More Independent: The End of Slavery in New York City, 1770–1810.* Athens: University of Georgia Press, 1991.

Williams, Vernon J. *Rethinking Race: Franz Boas and His Contemporaries.* Lexington: University of Kentucky Press, 1996.

Wood, Peter H. *Black Majority: Negroes in Colonial South Carolina from 1670 through the Stono Rebellion.* New York: W. W. Norton, 1974.

Woodward, C. Vann. "History From Slave Sources." *American Historical Review* 79 (April 1974): 470–481.

Wray, Matt, and Annalee Newitz. *White Trash: Race and Class in America.* New York: Routledge, 1997.

Yee, Shirley J. *Black Women Abolitionists: A Study in Activism, 1828–1860.* Knoxville: University of Tennessee Press, 1992.

Yetman, Norman. "The Background of the Slave Narrative Collection." *American Quarterly* 19 (Fall 1967): 534–553.

Young, James O. *Black Writers of the Thirties.* Baton Rouge: Louisiana State University Press, 1973.

Young, Melvina Johnson. "Exploring the WPA Narratives: Finding the Voices of Black Men and Women." In *Theorizing Black Feminisms: The Visionary Pragmatism of Black Women,* ed. Stanlie M. James and Abena P. A. Busia. New York: Routledge, 1993: 54–74.

Young, Robert J. C. *Colonial Desire: Hybridity in Theory, Culture, and Race.* New York: Routledge, 1995.

Index

DATE DUE

GRAD	JAN 30 '02		
APR 1	2 2005		
APR 1	2 2005		
DEC 1 2	2006		
SEP 2 9	2008		